Cyber Threat Intelligence

Cyber Threat Intelligence

Martin Lee
Oxford, UK

Library of Congress Cataloging-in-Publication Data

Names: Lee, Martin (Computer security expert), author.
Title: Cyber threat intelligence / Martin Lee.
Description: Oxford, UK ; Hoboken, NJ, USA : Wiley, 2023. | Includes
    bibliographical references and index.
Identifiers: LCCN 2022047002 (print) | LCCN 2022047003 (ebook) | ISBN
    9781119861744 | ISBN 9781119861751 (adobe pdf) | ISBN 9781119861768
    (epub)
Subjects: LCSH: Cyber intelligence (Computer security) |
    Cyberterrorism–Prevention. | Cyberspace operations (Military science)
Classification: LCC TK5105.59 .L47 2023 (print) | LCC TK5105.59 (ebook) |
    DDC 005.8/7–dc23/eng/20221205
LC record available at https://lccn.loc.gov/2022047002
LC ebook record available at https://lccn.loc.gov/2022047003

Cover Design: Wiley
Cover Image: © Yuichiro Chino/Getty images

Set in 9.5/12.5pt STIXTwoText by Straive, Pondicherry, India
Printed and bound by CPI Group (UK) Ltd, Croydon, CR0 4YY

Contents

Preface

Cyber Threat Intelligence describes the intelligence techniques and models used in cyber threat intelligence. It provides a survey of ideas, views, and concepts, rather than offering a hands-on practical guide. It is intended for anyone who wishes to learn more about the domain, possibly because they wish to develop a career in intelligence, and as a reference for those already working in the area.

The origins of this book lie in an awkward dinner conversation. I was on one side of the table, a software engineer who had fallen into the domain of cyber security more or less by accident. On the other was a uniformed senior military intelligence officer. A shared professional interest in cyber threat intelligence led to our being invited to the same event.

Keen to learn how better to analyse the attacks that I was encountering, I tried to learn all that I could about intelligence techniques from my neighbour. Naively, I had hoped that there might be a text book that set out the approaches that I could try to apply to identify attackers. At the very least, I was certain that there must be conceptual models, which I could adapt from the intelligence world to make better use of my data.

Instead, I discovered that military intelligence officers do not impart their knowledge to civilians easily, nor do they particularly appreciate lengthy questioning about the details of their profession. My conclusion was that I would have to develop my own body of knowledge regarding intelligence techniques and learn how to apply these to the emerging issue of cyber security.

This book is the result of that dinner. It is the book that I had hoped to discover when I started working in the nascent domain of cyber threat intelligence. It is the book that outlines the concepts and theories, which serve as the foundation of sound professional practice and the development of new practical applications.

Cyber threat intelligence is so much more than feeds of technical indicators relating to current cyber attacks. It is a discipline that is distinct from forensic cyber analysis, or malware analysis, seeking not necessarily to supply raw information detailing attacks, but to enrich such information to provide understanding.

Many working in the domain of cyber threat intelligence have been formally trained in intelligence through having followed careers in the military or law enforcement. However, professional obligations to protect sensitive operational details mean that it is often difficult to share knowledge and competences developed over long careers.

As a civilian working in the private sector, I have learned what I can about traditional threat intelligence theories and techniques from declassified or open-source material under the mentorship of formally trained senior colleagues. The nascent domain of cyber security has also had to develop its own specialised techniques and vocabulary derived from a large community of people working together to solve new problems.

This book is a collection of the techniques and theories that underpin the practice of cyber threat intelligence. The domain continues to evolve rapidly. The day-to-day tools and analyses performed by threat intelligence teams may change frequently, but the theory and frameworks in which these activities take place are well developed. It is these mature, evolved disciplines that this book seeks to describe.

This book approaches cyber threat intelligence from a perspective that is western and predominantly that of NATO and EU countries. Although the book is not partisan in nature, the reader should be aware that there are other perspectives.

I am indebted to a long line of people with whom I have worked over the years, who have helped me discover resources and techniques, and who have given me support and encouragement. This book has benefitted from the wisdom and oversight of Dr. Herb Mattord, Dr. Jonathan Lusthaus, Vanja Svajcer, Paul King, Wendy Nather, Don Taggart, and Natasha King who helped in the preparation of the manuscript.

About the Author

As EMEA Lead of the Strategic Planning and Communication team within Talos, Cisco's threat intelligence and security research organisation, Martin Lee researches the latest developments in cyber security and endeavours to ensure that organisations are aware of emerging threats and how to mitigate them.

Having worked in the field of detecting cyber threats since 2003, he has established and led threat intelligence teams on three continents. A Certified Information Systems Security Professional (CISSP) and a Chartered Engineer, Martin holds degrees from the Universities of Bristol, Cambridge, Paris-Sud, and Oxford. He is a member of the technical advisory board to Europol, and has delivered lectures on threat intelligence to students at the Universities of Oxford, Warwick, Kennesaw State, and l'Ecole Polytechnique, Paris.

An England Athletics licenced leader in running fitness, when not sat in front of a screen, Martin is often found running in the countryside or encouraging others to run for pleasure.

Abbreviations

$(ISC)^2$	Information System Security Certification Consortium
ABS	Anti-lock Braking System
AI	Artificial Intelligence
API	Application Programming Interface
APT	Advanced Persistent Threat
ARP	Address Resolution Protocol
AWS	Amazon Web Services
BCE	Before the Common Era
CAPEC™	Common Attack Pattern Enumeration and Classification
CE	Common Era
CERT	Computer Emergency Response Team
CERT/CC	Computer Emergency Response Team Coordinating Center
CIA	Central Intelligence Agency
CIDR	Classless Inter-Domain Routing
CISA	Cybersecurity and Infrastructure Security Agency
CISSP	Certified Information Systems Security Professional
COE	Council of Europe
COMINT	Communications Intelligence
COMSEC	Communications Secrecy
CPU	Central Processing Unit
CREST	Council of Registered Ethical Security Testers
CTI	Cyber Threat Intelligence
CVE	Common Vulnerabilities and Exposures
CVSS	Common Vulnerability Scoring System
CWE™	Common Weakness Enumeration
D3A	Decide, Detect, Deliver, Assess
DARPA	Defense Advanced Research Projects Agency
DNS	Domain Name System
DoS	Denial of Service

DPRK	Democratic People's Republic of Korea
EDRPOU	Unified State Registration Number of Enterprises and Organizations of Ukraine
ELINT	Electronic Intelligence
ENISA	European Network Information Security Agency
EU	European Union
F2T2EA	Find, Fix, Track, Target, Engage, Assess
F3EAD	Find, Fix, Finish, Exploit, Analyse, and Disseminate
FBI	Federal Bureau of Investigation
FIRST	Forum of Incident Response and Security Teams
FTP	File Transfer Protocol
GB	Gigabytes
GDPR	General Data Protection Regulation
GIAC	Global Information Assurance Certification
HSE	Health Services Executive (of Ireland)
HTTP	Hypertext Transfer Protocol
HTTPS	Hypertext Transfer Protocol Secure
HUMINT	Human Intelligence
HVAC	Heating, Ventilation, and Air Conditioning
ICAO	International Civil Aviation Organization
ICMP	Internet Control Message Protocol
ICS	Industrial Control System
IDE	Integrated Development Environment
IEC	International Electrotechnical Commission
IEEE	Institute of Electrical and Electronics Engineers
IESBA	International Ethics Standards Board for Accountants
IoCs	Indicators of Compromise
IODEF	Incident Object Description Exchange Format
IoT	Internet of Things
IP	Internet Protocol
IPS	Intrusion Protection System
IPSec	Internet Protocol Security
ISAC	Information Sharing and Analysis Center
ISO	International Organization for Standardization
ISP	Internet Service Provider
IT	Information Technology
JSON	JavaScript Object Notation
KGB	Committee for State Security (of Soviet Union)
MAEC	Malware Attribute Enumeration and Characterization
MIDI	Musical Instrument Digital Interface
MIME	Multipurpose Internet Mail Extensions

MISP	Malware Information Sharing Platform
MPEG	Motion Picture Experts Group
NASA	National Aeronautics and Space Administration
NATO	North Atlantic Treaty Organization
NCSC	National Cyber Security Centre (of the United Kingdom)
NICE	National Initiative for Cybersecurity Education
NIST	National Institute of Standards and Technology
NSA	National Security Agency
NSDD	National Security Decision Directive
ODNI	Office of the Director of National Intelligence
OECD	Organisation for Economic Co-operation and Development
OSI	Open System Interconnection
OSINT	Open Source Intelligence
OWASP	Open Web Application Security Project
PASTA	Process for Attack Simulation and Threat Analysis
PCI	Payment Card Industry
PCI DSS	Payment Card Industry Data Security Standards
PDD	Presidential Decision Directive
PMI	Project Management Institute
PPP	Point-to-Point Protocol
RAM	Random Access Memory
RAT	Remote Access Trojan
RC4	Rivest Cipher 4
RCE	Remote Code Execution
RJ45	Registered Jack 45
RS-232	Recommended Standard 232
SANS	SysAdmin, Audit, Network, and Security (Institute)
SCADA	Supervisory Control and Data Acquisition
SFIA	Skills Framework for the Information Age
SGAM	Structured Geospatial Analytical Method
SIGINT	Signals Intelligence
SLIP	Serial Line Internet Protocol
SMB	Server Message Block
SMBv1	Server Message Block version 1
SMS	Short Message Service
SMTP	Simple Mail Transfer Protocol
SOCKS	Socket Secure
SQL	Structured Query Language
STIX	Structured Threat Information eXpression
SVR	Foreign Intelligence Service of the Russian Federation
SWIFT	Society for Worldwide Interbank Financial Telecommunication

TAXII	Trusted Automated eXchange of Indicator Information
TCP	Transmission Control Protocol
TLP	Traffic Light Protocol
TLS	Transport Layer Security
TTPs	Tactics, Techniques, and Procedures
UDP	User Datagram Protocol
UEBA	User and Entity Behaviour Analytics
UEFA	Union of European Football Associations
UK	United Kingdom
UN	United Nations
URL	Uniform Resource Locator
USA / US	United States of America
USAF	United States Air Force
USB	Universal Serial Bus
UTC	Universal Time Coordinated
VERIS	Vocabulary for Event Recording and Incident Sharing
VoIP	Voice over Internet Protocol
WMIC	Windows Management Instrumentation Command
XML	eXtensible Markup Language

Endorsements for Martin Lee's Book

"Martin takes a thorough and focused approach to the processes that rule threat intelligence. But he doesn't just cover gathering, processing and distributing intelligence. He explains why you should care who is trying to hack you. And what you can do about it when you know."

—*Simon Edwards, Security Testing Expert,*
CEO SE Labs Ltd., Chair AMTSO

"I really enjoyed this engaging book, which beautifully answered one of the first questions I had coming into the profession of cyber security: "What is Cyber Threat Intelligence?"

It progressively walked me through the world of cyber threat intelligence, peppered with rich content collected through years' of experience and knowledge. It is satisfyingly detailed to make it an interesting read for those already in cyber security wanting to learn more, but also caters to those who are just curious about the prevalent cyber threat and where it may be headed.

One of the takeaways from this book for me is how finding threats is not the most important thing but how the effective communication of it is equally important so that it triggers appropriate actions at appropriate timing.

Moreover, as a penetration tester, we are used to looking at the little details so it was refreshing and eye-opening to learn about the macro view on cyber threat landscape."

—*Ryoko Amano, Penetration Tester*

"Cyber threats are a constant danger for companies in the private sector, which makes cyber threat intelligence an increasingly crucial tool for identifying security risks, developing proactive strategies, and responding swiftly to attacks. Martin Lee's new book is a comprehensive guide that takes the mystery out of using threat intelligence to strengthen a company's cyber defence. With a clear and concise explanation of the basics of threat intelligence, Martin provides a full picture of what's available and how to use it. Moreover, his book is packed with useful references and resources that will be invaluable for threat intelligence teams. Whether you're just starting in cybersecurity or a seasoned professional, this book is a must-have reference guide that will enhance your detection and mitigation of cyber threats."

—Gavin Reid, CISO VP Threat Intelligence at Human Security

"Martin Lee blends cyber threats, intel collection, attribution, and respective case studies in a compelling narrative. Lee does an excellent job of explaining complex concepts in a manner that is accessible to anyone wanting to develop a career in intelligence. What sets this book apart is the author's ability to collect related fundamentals and applications described in a pragmatic manner. Understandably, the book's challenge is non-disclosure of sensitive operational information. This is an excellent reference that I would highly recommend to cyber security professionals and academics wanting to deepen their domain expertise and broaden current knowledge. Threats indeed evolve and we must too."

—Dr. Roland Padilla, FACS CP (Cyber Security), Senior Cyber Security Advisor – Defence Program (CISCO Systems), Army Officer (AUS DoD)

"Cyber Threat Intelligence by Martin Lee is an interesting and valuable contribution to the literature supporting the development of cyber security professional practice. This well researched and thoroughly referenced book provides both practitioners and those studying cyber threats with a sound basis for understanding the threat environment and the intelligence cycle required to understand and interpret existing and emerging threats. It is supported by relevant case studies of cyber security incidents enabling readers to contextualise the relationship between threat intelligence and incident response."

—Hugh Boyes, University of Warwick

1

Introduction

Everything has a beginning. Chapter 1 sets out to define cyber threat intelligence and chart the development of the concept from antiquity to the present day. Despite cyber threat intelligence being a recent concept, the need to characterise threats and to understand the intentions of enemies has ancient roots.

1.1 Definitions

'Cyber Threat Intelligence' is a term which is readily understandable, but not necessarily easy to define.

There are a variety of different perspectives and experiences which lead to different understandings of the term. For some, cyber threat intelligence refers to the collection of data. For others the term refers to teams of analysts and the processes required to analyse data. For many it is the name of a product to be commercialised and sold.

Cyber threat intelligence encompasses all these perspectives, and more. This book addresses the many facets of the term, ranging from the historical development of intelligence through to the modern application of cyber threat intelligence techniques.

One area of threat intelligence is purposefully omitted. The covert collection of intelligence from human agents (HUMINT), often obtained from participants within underground criminal forums is beyond the scope of this book. This domain and the associated techniques are a distinct specialism with their own risks and dangers which merits a separate book.

To define what is meant by cyber threat intelligence we must start by understanding the meanings of the constituent terms, 'intelligence' and 'cyber threat'.

1.1.1 Intelligence

To better understand the concept of intelligence, we can examine the domain from the viewpoints of the different practitioners.

The field of Intelligence is most commonly associated with the military. The multi-national military organisation, North Atlantic Treaty Organization (NATO) defines Intelligence as:

> The product resulting from the directed collection and processing of information regarding the environment and the capabilities and intentions of actors, in order to identify threats and offer opportunities for exploitation by decision-makers.
>
> *(NATO 2017a)*

Intelligence is not exclusively military in nature. Intelligence activities may be undertaken by non-military governmental organisations, the Central Intelligence Agency (CIA) being one such example. Despite having the term 'intelligence' as part of its name, the early years of the agency were marked by much discussion debating the nature of what is meant by intelligence (Warner 2002). One document reflecting the uncertainties of the time, succinctly defines intelligence as:

> Intelligence is the official, secret collection and processing of information on foreign countries to aid in formulating and implementing foreign policy, and the conduct of covert activities abroad to facilitate the implementation of foreign policy.
>
> *(Bimfort 1958)*

Intelligence is not the exclusive preserve of the state. The private sector also engages in intelligence activities, such as conducting competitive intelligence, which may be defined as:

> ... actionable recommendations arising from a systematic process involving planning, gathering, analyzing, and disseminating information on the external environment for opportunities, or developments that have the potential to affect a company's or country's competitive situation.
>
> *(Calof and Skinner 1998)*

As with other forms of Intelligence, there is much debate regarding what is exactly meant by 'Competitive Intelligence'. Definitions range from those that could apply equally to military intelligence:

> A process that increases marketplace competitiveness by analysing the capabilities and potential actions of individual competitors as well as the overall competitive situation of the firm in its industry and in the economy.
>
> *(Pellissier and Nenzhelele 2003)*

Across the various disciplines and specialisations associated with the notion of 'intelligence', there are commonalities within definitions, namely:

- Intelligence is both a process and a product.
- The Intelligence process consists of gathering information, analysing this and synthesising it into an Intelligence product.
- Intelligence products are intended to be used by recipients in order to assist in decision making.

1.1.2   Cyber Threat

As a prefix, the term 'cyber' dates back to the 1940s, and was first used in the concept of 'cybernetics' relating to the communication and control interfaces between living things and machines (Coe 2015). Since this date the term has been used widely in the context of futuristic technology.

The term has undergone a rapid evolution. To Internet users of the mid to late 1990s, the term 'cyber' was used to describe the practice of conducting intimate relationships online (Newitz 2013). Yet in a relatively short time, the term has become closely associated with security and attacks against computing systems.

The origins of this evolution lie in the 1960s use of the term 'cyberspace' to refer to environments outside of normal experience (Ma et al. 2015; Strate 1999). Over time this notion of a separate domain came to be used to refer to the space created by the network of connected computing systems that comprises the Internet.

NATO defines cyberspace as:

> The global domain consisting of all interconnected communication, information technology and other electronic systems, networks and their data, including those which are separated or independent, which process, store or transmit data.
>
> *(NATO 2017b)*

Hence, the 'cyber domain' is a potentially contested space which is equivalent to the traditional militarily contested environments of the land, sea, and air (Crowther 2017). Following this logic, in the same way that there is an army to fight on land, a navy to fight on the sea, an air force for air battles, a cyber capability is required to defend and project national interests within this new domain (Ferdinando 2018; Emmott 2018).

Threats are to be found within the traditional domains of the land, sea, and air. These threats are diverse in nature, ranging from hostile adversaries who seek to cause harm, to adverse weather conditions which may damage ships or planes, or simply geographical features such as mountain ranges which might block routes.

A military commander wishing to operate in any of these domains must collect intelligence to understand the threats that may be encountered. This intelligence should be expected to describe where a threat is located, the specific danger that the threat may pose, and how the threat is changing over time.

In this respect, cyberspace is no different. Within this new domain hostile adversaries may be operating, physical features of the infrastructure may constrain operations, and software installations may change as frequently as the weather (Mavroeidis and Bromander 2017).

In order to operate in this cyber environment, we also must gather intelligence. Decision makers must remain abreast of the nature and risk posed by current threats so that an appropriate response can be orchestrated allowing everyday activities to be conducted safely and successfully.

1.1.3 Cyber Threat Intelligence

Clearly, cyber threat intelligence is the application of intelligence to threats that affect the cyber realm. This concept can be expressed in many different ways. The research organisation Gartner defines threat intelligence as several items that contribute to decision making:

> Threat intelligence is evidence-based knowledge, including context, mechanisms, indicators, implications and actionable advice, about an existing or emerging menace or hazard to assets that can be used to inform decisions regarding the subject's response to that menace or hazard.
>
> *(Gartner Research and McMillan 2003)*

The Forum of Incident Response and Security Teams (FIRST) emphasises the informational aspect of threat intelligence.

> Cyber Threat Intelligence is systematic collection, analysis and dissemination of information pertaining to a company's operation in cyberspace and to an extent physical space. It is designed to inform all levels of decision makers.
>
> *(FIRST 2018)*

The Bank of England's framework for threat intelligence-led operations, CBEST, states that an intelligence-based approach to cyber security should have the following goals:

> to prevent an attacker from successfully attacking;
>   to be able to recognise and respond effectively to an attack that has already happened.
>
> *(Bank of England 2016)*

Again, we can see common threads between these definitions. A working definition of cyber threat intelligence should combine definitions from the realm of traditional intelligence, emphasise the application to the notion of 'cyber', and state the use of intelligence.

Throughout this book I use the following as my working definition of cyber threat intelligence:

> The process and outcome of gathering and analysing information relating to threats that may cause damage to electronic networked devices, in order to assist decision making.

1.2 History of Threat Intelligence

This section is not intended to be an exhaustive study of history, but to highlight significant mileposts in the development of the discipline of intelligence, and to show how many of the issues faced by today's threat intelligence practitioners are not too different from those of the past.

1.2.1 Antiquity

The earliest recorded reference to Intelligence activities is found within the Biblical Book of Numbers. The book was probably written in the fifth century BCE describing events that took place many centuries earlier (McDermott 2002).

> And Moses sent them to spy out the land of Canaan, and said unto them, Get you up this way southward, and go up into the mountain;
> And see the land, what it is, and the people that dwelleth therein, whether they be strong or weak, few or many;
> And what the land is that they dwell in, whether it be good or bad; and what cities they be that they dwell in, whether in tents, or in strong holds;
>
> *(Numbers n.d.)*

Moses is the earliest example of a leader instructing teams to conduct an intelligence operation; gathering information regarding a domain in order to assist with decision making.

Also, during the fifth century BCE, the Chinese general Sun Tzu wrote his treatise on warfare, 'The Art of War'. This is one of the earliest descriptions of how to conduct warfare, although the text was not translated into English before the beginning of the twentieth century, it has become widely influential in the decades following the World War II onwards.

Sun Tzu recognised the importance of intelligence, and of having an understanding not only of the enemy's strengths and weaknesses, but also your own:

> If you know the enemy and know yourself, you need not fear the result of a hundred battles. If you know yourself but not the enemy, for every victory gained you will also suffer a defeat. If you know neither the enemy nor yourself, you will succumb in every battle.
>
> *(Giles 1910)*

Indeed, intelligence was fundamental to Sun Tzu's understanding of how to wage war. An entire chapter of his treatise was devoted to 'The Use of Spies', including descriptions of the different ways that intelligence can be gathered. Within this chapter, Sun Tzu emphasises the use of 'foreknowledge'.

> What enables the wise sovereign and the good general to strike and conquer, and achieve things beyond the reach of ordinary men, is *foreknowledge*. Now this foreknowledge cannot be elicited from spirits; it cannot be obtained inductively from experience, nor by any deductive calculation. Knowledge of the enemy's dispositions can only be obtained from other men.
>
> *(Giles 1910)*

It is informative to compare this quote on the importance of 'foreknowledge' with the multitude of definitions of Intelligence written twenty-five centuries later. Clearly the nature of intelligence has changed little over the years.

In tandem with the development of intelligence as the art of uncovering useful information, so the art of concealing useful information has also developed. Steganography is the science of hiding messages within other objects. Writing in the fifth century BCE, the Greek historian, Herodotus, described how messages could be tattooed on a slave's scalp before allowing the hair to grow and hide the message. Herodotus also described writing hidden messages on wooden backing of the wax tablets used by scribes to record and send messages (Fabien et al. 1999).

Discovering the hidden message required knowing how the message had been concealed. In the absence of this information, discovering the message was, by design, difficult. Uncovering hidden writing required a new skill set, that of cryptanalysis.

The first recorded cryptanalyst was Queen Gorgo of Sparta. A member of the Spartan royal family, Demaratus had been exiled to Persia. Upon learning of the Persian King Xerxes I's plans to invade Sparta, he sent a message inscribed on a wooden tablet hidden by a covering of wax to warn the Spartans.

However, the court of the Spartan king could make no sense of the apparently blank tablet until Gorgo correctly deduced that Demaratus would not have gone to the effort and danger of sending the item without good reason. She ordered the wax to be removed revealing the message concealed beneath (Baker 2022).

The fact that Gorgo's name is recorded along with her wisdom and insight in revealing the message demonstrates how highly regarded she and her actions were.

Through these snippets from prehistory we perceive glimpses of characters, and their efforts to gather intelligence and keep valued information secret. These illustrate how fundamental intelligence has been to humanity since the beginning of recorded time.

1.2.2 Ancient Rome

Rome was the dominant military power in the Mediterranean and Western Europe until the fourth century CE. Roman leaders made extensive use of intelligence in order to keep control over the empire and manage hostile borders (Austin and Rankov 1998).

Intelligence responsibilities were split between different functions, which changed and developed over time. In addition to scouts who operated to identify the location of the enemy for the legions, the *exploratores* operated at distance from the legions conducting reconnaissance and communicating with their generals by courier. Additionally, the enigmatic *speculatores* also conducted intelligence operations, including clandestinely listening to chatter within enemy camps, however detailed understanding of their function has yet to be determined (Campbell and Tritle 2013).

At the very least we know that Julius Caesar in the first century BCE made great use of intelligence. Contemporaneous reports describe Caesar as always reconnoitering the country when leading an army and seeking to understand the nature of his enemies from a geographical, economic, and even ethnographic point of view. He is known to have interrogated captured prisoners himself to understand how their customs and beliefs might affect their choice of how and when to conduct battle (Evov 1996).

We sense the presence of hostile intelligence operatives in the use of simple cryptography by Julius Caesar. Despite being the emperor, leading the largest and most efficient state apparatus in existence at the time, he found it necessary to write confidential matters using a substitution cypher (Reinke 1962).

The method of encrypting his messages is simplistic by modern standards. Caesar shifted the letters of the alphabet by four so that instead of writing the letter 'A', he would write 'D', and so forth. Nevertheless, the techniques necessary to reliably decrypt such messages were not described before the ninth century CE

(Lee 2014). In the Roman era, this was state of the art cryptography, indeed the technique would not be improved upon before the Renaissance.

In using cryptography, Caesar was clearly aware that his writing could be intercepted by operatives outside of his control, and potentially how the intelligence derived from his writings could be used against his interests. In this observation we sense an awareness of Communications Intelligence (COMINT) and the collection of intelligence from communications, alongside an awareness of the importance of Communications Secrecy (COMSEC) in the ancient world.

1.2.3   Medieval and Renaissance Age

During the eighth century CE, the Arabic philologist Al-Khalil ibn Ahmad al-Farahidi studied the nature of Arabic poetry, compiled the first Arabic dictionary, and studied cryptography, writing one of the first books on the subject, '*Kitab al-Mu'amma*' – 'The Book of Cryptographic Messages' (Broemeling 2011).

Although no copies of the book are known to have survived, the work influenced the Arabic philosopher Al-Kindi. Within a century of the publication of *Kitab al-Mu'amma*, Al-Kindi had expanded on Al-Khalil's ideas and developed the technique of frequency analysis in order to break the simple substitution cyphers in use at the time. Al-Kindi's book '*Risalah fi Istikhraj al-Mu'amma*' – 'A Manuscript on Deciphering Cryptographic Messages', detailed the techniques required in order to break any cryptographic cypher known at the time (Al-Kadit 1992).

Although the authors of the various medieval Arabic treatises on breaking cryptographic messages are clearly familiar with cyphertexts, little information remains of the content of the decyphered text, or who requested the decryption. A possible clue to the nature of the patrons of these works is to be found in the title of Ali ibd Adlan's manual of practical cryptanalysis '*Fi hall al-mutarjam*' – 'On Cryptanalysis', also known as '*al Mu'allaf Lil Malik al Ahraf*' – 'The Manual for King al Ahraf'. King al Ahraf being Al-Ashraf Musa, the Egyptian emir of Damascus, and a likely candidate for someone who would be interested in intercepting and decyphering messages.

Within Renaissance Italy, the associations between political power and cryptanalysis were clear. The first European cryptography manual was written in 1379 by Gabriele de Lavinde of Parma while working for Pope Clement VII. One hundred years later in 1474, Cicco Simonetta working for the Sforza, Dukes of Milan wrote the first European treatise on cryptanalysis and breaking cyphers (Bruen and Forcinto 2011).

Knowledge of how to hide messages quickly spread. Polydore Vergil observed in 1499 that *secret writing* (cryptography and steganography) had become widespread:

> But today this way of writing is so common that no one, sovereign or subject, is without his special signs, called cyphers in the vernacular.
>
> *(Marcus and Findlen 2019)*

Ambassadors, nobles, politicians, and their secretaries plotted and communicated in secret while keeping abreast of the plans and dispositions of other nation states or adversaries who, in turn, were also communicating and plotting in secret. Merchants communicated using 'secret writing' both to protect their trade secrets, but also to act as unofficial agents of the state, conducting diplomacy and collecting intelligence on foreign powers.

As Renaissance states developed, ensuring the confidentiality of communications became a state priority. Within Venice, cryptography developed into a professional branch of the civil service, with formal training and entry exams. This ensured that Venetian encrypted communications were as secure as possible, and that the Doge had a team of trained professionals who could decrypt intercepted documents (Iordanou 2018).

The breaking of cyphers was a technical problem; however, the collection of documents to decrypt was an operational problem. Networks of spies and informers could be tasked with collecting information from suspect individuals, or exiles. In Tudor England, Sir Francis Walsingham established a network of informers both within and outside the country, through which letters could be intercepted and potential threats to state security identified (Leimon and Parker 1996).

Walsingham's surveillance network, and his success in uncovering real or imagined Catholic plots against the nascently Protestant English nation helped secure Elizabethan England. At the same time, his network's infiltration of potential plots against the crown and their active involvement in instigating plots designed to uncover potential adversaries, helped temper the aspirations of those who might have preferred a change of political regime (Edwards 2007; Farhat-Holzman 2007).

The interception of private communications could be formalised as part of state functions. The *bullette* of Renaissance Siena was tasked with inspecting every letter sent from, or received within the city in order to identify any suspect contents (Shaw 2000). The establishment of the English postal service was strengthened by an ordinance of 1657, which included the provision that a national postal service *'will be the best means to discover and prevent many dangerous and wicked designs against the Commonwealth'*. Nevertheless, the secrecy of postal communication was not without protection. Postmasters were forbidden from opening any letter unless by warrant from the Secretary of State (Dugald et al. 1842).

Across seventeenth century Europe, *Cabinets noirs* or 'black chambers' were created by governments to intercept and monitor correspondence (Iordanou 2018; De Leeuw 1999). Intercepted encrypted messages could then be passed to the state cryptographers for decyphering. So efficient was the interception and decoding of the Viennese *Geheime Ziffernkanzle* (Secret Cypher Office) that the Viennese sold intercepted and decyphered diplomatic correspondence to France and Russia (Hillenbrand 2017).

The Snowden revelations of widespread state-sponsored monitoring of electronic communications during the twenty-first century should not have been a surprise (MacAskill and Dance 2013). Technology has facilitated and automated a state function that has already existed for many centuries.

1.2.4 Industrial Age

With the industrialisation of societies during the eighteenth and nineteenth centuries, Intelligence became an increasingly specialised function. Outside of the military, many states had some form of intelligence capacity, which included ensuring the secrecy of official communications, while seeking to compromise the secrecy of the communications of others. However, it was the upheaval of the French Revolution of 1798 which created an environment in which long-lasting intelligence innovations were made during the early industrial era.

The paranoia of the years following the revolution necessitated the surveillance of political agitators who sought to overthrow the new government. Joseph Fouché headed the Ministry of General Police *ministère de la police générale,* organising it into an effective surveillance engine. His daily *bulletin de police* provided the first known regular intelligence briefings by a state intelligence apparatus, supplying Napoleon Bonaparte with information relating to political opposition, public order, and crime throughout the French empire (Fijnaut and Marx 1995).

This high-level strategic intelligence may have been sufficient to inform the head of state, but it didn't meet the needs of those trying to secure personal property, or considering whether to enter into a financial relationship with another party.

In 1811, the ex-convict Eugène François Vidocq founded the *Brigade de la Sûreté* as part of the prefecture de police. He recruited ex-criminals to infiltrate the criminal underworld to collect intelligence on illicit activities, and provided his services as a private detective to those who wished to chase bad debts or establish the creditworthiness of potential business partners. Thus creating both the first criminal intelligence agency, and establishing the provision of financial intelligence as a business model (Vause 2014).

As the Industrial Revolution gathered pace technological advances provided opportunities for Intelligence gathering. The detailed reports of action in the Crimean War of 1854–1856 collected by journalists, sent by steam ship, and published by the newspapers could provide the enemy with more information, more rapidly than could be achieved with existing intelligence apparatus. This led Tsar Nicholas I to half-jokingly proclaim '*We have no need for spies. We have the Times*'. (Dylan 2012).

The ability of the telegraph to rapidly transmit reports and receive orders from high command proved invaluable for conducting military operations. However, messages sent over the telegraph were liable to interception. During the American

Civil War, both the Confederacy and the Union used the telegraph to send signals, both used cryptography to encrypt the contents of their messages, and both intercepted each other's communications.

Initially the Confederacy allowed commanders to choose their own cyphers. Unsurprisingly this proved insecure and unworkable. The Union demanded strict communications discipline and used an effective substitution cypher, which coupled with a lack of crypto-analysts on the Confederate side meant that although the Union could read Confederate messages, the Confederacy could not routinely decrypt Union messages, giving the Union a large intelligence advantage (Sapp 2009).

Interestingly, the importance of communications secrecy and the opportunities provided to the enemy through intercepting military communications and using intelligence against operations has been forgotten and re-invented more than once. One hundred years after the successful use of communications intercepts during the American Civil War, the US Air Force was surprised to find that the North Vietnamese forces had up to 24 hours advanced warning of air operations during the Vietnam War. The North Vietnamese were able to intercept poorly encrypted communications and take advantage of unencrypted voice communications of incoming air strikes both to reduce the effectiveness of the missions and to increase the effectiveness of anti-aircraft fire (Johnson 1995a).

During the nineteenth century the various world powers of the time created dedicated Intelligence arms within their militaries (Wheeler 2012). These were of great use in processing the information generated from technological advances such as aerial reconnaissance, reports of enemy activity sent by field telegraph, and most importantly by the emerging technology of radio.

1.2.5 World War I

The utility of effective Intelligence was demonstrated in one of the early battles of the World War I, the Battle of Tannenberg in August 1914. The Russian plan was to destroy the German army forces in East Prussia through a pincer movement using the Russian First and Second armies. This plan required coordination and planning between the two army groups.

The Russian armies lacked the necessary cables to construct wired telegraph communication infrastructure, so they relied heavily on the mobility and range of radio communication. Unfortunately, they lacked trained signal troops and cryptographers. Hence, in order to ensure that orders and reports were received clearly, the Russian troops routinely conducted radio communication without encryption. These communications were consistently intercepted by the German army, swiftly translated and used to understand the location, disposition, and intentions of the Russian units (Norwitz 2001).

In addition, the German army used aerial reconnaissance reports to understand the supply situation for the Russians, and to verify the accuracy of radio intercepts. As the Russians advanced, human intelligence from the populace and disguised soldiers also greatly benefitted the Germans.

Through their understanding of the situation, the German army was able to use their numerically smaller forces to destroy the Russian Second Army, before repositioning to attack and defeat the Russian First Army. Despite lacking numerical superiority, the Germans were able to develop informational superiority and use this to their advantage, striking a decisive blow on the Eastern front from which Imperial Russia never recovered (Kahn 2006).

Effective Intelligence wasn't confined to the Eastern front. Throughout 1917 onwards, the movement of German forces to and from the Western front was being monitored by the '*La Dame Blanche*' network of spies. This network conducted espionage within occupied Belgium and France; by the end of the war, it was reliably reporting the movement of all German troops to British military Intelligence (Decock 2014).

Thus, as the German Spring Offensive of 1918 was being prepared, Allied forces were aware of the build-up and that an attack was imminent. In March 1918, days before the German offensive began, the German Army switched to using a new cypher to encrypt their communications. This ADFGX cypher was derived from the signalling techniques used in ancient Greece, providing an encryption technique that was both simple to implement by radio operations and believed to be uncrackable (Dipenbroek 2019).

Within one month of the cypher being used, the French cryptanalyst Georges Painvin was able to decrypt some messages. The Germans made changes to their cypher in order to improve it, but again Painvin was able to crack the cypher. Painvin was also able to distinguish that the Germans only changed their encryption keys daily when a major offensive was planned. This allowed him to identify not only the location of the attack planned for June 1918 from decrypted messages, but from the fact that this attack was associated with daily key changes, that it was an attack of great significance (de Lastours 2014).

In response to this intelligence, the French high command was able to reinforce the area and repulse the attack, citing the intercepted communication as '*Le Radiotélégramme de la Victoire*' (the radiogram of victory) (de Lastours 2014). Successful execution of this offensive was vital to Germany before the full deployment of American troops could be achieved by the Allies.

The entry into the war by the United States was itself partly due to Intelligence. The Germans proposed to the Mexican government that if the United States joined World War I on the side of the allies that Germany and Mexico should form an alliance. As part of this alliance Germany would support Mexico in acquiring their 'lost' territory including Texas, Arizona, and New Mexico.

The encrypted telegramme containing this offer was transmitted via the diplomatic telegraph cables of neutral Sweden and the US. The British intercepted and decrypted the message, but could not pass the plain text to the US without disclosing that they monitored the communications of neutral countries. This dilemma was solved by the British Ambassador in Mexico who arranged for an official copy of the document to be 'acquired' by him in return for a sum of money. Presumably, a bribe was paid to someone with legitimate access to the document, or possibly a third party was contracted to steal a copy of the document.

Armed with a 'legitimately' procured version of the document, the British were able to pass the document to the American government. Publication of this intelligence coup caused a furore amongst the American public, helping to convince an until then sceptical public to enter the war on the side of the Allies (von Gathen 2007).

1.2.6 World War II

The story of Bletchley Park and the work done there building on the work of French and Polish cryptanalysts to break the German Enigma cypher has been well documented elsewhere (Ferris 2020). In passing, it is interesting to reflect that the first electronic computers built as part of the effort at Bletchley Park were designed to break the communications secrecy of a third party. This history of modern computers is inseparable from that of cyber security. Electronic computers have been used to compromise data since their first invention.

The contribution of Bletchley Park to traffic analysis is often overlooked. Gordon Welchman was one of the early recruits to Bletchley Park along with Alan Turing. He recognised that there was much useful intelligence to be gleaned from the traffic analysis of enemy signals identifying when and from where a signal had been sent, even without requiring the message to be decrypted.

The patterns of communication used between enemy units in the field could be used to identify command structures, the locations of headquarters as distinct from subordinate units. The frequency of communications, often referred to as 'chatter', tells much about the activity of units with the frequency of communications increasing before conducting operations as orders are issued and situational reports broadcast.

Welchman was able to create a fusion centre within Hut Six of Bletchley Park where the metadata from communications analysis was combined with the decrypted content of messages to create intelligence, which was more valuable than either source of intelligence on its own (Grey 2012; Welchman 2017). Indeed, combining intelligence from many different sources enriches reports since each independent source provides its own viewpoint on an issue. Many different perspectives and viewpoints help to provide a more complete picture.

> No-one else was doing anything about this potential goldmine; so, I drew up a comprehensive plan which called for close coordination of radio interception, analysis of the intercepted traffic, the breaking of Enigma keys, and extracting intelligence from the decodes. – G. Welchman
> *(Martin 2015)*

This intelligence process became known as SIXTA, derived from 'Hut Six Traffic Analysis'. The importance of this process to the war effort is emphasised by the fact that although the work of cryptographers, such as Alan Turing, in decoding the Enigma cypher is declassified, published and well described, the history of SIXTA at Bletchley Park remains classified as a state secret (National Archives 1945).

The use of radio detection equipment to triangulate the location of a radio transmitter had been developed during World War I as a method of locating U-Boats (Grant 2003). This technique named 'radiogoniometry', and later 'huff-duff', could pinpoint the source of radio transmissions from a ship or submarine to within a few miles (Markus 1946).

So successful was this technique that a series of radio direction finding stations were established throughout the UK, and abroad during World War II. This network of stations referred to as the Y Service, not only recorded the intercepted morse code signals, but provided intelligence regarding the locations of radio transmitters. Particularly skilled operators could distinguish characteristics in how the morse key was tapped while sending messages to recognise the individuals sending the message (McKay 2012).

The intercepted messages were sent to Bletchley Park for decryption. However, even before the content of the message was discovered, the Y Service and Traffic Analysis could provide the location from which the message was sent, the identity of the individual who sent the message, and the wider context of activity of which the message was part, thus providing even more enrichment to intelligence reports.

1.2.7 Post War Intelligence

At the end of World War II, the analysis of radio magnetic emissions had proved itself vital to the conduct of the war. This field of Signals Intelligence (SIGINT) was recognised as comprising two distinct disciplines: COMINT relating to the analysis of signals used for communications such as voice or text, and Electronic Intelligence (ELINT) relating to the analysis of non-communications signals such as radar emissions (NATO 2017c, NATO 2017d).

Analysis of the intelligence successes of the war identified that SIGINT had played a major part, and that the centralised intelligence function at Bletchley Park had greatly facilitated the production and dissemination of intelligence. On the other hand, German SIGINT efforts had floundered due to the existence of five separate cryptanalytic efforts, which competed for resources and refused to cooperate together (Johnson 1995b).

In the US the dangers of too many competing intelligence efforts were recognised leading to the creation of centralised intelligence agencies: the CIA in 1947, and the US National Security Agency (NSA) in 1952. Presumably, similar discussions were happening behind the Iron Curtain leading to the creation of the Soviet *Komitet Gosudarstvennoy Bezopasnosti* (KGB) in 1954, and the East German *Hauptverwaltung Aufklärung* foreign intelligence branch of the Ministry of State Security (Stasi) in 1955 (Johnston 2019).

Increasing SIGINT capabilities for gathering intelligence combined with awareness of how intelligence could assist decision making led to the development of management models by which intelligence efforts could be conceptualised and directed. Dating from this period, the Intelligence Cycle became the most widely known conceptual model of intelligence operations (Glass and Davidson 1948). This model remains in use today.

Beyond the immediate post war period, much of the history of the development of intelligence techniques remains classified and beyond the reach of civilian research in the private sector. However, the development of computing systems saw the interests of the largely civilian community of computer system operators overlap with those of security and intelligence agencies within the public sector. The former were seeking to assure the security and safety of the computer systems within their care, the latter seeking to assure the safety and security of nation states as part of their mission.

1.2.8 Cyber Threat Intelligence

The development of computers during the 1960s led to the deployment of the first multi-user systems within universities. Computing resources were limited and expensive, therefore username and password-enforced quotas and limits to users' access to these resources had to be implemented.

To a generation of young students gaining extra computing time proved a strong temptation, and password protection did not prevent illicit access (Walden and Van Vleck 2011). However, in an environment where everyone who could possibly access the device was known, the discovery and holding to account of the perpetrator could be expected, even if sanctions for the transgressor were mild (Yost 2012).

The existence of vulnerabilities in computer systems were known and widely shared within the system administrator community (Yost 2012). 'Tiger teams' were formed to hunt security vulnerabilities, so that they could be rectified. The weaknesses of such an approach and the prevalence of security vulnerabilities were recognised by the United States Air Force (USAF),

> ... the tiger team can only reveal system flaws and provide no basis for asserting that a system is secure in the event their efforts are unsuccessful. In the latter event, the only thing that can be stated is that the security state of the system is unknown. It is a commentary on contemporary systems that none of the known tiger team efforts has failed to date.
>
> *(Anderson 1972)*

Indeed, the USAF identified that,

> Based on current experience with penetration exercises, and assuming the availability of an individual with technical familiarity with the target system, the cost to find and exploit at least one design or implementation flaw in virtually any contemporary system is one man-month of effort or less.
>
> *(Anderson 1972)*

By the mid-1970s, computer security issues were discussed, and incidents of computer abuse shared within the computer security community. Motivations of early computer criminals ranged from theft of proprietary data, unauthorised access to services, through to financial fraud (Parker 1976). This set of motivations would seem remarkably familiar to today's cyber security teams.

By the mid-1970s, security practitioners had identified the fundamental tenets of computer security (Saltzer and Schroeder 1975). These included the importance of what we would now recognise as cyber threat intelligence,

> Detection and effective reporting of anomalous activity within a computer system and its environment is equally as important as prevention of unauthorized acts ...
>
> Monitoring the use of computers could be important for detecting the possible planning or practicing for attacks on computers.
>
> *(Parker 1973)*

By 1980 the techniques for analysing system data to identify anomalous activity by users or systems had been developed. The detection of anomalies within system data highlighted activity that was outside of that considered 'normal'. However, anomalous behaviour is not necessarily evidence of malicious behaviour.

Uncovering malicious acts requires investigation by a security operative to piece together the series of actions associated with the anomalous behaviour. Only with the context of the behaviour, identifying any actions that preceded or followed the anomaly, can any indication of malice and the potential source of the behaviour be uncovered (Anderson 1980).

Anderson's paper also made two observations that are as relevant today as when they were first published in 1980 (Anderson 1980). First, relating to the nature of the system data which we rely on to be able to identify malicious behaviour and incursions:

> security audit trails, if taken, are rarely complete and almost never geared to the needs of the security officers.

Second, relating to the difficulty of identifying the most sophisticated malicious users who have high-level access to a device, and who are able to use this access to erase their traces:

> The clandestine user who effects a technical penetration to obtain control of the most privileged state (of) the computer system, is not capable of being audited.

The 1983 film *WarGames*, in which a teenager played by Matthew Broderick succeeds in gaining unauthorised access to a Pentagon computer, and nearly brings about the world's destruction, brought the issue of computer security to the mainstream. The film captured the mood of the time, mixing themes of advances in computer technology and communications with cold war paranoia and the dangers of teenage 'hackers' (Schulte 2008).

The influence of the film extended to the White House, reportedly leading President Reagan to question his staff if such a scenario was possible. The reply that in reality, *'the situation is much worse than you think',* apocryphally led to the issuing of National Security Decision Directive (NSDD) 145 (White House 1984; Kaplan 2016).

NSDD 145 explicitly recognised that by the mid-1980s, computer and telecommunications systems were becoming inseparable. Despite increasing use of computer technology by the government and the private sector, *'the technology to exploit these electronic systems is widespread and is used extensively by foreign nations and can be employed, as well, by terrorist groups and criminal elements'.* (White House 1984). Significantly, the directive recognised that the solution to addressing these risks involved both the public and private sectors working together and sharing information, if only due to the recognition that many systems of key national interest were being operated within the private sector.

The wording of NSDD 145, *'widespread and is used extensively by foreign nations'* hints at the existence of many known but unpublished incidents of computer intrusions undertaken by hostile entities. There is an inherent conflict between the desire to keep such incidents classified as state secrets so as not to alert the attackers to cyber detection capabilities, and the possibility that publishing such reports might help develop detection capabilities within the private sector. This conflict has yet to be resolved.

The first in-depth description of the discovery, investigation, and identification of a hostile computer incursion over the Internet was published in 1988 when Clifford Stoll, a systems administrator at Lawrence Berkeley Laboratory was asked to investigate an accounting error. A new user account had been created, but the particular user did not have a billing address to which use of the computing facilities could be charged.

Over the following months, Stoll diligently collected information recording the activities of the unknown user, quickly identifying that this was a malicious attacker. The attacker was using the Lawrence Berkeley Laboratory computer system not only to search for and collect potentially sensitive information from the laboratory itself, but also as a site to launch further attacks on computer systems within the US, many of which were hosted by, or closely associated with the military (Stoll 1988).

Ultimately, the attacker was identified as a KGB agent based in Germany, and brought to justice. Stoll's publications characterised the method by which the attacker conducted their attack, allowing others to consider how they might detect and repel such an attack in the future, and provided detailed guidance on how the investigation was conducted, serving as a reference for how investigations should be conducted (Stoll 1987, 1989).

This incident served as a warning to the security community, illustrating that innocuous systems within the civilian sector may nevertheless become embroiled in activity, which may seem to have come straight from a spy film. Clearly, the nature of computer incidents, which administrators may have to resolve now included incursions by agents of nation state intelligence agencies.

As the volume of cyber attacks increased through the mid-2000s, it became steadily clear that a small percentage of these attacks were significantly different from the others (Lee and Lewis 2011). These attacks were distinguished by their sophistication, and by their persistence. Once the attacker had fixed on a target, the attacker patiently continued to launch attacks against the target for extended periods of time until they were successful (Thonnard et al. 2012).

The term Advanced Persistent Threat (APT) came to be used to refer to these sophisticated, patient, attackers. One characteristic of early APT attacks was that they did not appear to be conducted for clear financial gain. Indeed, many APT attacks appeared to be conducted in support of the objectives of a nation state. Although the identity of the attackers could not be discerned, the term APT came to be used as an umbrella term to refer to any attackers who appeared to be conducting a state-sponsored attack (Bejtlich 2010).

1.2.9 Emergence of Private Sector Intelligence Sharing

Not only was Stoll's uncovering of a KGB agent's infiltration of computer networks notable for being the earliest disclosure of nation state attacks against computer systems, but it was also a significant milestone in the development of threat intelligence outside of the state sector (Stoll 1988).

In its infancy, any issues with the operation of the Internet were resolved between administrators who for the most part, knew each other personally. This network of trust and interpersonal relationships was largely successful in managing risks. Online resources such as the Forum on Risks to the Public in Computers and Related Systems founded in August 1985, amongst other similar initiatives, provided a mechanism by which information regarding cyber risks and vulnerabilities could be shared amongst the community (Neumann 1985; Slayton and Clarke 2020).

This informal information sharing model was severely tested by the Morris Worm in 1988. The worm spread autonomously and rapidly between connected systems, infecting systems multiple times over leading to resource depletion and denial of service (Orman 2003). The worm severely affected many institutions bringing IT services to their knees. However, without a single point of contact offering authoritative information and advice, administrators were left struggling to manage the many sources of advice and remediation (Slayton and Clarke 2020).

In response, the Defense Advanced Research Projects Agency (DARPA) funded the creation of the Computer Emergency Response Team Coordinating Center (CERT/CC) at the Software Engineering Institute of Carnegie Mellon University. The team was established to provide advice and services to those affected by computer incidents, and ultimately to act as a middle-man between researchers who had identified software vulnerabilities, and the vendors of the affected software who needed to provide remediation (Allen and Pethia 2006). This model proved a successful template for national CERT organisations that was replicated globally (Slayton and Clarke 2020).

How the details of vulnerabilities should be handled proved to be a contentious issue. One group espoused that information regarding vulnerabilities was highly sensitive and should be kept secret until a suitable remediation was available. At the point of public disclosure, only a minimum of information should be released to ensure that attackers couldn't learn how to exploit the vulnerability. This was the model adopted by CERT/CC. Others believed that information about vulnerabilities should be shared early, widely, and with as much detail as possible so that administrators could take steps to protect their systems before official remediation was released.

This schism led to the creation of the Bugtraq mailing list in 1993, a public mailing list where computer security issues could be publicly discussed, and where researchers could disclose vulnerabilities that they had identified. The detail of technical discussion within the mailing list helped both vulnerability researchers and system administrators refine their skills. However, the potential price of such a discourse was that the same information could be used by attackers to refine and advance their own skills and create attack code quicker than may otherwise have been possible (Goerzen and Coleman 2022).

Yet, the development of detailed knowledge within the private sector was a source of strength. Discussions of vulnerabilities, security incidents, and protections developed organically into widely adopted practices for defending systems. The presidential commission on protecting critical infrastructure found that there was a need to improve information flow between the operators of critical infrastructure and the public sector. Operators would benefit from specialist knowledge within the public sector, and in turn the public sector could learn from the know-how and identification of cyber attacks within the private sector (Marsh 1997).

Aggregating and sharing threat intelligence both vertically between the private and public sectors, and horizontally amongst peers within industry sectors proved to be a compelling model for cooperation. The Presidential Decision Directive 63 (PDD-63) established Information Sharing and Analysis Centers (ISACs) by which trusted participants from industry could share intelligence together with representatives from law enforcement (White House 1998).

In parallel with the growing number of threats and attacks, private sector companies offering security solutions to detect and block threats also grew in number and capability. Protecting against the emerging threats such as computer viruses and trojans required collecting and analysing large numbers of the malware used in attacks (Kephart et al. 1997; Mezzour et al. 2016).

Over time, not only could providers of security services in the private sector detect distinct attacks, but also correlate many attacks against different victims into wider campaigns of activity carried out by a single threat actor. This intelligence gathering capability had previously been the preserve of the nation state.

In 2013, Mandiant had been able to collect sizable amounts of information relating to a single threat actor behind a large number of cyber attacks whom they referred to as APT1, which had been in operation since 2004. Unprecedentedly, Mandiant was able to identify the entity behind APT1, and feel secure enough in their conclusions to name the threat actor as a branch of the Chinese military (Mandiant Intelligence Center 2013).

In parallel, teams capable of performing in-depth investigations of cyber threats, and risks to human rights on the Internet developed within academia. The reports produced by entities such as Citizen Lab within the University of Toronto (Citizen Lab 2018), or the Georgia Tech Information Security Center (now part of the School of Cybersecurity and Privacy), provided balanced and open reporting and intelligence on emerging cyber security threats (Ahamad et al. 2008).

Stimulated by the ability of the private sector to generate cyber threat intelligence, and the hunger of organisations to understand cyber threats and to protect networks, commercial organisations such as Digital Shadows and Recorded Future were founded specifically to provide cyber threat intelligence to the private sector.

Alongside the commercial supply of threat intelligence, the non-profit organisation Bellingcat has emerged as an independent purveyor of intelligence, using the plethora of raw data and existing published intelligence reports to highlight human rights abuse and otherwise hidden conflicts.

Previously these capabilities were confined to national intelligence agencies. Intelligence agenies have not resisted the emergence of intelligence provision within the private sector. Indeed, the CIA has welcomed the work of Bellingcat as a means of discussing the policy implications of the attacks identified by the private sector without disclosing the classified intelligence gathering capabilities of the public sector (Mackinnon 2020).

1.3   Utility of Threat Intelligence

Put simply, you cannot protect against threats if you do not know that they exist, or do not understand their nature. This is the utility of threat intelligence, to describe what might cause harm so that decision makers can understand the threats they face and take appropriate action.

The process of generating threat intelligence results in information. On its own, this information is of little use. The ultimate utility of threat intelligence is in its application, putting the information to good use in support of an organisation's objectives.

These objectives should be set by the senior decision makers within the organisation and underpinned by a risk management strategy, which considers everything that might impede attaining those objectives.

Threat intelligence should inform and support the risk management process. Cyber threat intelligence specifically affects everything to do with risks relating to networked computer systems and the operations that these systems perform. As technology increasingly assists and enhances everything within our professional and personal lives, networked computer systems perform vital functions within our society. Cyber threat intelligence seeks to inform how we protect these vital systems against threats.

The threat landscape is dynamic and in constant flux. As an organisation's strengths and weaknesses change over time, so do those of attackers. The capabilities and ambitions of attackers evolve. Put bluntly, bad guys don't get any dumber. Threat intelligence reports on these changes, flowing into the risk management process so that our understanding of risk and the adequacy of our defences changes accordingly. With better understanding of our weaknesses and the emerging strengths of those who would do us harm, we can make decisions regarding the allocation of resources to best protect us from harm.

Organisations may already by conducting threat intelligence under a different name. Risk management processes such as NIST SP 800-39 or ISO/IEC 27005 may already be in use within an organisation, and activities related to keeping abreast of current threats may be in place.

The NIST SP 800-39 framework describes how organisations should frame risk, i.e. place it within the context of the business and its operations; assess risk, i.e. understand likelihoods and potential impact; respond to risk once determined and monitor risk as a continuous activity (NIST SP 800-39 2011) (Figure 1.1).

Threat intelligence drives the assessment of risk through the description of the threats, which may impact an organisation. Similarly, the monitoring of risk is also a threat intelligence activity since we seek to understand how threats and our exposure to them evolves (Figure 1.2).

The ISO/IEC 27005 risk management process is subtly different. Organisations identify and estimate risk as part of a risk analysis process, including this with risk evaluation to form a risk assessment process. If the risk assessment process is satisfactory, the identified risks are managed through risk treatment.

Threat intelligence should drive the risk assessment process, again through describing the threats which they may impact. Communicating information about these risks is a threat intelligence activity in itself, informing others so they can make appropriate decisions and modify behaviour if required. Similarly, the ongoing review and monitoring of risk is also threat intelligence. The threat landscape is constantly changing: monitoring these changes is part of threat intelligence.

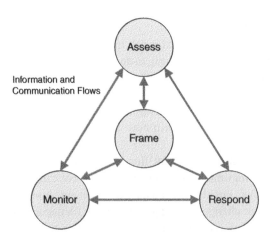

Figure 1.1 NIST SP 800-39 risk management process. *Source:* Adapted from NIST SP 800-39 2011.

Figure 1.2 Detail of ISO/IEC 27005 risk management process. *Source:* Adapted from ISO/IEC 27005 2018.

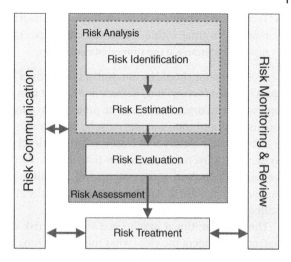

1.3.1 Developing Cyber Threat Intelligence

Cyber threat intelligence is concerned specifically with threats to networked electronic systems. Understanding the threats against these computer systems and the consequent risks to the organisation requires developing a cyber threat intelligence programme.

This programme can identify the relevant threats, feeding into the risk management process, and providing intelligence to manage these threats. However, as this programme is developed the goals and requirements of the programme need to be clearly stated, and a plan formulated to decide how the capabilities of the cyber threat intelligence function will be developed over time to reach the required standard. Organisations should have a clear idea of why intelligence is needed, exactly how the intelligence will be used, and how the success of the intelligence programme will be measured.

Similarly, an organisation should have an understanding of the limits of threat intelligence. An intelligence function cannot foresee the future or read the minds of adversaries. The unpredicted and unpredictable does happen. Threat intelligence can provide three types of insight as to what might happen, or what is currently happening:

- Strategic threat intelligence – Describing long term changes, and the long term objectives of adversaries. Intended to be read by senior executives to drive long term strategy and priorities.
- Operational threat intelligence – Describing short to medium term changes in the threat landscape, and the current techniques used by adversaries. Intended to be read by security teams to help manage short term priorities and the current situation.

- Tactical (or technical) threat intelligence – Describing what is happening at this moment in time within the threat landscape. Largely intended to be read by machine to manage the immediate situation.

Security teams should be mindful of the words of Frederick the Great of Prussia, *'he who defends everything, defends nothing'*. It is fanciful to expect that every system within an organisation can be protected to a maximum extent. Resources are not infinite, and compromises must be made trading off security against usability.

Every system deserves at least a minimum level of protection. However, some systems require more protection than others due to the risk they pose to the organisation. Indeed, some systems will constitute the 'crown jewels' of an organisation, to the point that if they were successfully attacked the organisation would suffer extreme consequences.

This is where threat intelligence augments risk management. While risk management considers the risk (what might go wrong), threat intelligence considers how an eventuality might be achieved (how might it happen). Threat intelligence allows security teams to focus on what is *likely* to happen rather than what *might* happen, and to take a proactive approach in responding to a changing threat environment.

Threat intelligence is uncertain. This degree of uncertainty must be quantified and expressed. Nevertheless, threat intelligence can increase understanding within an uncertain world, driving good decision making, and when the threat landscape changes, provide a rapid indication of the nature of these changes so that informed decisions can be swiftly taken.

Summary

Cyber threat intelligence is both the process and outcome of studying threats against networked computer systems. The goal of threat intelligence is to inform decision makers about threats so that better decisions can be made.

Threat intelligence has a long history dating back to antiquity. With the advent of the Internet, and the development of computer systems, cyber threat intelligence has emerged as a speciality and a capability within the private sector.

References

Ahamad, M., Amster, D., Barrett, M. et al. (2008). *Emerging Cyber Threats Report for 2009*. Georgia Tech Information Security Center. https://smartech.gatech.edu/bitstream/handle/1853/26301/CyberThreatsReport2009.pdf.

Al-Kadit, I.A. (1992). Origins of cryptology: the Arab contribution. *Cryptologia* 16 (2): 97–126.

Allen, J. and Pethia, R. (2006). *Lessons Learned: A Conversation with Rich Pethia, Director of CERT Transcript, Part 1: CERT History.* Carnegie Mellon University. https://apps.dtic.mil/sti/pdfs/AD1130301.pdf (accessed 13 January 2023).

Anderson, J.P. (1972). Computer Security Technology Planning Study. Report to USAF Deputy for Command and Management Systems, HQ Electronic Systems Division. https://csrc.nist.gov/csrc/media/publications/conference-paper/1998/10/08/proceedings-of-the-21st-nissc-1998/documents/early-cs-papers/ande72a.pdf (accessed 13 January 2023).

Anderson, J.P. (1980). *Computer Security Threat Monitoring and Surveillance.* James P. Anderson Company. https://csrc.nist.gov/csrc/media/publications/conference-paper/1998/10/08/proceedings-of-the-21st-nissc-1998/documents/early-cs-papers/ande80.pdf.

Austin, N.J.E. and Rankov, N.B. (1998). *Exploratio: Military and Political Intelligence in the Roman World from the Second Punic War to the Battle of Adrianople.* Psychology Press.

Baker, O.R. (2022). Gorgo: Sparta's woman of autonomy, authority, and agency. *Athens Journal of Humanities & Arts* 9 (2): 145–158.

Bank of England (2016). CBEST Intelligence-Led Testing Understanding Cyber Threat Intelligence Operations version 2.0. www.bankofengland.co.uk/-/media/boe/files/financial-stability/financial-sector-continuity/understanding-cyber-threat-intelligence-operations.pdf (accessed 13 January 2023).

Bejtlich, R. (2010). Understanding the advanced persistent threat. *Information Security Magazine Online* (13 July).

Bimfort, M.T. (1958). A definition of intelligence. *Studies in Intelligence* 2: 75–78.

Broemeling, L.D. (2011). An account of early statistical inference in Arab cryptology. *The American Statistician* 64 (4): 255–257.

Bruen, A.A. and Forcinto, M.A. (2011). *Cryptography, Information Theory, and Error-Correction: A Handbook for the 21st Century.* Wiley.

Calof, J.L. and Skinner, B. (1998). Competitive intelligence for government officers: a brave new world. *Optimum* 28 (2): 38–42.

Campbell, B. and Tritle, L.A. (2013). *The Oxford Handbook of Warfare in the Classical World.* Oxford University Press.

Citizen Lab (2018). *The Citizen Lab.* University of Toronto. https://citizenlab.ca/wp-content/uploads/2018/05/18033-Citizen-Lab-booklet-p-E.pdf (accessed 13 January 2023).

Coe, T. (2015). Where does the word cyber come from? *OUP Blog* (28 March). https://blog.oup.com/2015/03/cyber-word-origins (accessed 13 January 2023).

Crowther, G.A. (2017). The cyber domain. *The Cyber Defense Review* 2 (3): 63–78.

De Leeuw, K. (1999). The black chamber in the Dutch Republic during the war of the Spanish succession and its aftermath, 1707–1715. *The Historical Journal* 42 (1): 133–156. https://doi.org/10.1017/S0018246X98008292.

Decock, P. (2014). 'La Dame Blanche', *1914–1918-online. International Encyclopedia of the First World War*. https://doi.org/10.15463/ie1418.10241.

Dipenbroek, M. (2019). From fire signals to ADFGX. A case study in the adaptation of ancient methods of secret communication. *KLEOS Amsterdam Bulletin of Ancient Studies and Archaeology* 2 (Apr): 63–76.

Dugald, S., Playfair, J., Macintosh, J. et al. (1842). *Post Office*. Encyclopaedia Britannica. https://jstor.org/stable/10.2307/community.27604311.

Dylan, H. (2012). The joint intelligence bureau: (not so) secret intelligence for the post-war world. *Intelligence and National Security* 27 (1): 27–45.

Edwards, F. (2007). Review: Robert Hutchinson, Elizabeth's Spy Master. *Francis Walsingham and the Secret War that Saved England*, Weidenfeld and Nicolson, 2006, ISBN: 10 0 297 84613 2, pp. 399. *Recusant History* 28 (3): 483–488. https://doi.org/10.1017/S0034193200011535.

Emmott, R. (2018). NATO cyber command to be fully operational in 2023. *Reuters* (26 October). https://www.reuters.com/article/us-nato-cyber-idUSKCN1MQ1Z9 (accessed 13 January 2023).

Evov, A. (1996). The 'missing dimension' of C. Julius Caesar. *Historia: Zeitschrift Für Alte Geschichte* 45 (1): 64–94.

Fabien, A.P., Anderson, R.J., and Kuhn, M.G. (1999). Information hiding: a survey. *Proceedings of the IEEE* 87 (7): 1062–1078. https://doi.org/10.1109/5.771065.

Farhat-Holzman, L. (2007). Stephen Budiansky, *Her Majesty's spymaster: Elizabeth I, Sir Francis Walsingham, and the birth of modern espionage. Comparative Civilizations Review* 56 (56): 121–122.

Ferdinando, L. (2018). *Cybercom to Elevate to Combatant Command*. US Department of Defense Press Release. https://www.defense.gov/Explore/News/Article/Article/1511959/cybercom-to-elevate-to-combatant-command (accessed 13 January 2023).

Ferris, J. (2020). *Behind the Enigma: The Authorised History of GCHQ, Britain's Secret Cyber-Intelligence Agency*. Bloomsbury Publishing.

Fijnaut, C. and Marx, G.T. (1995). *Undercover, Police Surveillance in Comparative Perspective*. Kluwer Law International.

FIRST, Cyber Threat Intelligence SIG (2018). Introduction to CTI as a general topic. https://www.first.org/global/sigs/cti/curriculum/cti-introduction (accessed 13 January 2023).

Gartner Research and McMillan, R. (2003). Definition: Threat Intelligence. https://www.gartner.com/en/documents/2487216/definition-threat-intelligence (accessed 13 January 2023).

von Gathen, J. (2007). Zimmermann telegram: the original draft. *Cryptologia* 31 (1): 2–37.

Giles, L. (1910). *Sun Tzu on the Art of War*. Project Gutenberg. https://www.gutenberg.org/files/132/132-h/132-h.htm.

Glass, R.R. and Davidson, P.B. (1948). *Intelligence Is for Commanders*. The Telegraph Press.

Goerzen, M. and Coleman, G. (2022). *Wearing Many Hats. The Rise of the Professional Security Hacker*. Data & Society. https://datasociety.net/wp-content/uploads/2022/03/WMH_final01062022Rev.pdf.

Grant, R.M. (2003). *U-Boat Hunters, Code Breakers, Divers and the Defeat of the U-Boats, 1914–1918*. Periscope Publishing Ltd.

Grey, C. (2012). Understanding Bletchley Park's work. In: *Decoding Organization: Bletchley Park, Codebreaking and Organization Studies*, 213–244. Cambridge University Press.

Hillenbrand, T. (2017). *The King's NSA. From 1684 to 1984*. Epubli.

Iordanou, I. (2018). The professionalization of cryptology in sixteenth-century Venice. *Enterprise & Society* 19 (4): 973–1013. https://doi.org/10.1017/eso.2018.10.

ISO/IEC 27005:2018 (2018). *Information Technology – Security Techniques – Information Security Risk Management*. International Standards Organization. https://www.iso.org/standard/75281.html (accessed 13 January 2023).

Johnson, T.R. (1995a). From Tonkin to Tet – the heart of the war. In: *American Cryptology During the Cold War, 1945–1989. Book II: Centralization Wins, 1960–1972*, 528–558. Center for Cryptologic History. National Security Agency. https://nsarchive2.gwu.edu/NSAEBB/NSAEBB260/nsa-4.pdf.

Johnson, T.R. (1995b). AFSE and the creation of NSA. In: *American Cryptology during the Cold War, 1945–1989. Book 1: The Struggle for Centralization 1945–1960*, 23–59.

Johnston, M.K. (2019). The paradigm shifts in intelligence: from 1800 to present. *Illini Journal Of International Security* 5 (1): 56–64.

Kahn, D. (2006). The rise of intelligence. *Foreign Affairs* 85 (5): 125–134. https://doi.org/10.2307/20032075.

Kaplan, F. (2016). 'WarGames' and cybersecurity's debt to a Hollywood hack. *The New York Times* (19 February). https://www.nytimes.com/2016/02/21/movies/wargames-and-cybersecuritys-debt-to-a-hollywood-hack.html (accessed 13 January 2023).

Kephart, J.O., Sorkin, G.B., Chess, D.M., and White, S.R. (1997). Fighting computer viruses. *Scientific American* 277 (5): 88–93.

de Lastours, S. (2014). Les Travaux de la Section du Chiffre Pendant La Première Guerre Mondiale. *Cryptologie et mathématiques: Une mutation des enjeux* 87: 87–106.

Lee, M. (2014). History of hacking. *Engineering & Technology Reference* 1–7. https://doi.org/10.1049/etr.2014.0011.

Lee, M. and Lewis, D. (2011). Clustering disparate attacks: mapping the activities of the advanced persistent threat. *Proceedings of the 21st Virus Bulletin International Conference*.

Leimon, M. and Parker, G. (1996). Treason and plot in Elizabethan diplomacy: the 'Fame of Sir Edward Stafford' reconsidered. *The English Historical Review* 111 (44): 1134–1158.

Ma, J., Ning, H., Huang, R. et al. (2015). Cybermatics: a holistic field for systematic study of cyber-enabled new worlds. *IEEE Access* 3: 2270–2280.

MacAskill, E. and Dance, G. (2013). NSA Files: Decoded. What the revelations mean for you. *The Guardian*. https://www.theguardian.com/world/interactive/2013/nov/01/snowden-nsa-files-surveillance-revelations-decoded#section/1 (accessed 13 January 2023).

Mackinnon, A. (2020). Bellingcat can say what U.S. intelligence can't. *Foreign Policy* (17 December). https://foreignpolicy.com/2020/12/17/bellingcat-can-say-what-u-s-intelligence-cant (accessed 13 January 2023).

Mandiant Intelligence Center (2013). APT1: Exposing One of China's Cyber Espionage Units. https://www.fireeye.com/content/dam/fireeye-www/services/pdfs/mandiant-apt1-report.pdf (accessed 13 January 2023).

Marcus, H. and Findlen, P. (2019). Deciphering Galileo: communication and secrecy before and after the trial. *Renaissance Quarterly* 72 (3): 953–955.

Markus, J. (1946). Huff Duff. *Scientific American* 174 (4): 155–157.

Marsh, R.T. (1997). Critical Foundations Protecting America's Infrastructures. The Report of the President's Commission on Critical Infrastructure Protection. https://www.ojp.gov/ncjrs/virtual-library/abstracts/critical-foundations-protecting-americas-infrastructures (accessed 13 January 2023).

Martin, A.J. (2015). Bletchley Park remembers 'forgotten genius' Gordon Welchman. *The Register* (27 September). https://www.theregister.com/2015/09/27/gordan_welchman_bletchley_park_remembers/?page=1 (accessed 13 January 2023).

Mavroeidis, V. and Bromander, S. (2017). Cyber threat intelligence model: an evaluation of taxonomies, sharing standards, and ontologies within cyber threat intelligence. *2017 European Intelligence and Security Informatics Conference (EISIC)*, 91–98. IEEE. https://www.duo.uio.no/bitstream/handle/10852/58492/CTI_Mavroeidis%25282017%2529.pdf (accessed 13 January 2023).

McDermott, J.J. (2002). *Reading the Pentateuch: An Historical Introduction*. Paulist Press.

McKay, S. (2012). *The Secret Listeners. How the Y Service Intercepted the German Codes for Bletchley Park*. Arum Press Ltd.

Mezzour, G., Carley, L.R., and Carley, K.M. (2016). Longitudinal analysis of a large corpus of cyber threat descriptions. *Journal of Computer Virology and Hacking Techniques* 12 (1): 11–12. https://doi.org/10.4102/sajim.v15i2.559.

National Archives (1945). GC&CS Sixta History. An account of the work of the Traffic Analysis Party at Bletchley. https://discovery.nationalarchives.gov.uk/details/r/C11177401 (accessed 13 January 2023).

NATO Terminology Office (2017a). *Intelligence*. NATOTerm, The Official NATO Terminology Database. https://nso.nato.int/natoterm/content/nato/pages/home.html?lg=en (accessed 13 January 2023).

NATO Terminology Office (2017b). *Cyberspace*. NATOTerm, The Official NATO Terminology Database. https://nso.nato.int/natoterm/content/nato/pages/home.html?lg=en (accessed 13 January 2023).

NATO Terminology Office (2017c). *COMINT*. NATOTerm, The Official NATO Terminology Database. https://nso.nato.int/natoterm/content/nato/pages/home.html?lg=en (accessed 13 January 2023).

NATO Terminology Office (2017d). *ELINT*. NATOTerm, The Official NATO Terminology Database. https://nso.nato.int/natoterm/content/nato/pages/home.html?lg=en (accessed 13 January 2023).

Neumann, P.G. (1985). Welcome! *The RISKS Digest. Forum on Risks to the Public in Computers and Related Systems* 1 (1). https://catless.ncl.ac.uk/Risks/1/1#subj1.1.

Newitz, A. (2013). The bizarre evolution of the word 'Cyber'. *Gizmodo* (16 September). https://io9.gizmodo.com/today-cyber-means-war-but-back-in-the-1990s-it-mean-1325671487 (accessed 13 January 2023).

NIST SP 800-39 (2011). *NIST Special Publication 800-39. Managing Information Security Risk Organization, Mission, and Information System View*. National Institute of Standards and Technology, US Department of Commerce. https://nvlpubs.nist.gov/nistpubs/Legacy/SP/nistspecialpublication800-39.pdf (accessed 13 January 2023).

Norwitz, J.H. (2001). Leveraging Operational Intelligence: The Battle of Tannenberg and Masurian Lakes (1914). *NAVAL WAR COLL NEWPORT RI* [Preprint].

Numbers 13:17–19 (n.d.). *King James Bible*.

Orman, H. (2003). The Morris worm: a fifteen-year perspective. *IEEE Security & Privacy* 1 (5): 35–43.

Parker, D.B. (1973). Threats to Computer Systems. Report for US Atomic Energy Commission, Lawrence Libermore Laboratory. https://apps.dtic.mil/sti/pdfs/ADA587846.pdf (accessed 13 January 2023).

Parker, D.B. (1976). Computer abuse perpetrators and vulnerabilities of computer systems. *Proceedings of the June 7–10, 1976, National Computer Conference and Exposition*. AFIPS '76, 65–73. https://doi.org/10.1145/1499799.1499810.

Pellissier, R. and Nenzhelele, T.E. (2003). Towards a universal definition of competitive intelligence. *SA Journal of Information Management* 15 (2): 559. https://doi.org/10.4102/sajim.v15i2.559.

Reinke, E.C. (1962). Classical cryptography. *The Classical Journal* 58 (3): 113–121.

Saltzer, J.H. and Schroeder, M.D. (1975). The protection of information in computer systems. *Proceedings of the IEEE* 63 (9): 1278–1308.

Sapp, R. (2009). No room for gentlemen: cryptography in American history. *Historia* 21: 1–11.

Schulte, S.R. (2008). 'The WarGames scenario' regulating teenagers and teenaged technology (1980–1984). *Television & New Media* 9 (6): 487–513.

Shaw, C. (2000). Keeping track. In: *The Politics of Exile in Renaissance Italy*, 143–171. Cambridge University Press.

Slayton, R. and Clarke, B. (2020). Trusting infrastructure: the emergence of computer security incident response, 1989–2005. *Technology and Culture* 61 (1): 173–206.

Stoll, C. (1987). What do you feed a Trojan horse? *Proceedings of the 10th National Computer Security Conference*, 21–24.

Stoll, C. (1988). Stalking the wily hacker. *Communications of the ACM* 31 (5): 484–497.

Stoll, C. (1989). *The Cuckoo's Egg: Tracking a Spy Through the Maze of Computer Espionage*. Doubleday.

Strate, L. (1999). The varieties of cyberspace: problems in definition and delimitation. *Western Journal of Communication* 63 (3): 382–412. https://doi.org/10.1080/10570319909374648.

Thonnard, O., Bilge, L., O'Gorman, G. et al. (2012). Industrial espionage and targeted attacks: understanding the characteristics of an escalating threat. *International Workshop on Recent Advances in Intrusion Detection*, 64–85. Springer-Verlag.

Vause, E. (2014). 'The business of reputations': secrecy, shame, and social standing in nineteenth-century French Debtors' and Creditors' newspapers. *Journal of Social History* 48 (1): 47–71.

Walden, D. and Van Vleck, T. (ed.) (2011). *Compatible Time-Sharing System (1961–1973) Fiftieth Anniversary Commemorative Overview*. IEEE Computer Society. https://history.computer.org/pubs/2011-06-ctss.pdf.

Warner, M. (2002). Wanted: a definition of intelligence. *Studies in Intelligence* 46 (3): 15–22.

Welchman, G. (2017). Ultra revisited, a tale of two contributors. *Intelligence and National Security* 32 (2): 244–255. https://doi.org/10.1080/02684527.2016.125322.

Wheeler, D.L. (2012). A guide to the history of intelligence 1800–1918. *Intelligencer: Journal of U.S. Intelligence Studies* Winter/Spring: 47–50.

White House (1984). National Security Decision Directive Number 145. National Policy on Telecommunications and Automated Information Systems Security. https://fas.org/irp/offdocs/nsdd145.htm (accessed 13 January 2023).

White House (1998). Presidential Decision Directive 63. The White House. https://irp.fas.org/offdocs/pdd/pdd-63.htm (accessed 13 January 2023).

Yost, J.R. (2012). *Oral History Interview with Thomas Van Vleck*. Computer Security History Project, Charles Babbage Institute, University of Minnesota. https://conservancy.umn.edu/bitstream/handle/11299/144020/oh408tvv.pdf (accessed 13 January 2023).

2

Threat Environment

Every profession has a variety of commonly used technical terms and concepts. In this respect cyber threat intelligence is no different. Chapter 2 sets out many cyber security terms which are frequently encountered or used with a specific context within the domain of cyber threat intelligence.

2.1 Threat

Cyber threat intelligence is the study of threats. In order to explain and research threats we must be able to describe what is meant by the term.

Common usage covers three senses of the word:

- a suggestion that something unpleasant or violent will happen, especially if a particular action or order is not followed;
- a statement that someone will be hurt or harmed, especially if the person does not do something; and
- the possibility that something unwanted will happen, or a person or thing that is likely to cause something unwanted to happen.

(Cambridge Dictionary 2022)

Within cyber security the term is used specifically in the context of the final definition; a *threat* is something likely to cause an unwanted outcome in relation to computer systems.

Published definitions of the term within the cyber security industry can range from the very short:

potential violation of computer security – (ISO 2015)

Cyber Threat Intelligence, First Edition. Martin Lee.

To the verbose:

> Any circumstance or event with the potential to adversely impact organizational operations (including mission, functions, image, or reputation), organizational assets, individuals, other organizations, or the Nation through an information system via unauthorized access, destruction, disclosure, modification of information, and/or denial of service.
> – (NIST 2011)

Definitions may also be circular where terms are defined in relation to each other. In this definition, threat is defined in terms of the capacity to exploit a vulnerability, and vulnerabilities are defined in terms of their susceptibility to a threat:

> A circumstance or event that has or indicates the potential to exploit vulnerabilities and to adversely impact (create adverse consequences for) organizational operations, organizational assets (including information and information systems), individuals, other organizations, or society.
> – (US Cybersecurity & Infrastructure Security Agency [CISA] 2022)

In common with these definitions is the notion of a threat being something that can cause an unwanted effect on a computer system.

Importantly, threats do not necessarily need to be actively malicious. Threats can be accidental or forces of nature. For example, the landfall of Hurricane Sandy on Manhattan during 2012 caused extensive outages to communications infrastructure and caused disruption to many data centres (Kwasinski 2013). Clearly this meets our definition of a threat, since many computer systems were adversely affected, but it does not meet with the popular (mis)conception of a cyber threat being exclusively due to 'hackers'.

Providing guidance on how accidental data loss occurs, or the likely impact of an approaching weather system are both examples of relevant cyber threat intelligence. Remember that cyber threat intelligence relates to *things that may cause damage to electronic networked devices*. Therefore, information that is supplied to help improve decision making in relation to potentially severe threats, including physical threats such as severe weather is cyber threat intelligence.

Forces of nature can be studied and predicted without fear that observing the threat will cause it to change. A weather forecast may be right or wrong, but the action of studying the weather and releasing weather reports and forecasts does not cause the weather to change. This is not the case for the majority of cyber security threats.

The property of observing a phenomenon, which causes changes to that which is under observation is often referred to as the Hawthorne Effect (Landsberger 1958).

The effect was first described in studies on workplace productivity, where productivity seemed to improve without regard to the intervention being tested. Eventually the changes in productivity were explained as being due to the fact that the workers were being observed and investigated, and not due to any process or environmental change that was being researched as part of the study.

The Hawthorne Effect can have a large effect in cyber intelligence where threats are being controlled by people, or impacting people. When under scrutiny, users may become more diligent in their work and less prone to human error when they are aware that security teams are watching. However, close and intrusive scrutiny may not be welcomed by users leading to changes in behaviour, or even acting as a catalyst for someone to start acting to the detriment of their employer as a malicious insider (Whitty 2021).

Malicious threat actors frequently change their actions when they become aware that their presence or actions have been detected. They may seek to change their activity to evade detection, or act to remove evidence of their activities to prevent forensic analysis. In either case, this change in behaviour frustrates the gathering of evidence by threat intelligence teams.

Ideally, if we are to observe and understand a sentient threat, we do not wish the threat to be aware that it is under observation for fear that this will change its nature. Possibly, our actions may inform the threat that their activity has led to their detection. The disclosure of such information, even accidentally, may allow the malicious threat to refine and improve their techniques so that they become more difficult to detect in the future.

2.1.1 Threat Classification

Taxonomies of threats help drive the identification of threats, which might affect an organisation, and organise those that have already been found. Through considering the many types of threats listed in a taxonomy, organisations can identify the threats with which they may be faced.

The early information standard ISO/IEC 7498-2:1989 simply classified threats according to a two-dimensional grid as being either accidental or intentional, and active or passive.

Accidental threats are those that exist with no premeditated intent, whereas intentional threats have a purposeful motive. Passive threats do not modify any information within the system; active threats change the state of a computing device in some way (ISO 1989) (Figure 2.1).

Jouini et al.'s threat classification model considered the source of the threat, the threat agent, motivation, and intention. Showing that similar outcomes of a threat impacting such as the disclosure or destruction of information could have very different aetiology (Jouini et al. 2014).

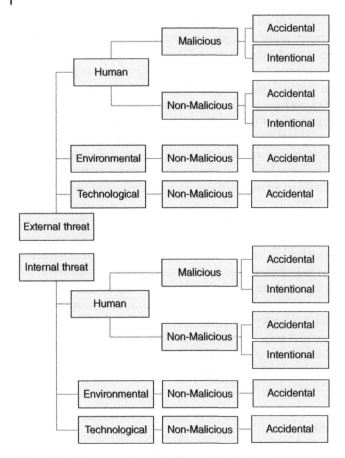

Figure 2.1 Taxonomy of threats. *Source:* Adapted from Jouini et al. (2014).

Taxonomies can be much more detailed than the above. The European Network Information Security Agency (ENISA) divides possible threats into eight high-level categories, then further subdivides into many more. The eight highest level categories consist of:

Physical attack (deliberate/intentional)
Unintentional damage/loss of information or IT assets
Disaster (natural, environmental)
Failures/Malfunction
Outages
Eavesdropping/Interception/Hijacking
Nefarious Activity/Abuse
Legal

(ENISA 2016)

Enumerating possible threat categories helps focus minds on identifying threats. Considering all the possible threats that might fit within a category is a very useful exercise. However, taxonomies can encourage analysts to look for certain types of threats at the risk of overlooking other threats that might not easily fit into the taxonomy.

Microsoft takes a different approach. Their STRIDE taxonomy of threats only considers threats against systems that fall under one of six categories:

Spoofing – Impersonating something or someone else.
Tampering – Modifying data or code.
Repudiation – Claiming not to have performed an action.
Information disclosure – Exposing information to someone not authorised to see it.
Denial of Service – Deny or degrade service to users.
Elevation of Privilege – Gain capabilities without proper authorisation.

(Shostack 2007; Microsoft 2009)

Clearly, the approach for identifying threats is radically different amongst these taxonomies. Many threat modelling methodologies can be applied to draw up a set of potential threats that might impact an organisation. Nevertheless, it is impossible for a threat intelligence programme or team to collect intelligence on a threat of which they are not aware.

Before a process of threat intelligence can be engaged, at the very least we need to have an idea of the threats that might impact us. Nevertheless, not every threat that can be imagined is going to be relevant to every organisation. We need to assess threats to consider if they are viable, and come to some degree of prioritisation so that the most urgent threats are addressed first.

2.2 Risk and Vulnerability

Cyber security is about managing risks. The consequences and likelihood of many risks are either so unlikely or inconsequential that it would be wasteful to devote resources to their management. Other risks necessitate mitigation, taking steps to reduce the likelihood of a risk occurring and/or measures to reduce the severity of the consequences if it were to happen (Figure 2.2).

This figure illustrates how risks can be evaluated. If both the likelihood and impact of a threat is low, then the organisation may just accept the risk. If the worst that can happen is that you get slightly wet feet when encountering the threat, then mitigation may not be required. An informal countermeasure, such as stepping over the gap may suffice. Although if the low impact consequences of the threat are frequently incurred, so that the cumulative effects become significant then a mitigation measure might be considered.

IMPACT

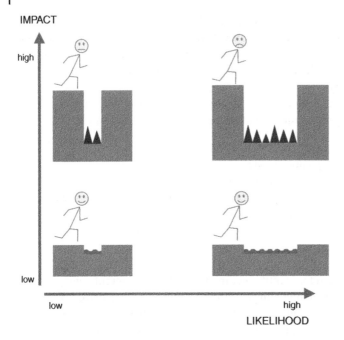

Figure 2.2 Illustration of threat impact vs likelihood of the threat impacting.

Where the potential impact is much higher, although the likelihood of harm being incurred remains low, then an improved protection such as building a bridge to span the gap may be necessary. Where both the consequences of the threat and the likelihood of incurring those consequences are high, then clearly a countermeasure to reduce the impact and likelihood is required.

In terms of cyber security, NATO defines a risk as the possibility that a particular threat will exploit a particular vulnerability of a data processing system (NATO 2017a). Note that other sources may choose to define risk differently (Figure 2.3).

Following NATO's definition, even if the vulnerability exists but there is no meaningful threat, then there is no risk. It would be wasteful to devote resources to mitigating this risk because the likelihood of exploitation of the vulnerability is minimal. The resources would be better allocated elsewhere.

Figure 2.3 Risk = threat + vulnerability.

Making such an assertion requires understanding both the risks and the relevant threats. The nature of threats is constantly changing. A new threat may become apparent that does exploit the vulnerability, in which case the level of risk will rise and may require addressing.

The understanding and characterisation of threats is an important component of understanding risk. Threat intelligence provides the relevant information necessary to make informed decisions regarding the nature of threats and how these interact with vulnerabilities.

Nevertheless, we must be aware of the limitations of our capabilities. It is impossible to collect useful intelligence about every single threat. Similarly, there is little point in collecting intelligence regarding threats that in practice will not affect a system, or will not result in harm. Threat intelligence must focus on providing understanding of the most relevant threats, which can provide the most benefit to senior decision makers.

The relationship between risk management and threat intelligence is circular in nature and mutually supportive. The risk management process determines the threats a threat intelligence programme should prioritise for investigation. In turn, the threat intelligence programme identifies the threats that pose the greatest risk to an organisation, which feeds back to the risk management process, driving the prioritisation.

Threats must be assessed to determine if a target is vulnerable to the threat. That is to say that there exists a weakness that a threat may exploit that could result in harm. For instance, a major earthquake may have drastic effects on the availability of a computing system, and as such poses a major risk. However, this is only a relevant threat if the computing system is located in an area where the local geology is vulnerable to earthquakes. If the physical area is not prone to earthquakes, then although a major earthquake may cause large amounts of damage, the area is not vulnerable to such a threat, therefore there is no risk.

The analysis and management of risk is a science in its own right, which to describe in any detail is beyond the scope of this book. The UK's National Cyber Security Centre (NCSC) provides an excellent introduction to risk management (NCSC 2016). There are many published standards and frameworks relating to risk management. The ISO 31000 family of standards provide guidelines relating to the implementation of risk management (ISO 2018b). The ISO/IEC 27005 (ISO 2018a) and NIST SP 800-37 (NIST 2018) standards provide more specific guidelines relating to the management of cyber risks.

In terms of cyber security, NATO defines a vulnerability as 'a *weakness or flaw in a data processing system*' (NATO 2017b). Vulnerabilities come in many shapes and forms. For a computer system, the weakness may be related to how the system is operated, how it was installed or configured, or within the software or hardware of the system. It is these flaws which can be exploited by a threat in order to adversely affect the confidentiality, integrity, or availability of the system that concern cyber security programmes.

The MITRE Corporation has developed a comprehensive list of common weaknesses in systems and regularly reports on the most dangerous (in that they are commonly found and easy to exploit) weaknesses (MITRE 2022a). Similarly, the Open Web Application Security Project (OWASP) reports on the most critical weaknesses within web applications (OWASP 2022).

2.2.1 Human Vulnerabilities

Human beings are intelligent and creative creatures who can achieve amazing feats through collaboration. However, they are also fallible, sometimes failing to successfully achieve what might be considered a simple routine task due to human error.

Analysis of data breaches identifies that one of the most common weaknesses in the unauthorised disclosure of information is in the operation of systems, and due to human error. Verizon finds that 85% of data breaches involve a human element, and that the single most common reason for a data breach is social engineering (Verizon 2021).

Nevertheless, humans fail in predictable ways:

Errors of action – attempting to do the right thing, but failing in correct execution.
Errors of thinking – misunderstanding a situation and executing the wrong course of action.
Non-compliance – wilfully choosing not to execute the correct task (Table 2.1).

Table 2.1 Classification of types of human error.

Error	Error class	Error type
Errors of action	Slips	Correct action performed incorrectly.
	Lapses	Correct action attempted, but with omissions.
Errors of thinking	Rule-based mistakes	Incorrect action due to mis-application of an otherwise correct procedure.
	Knowledge-based mistakes	Incorrect action due to applying best efforts to an unfamiliar situation.
Non-compliance	Routine	Incorrect action routinely performed due to tolerance of the action.
	Situational	Incorrect action performed due to extrinsic factors or constraints.
	Exceptional	Incorrect action performed due to extraordinary circumstances.

Source: Adapted from HSE (n.d.).

Training is often touted as the means by which human error can be minimised. Yet, people who have not been trained to be aware of the dangers of phishing attacks, or not taught about the dangers of clicking links in unexpected emails are few and far between. Nevertheless, phishing attacks remain successful due to human error. Despite knowing the correct course of action in response to a phishing email, users are prone to errors of thinking, mistaking malicious emails for genuine communications and incorrectly responding as if the approach was legitimate.

Threat actors actively exploit human errors through social engineering, making their malicious activities appear legitimate and so tricking victims into following an inappropriate course of action.

2.2.1.1   Example – Business Email Compromise

The business email compromise is a type of scam that relies on human error. In one common variation of the scam, the attacker identifies when a senior executive of an organisation is scheduled to speak at a conference, and will be away from the office. The attacker then contacts someone with financial authority within the target organisation purporting to be the executive requesting funds to be urgently transferred due to the non-payment of an invoice for the conference. The intended victim is urged to bypass financial controls because the money is required immediately.

The target is tricked into believing that the request is genuine, and consequently bypasses usual procedures due to the urgent nature of the request, transferring funds to the attacker. The target exhibits both rule-based human error in misrecognising the situation, and non-compliance through believing there to be an exceptional situation.

The Federal Bureau of Investigation (FBI) measures that in the US alone during 2020, such scams resulted in losses of $1.8 million per year (FBI 2020).

Threat intelligence professionals can help staff members with financial authority recognise and resist these scams by spreading awareness of how the scams work, and report any newly discovered variations in the scam. Similarly, intelligence teams can work together with financial teams to ensure that processes are robust enough to resist these attacks, yet also flexible enough so that unexpected events can be accommodated.

2.2.2   Configuration Vulnerabilities

Complex systems require configuration. However, configuring such systems to provide the required functionality is also a source of vulnerabilities. The OWASP top 10 list of vulnerabilities in web applications places security configuration as number six on the list, but warns that this '*is the most commonly seen issue*' (OWASP 2022).

The default settings on some software are inherently insecure. This means that the software must actively be configured to render it into a secure state. For example, some versions of the NoSQL database MongoDB were configured to not require authentication by default (Kirkpatrick 2013). This resulted in many thousands of unsecured databases being installed and left visible across the Internet (Matherly 2015). Predictably, this led to attackers compromising 27 000 instances of the database with ransomware (Claburn 2017).

Threat intelligence professionals have a key role in identifying common misconfigurations, and informing system administrators of these. Insidiously, some misconfigurations may give rise to latent risks where the risk is not immediately obvious, but may only become apparent under certain circumstances.

The simplest approach to managing this issue is to disable any functionality or services that aren't required. This is especially true if the software is not used and also difficult to configure securely. This is also a strong argument for conducting regular penetration testing exercises where security testers under contract to the organisation search for misconfigured, vulnerable systems. These systems can then be remediated and hardened before they are identified by malicious threat actors.

2.2.2.1 Example – Misconfiguration of Cloud Storage

Hosting data in cloud-based systems has many advantages. Notably, such systems are easy to use and set up, the storage provider takes care of the administration of the platform, leaving the user to concentrate on the functionality that is important to them. Cloud file storage systems can be configured to only serve files to authenticated users presenting authorised credentials, or to serve files without authentication in the same way as a web server.

However, misconfiguration of cloud storage is relatively common. Studies have identified that between 7% and 14% of AWS S3 buckets are unsecured (Cimpanu 2017; Continella et al. 2018). These misconfigured, unsecured data storage systems have been behind data breaches that have resulted in hundreds of gigabytes of personal data being disclosed (Seals 2017; Scroxton 2020; Leyden 2022).

Threat intelligence professionals remaining abreast of common misconfiguration errors can highlight these to system administrators and users to reduce their incidence, and actively search for misconfigured systems affecting their organisation. Most importantly, intelligence teams can inform senior decision makers regarding the risk so that decisions can be made on how the risk can be managed. Potentially, management can require that new cloud file storage systems undergo mandatory testing and sign-off before deployment so that such errors can be identified.

2.2.3   Software Vulnerabilities

Writing software is hard. Developing software that is delivered on time, within budget, and that provides the requested functionality is the goal which the discipline of software engineering strives to reach. However, roughly 65% of software development projects are counted as failures, despite many years of research and some success in reducing project failure rates (Ibraigheeth and Fadzil 2019).

Given that it is so difficult to bring a software project to fruition, it can be no surprise that software is rarely perfect. The most egregious software bugs that prevent functionality from working at all are often caught as part of the development process. Whereas more subtle bugs, which may only manifest under certain circumstances that would never be expected to occur during normal operation are likely to persist within source code simply because they are not encountered during testing.

It is these subtle bugs that may not be immediately apparent, but which can be exploited by a threat in order to affect the operation of the system which poses the greatest danger. Nevertheless, not all vulnerabilities are considered equal.

Since 1999 the Common Vulnerabilities and Exposures (CVE) project has tracked software vulnerabilities and provided an identifier (CVE id) by which vulnerabilities can be uniquely referenced (CVE 2018). In turn the Common Vulnerability Scoring System (CVSS) project was initiated to create a framework by which the severity of vulnerabilities could be scored to allow triage and prioritisation of vulnerability remediation (FIRST 2005).

The CVSS system can be applied to calculate a base metric for a vulnerability based on how easy it may be to exploit the vulnerability, and the consequences of successful exploitation. For instance, a vulnerability that can only be exploited by an authenticated user with access to a vulnerable device, which results in a denial of service affecting only the vulnerable software will have a much lower CVSS score than a vulnerability that can be exploited by an unauthenticated user over the network resulting in the execution of arbitrary code supplied by the attacker.

Although the base metric for a vulnerability may be expected to be static, the risk posed by a vulnerability will change over time, as the threat landscape evolves. This change in risk is reflected in the temporal metric that changes with the threat environment. A vulnerability for which exploit code is available and being used in the wild is a much greater risk than a vulnerability for which working exploit code is difficult to develop. Conversely, the availability of a patch that can be applied to remove the vulnerability from affected software reduces the risk.

The base metric and the temporal metric are combined with an environmental metric reflecting the security requirements of the affected system to create a CVSS score. This scale ranks the severity of vulnerabilities from a minimum of 0 to a maximum of 10.0. Any vulnerability with CVSS score of 9.0 or greater is rated as 'critical' and should be prioritised for immediate remediation (FIRST 2019). CVSS scores are used to triage and prioritise the remediation and mitigation of vulnerabilities.

Ideally, software vulnerabilities should be remediated by the application of a patch from the vendor, removing or correcting the erroneous code and removing the vulnerability. However, vendors differ in their responsiveness to the discovery of vulnerabilities, and patching is not necessarily a straightforward process. Critical systems may not be able to be rebooted to apply a patch due to availability constraints, or the risks of making alterations to complex systems may be judged to be too high.

In such cases, vulnerabilities may be mitigated rather than remediated by the application of additional security measures. This may include filtering network traffic to a vulnerable system through an appropriately configured Intrusion Protection System (IPS), which can detect and block attempts at exploitation, or through additional monitoring of the vulnerable system to identify malicious activity which may be the precursor to exploitation.

Threat intelligence has an important part to play in identifying which vulnerabilities are actively being exploited, or which vulnerabilities may become exploited to serious effect. Effectively communicating such risks and ensuring that appropriate mitigation strategies are in place is a key part of the profession. Rarely is a CVSS score on its own enough to convey the particular risk faced by an organisation to a significant vulnerability. Threat intelligence teams may be able to identify specific weaknesses within an organisation that could leave them more exposed to exploitation than others, and increase the priority of a vulnerability appropriately.

The security industry has spawned an entire ecosystem of researchers hunting for software vulnerabilities who work with vendors in order to get vulnerabilities resolved. However, in parallel, an ecosystem of researchers hunting for such vulnerabilities in order to develop exploit code so that vulnerable systems can be compromised also exists. The vast majority of vulnerabilities have patches released before exploit code for the vulnerability becomes available. The issue of whether the necessary patch has been applied in time is another matter.

Occasionally, a vulnerability will be discovered by an attacker and exploit code developed before the vulnerability becomes known to the wider security community, or exploit code will be developed before a patch is available. In this scenario, the vulnerability is known as a zero-day vulnerability. In such circumstances, organisations with vulnerable systems should carefully consider their exposure to the vulnerability, and establish if additional mitigation strategies should be deployed. Identifying when this occurs and communicating the consequent risk is very much part of the cyber threat intelligence teams' responsibilities.

Table 2.2 Timeline of disclosure and exploitation of CVE-2021-44228.

24 November 2021	Log4j Remote Code Execution (RCE) vulnerability first reported to Apache (Talos 2021).
30 November 2021	Presence of the vulnerability in Log4j disclosed through changes made in open-source code (Github 2021).
1 December 2021	First exploitation of vulnerability observed (Graham-Cumming and Martinho 2021).
9 December 2021	Patch for vulnerability released and public notification of the vulnerability (Talos 2021).
9 December 2021	Proof of concept exploit code published.
10 December 2021 onwards	Widespread exploitation observed (Graham-Cumming and Martinho 2021; Talos 2021).

2.2.3.1 Example – Log4j Vulnerabilities

The software vulnerability CVE-2021-44228 affected various versions of Log4j, a popular logging application released by Apache. The vulnerability allows attackers to interact with systems that use Log4j so that malicious code is processed and executed by the logging system, allowing an attacker to steal Information from the vulnerable system, or download and execute code from remote servers over the Internet (CISA 2021).

The vulnerability was assigned the highest possible CVSS score of 10.0 and was widely exploited by threat actors (Wisniewski 2022).

The timeline of disclosure and exploitation of the vulnerability demonstrates the importance of cyber threat intelligence teams in highlighting vulnerabilities that are actively being exploited and need prioritising for patching (Table 2.2).

Realistically, cyber threat intelligence teams would have been unaware of the vulnerability before public disclosure on 9 December. Given the severity of the vulnerability, the ease of exploitation and the publication of proof of concept code, intelligence teams were able to inform decision makers of the risk and the importance of immediately implementing mitigation measures and patching.

Intelligence teams can keep abreast of reports of exploitation, and official advice regarding the vulnerability, such as that given by the UK National Cyber Security Centre who provided guidance in managing the situation (NCSC 2021).

2.3 Threat Actors

Not all threats are malicious, some may be accidental or due to forces of nature, but behind every malicious threat is an attacker. This may be an individual or group of individuals, who are seeking to meet objectives through adversely affecting a computer system.

Table 2.3 Threat actor attributes.

Attribute	Description
Target	The nature of the targets of the threat actor. Some threat actors preferentially target individuals, other companies, or governments.
Expertise	The technical capability of the threat actor. Less sophisticated threat actors are only able to launch attacks using tools written by others, the most sophisticated develop their own malicious tools and may identify previously unknown vulnerabilities.
Resources	The budget and time available to the threat actor. Even threat actors with relatively little expertise may be able to assemble and coordinate large networks of computers under their control as part of a botnet.
Organisation	The nature of relationship between individuals within a group. Threat actors may be 'lone wolves' acting without coordinating with others, may be part of a tightly disciplined military-like structure, part of a flexible gang united by personal relationships and trust, or members of a collective united by shared interests.
Motivation	The reason the threat actor is conducting an attack. For the majority of attacks, the reason is illicit financial gain. However, some attacks may be due to personal reasons such as for self-gratification or due to holding a grudge, or due to furthering an ideology, or to support geopolitical aims.

Source: Adapted from de Bruijne et al. (2017).

Threat actors can range from individuals working on their own who attack systems for no other motivation than to have fun or to demonstrate their technical prowess, to teams of salaried government employees who launch attacks to further the geopolitical aims of a nation state.

In practice, threat actors can be considered to exhibit a number of attributes, such as those shown in Table 2.3.

The Threat Actor Library developed by Intel defines seven attributes of threat actors (Table 2.4).

Casey arranges the various agent attributes to enumerate the following list of potential threat actors: *anarchist, civil activist, competitor, corrupt government official, cyber vandal, data miner, government spy, government cyberwarrior, internal spy, irrational individual, legal adversary, mobster, radical activist, sensationalist, terrorist, thief, vendor, employee (disgruntled), employee (reckless), employee (untrained), information partner* (Casey 2007).

Threat actors are often referred to as falling into one of the following categories:

Script kiddie – An unsophisticated individual with low expertise and low resources who conducts attacks for personal gratification, or to demonstrate prowess within a peer group.

Table 2.4   Agent attributes.

Attribute	Description
Intent	The nature of the actor's intent: actively hostile or causing harm by accident or mistake.
Access	The level of system access of the actor, either external or internal.
Limits	Any legal or ethical frameworks applied by the actor which may limit their activities. The actor may follow laws, adhere to a code of conduct, may break laws in a minor manner, or may operate without any regard for laws.
Resource level	The format of association of the actor. An actor may be a single individual, a member of a loosely defined club, or a more tightly defined team. The actor may be acting as part of a short acting contest, or part of a formal organisation, or acting as part of a government.
Skill level	The level of ability of the actor ranging from none to adept.
Objective	The nature of the objective of an actor. This may be to injure or destroy an asset, to copy or take possession of it. Occasionally the actor may not have a specific objective in mind and takes opportunities as they present.
Visibility	The actor may act in a clandestine manner to hide their identity and actions as much as possible, or less with care to act in a clandestine manner. Alternatively, the actor may act overtly without regard to their visibility or simply not care about their discovery.

Source: Adapted from Casey (2007), Casey et al. (2010).

Hacktivist – A collective of individuals united by shared interests or ideology who may have some degree of technical competence, and who may be able to muster significant resources, in order to conduct attacks to further their ideology.

Criminal – A catch-all term used to refer to any group that is motivated by illicit financial gain. Some criminal gangs may be relatively unsophisticated with little expertise or resources, using tools developed by others to conduct attacks. Other criminal groups may be highly organised crime groups with access to significant technical expertise and large quantities of resources.

State sponsored – Some threat actor groups exhibit great expertise and clearly have access to many resources, yet do not appear to be financially motivated. The victims they target often appear to point towards the group conducting espionage, or seeking to support the geopolitical aims of a nation state.

APT (advanced persistent threat) – This term is often used synonymously with state sponsored to refer to threat actors that are supported by a nation state. However, it was first used to refer to threat actors that were highly sophisticated and well resourced, who carefully target their victims and are patient and persistent in launching attacks. As such, the term can be used to refer to both state-sponsored and the most sophisticated criminal groups who may have levels of expertise and resources at least equal to those of many state-sponsored threat actors.

Insider – An individual who may have legitimate access to a system, or deep knowledge of a system gained through legitimate access, who chooses to use these to the detriment of the legitimate system owner.

These are not the only possible taxonomies of threat actors. The criminologist, David Wall classified threat actors according to their behaviour types:

Cyber-trespass or *hacking* – Transgressing computer boundaries to intrude in spaces that are owned by others.

Cyber-deceptions/thefts – Acquisitive crime over the internet, including the abuse of financial instruments or details to obtain monetary gain, and the unauthorised obtention of digital property, such as music piracy.

Cyber-pornography/obscenity – The acquisition and distribution of illegal pornographic material, including images of child abuse.

Cyber-violence – Using networked systems to inflict psychological harm on others. This term includes activities such as publishing hate speech or cyberstalking where a perpetrator seeks to affect another through persistent tracking or sending unwanted communications.

(Wall 2001)

Understanding the potential threat actors, their motivations, and capabilities allows us to consider how and if a class of threat actor might attack a system. Consequently we can implement the defences, which might frustrate that attack and the detection capabilities that identify the attack happening.

2.3.1 Example – Operation Payback

The hacktivist collective Anonymous launched Operation Payback in September 2010. As part of this operation, the collective provided instructions for others to install the network stress testing tool Low-Orbit Ion Cannon and coordinated the websites that should be 'stressed' with the tool. The resulting large amounts of network traffic rendered the target websites unavailable through a denial of service attack (Osborne 2013).

Thus, the group was able to enlarge their resources by recruiting others who were sympathetic to the group's aims to contribute network capacity to the attack by using a third-party tool. The group did not need to deploy sophisticated technical expertise, but could use their ideology and communication skills to further their attacks and goals.

Hacktivist operations are often very open regarding the identity of their intended targets, and the reasons for the operations. This gives intelligence teams prior warning of the attack so that operational teams can be primed to expect the attack and mitigation strategies prepared.

2.3.2 Example – Stuxnet

In June 2010, an extremely sophisticated piece of malware ultimately named Stuxnet was discovered. The malware contained code to exploit four previously unidentified (zero-day) vulnerabilities, and could spread autonomously over networks searching for systems with very specific industrial control system software installed (Falliere et al. 2011). Once a machine with the right profile was discovered, the malware would inject its payload into the control software before identifying if the system was controlling a high speed frequency converter and subsequently changing the operating frequency of the attached motor along with opening and closing valves. The malware appeared designed to disrupt Iranian nuclear enrichment activity, and was subsequently attributed to a joint US–Israeli operation (Lindsay 2013).

Planning, developing, and executing such an attack requires an extremely high degree of technical expertise, access to huge resources (reportedly including a duplicate nuclear processing facility for testing purposes [Lindsay 2013]), and outstanding organisational skill to coordinate the various teams within the project while maintaining secrecy. Clearly, such an attack can only have been carried out with the resources of a nation state threat actor, even before the apparent motivation of disrupting nuclear processing by a third-party nation state is taken into consideration.

Prior to this attack, cyber threat intelligence teams had no indication that such an operation was possible. Since Stuxnet, threat intelligence organisations must remain cognisant of the risk to operational technology systems, and threat actors seeking to disrupt systems that interact with the physical world.

The capability to conduct such an audacious attack almost certainly remains limited to well-resourced state-sponsored threat actors. However, criminal threat actors have targeted the information technology systems of operational technology and caused disruption. In May 2021, the criminal gang DarkSide disrupted the financial billing systems of the Colonial Pipeline company resulting in the closure of a fuel pipeline causing fuel outages across the Southeast United States (Chan 2021).

2.3.3 Tracking Threat Actors

Although it's not possible to identify and track every single individual involved in malicious cyber activity, it is possible to identify commonalities amongst many attacks and to attribute these to previously identified threat actor groups. The activities of these groups are followed by many organisations in both the private and public sectors. Comprehensive lists of known threat actor groups are published by the MITRE Corporation® ATT&CK team and the Malware Information sharing Platform (MISP) Galaxy Project who identify 122 and 364 active threat actor groups, respectively (MITRE 2022b; Fraunhofer Institute and MISP Galaxy Project 2022).

Tracking threat actor groups is not an exact science. Only the threat actors themselves know the exact composition of their groups and the attacks which they have carried out. External entities may mis-attribute attacks, consider two separate threat actors as one, or misidentify a single group as two threat actors. Confusingly, there is no single accepted naming convention for threat actors, many different names may refer to the same threat actor group.

For example, the suspected Chinese threat actor, Deep Panda is also referred to as Shell Crew, WebMasters, KungFu Kittens and PinkPanther. The same group may also be tracked as Black Vine or APT19, but this connection is less clear (MITRE 2022c).

Distinctions between threat actor groups may be blurred through different groups sharing tools and techniques, or attacking similar targets. Groups may have close links and associations to other groups. Many threat actors considered to be associated with China have been linked to a common 'digital quartermaster' who is suspected of providing supporting services to different threat actor groups (FireEye 2014).

Criminal entities may form and disband, blurring exactly which group was responsible for what attack. Or they may outsource components of an attack to a third party that links many different attacks from separate threat actors.

The distinction between criminal and state-sponsored groups should be considered as a spectrum of activity rather than necessarily as a binary division. Some criminal threat actors may act with various degrees of state sponsorship ranging from tacit tolerance of their activity through to state direction in the choice of their targets. In many ways, these primarily criminal threat actors acting under state direction and protection are analogous to privateers of the seventeenth and eighteenth centuries. Privateers were pirates who acted on behalf of a nation state as an adjunct to national armed forces, in return gaining respectability and protection for their otherwise criminal activities (Egloff 2015).

Similarly some state-sponsored threat actors may also engage in criminal activity. For example, the NotPetya destructive worm is widely believed to be part of a geopolitical campaign developed by a sophisticated state-sponsored threat actor (NCSC 2018). Yet the subsequent ransomware BadRabbit, which appears to be an illicit financial gain criminal malware, shows evidence of having been developed by the same actors responsible for NotPetya (Greenberg 2017).

Many hypotheses to explain such an observation are possible. At the very least, this shows that there is some fluidity between state-sponsored and criminal endeavours. Indeed, we can imagine the career path of a hypothetical individual who starts their career as a script kiddie before becoming a career criminal cyber threat actor, who increasingly comes under state influence, before graduating to become a salaried state-sponsored actor. We can also imagine the career paths of individuals within state-sponsored groups who may move between different threat actor teams within their country before branching out to become a private sector consultant selling services to whomever is buying, including criminal entities.

Suffice to say that threat actors should not be thought of as monolithic entities whose motivations and modes of action are static and set in stone, but as fluid entities whose allegiances, associations, and motivations may change over time.

2.4 TTPs – Tactics, Techniques, and Procedures

Everyone has certain skills, abilities, and preferences that they apply in their day-to-day lives in order to get things done. Many of these skills may have been developed over years of practice, and require the use of tools that have been acquired to assist these skills. We're unlikely to abandon tried and tested skills, and an investment in tools, in order to attempt to fulfil a task using an entirely different approach.

Threat actors are no different. The way that they go about their business tends to remain the same time after time. Certainly, the skills of threat actors develop, and tools are upgraded or swapped out over time, but the approach to conducting their business is consistent. These methods that are applied by threat actors are referred to as Tactics, Techniques, and Procedures (TTPs). Often these form a kind of fingerprint unique to a threat actor, which can be used for identification.

TTPs are descriptions of how a threat actor goes about attempting to achieve their desired goal. 'Tactics' refers to the high-level description of the goal of actions being executed by an attacker. 'Techniques' refers to a more detailed description of the actions themselves. 'Procedures' refers to the in-depth detail of the instructions that the attacker is using to implement a specific technique (NIST n.d.; Strom et al. 2020).

Tactics and techniques can be thought of as the framework necessary in order for an attacker to conduct a successful attack, with procedures as the implementation details. Many of the tactics used in an attack will be common to a variety of threat actors and their many campaigns. However there are likely to be differences in the choice of techniques used to succeed in achieving a tactic between threat actors, and there will certainly be differences at the procedural level where techniques are implemented using different tools and approaches.

Everyone has tried and tested routines and methods by which they get their work done. Successfully adopting new practices can be a long and disruptive process. It is frequently much easier for everyone involved to stick with what they know, and if changes need to be made, to make these changes incrementally rather than scrapping everything and starting again.

The same can be expected for threat actors. Threat actors appear to have preferences for how they go about conducting attacks. Techniques and procedures are reused repeatedly, or with small incremental changes. Presumably these repeat behaviours reflect the investments in time and resources necessary for individuals to become familiar with tools and processes, as well as the cost and effort necessary to develop specific tooling such as exploit code. Such investments are unlikely to be discarded following a single attack and tend to be reused between malicious campaigns.

This means that the specific procedures and techniques which are implemented as part of an attack can be used to help identify the threat actor group behind an attack, and to help build up the patterns of activity associated with the threat actor.

The complexities of behaviour which may be observed within an attack necessitates a common vocabulary that can be used consistently to describe the actions of threat actors. There have been various attempts at creating ontologies that describe security concepts to allow the cross referencing of threats and incidents (Iannacone et al. 2015; Mavroeidis and Bromander 2017). There are also tools to parse textual descriptions of attacks to automatically identify TTPs and key terms (Ayoade et al. 2018; Husari et al. 2018; Li et al. 2019).

However, these have not been widely adopted in comparison with MITRE ATT&CK. This curated framework enumerates the tactics, techniques, and sub-techniques observed in attacks (MITRE 2022d). The widespread use of this taxonomy, and the related MITRE catalogues: CAPEC and CWE, discussed at the end of this section, provide a common vocabulary for describing attacks and threats.

The relationship between threat actor groups, techniques, and tactics can be visualised (as seen in Figure 2.4).

The ATT&CK framework for enterprise systems only contains 14 tactics, with separate tactics described for mobile and for ICS systems. These 14 tactics are as seen in Table 2.5.

Common Attack Pattern Enumeration and Classification (CAPEC™) is a separate initiative that seeks to enumerate the attack patterns used by attackers, listing the approaches used to exploit weaknesses within systems (US Department of Homeland Security and MITRE n.d.). The Common Weakness Enumeration (CWE™) site lists weaknesses in systems presenting a defender's viewpoint of vulnerabilities; CAPEC presents an attacker's point of view of these weaknesses and how they may be exploited (MITRE 2022e).

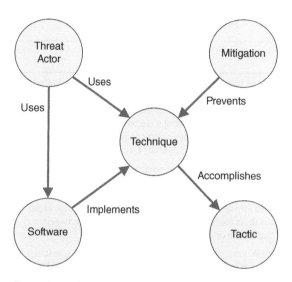

Figure 2.4 ATT&CK Model Relationship. *Source:* Adapted from Strom et al. (2020).

Table 2.5 ATT&CK framework tactics.

Tactic	Explanation
Reconnaissance	Reconnaissance consists of techniques that involve adversaries actively or passively gathering information that can be used to support targeting. Such information may include details of the victim organisation, infrastructure, or staff/personnel. This information can be leveraged by the adversary to aid in other phases of the adversary lifecycle, such as using gathered information to plan and execute Initial Access, to scope and prioritise post-compromise objectives, or to drive and lead further Reconnaissance efforts.
Resource development	Resource Development consists of techniques that involve adversaries creating, purchasing, or compromising/stealing resources that can be used to support targeting. Such resources include infrastructure, accounts, or capabilities. The adversary can leverage these resources to aid in other phases of the adversary lifecycle, such as using purchased domains to support Command and Control, email accounts for phishing as a part of Initial Access, or stealing code signing certificates to help with Defence Evasion.
Initial access	Initial Access consists of techniques that use various entry vectors to gain their initial foothold within a network. Techniques used to gain a foothold include targeted spear phishing and exploiting weaknesses on public-facing web servers. Footholds gained through initial access may allow for continued access, like valid accounts and use of external remote services, or may be limited-use due to changing passwords.

(Continued)

Table 2.5 (Continued)

Tactic	Explanation
Execution	Execution consists of techniques that result in adversary-controlled code running on a local or remote system. Techniques that run malicious code are often paired with techniques from all other tactics to achieve broader goals, like exploring a network or stealing data. For example, an adversary might use a remote access tool to run a PowerShell script that does Remote System Discovery.
Persistence	Persistence consists of techniques that adversaries use to keep access to systems across restarts, changed credentials, and other interruptions that could cut off their access. Techniques used for persistence include any access, action, or configuration changes that let them maintain their foothold on systems, such as replacing or hijacking legitimate code or adding startup code.
Privilege escalation	Privilege Escalation consists of techniques that adversaries use to gain higher-level permissions on a system or network. Adversaries can often enter and explore a network with unprivileged access but require elevated permissions to follow through on their objectives. Common approaches are to take advantage of system weaknesses, misconfigurations, and vulnerabilities.
Defence evasion	Defence Evasion consists of techniques that adversaries use to avoid detection throughout their compromise. Techniques used for defence evasion include uninstalling/disabling security software or obfuscating/encrypting data and scripts. Adversaries also leverage and abuse trusted processes to hide and masquerade their malware. Other tactics' techniques are cross-listed here when those techniques include the added benefit of subverting defences.
Credential access	Credential Access consists of techniques for stealing credentials like account names and passwords. Techniques used to get credentials include keylogging or credential dumping. Using legitimate credentials can give adversaries access to systems, make them harder to detect, and provide the opportunity to create more accounts to help achieve their goals.
Discovery	Discovery consists of techniques an adversary may use to gain knowledge about the system and internal network. These techniques help adversaries observe the environment and orient themselves before deciding how to act. They also allow adversaries to explore what they can control and what's around their entry point in order to discover how it could benefit their current objective. Native operating system tools are often used towards this post-compromise information-gathering objective.
Lateral movement	Lateral Movement consists of techniques that adversaries use to enter and control remote systems on a network. Following through on their primary objective often requires exploring the network to find their target and subsequently gaining access to it. Reaching their objective often involves pivoting through multiple systems and accounts to gain. Adversaries might install their own remote access tools to accomplish Lateral Movement or use legitimate credentials with native network and operating system tools, which may be stealthier.

Table 2.5 (Continued)

Tactic	Explanation
Collection	Collection consists of techniques adversaries may use to gather information and the sources information is collected from that are relevant to following through on the adversary's objectives. Frequently, the next goal after collecting data is to steal (exfiltrate) the data. Common target sources include various drive types, browsers, audio, video, and email. Common collection methods include capturing screenshots and keyboard input.
Command and control	Command and Control consists of techniques that adversaries may use to communicate with systems under their control within a victim network. Adversaries commonly attempt to mimic normal, expected traffic to avoid detection. There are many ways an adversary can establish command and control with various levels of stealth depending on the victim's network structure and defences.
Exfiltration	Exfiltration consists of techniques that adversaries may use to steal data from your network. Once they've collected data, adversaries often package it to avoid detection while removing it. This can include compression and encryption. Techniques for getting data out of a target network typically include transferring it over their command and control channel or an alternate channel and may also include putting size limits on the transmission.
Impact	Impact consists of techniques that adversaries use to disrupt availability or compromise integrity by manipulating business and operational processes. Techniques used for impact can include destroying or tampering with data. In some cases, business processes can look fine, but may have been altered to benefit the adversaries' goals. These techniques might be used by adversaries to follow through on their end goal or to provide cover for a confidentiality breach.

Source: Reproduced from MITRE Corporation (2022f).

Although the patterns listed by CAPEC are strictly speaking distinct from the TTPs listed by the ATT&CK project, many of the approaches contained in CAPEC may be identified within procedures as defined by ATT&CK.

2.5 Victimology

In the context of cyber threat intelligence, victimology is the study of the profile of the targets and victims of threat actors and their campaigns. The term is borrowed from criminology and research into the nature of criminal motivation.

In popular culture at the very least, there is the concept that a criminal must possess the means, motivation, and opportunity in order to commit a crime. This is a relevant observation for malicious cyber activity. The threat actor must possess the necessary technical means to perpetrate the act; not every threat actor has the capability to conduct every attack.

There should be some notion of the motivation of the attacker. This may be due to the desire to make illicit financial gain, to gain access to confidential information for reasons of state espionage, or a whole range of other motivations. At some point during the attack, the target and the perpetrator must have had some form of interaction, although this might occur via a third party.

Routine activity theory explains crime as happening when a motivated offender and a suitable victim intersect in time and space, in the absence of a capable guardian who is able to prevent a crime from happening (Cohen and Felson 1979). One facet of this theory is that it is an individual's behavioural choices that exposes them to the situations when crime may occur (Ngo and Paternoster 2011). At the very least, the potential victim must be visible in some way to the attacker (Leukfeldt and Yar 2016). If the attacker cannot interact with the victim in some way, then the crime cannot take place. This is not to blame the victim. Individuals and organisations should be free to conduct their lawful business without fear of crime. Yet our activities influence the threats to which we are exposed. Recognising this helps us understand and predict the threats that we will encounter.

Individuals who conduct online purchases or who use online banking are more at risk of fraud and identity theft (Junger et al. 2017). One can imagine that someone who does not conduct banking online would be immune to banking trojans that seek to steal online banking credentials, since the opportunity to commit a crime is absent.

Many routine activities carried out on the Internet offer opportunities for threat actors to conduct attacks against us. Hence, the importance of providing strategies (known as 'guardians' in the terminology of routine activity theory) to frustrate cyber attacks (Reyns and Henson 2016). These strategies may range from better system design, routine encryption of data, to the use of anti-virus software on client systems, or using unique complex passwords as system access credentials.

Not all threat actors select their victims in the same way. Many threat actors do not actively select their victims, but launch attacks against any potential victim whom they encounter. These attacks may succeed if the victim is susceptible to the vulnerabilities exploited as part of the attack or fail if the intended victim is not exploitable.

Some threat actors seek to specifically select their intended victims based on criteria defined by the attacker (Thonnard et al. 2012). These criteria may be related to the job role of an individual, their industrial sector (Thonnard et al. 2015), political exposure (Hardy et al. 2014), or probability and size of financial gain due to an attack (FE Centre for Cyber Security 2020).

Cyber threat intelligence teams should have an understanding of the scope of their own organisation's activities, how these may influence their visibility to threat actors and the attacks to which they are subjected.

2.5.1 Diamond Model

The Diamond Model of Intrusion Analysis describes both how an adversary launches attacks against a victim, and in doing so disclosing information about themselves (Caltagirone et al. 2013) (Figure 2.5).

The threat actor (adversary) conducts an attack against a victim applying a capability they possess and infrastructure to which they have access. The infrastructure and capability are connected, since the model assumes that a capability cannot be applied without supporting infrastructure.

When an attack is discovered, although the victim may be unaware of the identity and nature of the attacker, the victim can identify the attacker's capabilities that have been used against them. The victim may be in the position to identify some of the attacker's infrastructure that has been used as part of the attack.

The capabilities used in the attack will be part of the attacker's TTPs. The victim will be aware of at least some of the attacker's procedures, deduce the techniques used as part of the attack, and possibly identify the tactic that the attacker applied. The nature of the victim, whether the victim is an individual or system, also discloses information regarding the attacker's interests and capabilities. Thus, defenders can start to build a picture of their adversary.

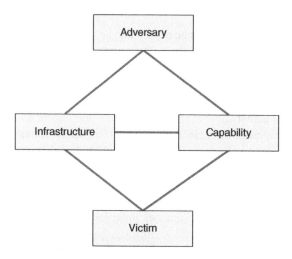

Figure 2.5 The Diamond model. *Source:* Adapted from Caltagirone et al. (2013).

The infrastructure used during the attack comprises part of the attacker's resources. Even the most sophisticated attackers do not have infinite resources; it is probable that additional attacks will (or have) used the same infrastructure. Searching for further malicious activity involving the same infrastructure is likely to uncover further capabilities of the attacker.

Sharing information with relevant authorities, including other potential victims, can uncover additional attacks using the same infrastructure or further commonalities, thus aiding the compilation of the attacker's portrait. Ultimately, enough information may be gathered to associate the attacks with a known threat actor. Keeping abreast of any new infrastructure, resources, or capabilities of a threat actor allows defenders to prepare their defences in advance and prime their capacity to detect future attacks.

Threat intelligence professionals should be aware of the particular victimology of their own organisation. Teams should know the nature and preferred TTPs of the threat actors that may be targeting their organisation, and be aware of the systems and individuals to whom attacks may be directed. This intelligence can be used to direct resources to areas that are most likely to be targeted.

2.6 Threat Landscape

The nature of the cyber threats across the world at any one time comprises the threat landscape. This comprises the many threat actors, their goals, the vulnerabilities open to exploitation, the malware, malicious techniques, not forgetting the victims, their many defences and countermeasures available to them to defeat the bad guys.

This mix is in constant flux. Threat actors can be expected to be constantly looking to achieve their objectives while minimising their efforts and costs. Defenders, and the cyber security industry in general, are always looking at deploying new defences and countermeasures. Service providers and law enforcement act to take down malicious infrastructure, in addition law enforcement seeks to hold threat actors to account and halt their activity.

As a consequence the risk exposure of organisations is also constantly changing. Decisions based on the understanding of risk for the threat landscape in the past may no longer be valid as the nature of the threat landscape changes. Previously, well-characterised threat actors may develop new TTPs or may be usurped by new threat actors pursuing new objectives. A new vulnerability, or exploit code may cause sudden changes as attackers seek to exploit the opportunities this affords them.

Threat intelligence professionals need to keep abreast of changes within the threat landscape and the changing nature of risks facing their organisation.

Decision makers within the organisation are unlikely to be aware of evolutions of the threat landscape and the consequences of these without input from the threat intelligence team.

2.6.1 Example – Ransomware

Prior to 2016, ransomware was a threat distributed by criminal threat actors widely across the Internet without regard to the nature or identity of the victim. The malware encrypts the files of compromised systems rendering them inaccessible to the victim. If the victim wished to gain access to their files, the victim was encouraged to pay a ransom to the threat actor to retrieve the cryptographic key necessary to decrypt and access their files.

This criminal business model relies on a certain percentage of victims being vulnerable to the exploit used to install the ransomware, lacking countermeasures to block the action of the ransomware or to recover files, and being willing to pay the ransom. In essence, the model was akin to that of 'kidnap', taking something of value away from the victim, and demanding money for its safe return.

In 2016, a criminal gang using a new ransomware variant named SamSam tested an innovation in the business model. Instead of distributing their ransomware according to a 'mass market' model, they targeted specific organisations, notably within the health care sector, infiltrated the networks of their victims and executed the ransomware on key systems within their victim's infrastructure. By encrypting files on systems vital to the operation of their victim organisations the threat actors disrupted the activity of their victims, and were able to demand a larger ransom than that typically requested from victims of untargeted ransomware. Although there is no available data, the presumption is that the likelihood of the ransom being paid was higher for the targeted victims (CISA 2018a; Biasini 2016).

This innovation changed the nature of ransomware and changed the risk exposure of organisations to the threat. Organisations that were perceived by threat actors as being profitable victims of targeted ransomware attacks massively increased their risk of being subject to ransomware attacks in comparison with previously when ransomware remained being distributed as a 'mass market' attack.

Cyber threat intelligence teams should have perceived this strategic shift in the threat landscape and explained it to decision makers. Many of the assumptions upon which risk management decisions were taken, such as ransomware only ever affecting end point systems because it is only ever distributed via email or compromised websites, were no longer true. Threat actors were looking to penetrate corporate networks, identify key systems critical for business operations to target these with ransomware. This change in risk exposure required a consequent change in mitigation strategies.

2.7 Attack Vectors, Vulnerabilities, and Exploits

Malicious attacks require a target to possess a vulnerability, an exploit in order to take advantage of the vulnerability, and an attack vector, a means of delivering the exploit to the vulnerability. Vulnerabilities do not exploit themselves. The attacker must have a means to ensure that their exploit impacts the vulnerable system in the correct way.

The attack vector may be physical in nature. Someone with access to a system may deliver malicious code via a USB stick. A malicious insider may need no other vector than the device's keyboard in order to deliver an attack.

In terms of cyber security, we are mostly concerned with attack vectors delivered by network connections. Vulnerable applications being exploited through malicious data files transferred over the network are frequently considered as the greatest risk. It is important to consider that vulnerabilities may be exploited at every layer within the Open System Interconnection (OSI) model, and that any network protocol may be open to abuse (Table 2.6).

Although the OSI model is strictly speaking only applicable to networks, the principle that threats can be delivered via different layers within a stack is very useful for identifying potential threat delivery vectors. For example, the physical layer is relevant to USB or any other peripheral device, the data link layer could encompass Bluetooth connections or data exchange using near-field communications. The application layer acts as a reminder that potentially any file opened or accessed by any application could contain malicious content.

If a vulnerability is present and exploitable, sooner or later a threat actor can be expected to attempt exploitation. Even if there are no vulnerabilities in the software or hardware, the threat actor may still attempt to exploit the user's human vulnerabilities.

Table 2.6 The OSI network model.

Layer no.	Layer name	Example TCP/IP protocols	Other example protocols
7	Application	HTTP, HTTP2, FTP, SMTP	Modbus
6	Presentation	MIME, TLS	MIDI, MPEG
5	Session	Sockets	Named pipes, SOCKS
4	Transport	TCP, UDP	
3	Network	IP, IPSec, ICMP	
2	Data link	PPP, SLIP	ARP, IEEE 802.3 (Ethernet), IEEE 802.11 (Wi-Fi)
1	Physical	–	RS-232, RJ45, 1000BASE-T

2.7.1 Email Attack Vectors

Email is a popular vector for attackers. The protocols involved in sending, receiving, and opening emails do not verify the email sender's identity by default, which allows attackers to spoof the identity of the sender or to disguise the email's origin.

Various standards have added additional layers of authentication to email that make it more difficult for attackers to falsify the domain from which an email was sent. However, the plethora of free email providers has meant that attackers are able to access legitimate email sending facilities with ease. Malicious emails sent from free email providers pass verification checks because the messages have genuinely been sent from the infrastructure of the email provider. Nevertheless, the emails may still be malicious and the identity of the sending user may have been crafted to impersonate a third party.

More sophisticated attackers may attempt a different approach. An attacker may craft a phishing attack in order to obtain the credentials of a legitimate user of a legitimate organisation. Then use these stolen credentials to access the email system of the organisation and send malicious emails on behalf of the user whose credentials have been stolen.

Such abuse is particularly difficult to detect since the emails have been sent from the genuine and legitimate email system of a genuine user. Crafty attackers may choose to send their emails to targets selected from the contacts list or harvested from the inbox of the compromised account, adding an additional veil of legitimacy to their attacks.

The primary vulnerability targeted by email is human weakness. Convincing social engineering within the malicious email can trick the target into interacting with the attack. This interaction can take many forms:

> The attacker may wish the target to engage in conversation to develop a rapport, before attempting fraud or sending malware. This is frequently the case in romance scams, where the attacker may go to great lengths to establish a relationship with the victim before concocting a scenario where the victim is requested to transfer money to the scammer.
>
> The attacker may seek to trick the target into 'clicking the link' and opening a URL within the email. Subsequently, the attacker can exploit a vulnerability within the web browser before uploading and installing malware on the victim's device.
>
> More simply, the attack may include a malicious attachment to the email and invite the recipient to open the attachment in order to exploit a software vulnerability to install malware, or politely request that the user install the malware themselves.

Email attacks may be very convincing. Phishing attacks may copy corporate branding and templates and appear identical to genuine emails to all but the closest scrutiny. Emotet malware has taken to stealing snippets of conversations from the email threads of previously compromised individuals. The use of genuine conversations within emails makes it incredibly difficult for unsuspecting victims to identify that the email is malicious, simply because the email content is genuine, apart from a single malicious link (Cimpanu 2019).

Attackers may use other messaging systems in the same way. Messages sent via social media, SMS messages, or any form of instant messaging can all be abused. Voice phone calls are used to purport to be from a trusted organisation and used to trick victims into divulging information such as user credentials or financial details.

2.7.2   Web-Based Attacks

If a victim can be tricked into clicking a link, then the victim can be directed to visit a server under the control of the attacker. From this platform, additional social engineering attacks can be carried out to trick the victim into acting against their interests. The attacker may choose to exploit a vulnerability in the web browser itself or a third-party plug-in installed in the browser. Alternatively, the victim can be tricked into downloading and executing malicious code, under the pretence that it is a legitimate program.

Attackers may set up exploit kits on web servers. In these systems, software profiles the visitor's web browser and any browser plug-ins that may be installed to identify potential vulnerabilities, then selects exploit code to execute from a range of options available on the server. In this way the attacker can maximise their chance of successfully compromising a visitor.

There are many ways to entice a victim to a malicious website, of which clicking a link is but one. Attackers may conduct typosquatting attacks, registering domain names that are similar to legitimate sites, but which contain a spelling error that may be made by a user mis-keying the genuine domain name. The advertising networks are also a target of abuse. Attackers can buy web adverts (or compromise the advertising platform) in order to deploy malicious code to browsers via adverts displayed within legitimate websites.

Another avenue of attack is to compromise legitimate websites in order to include malicious code on an otherwise genuine website. This is often referred to as a watering hole attack. In these attacks, the attacker patiently lies in wait for the victims to come to them before exploiting their browser or tricking the victim to install malware.

For example, the Magecart malware when included on an ecommerce website is able to collect financial data as it is being entered by the victim. This data is exfiltrated to the attacker as the victim makes a legitimate purchase, ultimately allowing the attacker to make further purchases using the stolen data (Montalbano 2020).

Attackers may seek to redirect the victim's connection to their intended website. In such an attack, the victim makes a legitimate connection to a genuine website, but along the way the attacker redirects the connection to a malicious server under the control of the attacker. Threat actors have been observed compromising the network routing infrastructure, which allows network traffic to be redirected (CISA 2018b). Additionally, threat actors have tampered with DNS records meaning that the IP addresses for malicious systems would be returned in response to genuine DNS requests made to legitimate DNS servers (CISA 2019).

2.7.3 Network Service Attacks

Network services that accept remote connections to an open TCP port are also vulnerable to abuse. The software within the network service that listens for and processes incoming connections may contain mistakes that give rise to vulnerabilities that can be exploited over the network.

For example, the Heartbleed vulnerability CVE-2014-0160 allowed attackers to communicate with vulnerable TLS implementations in order to read the memory of the TLS software and extract cached usernames, passwords, and keys.

The Server Message Block (SMB) vulnerability CVE-2017-0144 was exploited to great effect by the WannaCry worm, which was able to execute malicious code on vulnerable devices to allow the worm to spread across networks.

2.7.4 Supply Chain Attacks

Attackers may also distribute malware through piggybacking on the distribution of legitimate software. If an attacker can compromise the source code or build process of legitimate software, the attacker can include their malicious code as part of the legitimate software. Alternatively, through compromising the update system of legitimate software, malicious code can be distributed as an update to a legitimate package.

For example, the NotPetya malware was distributed with the help of malicious functionality integrated in the source code of M.E.Doc, a tax accounting package widely used in Ukraine. The malicious code was distributed through the legitimate software update system of the accounting software. This allowed the attackers to ensure that their malicious code was distributed for a number of months, before the attacker instructed the affected systems to download and execute the NotPetya payload which spread autonomously across networks wiping systems as it spread (Cherepanov 2017; Maynor et al. 2017).

Threat intelligence professionals should be aware of common attack vectors, and how the use of attack vectors is changing. Understanding how threat actors penetrate systems allows defenders to block routes of entry and hunt for attacks that may have breached defences.

2.8 The Kill Chain

Attacks do not happen instantaneously. A number of distinct steps must be successfully executed before the attacker can realise their goals. The sequence of these steps is referred to as the Kill Chain.

The concept of the kill chain has its origins in the US Air Force doctrine of Find, Fix, Track, Target, Engage, Assess (F2T2EA) (Boyne 2004). In order to engage an enemy, the attacker must first find the likely location of the enemy, fix their position, track their movements so as to maintain situational awareness, finalise the target before engaging, then assess the results (Headquarters, Department of the Army 2015). Thus, an operation to engage an enemy must progress through a number of phases before it can be completed.

This idea was developed by researchers at Lockheed Martin into the Cyber Kill Chain® framework, setting out the steps that an attacker must progress through in order to complete an offensive cyber operation (Hutchins et al. 2011) (Table 2.7).

Considering the different steps within the kill chain is very useful for defenders as a method of walking backwards through the kill chain from the point of discovery of an attack to identify the attacker's prior behaviour. This can allow defenders

Table 2.7 Phases of the kill chain.

Kill chain phase	Explanation
Reconnaissance	Relevant targets must be identified and selected.
Weaponisation	Malicious code coupled with an exploit must be crafted into a deliverable payload.
Delivery	This payload must be delivered to the target.
Exploitation	A vulnerability of the target system is exploited by the payload.
Installation	Malicious code is installed within the target system.
Command and control	A communication channel between the attacker and compromised system is established so that further commands can be executed, and information exfiltrated.
Actions on objective	The goals of the attacker can be fulfilled.

Source: Adapted from Hutchins et al. (2011).

to uncover further malicious activity and build up a picture of the threat actor's capabilities and infrastructure.

With a better understanding of the threat actor, defenders can move forwards through the kill chain to predict what additional steps the attacker may have taken, to investigate if there is evidence that these activities have occurred, or to consider what defences may be installed to detect these.

Indeed, the kill chain provides a means by which defences can be reviewed by considering each step in the chain.

Reconnaissance – Reducing the visibility of assets to reconnaissance may make it less likely that they will be the target of attacks, or make the attack more difficult.

Weaponisation – Detecting the delivery and presence of malicious payloads will block or uncover attacks in progress.

Exploitation – Improving the time taken to deploy patches will reduce exposure to the exploitation phase and reduce the likelihood that attackers can compromise systems.

Command and Control – Detecting and blocking command and control traffic will help uncover attacks and prevent attackers from issuing commands to compromised systems or exfiltrating stolen data.

Actions on Objectives – Depending on the attackers' goals, the final phases of an attack may be discovered and disrupted before the attackers can complete their objectives. For example, the exfiltration of large volumes of data can be detected, encryption of files as part of a ransomware attack can be identified before the device is fully encrypted.

By spreading defences and detections across the many components of the kill chain, defenders can increase their ability to detect and block intruders. Focusing too much on one single link within the kill chain means that if attackers are able to bypass those defences, there will be little to prevent them achieving their attack objectives.

Nevertheless, the Cyber Kill Chain is not without criticism. It is simplistic to expect all attacks to implement every step within the kill chain. The model was initially developed to relate to targeted attacks carried out by APT threat actors, although it is now applied to many different types of attack to which it may not be relevant.

Attacks may skip the reconnaissance phase entirely. Untargeted attacks don't necessarily need to reconnoitre targets. Attacks using compromised credentials don't require the attacker to deploy a payload, the attack may be carried out through the attacker directly typing in instructions via a compromised account. Destructive wiper attacks that seek to destroy systems don't need to communicate with the attacker and can omit command and control.

In practice, many attacks consist of multiple instances of the kill chain, where an attacker identifies, exploits, and compromises an initial system before reconnoitring and targeting additional systems in order to compromise them. This process of pivoting through compromising many systems may be repeated many times until the attacker reaches a system that allows them to finalise the goals of the attack.

Many variations on the kill chain have been published with different steps, and variations. Although the kill chain is not perfect, it remains a useful model by which attacks can be modelled.

2.9   Untargeted versus Targeted Attacks

Threat actors have specific objectives that they are trying to achieve with their attacks. These objectives dictate the different approaches used by the attacker. A threat actor who wishes to gain access to a specific system in order to gain access to a high-value piece of information will adopt a different approach to a threat actor who wishes to infect as many systems as possible with ransomware. In the former, the attacker is seeking to conduct a *targeted* attack against a single identified target. In the latter, the attacker is not overly concerned which systems they infect, so long as the attack is successful. This is described as an *untargeted* attack.

These different approaches can be thought of as akin to 'business models'. Some threat actors apply a 'bespoke' business model devoting time and resources into conducting a one-off attack against a single target. Others may adopt a 'mass market' business model seeking to deploy a 'one size fits all' attack attempting to compromise as many systems as possible.

Between these two extremes are a whole range of approaches. If there is evidence that the targets of the attack have been selected according to some criteria by the threat actor, then the attack is referred to as targeted. If there is little or no evidence that the attacker has a preconceived notion of the identities of their victims, then the attack is referred to as untargeted.

Typically, as the name suggests, APT threat actors are more likely to conduct targeted attacks, specifically identifying their intended victims in advance, and launching attacks tailored to vulnerabilities likely to be found within their target's systems. This may include the use of social engineering within attacks that have been selected so as to be relevant to the interests of the target.

On the other hand, criminal threat actors are more likely to conduct untargeted attacks, almost certainly seeking to compromise as many systems as possible in order to extract whatever value they can from the affected systems. Their attack vectors may include malicious email campaigns with generic social engineering that might be relevant to many recipients, or compromising websites in order to launch attacks against any visitor to the site.

However, criminal actors can partake in targeted attacks, and APT threat actors can launch untargeted attacks. Criminal threat actors may identify and select specific targets such as launching ransomware attacks against businesses where the attacker suspects that a large ransom is likely to be paid, or researching entities in the financial sector to hit with attacks aimed at syphoning off money.

Conversely, the NotPetya attack of 2017 was a self-propagating destructive worm that spread across networks causing large amounts of damage across the globe. This attack was publicly attributed to Russian military threat actors. Normally, we would expect sophisticated threat actors to carefully identify and target their victims rather than cause widespread harm (Greenberg 2018).

What appears to be the same attack vector can be used both for targeted and untargeted attacks depending on the motivation and operation of the threat actor. In 2016 the website of the International Civil Aviation Organization (ICAO) was subject to a watering hole attack by an APT threat actor (Paganini 2019).

In watering hole attacks, the threat actor compromises a website that is suspected to be visited by high-value targets. The threat actor places malicious code on the compromised website, which attempts to exploit vulnerabilities on visitors' browsers as they visit the site. The assumed goal of such an attack is to conduct espionage against the type of user expected to visit the website.

In 2018 the website of British Airways was compromised, but this attack was assessed as being criminal in nature. Instead of deploying malicious code to compromise users' systems, the attackers installed credit card skimming malware to collect financial details from users of the site (Corfield 2020; Leyden 2018). Although the ICAO and British Airways attacks both involved the compromise of a website, the nature of the threat actors and their presumed goals are different.

2.10 Persistence

This is listed as one of many tactics in the MITRE ATT&CK framework, but is worth considering in some detail since it is not only a commonly used technique by threat actors, but also one of their weaknesses.

Threat actors must eat and sleep. There is only so much value that can be extracted from a compromised system during the hours of a single working day. If a threat actor wishes to gain long term value from a compromised system, they must find a mechanism by which they can persist on the system.

Insider threats may have day-to-day access to the system that they are abusing and not require an additional persistence mechanism. Similarly, an attacker who abuses compromised credentials may assume that the credentials can be used for many days. However, if the credentials are reset or remote access blocked, then the attacker may be locked out of the system and be unable to complete their objectives. Therefore an attacker may wish to achieve long term persistence within a system to ensure access, even if they are confident in being able to access a system repeatedly.

Running malicious tools in memory without touching any form of persistent storage, such as disk drives, might avoid detection methods that scan these systems, but residing in volatile memory is risky for attackers. Any reboot of the device will wipe volatile memory and remove the attacker from the system.

Hence, attackers often seek to achieve a presence within persistent storage of a compromised system. Conversely, for a defender this can render detection easier. There are only so many features within an operating system that an attacker can use to achieve persistence. These techniques are well known and described for both enterprise systems (MITRE 2018a) and mobile systems (MITRE 2018b).

Searching for attempts at achieving persistence can be a powerful technique to discover compromise. Awareness of common methods for gaining persistent access to systems, such as creating new administrator accounts on a domain controller can help direct resources for protection of systems that might be targeted. Additionally, this can help guide detection of network attacks where attackers may seek to specifically compromise systems in order to achieve a long term presence within a network.

2.11 Thinking Like a Threat Actor

Threat actors and their actions comprise a large part of the threat landscape. Although the threat landscape is constantly changing, by understanding the likely objectives of a threat actor, and how they might go about achieving those objectives, we can predict the nature of future attacks.

Through thinking like a threat actor, considering their TTPs, and using the kill chain to describe possible attack scenarios, defenders can identify areas where defences may need to be augmented, or other attack mitigation techniques deployed.

The set of threat actors who wish to do us harm is not infinite, neither are the means that they have at their disposition to conduct attacks. Recognising this, and planning for the most likely, or potentially most damaging, attacks helps defenders plan their defences.

Summary

Cyber threat intelligence is the study of threats, which are a function of risk and vulnerability. Threats exist in many forms and may be accidental or a force of nature as well as malicious. Behind every malicious threat is a threat actor, an individual or group who is seeking to cause harm to their intended victim.

Threat actors conduct their attacks using Tactics, Threats, and Procedures (TTPs), which can be arranged in sequence to construct a kill chain describing how the attack was conducted. Potentially, any computer protocol or file format can be used to conduct attacks. Exactly how an attack is conducted depends on the goals of the threat actor and the nature of their intended targets.

References

Ayoade, G., Chandra, S., Kahn, L. et al. (2018). Threat report classification over multi-source data. *2018 IEEE 4th International Conference on Collaboration and Internet Computing (CIC)*, 236–245. IEEE. http://dx.doi.org/10.1109/CIC.2018.00040.

Biasini, N. (2016). SamSam: the doctor will see you, after he pays the ransom. *Cisco Talos Threat Intelligence* (23 March). https://blog.talosintelligence.com/2016/03/samsam-ransomware.html (accessed 13 January 2023).

Boyne, W.J. (2004). *The Influence of Air Power upon History*. Leo Cooper Ltd.

de Bruijne, M., van Eeten, M., Hernández, Gañán C., and Pieters, W. (2017). Towards a new cyber threat actor typology. A hybrid method for the NCSC cyber security assessment. Faculty of Technology, Policy and Management, Delft University of Technology. https://repository.wodc.nl/bitstream/handle/20.500.12832/2299/2740_Volledige_Tekst_tcm28-273243.pdf (accessed 13 January 2023).

Caltagirone, S., Pendergast, A., and Betz, C. (2013). *The Diamond Model of Intrusion Analysis*. US Department of Defense. https://apps.dtic.mil/dtic/tr/fulltext/u2/a586960.pdf (accessed 13 January 2023).

Cambridge Dictionary (2022). Threat. https://dictionary.cambridge.org/dictionary/english/threat (accessed 30 October 2022).

Casey, T. (2007). *Threat Agent Library Helps Identify Information Security Risks*. Intel Information Technology. https://www.oasis-open.org/committees/download.php/66239/Intel%20Corp_Threat%20Agent%20Library_07-2202w.pdf (accessed 13 January 2023).

Casey, T., Koeberl, P., and Vishik, C. (2010). Threat agents: a necessary component of threat analysis. *Proceedings of the 6th Annual Workshop on Cyber Security and Information Intelligence Research*, 1–4. http://dx.doi.org/10.1145/1852666.1852728.

Chan, D. (2021). *Colonial Pipeline Ransomware Attack (2021)*. NATO Cooperative Cyber Defence Centre of Excellence. https://cyberlaw.ccdcoe.org/wiki/Colonial_Pipeline_ransomware_attack_(2021).

Cherepanov, A. (2017). Analysis of TeleBots' cunning backdoor. *WeLiveSecurity by Eset*, July. https://www.welivesecurity.com/2017/07/04/analysis-of-telebots-cunning-backdoor (accessed 13 January 2023).

Cimpanu, C. (2017). 7% of all Amazon S3 servers are exposed, explaining recent surge of data leaks. *Bleeping Computer* (25 September). https://www.

bleepingcomputer.com/news/security/7-percent-of-all-amazon-s3-servers-are-exposed-explaining-recent-surge-of-data-leaks (accessed 13 January 2023).

Cimpanu, C. (2019). Emotet hijacks email conversation threads to insert links to malware. *ZDNet* (11 April). https://www.zdnet.com/article/emotet-hijacks-email-conversation-threads-to-insert-links-to-malware (accessed 13 January 2023).

Claburn, T. (2017). How to secure MongoDB – because it isn't by default and thousands of DBs are being hacked. *The Register* (11 January). https://www.theregister.com/2017/01/11/mongodb_ransomware_followup (accessed 13 January 2023).

Cohen, L.E. and Felson, M. (1979). Social change and crime rate trends: a routine activity approach. In: *Classics in Environmental Criminology (2010)* (ed. M.A. Andresen, P.J. Brantingham and J.B. Kinney), 203–232. Routledge.

Continella, A., Polino, M., Pogliani, M., and Zanero, S. (2018). There's a hole in that bucket! A large-scale analysis of misconfigured s3 buckets. *Proceedings of the 34th Annual Computer Security Applications Conference*, 702–711.

Corfield, G. (2020). British Airways fined £20m for Magecart hack that exposed 400k folks' credit card details to crooks. *The Register* (16 October). https://www.theregister.com/2020/10/16/british_airways_ico_fine_20m (accessed 13 January 2023).

CVE Project (2018). History. https://cve.mitre.org/about/history.html (accessed 13 January 2023).

Egloff, F. (2015). *Cybersecurity and the Age of Privateering: A Historical Analogy.* University of Oxford, Cyber Studies Programme, Working Paper Series, 1 (1). https://www.politics.ox.ac.uk/materials/centres/cyber-studies/Working_Paper_No.1_Egloff.pdf (accessed 13 January 2023).

ENISA European Union Agency for Cybersecurity (2016). Threat taxonomy. https://www.enisa.europa.eu/topics/threat-risk-management/threats-and-trends/enisa-threat-landscape/threat-taxonomy/view (accessed 13 January 2023).

Falliere, N., O'Murchu, L., and Chien, E. (2011). W32.Stuxnet Dossier. White paper, Symantec Corp. Symantec.

FE Centre for Cyber Security (2020). Investigation Report. The Anatomy of Targeted Ransomware Attacks. Targeted ransomware attacks and how to defeat them. https://cfcs.dk/globalassets/cfcs/dokumenter/rapporter/en/cfcs-report--the-anatomy-of-targeted-ransomware-attacks.pdf (accessed 13 January 2023).

Federal Bureau of Investigation, Internet Crime Complaint Center (2020). 2020 Internet Crime Report. https://www.ic3.gov/Media/PDF/AnnualReport/2020_IC3Report.pdf (accessed 13 January 2023).

FireEye (2014). Supply chain analysis: from quartermaster to sunshop. https://www.fireeye.com/content/dam/fireeye-www/global/en/current-threats/pdfs/rpt-malware-supply-chain.pdf (accessed 13 January 2023).

Forum of Incident Response and Security Teams, CVSS-SIG (2005). Common Vulnerability Scoring System v1 Archive. https://www.first.org/cvss/v1 (accessed 13 January 2023).

Forum of Incident Response and Security Teams, CVSS-SIG (2019). Common Vulnerability Scoring System v3.1: Specification Document. https://www.first.org/cvss/v3.1/specification-document (accessed 13 January 2023).

Fraunhofer Institute & MISP Galaxy Project (2022). Malpedia actors. https://malpedia.caad.fkie.fraunhofer.de/actors (accessed 13 January 2023).

Github (2021). Restrict LDAP access via JNDI #608, Github, logging-log4j2. https://github.com/apache/logging-log4j2/pull/608 (accessed 13 January 2023).

Graham-Cumming, J. and Martinho, C. (2021). Exploitation of Log4j CVE-2021-44228 before public disclosure and evolution of evasion and exfiltration, 14 December. https://blog.cloudflare.com/exploitation-of-cve-2021-44228-before-public-disclosure-and-evolution-of-waf-evasion-patterns (accessed 13 January 2023).

Greenberg, A. (2017). New ransomware linked to NotPetya sweeps Russia and Ukraine "BadRabbit," linked to the authors of NotPetya, hits hundreds of victims, including subways, an airport, and media firms. *Wired* (24 October). https://www.wired.com/story/badrabbit-ransomware-notpetya-russia-ukraine (accessed 13 January 2023).

Greenberg, A. (2018). The White House blames Russia for NotPetya, the 'Most Costly Cyberattack In History'. *Wired* (15 February). https://www.wired.com/story/white-house-russia-notpetya-attribution (accessed 13 January 2023).

Hardy, S., Crete-Nishihata, M., Kleemola, K. et al. (2014). Targeted threat index: characterizing and quantifying politically-motivated targeted malware. *Proceedings of the 23rd USENIX Security Symposium. {USENIX} Security 14*, 527–541. https://www.usenix.org/system/files/conference/usenixsecurity14/sec14-paper-hardy.pdf (accessed 13 January 2023).

Headquarters, Department of the Army (2015). Army Techniques Publication No. 3-60, Targeting. https://armypubs.army.mil/epubs/DR_pubs/DR_a/pdf/web/atp3_60.pdf (accessed 13 January 2023).

Health and Safety Executive (n.d.). Human factors: managing human failures. https://www.hse.gov.uk/humanfactors/topics/humanfail.htm (accessed 13 January 2023).

Husari, G., Niu, X., Chu, B., and Al-Shaer, E. (2018). Using entropy and mutual information to extract threat actions from cyber threat intelligence. *2018 IEEE International Conference on Intelligence and Security Informatics (ISI)*. IEEE. http://dx.doi.org/10.1109/ISI.2018.8587343.

Hutchins, E.M., Cloppert, M.J., and Amin, R.M. (2011). Intelligence-driven computer network defense informed by analysis of adversary campaigns and intrusion kill chains. *Proceedings of the 6th International Conference on Information Warfare and*

Security. 6th International Conference on Information Warfare and Security ICIW 2011, 113–125. https://www.lockheedmartin.com/content/dam/lockheed-martin/ rms/documents/cyber/LM-White-Paper-Intel-Driven-Defense.pdf (accessed 13 January 2023).

Iannacone, M., Bohn, S., Nakamura, G. et al. (2015). Developing an ontology for cyber security knowledge graphs. *Proceedings of the 10th Annual Cyber and Information Security Research Conference*. Association for Computing Machinery, 1–4. http://dx.doi.org/10.1145/2746266.2746278.

Ibraigheeth, M. and Fadzil, S.A. (2019). Core factors for software projects success. *JOIV: International Journal on Informatics Visualization* 3 (1): 69–74.

ISO 31000 (2018b). *Risk management*. International Standards Organization. https:// www.iso.org/iso-31000-risk-management.html (accessed 13 January 2023).

ISO 7498-2:1989 (1989). *Information Processing Systems – Open Systems Interconnection – Basic Reference Model - Part 2: Security Architecture*. International Standards Organization. https://www.iso.org/standard/14256.html (accessed 13 January 2023).

ISO/IEC 2382:2015(en) (2015). *Information Technology – Vocabulary – Threat*. International Standards Organization. https://www.iso.org/obp/ui/#iso:std:iso-iec:2382:ed-1:v1:en (accessed 13 January 2023).

ISO/IEC 27005:2018 (2018a). *Information Technology – Security Techniques – Information Security Risk Management*. International Standards Organization. https://www.iso.org/standard/75281.html (accessed 13 January 2023).

Joint Task Force, National Institute of Standards and Technology, US Chamber of Commerce (2018). *Risk Management Framework for Information Systems and Organizations. A System Life Cycle Approach for Security and Privacy*. NIST Special Publication 800-37 revision 2. http://dx.doi.org/10.6028/NIST. SP.800-37r2.

Jouini, M., Rabai, L.B.A., and Aissa, A.B. (2014). Classification of security threats in information systems. *Procedia Computer Science* 32: 489–496.

Junger, M., Montoya, L., Hartel, P., and Heydari, M. (2017). Towards the normalization of cybercrime victimization. A routine activities analysis of cybercrime in Europe. *2017 International Conference on Cyber Situational Awareness, Data Analytics And Assessment (Cyber SA)*, 1–8. http://dx.doi. org/10.1109/CyberSA.2017.8073391.

Kirkpatrick, D. (2013). Mongodb – Security Weaknesses in a typical NoSQL database. *Trustwave - SpiderLabs Blog* (21 March). https://www.trustwave.com/en-us/ resources/blogs/spiderlabs-blog/mongodb-security-weaknesses-in-a-typical-nosql-database (accessed 13 January 2023).

Kwasinski, A. (2013). *Lessons from Field Damage Assessments about Communication Networks Power Supply and Infrastructure Performance during Natural Disasters with a Focus on Hurricane Sandy*, 1–36. FCC Workshop Network Resiliency.

Landsberger, H.A. (1958). *Hawthorne Revisited. Management and the Worker: Its Critics, and Developments in Human Relations in Industry.* Cornell University.

Leukfeldt, E.R. and Yar, M. (2016). Applying routine activity theory to cybercrime: A theoretical and empirical analysis. *Deviant Behavior* 37 (3): 263–280. https://doi.org/10.1080/01639625.2015.1012409.

Leyden, J. (2018). British Airways hack: Infosec experts finger third-party scripts on payment pages. *The Register* (11 September). https://www.theregister.com/2018/09/11/british_airways_website_scripts (accessed 13 January 2023).

Leyden, J. (2022). Insecure Amazon S3 bucket exposed personal data on 500,000 Ghanaian graduates. *The Daily Swig* (6 January). https://portswigger.net/daily-swig/insecure-amazon-s3-bucket-exposed-personal-data-on-500-000-ghanaian-graduates (accessed 13 January 2023).

Li, M., Zheng, R., Liu, L., and Yang, P. (2019). Extraction of threat actions from threat-related articles using multi-label machine learning classification method. *2019 2nd International Conference on Safety Produce Informatization (IICSPI)*, 428–431. IEEE. http://dx.doi.org/10.1109/IICSPI48186.2019.9095885.

Lindsay, J.R. (2013). Stuxnet and the limits of cyber warfare. *Security Studies* 22 (3): 365–404.

Matherly, J. (2015). It's the Data, Stupid! *Shodan Blog* (11 July). https://blog.shodan.io/its-the-data-stupid (accessed 13 January 2023).

Mavroeidis, V. and Bromander, S. (2017). Cyber threat intelligence model: an evaluation of taxonomies, sharing standards, and ontologies within cyber threat intelligence. *2017 European Intelligence and Security Informatics Conference (EISIC)*, 91–98. IEEE. http://dx.doi.org/10.1109/EISIC.2017.20.

Maynor, D., Nikolic, A., Olney, M., and Younan, Y. (2017). The MeDoc Connection. *Talos Intelligence*, July. https://blog.talosintelligence.com/2017/07/the-medoc-connection.html (accessed 13 January 2023).

Microsoft (2009). The STRIDE threat model, 12 November. https://learn.microsoft.com/en-us/previous-versions/commerce-server/ee823878(v=cs.20) (accessed 13 January 2023).

MITRE Corporation (2018a). MITRE ATT&CK – enterprise persistence. https://attack.mitre.org/tactics/TA0003 (accessed 13 January 2023).

MITRE Corporation (2018b). MITRE ATT&CK – mobile persistence. https://attack.mitre.org/tactics/TA0028 (accessed 13 January 2023).

MITRE Corporation (2022a). CWE top 25 most dangerous software weaknesses. https://cwe.mitre.org/top25/archive/2022/2022_cwe_top25.html (accessed 13 January 2023).

MITRE Corporation (2022b). ATT&CK Groups. https://attack.mitre.org/groups/ (accessed 13 January 2023).

MITRE Corporation (2022c). Deep Panda. https://attack.mitre.org/groups/G0009 (accessed 13 January 2023).

MITRE Corporation (2022d). ATT&CK. https://attack.mitre.org (accessed 13 January 2023).

MITRE Corporation (2022e). Common Weakness Enumeration. https://cwe.mitre.org (accessed 13 January 2023).

MITRE Corporation (2022f). MITRE ATT&CK – enterprise tactics. https://attack.mitre.org/tactics/enterprise (accessed 13 January 2023).

Montalbano, E. (2020). Magecart attack convincingly hijacks PayPal transactions at checkout. *Threat Post* (1 December). https://threatpost.com/magecart-hijacks-paypal-transactions/161697 (accessed 13 January 2023).

National Institute of Standards and Technology (2011). *NIST Cyber Threat – CNSSI 4009-2015 under threat from NIST SP 800-30 Rev. 1*. Computer Security Resource Centre, Glossary. https://csrc.nist.gov/glossary/term/Cyber_Threat (accessed 13 January 2023).

NATO Terminology Office (2017a). *Risk*. NATOTerm. The Official NATO Terminology Database. https://nso.nato.int/natoterm/content/nato/pages/home.html?lg=en (accessed 13 January 2023).

NATO Terminology Office (2017b). *Vulnerability*. NATOTerm. The Official NATO Terminology Database. https://nso.nato.int/natoterm/content/nato/pages/home.html?lg=en (accessed 13 January 2023).

Ngo, F.T. and Paternoster, R. (2011). Cybercrime victimization: an examination of individual and situational level factors. *International Journal of Cyber Criminology* 5 (1): 773–793.

Osborne, C. (2013). 13 Anonymous members indicted over Operation Payback. *ZDNet, Zero Day* (4 October). https://www.zdnet.com/google-amp/article/13-anonymous-members-indicted-over-operation-payback/ (accessed 13 January 2023).

OWASP (2022). OWASP Top Ten. https://owasp.org/www-project-top-ten (accessed 13 January 2023).

Paganini, P. (2019). Only now we know that International Civil Aviation Organization (ICAO) was hacked in 2016. *Security Affairs* (1 March). https://securityaffairs.co/wordpress/81790/apt/icao-hack-2016.html (accessed 13 January 2023).

Reyns, B.W. and Henson, B. (2016). The thief with a thousand faces and the victim with none: identifying determinants for online identity theft victimization with routine activity theory. *International Journal of Offender Therapy and Comparative Criminology* 60 (10): 1119–1139.

Scroxton, A. (2020). Leaky AWS S3 bucket once again at centre of data breach. *Computer Weekly* (10 November). https://www.computerweekly.com/news/252491842/Leaky-AWS-S3-bucket-once-again-at-centre-of-data-breach (accessed 13 January 2023).

Seals, T. (2017). Every single American household exposed in massive leak. *Infosecurity Magazine* (19 December). https://www.infosecurity-magazine.com/news/every-single-american-household (accessed 13 January 2023).

Shostack, A. (2007). STRIDE chart, 11 September. https://www.microsoft.com/
security/blog/2007/09/11/stride-chart (accessed 13 January 2023).

Strom, B.E., Appebaum, A., Miller, D.P. et al. (2020). *MITRE Corporation: Design and Philosophy*. MITRE Corporation. https://attack.mitre.org/docs/ATTACK_Design_and_Philosophy_March_2020.pdf.

Talos (2021). Threat Advisory: Critical Apache Log4j vulnerability being exploited in the wild. *Talos Intelligence* (10 December). https://blog.talosintelligence.com/2021/12/apache-log4j-rce-vulnerability.html (accessed 13 January 2023).

Thonnard, O., Bilge, L., O'Gorman, G. et al. (2012). Industrial espionage and targeted attacks: understanding the characteristics of an escalating threat. *International Workshop on Recent Advances in Intrusion Detection*, 64–85. Springer-Verlag.

Thonnard, O., Bilge, L., Kashyap, A., and Lee, M. (2015). Are you at risk? Profiling organizations and individuals subject to targeted attacks. Lecture Notes in Computer Science. *Financial Cryptography and Data Security. FC 2015*. http://dx.doi.org/10.1007/978-3-662-47854-7_2.

UK National Cyber Security Centre (2016). Risk management guidance. www.ncsc.gov.uk/collection/risk-management-collection (accessed 13 January 2023).

UK National Cyber Security Centre (2018). Russian military 'almost certainly' responsible for destructive 2017 cyber attack. *National Cyber Security Centre News* (14 February). www.ncsc.gov.uk/news/russian-military-almost-certainly-responsible-destructive-2017-cyber-attack (accessed 13 January 2023).

UK National Cyber Security Centre (2021). Alert: Apache Log4j vulnerabilities. National Cyber Security Centre. www.ncsc.gov.uk/news/apache-log4j-vulnerability (accessed 13 January 2023).

US Cybersecurity & Infrastructure Security Agency (2018a). Alert (AA18-337A) SamSam Ransomware. National Cyber Awareness System. https://us-cert.cisa.gov/ncas/alerts/AA18-337A (accessed 13 January 2023).

US Cybersecurity & Infrastructure Security Agency (2018b). Alert (TA18-106A) Russian State-Sponsored Cyber Actors Targeting Network Infrastructure Devices. National Cyber Awareness System. https://us-cert.cisa.gov/ncas/alerts/TA18-106A (accessed 13 January 2023).

US Cybersecurity & Infrastructure Security Agency (2019). Alert (AA19-024A) DNS Infrastructure Hijacking Campaign. National Cyber Awareness System. https://us-cert.cisa.gov/ncas/alerts/AA19-024A (accessed 13 January 2023).

US Cybersecurity & Infrastructure Security Agency (2021). Apache Log4j Vulnerability Guidance. https://www.cisa.gov/uscert/apache-log4j-vulnerability-guidance (accessed 13 January 2023).

US Cybersecurity & Infrastructure Security Agency (2022). CISA.gov threat definition. https://niccs.cisa.gov/about-niccs/cybersecurity-glossary#T (accessed 13 January 2023).

US Department of Commerce, National Institute of Standards and Technology (n.d.). *Tactics, Techniques, and Procedures (TTP)*. Computer Security Resource Centre, Glossary. https://csrc.nist.gov/glossary/term/Tactics_Techniques_and_Procedures (accessed 13 January 2023).

US Department of Homeland Security and The MITRE Corporation (n.d.). Common Attack Pattern Enumeration and Classification (CAPEC). https://capec.mitre.org/about/index.html (accessed 13 January 2023).

Verizon (2021). DBIR 2021 Data Breach Investigations Report. https://www.verizon.com/business/resources/reports/2021-data-breach-investigations-report.pdf (accessed 13 January 2023).

Wall, D. (2001). Cybercrimes and the Internet. In: *Crime and the Internet*, 18–28. Routledge.

Whitty, M. (2021). Developing a conceptual model for insider threat. *Journal of Management & Organization* 27 (5): 911–929. https://doi.org/10.1017/jmo.2018.57.

Wisniewski, C. (2022). Log4Shell: No mass abuse, but no respite, what happened? *Sophos News* (24 January). https://news.sophos.com/en-us/2022/01/24/log4shell-no-mass-abuse-but-no-respite-what-happened (accessed 13 January 2023).

3

Applying Intelligence

Threat Intelligence is a practical discipline gathering and utilising information. Before considering how intelligence is used in practice, we must identify the nature of the intelligence that is required and the framework in which this intelligence will be applied. To be a useful adjunct to cyber security protection, the correct threat intelligence must be applied, and its utility measured.

Chapter 3 describes the threat intelligence cycle, the most commonly described framework for organising and applying intelligence, as well as the many elements that comprise the threat intelligence programme.

3.1   Planning Intelligence Gathering

In Chapter 1, Cyber Threat Intelligence was defined as:

> The process and outcome of gathering and analysing information relating to the people or things that may cause damage to electronic networked devices, in order to assist decision making.

This definition poses some immediate questions – what intelligence does decision making require? How will the delivered intelligence be used? How will we know if the intelligence supplied is useful and fulfilling its purpose?

Threat intelligence cannot exist in a vacuum. Intelligence production must be part of a wider process of supporting the cyber security posture of an organisation as part of a developed security structure. Unplanned and undirected intelligence activities are unlikely to be productive. To provide value to an organisation, threat intelligence needs to be part of a defined operational programme.

Cyber Threat Intelligence, First Edition. Martin Lee.
© 2023 John Wiley & Sons, Inc. Published 2023 by John Wiley & Sons, Inc.

Although the circular relationship between threat intelligence and the risk management programme was discussed in Chapter 2, cyber threat intelligence is more frequently thought of as supporting the organisation's cyber security programme.

The US National Institute of Standards and Technology (NIST) Cyber Security Framework describes the components necessary for an effective cyber security programme (NIST 2018). Although specifically created to improve cyber security activities within critical national infrastructure, the framework has been applied to all industrial sectors and all sizes of organisation (Mahn 2018).

The framework provides five high-level cyber security functions against which activities can be directed and oriented (Table 3.1).

Clearly cyber threat intelligence can assist with all these functions. Threat intelligence clearly helps identify and characterise threats. Intelligence provides indicators that allow security teams to identify threats as they impact organisations, and understand how any cyber security events relate to specific threats. Additionally, intelligence provides information regarding how other organisations have protected systems against threats, and how they have responded to actual threats. Finally, threat intelligence helps in understanding what has happened during response and recovery activities.

The ISO/IEC 27000 family of standards supplies best practices for managing information security risks (OGCIO 2022). The security controls described within ISO/IEC 27002 include threat intelligence. The standard recommends that organisations have the capability to identify and analyse the changing threat landscape, identify the threats relevant to the organisation, and develop suitable mitigations for these. This intelligence can then be used to feed into additional controls,

Table 3.1 Functions of the cyber security function (NIST 2018).

Function	Description
Identify	Develop and identify the requirements, processes, and people necessary to provide cyber security; the assets that require protecting; the existing cyber security capabilities; and the threats that may impact the organisation.
Protect	Develop and implement the necessary protections in order to protect assets against threats, and to be able to contain the impact of potential cyber security events.
Detect	Develop and implement the necessary processes, systems, and people in order to detect cyber security events.
Respond	Develop and implement the capability to respond appropriately to cyber security events and incidents.
Recover	Develop and implement the ability to be able to restore business functionality that may be impaired by a cyber security incident.

notably monitoring activities and decision making regarding security events and their triage (ISO 2022).

Clearly there are many functions that threat intelligence can support, however which of these should be prioritised? Spreading resources too thinly, especially when an intelligence function is being established, risks threat intelligence making little or no difference to the security goals of the organisation. To muster intelligence resources and direct them where they can be most effective, requires an intelligence programme.

3.1.1 The Intelligence Programme

Threat intelligence means different things to different people. Through creating a defined threat intelligence programme expectations can be managed, the form and nature of the intelligence can be decided, and most importantly the intelligence product created so that it is relevant to the intended use.

Threat intelligence products are often considered as comprising three different types: tactical, operational, and strategic. Each product has a different target audience, who have their own unique needs. Intelligence products may be briefing documents, machine readable lists of indicators of compromise (IoCs), a mixture of the two, or consist of another format entirely. All of these formats are equally valid, but intended for different audiences and consumed in different ways.

These features and expectations must be decided in advance of collecting threat intelligence so that the needs of the consumers of the intelligence will be met, and relevant metrics that demonstrate the utility of the intelligence can be agreed upon. Metrics help show how threat intelligence is benefitting the organisation's cyber security activities, how the cyber security objectives are being met, highlight successes so that they can be recognised, and identify weaknesses to be addressed.

Coherent metrics are important for identifying any intelligence gaps, and areas where the intelligence programme can be improved, and vital for communicating the importance of the programme to senior decision makers who may otherwise decide to allocate resources elsewhere.

Intelligence programmes, like all elements of an organisation, will vary in their maturity. Growing an intelligence capability incrementally helps organisations better understand their needs, and develop their resources in line with awareness of what is required from an intelligence team. Developing a threat intelligence team too quickly risks delivering more intelligence than other teams can process, or worse delivering intelligence that is of no use to the intended consumers.

Verisign describes four stages of threat intelligence maturity (Table 3.2) (Verisign iDefense Security Intelligence Services 2012).

It is not only the threat intelligence teams producing intelligence that mature their capabilities, but the consumers of intelligence can also be expected to

Table 3.2 Stages of threat intelligence maturity.

Stage	Description
Ad hoc	Organisations handle tasks manually with little or no defined process. They may handle recurring tasks inconsistently.
Formal	Expectations, capabilities, and processes are all documented and understood. Tasks at this level are repeatable and have consistent outputs, though they are largely handled manually.
Efficient	Automated processes streamline handling of tasks and data, including prioritisation. There is increased visibility into operations through reporting metrics.
Proactive	Organisations can identify intelligence gaps and anticipate future needs.

Source: Verisign iDefense Security Intelligence Services 2012 / VeriSign, Inc.

develop their own maturity as well. The Bank of England presents a maturity model for threat intelligence consumption (Bank of England 2016) (Table 3.3).

Organisations may assess their maturity as consumers of intelligence and come to the conclusion that the cyber security posture of the organisation may be better served through adding resources to bolster existing security activities or to allocate resources to immediate concerns rather than to create a threat intelligence function.

In any case, even having a minimal threat intelligence function that is able to provide basic information enriching understanding of current threats and how these might be addressed is likely to provide benefit. Organisations do not necessarily need to develop a large mature intelligence capacity (however this may be defined) immediately, but seek to expand capabilities over time as the utility of threat intelligence is recognised, and the ability to put it to good use developed.

3.1.2 Principles of Intelligence

Intelligence should maintain certain guiding principles that define how threat intelligence activities are undertaken and how intelligence products are used.

ISO/IEC 27002 states that threat intelligence should be '*relevant, perceptive, contextual, and actionable*' (ISO 2022). Clearly, these are noble goals, however other organisations have gone further in specifying intelligence principles.

CREST, the non-profit association for the cyber security industry, defines eight principles of intelligence known by the mnemonic CROSSCAT (Table 3.4).

These principles are similar to those used in military intelligence doctrine, as described by the British Ministry of Defence (Table 3.5).

Table 3.3 Bank of England maturity model for threat intelligence consumption. (Bank of England 2016)

Stage	Description
Report	Consumers use intelligence that describes what has happened to piece together the anatomy and symptoms of an attack.
	This is a reactive stance based on hindsight.
Diagnose	Consumers use intelligence to diagnose why an attack occurred. Building on intelligence to understand who launched an attack and why.
	This responsive stance requires strategic insight and awareness of what is not known regarding an attack or threat actor.
Predict	The consumer uses advanced forms of intelligence to make predictions about what will happen.
	This responsive stance employs strategic foresight to focus monitoring and mitigation activities.
Operationalise	Intelligence processes are tightly coupled with the consumer to enable real time intelligence in support of tactical decision making.
	This responsive stance employs tactical insight regarding what is happening now.
Activate	Intelligence and operations are tightly coupled so that intelligence triggers an automated operational response.
	This proactive stance allows a consumer to consider 'what do I want to happen?'

Table 3.4 CROSSCAT principles of intelligence.

Principle	Description
Centralised	Centralisation of control allows for efficient resource allocation, minimises risk of duplication of effort, and allows for a primary point of contact.
Responsive	Intelligence should be responsive to consumers with clearly defined reporting lines.
Objective	Analysts should remain impassive with assessments which should be made independently from the policy process.
Systematic	Source, data, and information should be methodically exploited in a coherent and coordinated fashion.
Sharing	Intelligence should be shared according to protective markings that clearly describe how sharing is limited, while protecting sources when required.
Continuous review	Assessments should be continually tested against new information, while feedback should spread through the cycle of gathering, analysing, and disseminating intelligence.
Accessible	Intelligence products should be designed and delivered with its intended audience in mind.
Timely	Intelligence is useless if delivered too late. Less than perfect outputs delivered on time are preferable to outdated material.

Source: Adapted from CREST (2019).

Table 3.5 Principles of military intelligence.

Principle	Description
Command led	Good intelligence flows from a command led process that constantly defines (and re-defines) what is important as well as what is urgent.
	Commanders should foster a command climate that empowers their staff, particularly the intelligence staff, to work in a spirit of cooperation.
Objectivity	Intelligence must be unbiased, undistorted, intellectually honest, and free of prejudice.
	Intelligence staff should not distort their assessments to fit preconceived ideas to provide the answer that they think the commander wants, or conform to fit existing plans.
Perspective	Get inside the mindset of the key actors, particularly adversaries; try to think like them.
	Intelligence analysts must seek to understand the likely perspective of adversaries and other key actors in the operational theatre. They must continuously refine their ability to think like them and to understand their fears, motivations, intentions, capabilities, and narratives.
Agility	Look ahead, identify threats and opportunities, develop the flexibility to react to changing situations, and be ready to exploit opportunities as they arise. Agility is not about absolute speed: it is an ability to exploit information in context at the right tempo.
Timeliness	Providing intelligence on time, even if incomplete, to enable commanders to make decisions at a pace that maintains the initiative.
Collaboration	Sharing individual understanding to achieve greater collective and common understanding is a powerful tool in joint and coalition operations.
	For operational security, the need-to-know principle endures, but a collaborative environment relies on a duty to share culture across and possibly outside government, underpinned by pragmatic risk management.
Continuity	Maintaining subject matter experts in post, both at home and on operations, is one way to achieve continuity of understanding. The commander should ensure that sufficient continuity of expertise is maintained within his intelligence staff, but also recognise the valuable insights sometimes gained from a fresh perspective.
Security	Security must permeate the entire intelligence enterprise, but should balance the need to share with the need to protect people and plans.

Source: Adapted from Development, Concepts and Doctrine Centre, UK MoD (2011).

Similar principles are described in the US Joint Chiefs of Staff's joint intelligence doctrine (JCS 2013).

Organisations should not adopt such principles without challenge or reflection. Developing similar guiding principles that are appropriate to the needs of the organisation will help developing a healthy culture in which threat intelligence activities can flourish.

3.1.3 Intelligence Metrics

A threat intelligence programme should meet the programme's stated requirements and satisfy the intelligence needs of the customers. Different types of intelligence will have different requirements, and hence different metrics, but broadly speaking there will be two types of metrics for intelligence: team productivity and intelligence utility.

Metrics will depend on the maturity of the intelligence capability. A programme focused on developing the team's capability may wish to focus on measuring the team's ability to produce intelligence, a mature team may wish to focus on how intelligence is assisting in reducing the time to detection for threats.

In either case, involving the teams generating and consuming the intelligence in devising metrics and providing feedback on the quality of the intelligence is likely to result in better measures of quality and also perception of quality of the intelligence (Schlette et al. 2021).

The commercial cyber threat intelligence organisation Flashpoint describes intelligence metrics as falling into one of three categories.

- Operational metrics describing the speed and efficiency of teams and how intelligence contributes to this by allowing teams to process threats faster, or discover relevant threats with less effort.
- Tactical metrics following the efficacy of intelligence. This includes measures such as the false negative rate: the number of threats that impacted the organisation for which intelligence did not contribute, and the false positive rate: the number of falsely attributed threats that intelligence suggested were malicious, but which were identified not to be malicious.
- Strategic metrics describing how the intelligence programme has helped the business achieve its goals. This may include measures such as how intelligence has reduced risk, or money saved through detecting or resolving threats faster due to the contributions of intelligence.

(Flashpoint 2021)

Recorded Future, another commercial threat intelligence organisation, recommends using metrics as a method of illustrating the story of the threat intelligence team rather than becoming overly driven by metrics (Reid 2018).

They recommend focusing on metrics that are directly affected by the intelligence team, namely the inputs to the team, the analyses that the team performs, the output that the team creates, and the impact that the intelligence has on the cyber security function.

3.2 The Intelligence Cycle

The process of gathering data, transforming it into intelligence, and disseminating that information is referred to as the Intelligence Cycle (Figure 3.1).

Various versions of the intelligence cycle have been published with the number of phases within the cycle ranging from four (CREST 2019) to seven (Lahneman and Naval Postgraduate School 2018), with different variations on the names of the phases. Nevertheless, although the number of and names of steps may differ between the many versions, the principle of the cycle remains essentially the same.

The phases within the cycle should not be thought of as separate distinct steps, but as a continuum of overlapping steps. The activities of a subsequent step in the cycle may begin before the previous step has been completed. Simultaneous activity conducted as parallel streams of word is to be expected. For example, as data is collected, analysis and processing of the data can begin. There is no need to wait for all data to be collected before beginning analysis.

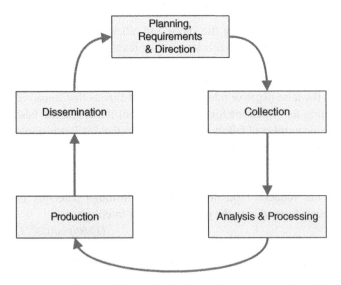

Figure 3.1 The Intelligence Cycle. *Source:* Image adapted from The Interagency OPSEC Support Staff (1996); NATO (2017).

Similarly, activity may be backwards facing. For example, as analysis and processing progresses, it may become clear that additional data needs to be collected, hence a new collection process may be initiated. The focus should be on delivering an intelligence product that meets the requirements of the end user rather than strictly following a notional process.

3.2.1 Planning, Requirements, and Direction

The intelligence cycle commences with a clear articulation of the intelligence that is required to be delivered. Ultimately, this is likely to be a variation or derivation of the main intelligence questions of *'what, where, why, how, who and when'* (Development, Concepts and Doctrine Centre, UK MoD 2011). That is to say what is happening, where is it happening, why is it occurring and who or what is causing the event, and when did this begin? The same intelligence questions can be asked in the past tense: what happened, etc., or in the future tense: what will happen, etc.

At this stage of the cycle the requirements for the intelligence should be defined. There should be no doubt as to for whom the intelligence is intended, the format in which the intelligence will be delivered, the timeliness by which the intelligence is required, and the nature of the expected product, which may be strategic, operational, or tactical intelligence.

The manager responsible for delivering the intelligence should engage with the individual requesting the intelligence and the eventual customer to ensure that the requirements have been correctly specified and understood. It is also the duty of the intelligence manager to ensure that the intelligence team is able to fulfil the request, that the team has the necessary resources and capabilities to deliver the required product.

Hence, planning for delivery of the request may start before the request is fully finalised so that the intelligence manager is aware of what is required in order to satisfy the request. The planning process may uncover that it is impossible to deliver the required product, or that some of the requirements are mutually incompatible. For instance, the requirements might specify that the product is to be delivered on a tight deadline, but the data collection process would not be complete before the deadline.

Some to-ing and fro-ing between the intelligence manager and the requestor is to be expected so that the request can be refined to both satisfy the customer's requirements and the intelligence team's capabilities. Occasionally, the requestor may need educating regarding the limits of what intelligence can provide, and the realities of an intelligence team of finite resources.

Once the request is understood by all parties and decided, the activities within the subsequent phases of the cycle can be finalised and resources allocated.

3.2.2 Collection

This phase involves the collection of the data and information that is relevant to the intelligence task and delivering them in an appropriate format to the analysis team for the next phase in the cycle.

Data may come from external sources. Third party intelligence reports can act as source data for intelligence teams to ingest, analyse, and use to create new intelligence reports with additional context and relevance to their own organisations. Trusted sources of data, such as members of an industry group or intelligence partners are also valuable sources of data.

Media publications should not be discounted as a valuable source of information. The motivations of threat actors are varied, some may seek a high profile and actively publicise their actions, or journalists may have published investigative reports relevant to the intelligence request.

Data may also originate from internal sources. Notably, technical data derived from network or system monitoring, forensic analysis of compromised systems, analysis of malware, or incident response reports.

Human intelligence, where an intelligence operative engages directly or indirectly with a threat actor is another possibility. Malicious campaigns or capabilities may be discussed within criminal forums, or over social media. Specialist commercial organisations are available who specialise in collecting and supplying such information.

Communications by threat actors are a further source of intelligence. The language, sentences, paragraphs used in demands for payment by ransomware gangs can be used to spot similarities with previous attacks. The phrases and language particularities of threat actors can be indicative of their native language. Metadata, such as email addresses, sending IP addresses, or even time of day may also be disclosed during communication and disclose information regarding the threat actor.

3.2.3 Analysis and Processing

This phase involves the transformation of raw data and information into intelligence through the application of the intelligence analyst's skill in combining and synthesising the inputs into intelligence analysis that meets the customer's requirements.

Key considerations within this phase are evaluating the reliability, accuracy, and veracity of sources and data. Sophisticated threat actors may seed purposely incorrect information to lead analysts astray.

Analysts should ensure their own objectivity remaining aware of any overt or subconscious biases they may bring to their analysis, and reprocess their analyses as new information or intelligence becomes available.

3.2.4 Production

The analyses are transformed into a final intelligence product that meets the original requirements. At this stage, any gaps in the intelligence can be identified, and an additional intelligence process initiated to fill these.

The intelligence product should succinctly present the information necessary to fulfil the request. Within the content, known facts should clearly be presented as such, with any assumptions, hypotheses, and conjecture clearly identified. Intelligence gaps or information that is relevant but unknown should also be clearly stated.

3.2.5 Dissemination

Finally, the intelligence product can be disseminated to the target audience. The intelligence should be timely, '*It is better to provide 80% of the intelligence on time rather than 100% of the intelligence too late*' (Development, Concepts and Doctrine Centre, UK MoD 2011).

The security level of the product and distribution restrictions should also be indicated. State intelligence apparatuses have formal classifications for the confidentiality of reports and limit distribution appropriately. Being in possession of classified material without appropriate clearance can carry severe legal penalties.

Other organisations are unlikely to possess the means to restrict distribution in the same way as the government, or have a culture that is used to handling sensitive material. The customers of intelligence reports may not be aware of the sensitivity of an intelligence product, or the importance of not accidentally disclosing information regarding an incident to a threat actor.

Hence, intelligence reports need to clearly indicate restrictions on the distribution of reports and the importance of keeping the report confidential, if this is necessary. Nevertheless, intelligence is only useful if it is used. Circulation should not be overly restrictive in such a way to prevent intelligence reaching those who require access or who would benefit from having access.

3.2.6 Review

Often included in the intelligence cycle is the notion of an additional phase of 'review'. In this phase the effectiveness and performance of the intelligence process is reviewed; areas that require improvement are appropriately addressed. Similarly, the effectiveness and performance of the intelligence product can be reviewed against the requirements and expectations of the request. If the intelligence product did not meet requirements, or the requirements did not lead to an effective outcome, these can be reviewed with the customer and appropriate changes made.

By including such a phase, quality management can be built into the intelligence cycle with the concept of continuous improvement integrated into the production of intelligence. In an ideal world, each iteration of the production of intelligence should better fit the requirements of the customer, while at the same time, the customer improves the definition and articulation of their requirements.

3.3 Situational Awareness

The intelligence cycle describes how to go about producing intelligence, but it says nothing about the subjects for which intelligence should be gathered. Good intelligence begins with asking good questions. But which questions to ask?

Situational awareness refers to the mental models we construct relating to our position in the environment and our relationships with other entities around us. In our daily lives we don't need to constantly keep track of everything around us, only that which is significant or important. If we are walking through a doorway, we need to be aware of where the doorway is physically, our trajectory towards that space, if the door is open or closed, and if there are any immediate hazards that may impact our route.

If our mental model closely matches what is happening in the environment, our situational awareness is good, there is little difference between our understanding of reality and reality itself. However, if our perception of reality diverges from the actual environment then our situational awareness may be poor. We may trip on the rucked carpet that we missed before we reach the doorway, or risk having the door shut in our face because we failed to realise that someone was in the process of closing the door as we were walking towards it.

Formally situational awareness is defined as:

> the perception of the elements in the environment within a volume of time and space, the comprehension of their meaning and the projection of their status in the near future.
>
> *(Endsley 1995)*

And less formally as:

> the degree of accuracy by which one's perception of his current environment mirrors reality.
>
> *(Nofi 2000)*

Situational awareness is vital for cyber security. Decision makers need to be aware of what they are responsible for protecting, the threats that these assets face, the

Table 3.6 Situational awareness and threat intelligence maturity.

Threat intelligence maturity	Situational awareness level	Description
Ad hoc Formal	1 – Perception of Elements in the Environment	Awareness of attributes and dynamics of relevant elements in the environment. Perception of critical dangers and threats.
Efficient	2 – Comprehension of the Current Situation	Forming a holistic picture of the environment, comprehending the significance of objects and events. Prioritising threats and information with respect to the decision maker's objectives.
Proactive	3 – Projection of Future Status	The ability to project the future actions of elements in the environment. Understanding how the current environment will evolve.

Source: Adapted from Endsley (1995); Harrald and Jefferson (2007); Verisign iDefense Security Intelligence Services (2012).

threat actors that may attack the assets, and the relative vulnerabilities and protections in place. The threat intelligence programme is a key part of developing situational awareness. However, this ability must be developed as the intelligence programme grows in maturity.

Endsley describes three levels of situational awareness that we can map to stages of maturity of the threat intelligence programme (Table 3.6).

Decision makers in cyber security should be constantly assessing the ability of the organisation to provide situational awareness and seeking where resources can be directed to improve weaknesses in awareness.

A base line of situational awareness must be achieved before more complex questions can be asked. However, through tasking threat intelligence teams with pertinent questions, intelligence analysts can both practise and refine their skills, while producing intelligence that adds to the situational awareness of the organisation and how the organisation sits within the changing threat landscape.

Developing situational awareness is not without risks. The understanding of the environment may increasingly diverge from reality especially if the team succumbs to one or more common pitfalls:

> *Attentional Tunnelling* – the user locks in on certain aspects/features of the environment they are trying to process and begin to exclude other information sets.
> *Requisite Memory Trap* – the user reaches their limit in working memory.
> *Workload, Anxiety, Fatigue, and Other Stressors* – these factors will decrease the user's limited working memory, diminishing their ability to collect and filter information, resulting in erroneous decision making.

Data Overload – the user's ability to process information becomes saturated.

Misplaced Salience – false alarms, less important information, etc., distract from vital information.

Complexity Creep – as systems become more and more complex the user's ability to understand the information offered prevents them from forming appropriate mental models.

Errant Mental Models – errant mental models result in limited comprehension and the inability to anticipate future events.

Out-of-the-loop Syndrome – as the system becomes more automated individuals are left out of the loop, thereby reducing the overall situational awareness (Endsley et al. 2003; Harrald and Jefferson 2007).

It may seem that the answer to weaknesses in situational awareness is simply to gather more information. However, there is a point where a decision maker has all the information that they are able to process, adding more information at this point decreases the ability to make decisions (Ruff 2002; Karr-Wisniewski and Lu 2010).

In supplying decision makers with strategic or operational intelligence, the goal of the intelligence team must not only be to supply pertinent intelligence to form good situational awareness, but to supply just enough information and no more.

However, computer systems have no such cognitive limits. In supplying tactical intelligence, which is ingested by an automated system, intelligence teams can seek to deliver everything that is relevant and accurate without fear of overloading recipients. Nevertheless, human oversight is required to ensure the veracity of the tactical intelligence, and whether it contributes to improving the security posture.

3.3.1 Example – 2013 Target Breach

For example, although the exact details of what happened during the 2013 Target breach are known only to the attacker and victim, the published details of the incident have become an excellent case study in cyber security. Ultimately the breach resulted in the financial data of up to 70 million individuals becoming compromised by attackers.

Target had a cyber security centre providing round the clock monitoring of cyber threats on their network. Reportedly, security operations personnel raised alerts due to the detection of malicious activity on 30 November 2013 and again on 2 December. However, it wasn't until 12 December 2013 when US Department of Justice personnel contacted Target to report a possible data breach that reportedly an investigation began in earnest (Plachkinova and Maurer 2018).

The significance of the malicious activity would appear to have been missed by decision makers. It is very tempting to frame this supposition in the context of situational awareness and to consider that this might have been an intelligence failure due to a lack of context. Possibly the alerts were depriorisited, because the significance of these alerts and the importance of the environment in which they were occurring were not recognised.

A further possibility is that the relevant alerts relating to the attack may have been overlooked due to information overload; there were simply too many alerts for each one to be considered adequately. Situational awareness may have been lost due to too much information overwhelming security teams.

This breach is examined in more detail in Chapter 9.

3.4 Goal Oriented Security and Threat Modelling

For complex environments it is unrealistic to envisage providing detailed operational intelligence regarding every threat that is likely to impact the organisation. Even to try to do so is likely to prove to be counterproductive, because the amount of information would be expected to overload operational teams who would need to make use of the intelligence.

In order to provide effective threat intelligence, we must focus on identifying that which is important so that a detailed understanding of a situation can be developed where and when it is needed. A very good start in identifying what is important is to ask the question: 'what is the worst thing that could happen?'

Goal oriented requirements engineering is a technique used to understand what users are trying to do, so that requirements that describe their activity can be collected (Horkoff et al. 2019). The same approach can be applied to cyber security by considering what it is that we don't want to happen. This can help identify scenarios that would cause large amounts of harm to an organisation. There are certainly situations that can be considered as 'important'.

From a different point of view, we can consider goals of threat actors, and think what it is that they might wish to achieve. There are enough case studies or organisations that have been attacked, and enough known about specific threat actors, to put together several scenarios regarding what a malicious threat actor might seek to achieve.

Armed with these scenarios, we can imagine the steps that might lead to the occurrence of such a scenario, defining these steps by applying the Kill Chain, the ATT&CK framework, and threat graphs.

Threat graphs are a way of describing visually the various different options that an attacker has available to them in order to fulfil an objective.

For example, maintaining the confidentiality of the customer database is a security goal that an organisation must achieve, we can envisage a scenario where an attacker wishes to compromise the database, and exfiltrate the customer data.

Working backwards, the attacker must succeed in applying the ATT&CK tactic:

Exfiltration – TA0010

Almost certainly through applying one of the following techniques:

Exfiltration Over C2 Channel – TA1041
Exfiltration Over Alternative Protocol – TA1048
Exfiltration Over Web Service – TA1567
Exfiltration Over Physical Medium – TA1052

To achieve TA1041 or TA1048, the attacker would need to gain access to the database server through applying one or more of the tactics:

Credential Access – TA0006
Lateral Movement – TA0008 followed by Execution TA0002 (Figure 3.2)

The focus of threat modelling of cyber security tools is typically to understand how the attacker may carry out attacks so that mitigation strategies can be put in place to block the attackers. Cyber threat intelligence teams have a different focus; their role is to understand malicious activity. If the cyber security team is asking the question, 'if this were to happen to us, how would we block it?', the cyber

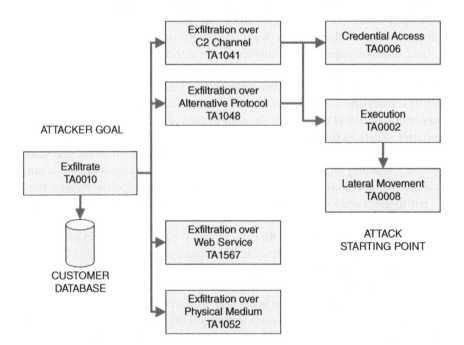

Figure 3.2 Illustration of choice of tactics for an attacker to exfiltrate a database.

threat intelligence team should be asking, 'if this were to happen to us, how would we identify it?'

The techniques of how to identify incursion through telemetry are covered in more detail in Chapter 5. Nevertheless, the cyber threat intelligence analyst should always be looking to consider what traces an attacker may leave in their malicious activity and how these traces might be detected.

For this example, lateral movement may leave traces in network logs, execution of malware or malicious commands will leave traces in system logs, attempts at using credentials will leave traces in access logs. Exfiltration over networks will require connecting to remote systems that may already be known to be malicious or at least suspicious, the exfiltration of large amounts of data will leave traces in network logs, etc.

Strategic threat intelligence can give an overview of current threats, what threat actors are trying to achieve, and how they are going about reaching these goals. For operational teams, this intelligence can be transformed into IoCs that might be apparent within logs or in alerts. Enriching these with the assistance of intelligence helps provide context, allowing teams to understand better what is happening, and to prioritise alerts appropriately.

Methods such as Quantitative Threat Modelling (Potteiger et al. 2016) or Process for Attack Simulation and Threat Analysis (PASTA) (UcedaVelez and Morana 2015) describe processes for threat modelling. A complete threat model allows teams to identify the steps by which threats can be blocked, mitigated, and detected.

The CBEST assessment framework for evaluating the cyber protections of financial institutions uses a similar approach by deriving realistic attack scenarios from threat intelligence. These scenarios then form the basis for penetration testers to attempt to penetrate cyber defences (Bank of England 2022).

3.5 Strategic, Operational, and Tactical Intelligence

Broadly speaking, cyber threat intelligence reports take three separate forms destined to support the requirements of three different types of end users. As part of the requirements process, intelligence teams need to assess the most appropriate form (or mix of forms) of intelligence for the request, and what will best help the recipient.

3.5.1 Strategic Intelligence

This intelligence is produced to provide a strategic view regarding a threat and is by nature a high-level overview of a particular threat. Such information is useful for anyone who needs a big-picture understanding of a threat, but it is particularly useful to assist senior decision makers in making informed long term decisions regarding priorities and allocation of resources.

Strategic intelligence should include the information that senior leaders need in order to make strategic decisions including: the nature of the threat, what is at risk from the threat, the consequences if the threat impacts the organisation, and what is the current security posture to the threat (INSA 2014a).

3.5.1.1 Example – Lazarus Group

Strategic intelligence on the Lazarus Group threat actor would be very relevant to senior decision makers in financial services organisations. The Lazarus Group is a sophisticated threat actor believed to be working under the direction of, and on behalf of, the North Korean state. The group is thought to be behind the attempted theft of approximately $1 billion from the national bank of Bangladesh in 2016.

In this attack, the threat actors infiltrated the bank's systems and issued Society for Worldwide Interbank Financial Telecommunication (SWIFT) instructions to transfer funds from one account to various third party accounts. The group succeeded in transferring $81 million to accounts under their control.

Although the threat actors were not fully successful in their goals, the consequences of the attack were severe for those involved. The governor of the Bangladesh Bank resigned following the theft. One of the banks to which stolen funds were transferred was fined for non-compliance with banking regulations leading to additional executive resignations (White 2021; Cordero 2016).

Senior managers in financial organisations should be aware of the threat from this particular threat actor, and of audacious attacks of this nature. Detecting and blocking these kinds of thefts requires actions to be taken at an executive level since the attacks leverage the trust between banks and abuse the protocols that underpin the global financial network.

Senior managers do not necessarily need to know the details of how the target's systems are compromised. However, understanding who was behind the attack, why and how the attack was carried out, is vital to prompt senior decision makers to consider how transfers of large sums of money are verified, validated, and authorised. Other threat actors may take inspiration from the attack and attempt to subvert the SWIFT system through similar attacks.

The Lazarus Group are unlikely to content themselves with this single attempt to steal a large sum of money. Such an attack should prompt senior decision makers to review potential vulnerabilities in their systems that could be exploited to transfer or take control of large sums of money.

Indeed, subsequent thefts have been attributed to the Lazarus Group, and a service that is believed to have been involved in laundering proceeds by the group has been sanctioned by the US government (US DoT 2022).

3.5.2   Operational Intelligence

This is intelligence that supports the day-to-day and week-to-week operating environment. The intelligence provides operational managers with the intelligence necessary to protect their organisations against current and potential threats in the short to medium term.

Operational intelligence should take into consideration the operating environment of the organisation, describing how the nature and capabilities of a threat may impact that operating environment. If strategic intelligence is concerned with the 'who' and 'why' of threats, operational intelligence is concerned with the 'how' and 'when' (INSA 2014b).

3.5.2.1   Example – SamSam

In 2016, a new variant of ransomware, SamSam, was identified that was spread with a different methodology to previous ransomware campaigns. Notably, this ransomware was observed affecting health care organisations. As such, cyber security managers within the health care sector needed to take note of this new threat.

The threat actor using SamSam adopted a different business model to previous ransomware threat actors. Instead of distributing the ransomware without regard to the nature of the victim, the threat actor apparently identified specific organisations in the health care and education industry sectors. Instead of infecting the systems of end users through distributing malware via emails or through compromised websites, the threat actor exploited vulnerable Internet-facing JBoss application servers to gain a foothold within the organisation.

Once the threat actor had gained access, they would conduct network reconnaissance to identify key systems within the organisation before exploiting them and installing then executing ransomware on these systems. The execution of ransomware on systems identified as vital to operations by the threat actor, brought the systems, and consequently the entire organisation to a halt. At this point the threat actor demanded a ransom in the order of tens of thousands of dollars in order to restore the affected systems (Biasini 2016; CISA 2018).

Managers responsible for cyber security within the health care industry needed to be aware of this change in the threat landscape and the adoption of a new business model for ransomware, which directly affected their industry. Detecting and blocking this threat required evaluation of the state of defences, verification of business continuity, and incident response plans in relation to the risk of ransomware hitting key systems. Intelligence regarding the active exploitation of vulnerabilities in JBoss software should have triggered the prompt patching of vulnerable systems.

The intelligence identified a new threat in the shift of threat actor methodology. This threat did not necessarily require immediate action, although intelligence relating to active vulnerability exploitation did warrant urgent patching of vulnerable systems, however defences against this evolving threat should have been promptly reviewed without undue delay.

3.5.3 Tactical Intelligence

This is intelligence relating to the immediate threat landscape that provides operational teams with intelligence regarding current threats. This intelligence provides hands-on teams with intelligence to allow them to detect or block threats that may be affecting the organisation currently or in the immediate future.

Tactical intelligence is not concerned with the long term view, and indeed may not give information regarding who is behind threats. Instead, the intelligence is focused on the 'what' and 'how' of threats. Indeed, tactical intelligence reports may not necessarily be created in order to be read by human operations, but consist of lists of IoCs such as hash values of malware, IP addresses, or domain names that are used to distribute attacks or used as part of the command and control network. These lists of IoCs can be ingested by security systems to rapidly block communications with known malicious systems, or identify the presence of malicious software within the organisation's IT estate.

3.5.3.1 Example – WannaCry

The WannaCry destructive worm of 12 May 2017 caused enormous damage to IT systems across the globe due to its ability to autonomously spread across networks to infect Windows systems that had not installed the most recent operating system update prior to the attack.

Security analysts were quick to identify that the worm was spreading across networks by exploiting a vulnerability in SMB protocol implementation, which was bound to TCP port 139 and port 445. Hashes for the components of the malware were also quickly identified. These IoCs were widely shared allowing security teams to take appropriate action to block the work from spreading (CISA 2017).

However, there were incorrect intelligence reports circulating at the same time. Reports suggested that the worm had been initially spread by malicious emails (Jones 2017). This incorrect intelligence diverted many security teams to hunt for non-existent emails instead of focusing on the remediation and patching of unaffected devices. It is wise to remember that in the immediacy of a difficult and fast developing situation, not every intelligence report will be accurate.

3.5.4 Sources of Intelligence Reports

A thriving community and an entire industry have grown up around the provision of cyber threat intelligence reports. Many major business service providers, cyber security providers, and specialist providers offer strategic, operational, and tactical intelligence reports and feeds as a paid service, as well as bespoke research.

Many reports are freely shared without charge. Security organisations in both the private and public sectors publish blogs, longer whitepapers, and in-depth reports on threat actors, malicious campaigns, or any threat that they believe to be noteworthy. Similarly, independent security researchers share observations and IoCs over social media and in online forums.

Peer contributions are often well received, analysts and researchers frequently share ideas and IoCs and can help develop understanding of the wider picture of a campaign, of which any one victim may have only a small view. This peer support model of cyber threat intelligence has proved so successful that many nations have created information exchanges where vetted representatives of organisations who may in other contexts be competitors can meet and share information regarding threats and vulnerabilities (ENISA 2018).

Intelligence may be derived from press reports. The consequences of individual cyber attacks make the national press typically only in the most severe or egregious occasions, but can be regularly found in local press or industry press reports. Within each tale of an organisation being hit by a cyber attack are nuggets of information that can be combined into intelligence.

The collection of intelligence material from publicly available information is frequently referred to as Open Source Intelligence or OSINT. The nature of electronic publishing on the Internet, and especially the self-publishing platform model of social media means that there is a vast amount of raw information available for analysis and processing (Williams and Blum 2018).

Even the most diligent of organised criminals can leave traces of their activities in open sources of information (Larsen et al. 2017). Researchers can monitor or gain access to environments where criminal acts are prepared to collect information (Décary-Hétu and Aldridge 2015). Or datasets related to criminal activity may be released, such as the publication of the chat server logs relating to the Conti ransomware gang (Corfield 2022).

International news can also impart strategic-level intelligence. As the allegiances and priorities of nation states change, so do the targets of nation state related threat actors. A changing geopolitical situation can provoke cyber attacks, and act as an indicator.

Keeping abreast of international tensions and the policy goals of the state sponsors of threat actors can give advance warning of where nation state related attacks might fall.

3.5.4.1 Example – Shamoon

Amid worsening relations between Saudi Arabia and Iran in 2012, the Saudi Arabian Oil Minister offered to increase Saudi oil production to compensate for the loss of Iranian oil production due to potential international sanctions. This stance was criticised by Iran, leading an Iranian official to pronounce:

> Our Arab neighbor countries should not cooperate with these adventurers... These measures will not be perceived as friendly.
>
> *(Reuters 2012)*

Some months later, a wiper malware named Shamoon hit Saudi Aramco, reportedly destroying 35 000 computer systems within the organisation. The attack risked seriously disrupting oil supply, and led to the disruption to the supply of hard disk drives globally, as the targeted organisation sought to recover from the attack by buying large numbers of hard disk drives to replace those destroyed by the attack (Pagliery 2015). Ultimately, the US government and others attributed the attack to Iranian nation state threat actors (Osborne 2018; CISA 2021).

The escalating international tensions in the region could have led to a strategic assessment of a heightened risk of cyber attack by Iran or Iranian inspired threat actors against organisations and countries that were perceived by the Iranian government as acting against their interests.

3.6 Incident Preparedness and Response

Threat intelligence feeds into the risk management process, so that relevant threats may be 'managed'. This can result in the risk due to a threat being transferred or shared, avoided, accepted, or reduced through applying mitigation measures.

These mitigation measures fall into one or more of the following categories known as the four Ds: *Deter, Deny, Detect, Delay* (Peterson 2010). Threat intelligence can help in optimising these measures. Identifying the vulnerabilities most likely to be exploited and prioritising these for patching helps deny threat actors access to systems. Ensuring that the key systems most likely to be attacked by threat actors are subject to appropriate levels of protection and suitably defensive network topology, helps frustrate attacks and delay their success.

Denying and delaying attacks gives defenders more chances to detect attacks in progress since the attackers need to be more active to achieve their objectives, which leaves more traces by which attacks can be identified. Data that is enriched with threat intelligence also helps defenders develop situational awareness and quickly identify malicious behaviour.

An environment that denies and delays attacks, leading to early detection of the attack will tend to deter attackers. Profit motivated criminal threat actors seek to maximise the return on their investment. It is more profitable for them to attack soft targets rather than those that are well protected. State-sponsored threat actors prefer to conduct their work without the spotlight falling on them and their activities being disclosed. Even hacktivists seeking high profile disruption or data can be expected to get bored or become wary of detection and law enforcement engagement and prioritise other targets if attacking a target is too frustrating.

However, no mitigation strategy, or set of cyber defences is ever perfect. There will always be a residual risk that an attack will bypass a defensive measure or be missed. Hence, security teams must deploy multiple overlapping layers of protective measures to maximise protection against threats so that if one protection fails, another protection has a chance of succeeding.

The Swiss Cheese Model of accident causation is a useful approach for visualising the potential gaps in defences. Each layer of defence is like a slice of Swiss cheese, with the deficiencies in the defence represented by the holes in the cheese. If the holes in the layers of cheese align, then a threat may impact on the organisation and cause harm (Reason et al. 2006) (Figure 3.3).

History is full of examples of hubris and flat-out denial that anything bad could happen. In cyber security we can reduce the risk of an attacker breaching systems, but we can never completely absolve the risk. Therefore, although the risk may be small, we must prepare for defences to fail, and to result in a cyber security incident. Efficient planning is required for how such incidents will be detected and resolved.

The incident response process includes four activities:

Detecting events – the ability to detect events that impact on the organisation, including incursions and security breaches.
Triage and analyse – the ability to analyse the events impacting the organisation, and identify those that qualify as an 'incident' requiring additional resources to resolve.

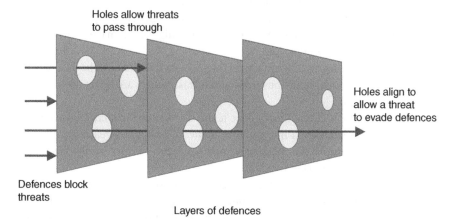

Figure 3.3 The Swiss Cheese Model of threats evading defences. *Source:* Adapted from Reason et al. (2022).

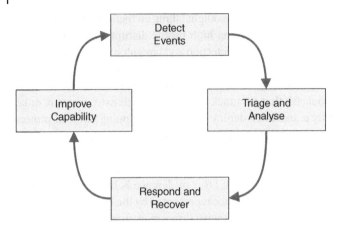

Figure 3.4 The incident response process. *Source:* Adapted from Carnegie Mellon University (2016).

Respond and recover – marshal, direct, and coordinate additional resources required to restore normal functions following an incident.

Improve capability – identify the root cause that led to the incident, remediate the root cause and any deficiencies identified during the response (Figure 3.4).

Each of these activities needs to be planned to detail the different roles and responsibilities that are required. Threat intelligence teams are required for each phase of the process.

Detecting events – Threat intelligence teams identify the tactics, techniques, and procedures (TTP) that threat actors are likely to employ. Through considering the traces that these TTPs might leave if deployed against an organisation, and how these traces might be spotted the threat intelligence team can help identify security events within raw data.

Threat intelligence teams collect tactical intelligence IoCs that can be used to find events where known malicious tools and infrastructure are being used against the organisation.

Triage and analyse – Threat intelligence teams add context to identified events to transform raw event data into notions of the TTPs that a threat actor may be using, the nature of the attacker's goals, and the priority of the resources required to respond to the incident.

Respond and recover – Threat intelligence teams enrich information uncovered during the response phase to compile an intelligence-based understanding of the incident that can be used to brief teams involved in the response. Furthermore, with understanding of the information needs of various stakeholders, intelligence teams can work with external facing teams to assemble briefings that can be used to keep external stakeholders such as the press, customers, partners, and law enforcement, etc., abreast of the incident.

Improve capability – threat intelligence teams can assemble the findings of the incident investigation, along with other sources of intelligence to assemble a full intelligence report of the incident. This can then be used to help identify the root cause of the incident, and opportunities where the threat may have been detected and blocked before harm was incurred. This understanding helps in the detection, triage, and analysis of subsequent events.

3.6.1 Preparation and Practice

Incident response plans should be tested long in advance of any genuine incident so that any deficiencies or false assumptions in the plan can be identified and remedied. Threat intelligence teams can use their understanding of the threat landscape to put together realistic, representative scenarios that can be used to conduct desktop war gaming exercises.

Representative scenarios can be devised that are relevant to the organisation, their systems, and the particular threats they face. Scenarios can be updated as the threat landscape evolves, incorporating elements from attacks that have affected similar organisations.

War gaming exercises help security teams familiarise themselves with the tactics and techniques that sophisticated attackers may deploy against them. Teams can consider how they might detect such an attack, triage it appropriately, and respond free from the stress and distractions of the 'live' environment.

Representative scenarios can also be used to brief penetration testing teams and used to test responses to 'genuine' attacks against the organisation. Managers can then observe how security operations teams are able to put to good use the skills that they have refined during gaming exercises.

Ultimately, attacks by sophisticated attackers are rare events. Security teams that have never considered or practised against such an attack are unlikely to be prepared to effectively counteract the attack. Sophisticated attackers constantly refine their attacks against defenders, whereas any given security team may never encounter such an attack over many years.

Every form of preparation and attack simulation helps train teams. Simple walk-through exercises where the sequence of events that may be expected to be encountered in an attack help in considering and rehearsing attack techniques. Even discussing recent attacks as a team helps focus minds on what might happen, and uncover any potential gaps in protection or response before an attack is encountered.

Only through practice and training can security operations teams hope to develop the capability to defend against sophisticated threat actors as a matter of routine. One of the many roles of threat intelligence is to direct preparations and practice so that the cyber security function is more than equal to the most severe, but mercifully rare, threats.

Summary

Threat intelligence must meet the needs of the consumers of that intelligence, and be able to show support for the overall security goals of the organisation. Typically, this is achieved by providing situational awareness of the threat landscape.

This awareness may be at a strategic level providing intelligence about the long term aims and tactics of threat actors, at an operational level presenting the current state and near future of the threat environment, or at a tactical level supplying indicators of immediate threats.

Intelligence is produced and disseminated according to a number of steps that comprise the Intelligence Cycle. The cycle describes how the process of generating intelligence is separated into distinct steps, each of which may be a separate activity. Ultimately threat intelligence teams must strive to ensure that they are contributing to the wider security effort through continuous improvement.

References

Bank of England (2016). *CBEST Intelligence-Led Testing Understanding Cyber Threat Intelligence Operations Version 2.0.* https://www.bankofengland.co.uk/-/media/boe/files/financial-stability/financial-sector-continuity/understanding-cyber-threat-intelligence-operations.pdf (accessed 13 January 2023).

Bank of England (2022). *CBEST Threat Intelligence-Led Assessments. Implementation Guide.* https://www.bankofengland.co.uk/-/media/boe/files/financial-stability/financial-sector-continuity/cbest-implementation-guide.pdf (accessed 13 January 2023).

Biasini, N. (2016). SamSam: the doctor will see you, after he pays the ransom. *Cisco Talos Threat Intelligence* (23 March). https://blog.talosintelligence.com/2016/03/samsam-ransomware.html (accessed 13 January 2023).

Carnegie Mellon University (2016). CRR implementation guide. Volume 5 incident management. https://us-cert.cisa.gov/sites/default/files/c3vp/crr_resources_guides/CRR_Resource_Guide-IM.pdf (accessed 13 January 2023).

Cordero, T. (2016). Bangko Sentral slaps P1-B fine on RCBC for stolen Bangladesh Bank fund. *GMA News Authority* (5 August). https://www.gmanetwork.com/news/money/companies/576498/bangko-sentral-slaps-p1-b-fine-on-rcbc-for-stolen-bangladesh-bank-fund/story (accessed 13 January 2023).

Corfield, G. (2022). Conti ransomware gang leak: 60,000 messages online. *The Register* (28 February). https://www.theregister.com/2022/02/28/conti_ransomware_gang_chats_leaked (accessed 13 January 2023).

CREST (2019). What is Cyber Threat Intelligence and how is it used? https://www.crest-approved.org/wp-content/uploads/2022/04/CREST-Cyber-Threat-Intelligence.pdf (accessed 13 January 2023).

Décary-Hétu, D. and Aldridge, J. (2015). Sifting through the net: monitoring of online offenders by researchers. *European Review of Organised Crime* 2 (2): 122–141.

Development, Concepts and Doctrine Centre, UK Ministry of Defence (2011). *Joint Doctrine Publication 2–00. Understanding and Intelligence Support to Joint Operations.* 3rd Edition. https://assets.publishing.service.gov.uk/government/uploads/system/uploads/attachment_data/file/311572/20110830_jdp2_00_ed3_with_change1.pdf (accessed 13 January 2023).

Endsley, M.R. (1995). Toward a theory of situation awareness in dynamic systems. *Human Factors* 27 (1): 32–64.

Endsley, M.R., Bolte, B., and Jones, D.G. (2003). *Designing for Situation Awareness. An Approach to User-Centered Design.* Taylor & Francis.

European Union Agency For Network and Information Security (2018). Information sharing and analysis centres (ISACs) cooperative models. https://cryptome.org/2014/11/insa-sci.pdf (accessed 17 October 2022).

Flashpoint (2021). 3 threat intelligence KPIs to win your ROI business case, 22 March. https://www.flashpoint-intel.com/blog/3-threat-intelligence-kpis-for-roi-business-case (accessed 13 January 2023).

Harrald, J. and Jefferson, T. (2007). Shared situational awareness in emergency management mitigation and response. 2007 *40th Annual Hawaii International Conference on System Sciences. HICCS'07*, 23–23. http://dx.doi.org/10.1109/HICSS.2007.481.

Horkoff, J., Audemir, F.B., Cardoso, E. et al. (2019). Goal-oriented requirements engineering: an extended systematic mapping study. *Requirements Engineering* 24: 133–160.

Intelligence and National Security Alliance, Cyber Intelligence Task Force (2014a). Strategic cyber intelligence. https://cryptome.org/2014/11/insa-sci.pdf (accessed 17 October 2022).

Intelligence and National Security Alliance, Cyber Intelligence Task Force (2014b). Operational cyber intelligence. https://cryptome.org/2014/11/insa-oci.pdf (accessed 13 January 2023).

ISO/IEC 27002:2022 (2022). *Information Security, Cybersecurity and Privacy Protection – Information Security Controls.* International Standards Organization. https://www.iso.org/standard/75652.html (accessed 13 January 2023).

Jones, S. (2017). Timeline: how the WannaCry cyber attack spread. *Financial Times* (14 May). https://www.ft.com/content/82b01aca-38b7-11e7-821a-6027b8a20f23 (accessed 13 January 2023).

Karr-Wisniewski, P. and Lu, Y. (2010). When more is too much: operationalizing technology overload and exploring its impact on knowledge worker productivity. *Computers in Human Behavior* 26 (5): 1061–1072.

Lahneman, W. and Naval Postgraduate School, Center from Homeland Defense and Security (2018). The seven step intelligence process. https://www.chds.us/coursefiles/NS4156/lectures/intel_7_step_intel_cycle/script.pdf (accessed 13 January 2023).

Larsen, H.L. et al. (ed.) (2017). *Using Open Data to Detect Organized Crime Threats.* Springer.

Mahn, A. (2018). Identify, protect, detect, respond and recover: the NIST cybersecurity framework. *NIST Taking Measure, Just a Standard Blog* (23 October). https://www.nist.gov/blogs/taking-measure/identify-protect-detect-respond-and-recover-nist-cybersecurity-framework (accessed 13 January 2023).

National Institute of Standards and Technology (2018). *Framework for Improving Critical Infrastructure Cybersecurity Version 1.1.* National Institute of Standards and Technology. https://www.nist.gov/cyberframework/framework (accessed 6 March 2023).

NATO Terminology Office (2017). *Intelligence Cycle.* NATOTerm, The Official NATO Terminology Database. https://nso.nato.int/natoterm/content/nato/pages/home.html?lg=en (accessed 13 January 2023).

Nofi, A.A. (2000). *Defining and Measuring Shared Situational Awareness.* Center for Naval Analyses. https://www.cna.org/cna_files/pdf/D0002895.A1.pdf (accessed 28 March 2023).

Office of the Government Chief Information Officer (2022). *An Overview of ISO/IEC 27000 Family of Information Security Management System Standards.* The Government of the Hong Kong Special Administrative Region of the People's Republic of China. www.ogcio.gov.hk/en/our_work/information_cyber_security/collaboration/doc/overview_of_iso_27000_family.pdf (accessed 13 January 2023).

Osborne, C. (2018). Shamoon data-wiping malware believed to be the work of Iranian hackers. *ZDNet, Zero Day* (20 December). https://www.zdnet.com/article/shamoons-data-wiping-malware-believed-to-be-the-work-of-iranian-hackers (accessed 13 January 2023).

Pagliery, J. (2015). The inside story of the biggest hack in history. *CNN Business* (5 August). https://money.cnn.com/2015/08/05/technology/aramco-hack/index.html (accessed 13 January 2023).

Peterson, K.E. (2010). Security risk management. In: *The Professional Protection Officer*, Chapter 27 (ed. S.J. Davies and L.J. Fennelly), 315–330. Butterworth-Heinemann. https://www.sciencedirect.com/science/article/pii/B9781856177467000274 (accessed 28 March 2023).

Plachkinova, M. and Maurer, C. (2018). Teaching case security breach at Target. *Journal of Information Systems Education* 29 (1): 11–20.

Potteiger, B., Martins, G., and Koutsoukos, X. (2016). Software and attack centric integrated threat modeling for quantitative risk assessment. *HotSos '16: Proceedings of the Symposium and Bootcamp on the Science of Security*, 99–108. http://dx.doi.org/10.1145/2898375.2898390.

Reason, J., Hollinagel, E., and Paries, J. (2006). *Revisiting The « Swiss Cheese » Model of Accidents*. Eurocontrol. https://www.eurocontrol.int/sites/default/files/library/017_Swiss_Cheese_Model.pdf (accessed 28 March 2023).

Reid, G. (2018). Key threat intelligence metrics for your security strategy. *Recorded Future* (24 January). https://www.recordedfuture.com/threat-intelligence-metrics (accessed 13 January 2023).

Reuters (2012). Iran warns gulf countries not to replace its oil. *Haaretz* (15 January). https://www.haaretz.com/1.5165402 (accessed 13 January 2023).

Ruff, J. (2002). *Information Overload: Causes, Symptoms and Solutions*. Learning Innovations Laboratories, Harvard Graduate School of Education. https://workplacepsychology.files.wordpress.com/2011/05/information_overload_causes_symptoms_and_solutions_ruff.pdf (accessed 28 March 2023).

Schlette, D., Böhm, F., Caselli, M., and Pernul, G. (2021). Measuring and visualizing cyber intelligence threat quality. *International Journal of Information Security* 20: 21–38. https://doi.org/10.1007/s.10207-020-00490-y.

The Interagency OPSEC Support Staff (1996). Operations security intelligence threat handbook. https://fas.org/irp/nsa/ioss/threat96/index.html (accessed 13 January 2023).

UcedaVelez, T. and Morana, M.M. (2015). *Risk Centric Threat Modelling: Process for Attack Simulation and Threat Analysis*. Wiley.

US Cybersecurity & Infrastructure Security Agency (2017). *Alert (TA17-132A) Indicators Associated With WannaCry Ransomware*. National Cyber Awareness System. https://us-cert.cisa.gov/ncas/alerts/TA17-132A (accessed 6 March 2023).

US Cybersecurity & Infrastructure Security Agency (2018). *Alert (AA18-337A) SamSam Ransomware*. National Cyber Awareness System. https://us-cert.cisa.gov/ncas/alerts/AA18-337A (accessed 28 March 2023).

US Cybersecurity & Infrastructure Security Agency (2021). *ICS Joint Security Awareness Report (JSAR-12-241-01B)*. National Cybersecurity and Communications Integration Center. https://us-cert.cisa.gov/ics/jsar/JSAR-12-241-01B (accessed 28 March 2023).

US Department of the Treasury (2022). U.S. Treasury issues first-ever sanctions on a virtual currency mixer, targets DPRK cyber threats. https://home.treasury.gov/news/press-releases/jy0768 (accessed 13 January 2023).

US Joint Chiefs of Staff (2013). JP 2–0, Joint intelligence. https://irp.fas.org/doddir/dod/jp2_0.pdf (accessed 13 January 2023).

Verisign iDefense Security Intelligence Services (2012). *Establishing a Formal Cyber Intelligence Capability.* Verisign. https://www.verisign.com/assets/whitepaper-idefense-cyber-intel.pdf (accessed 6 March 2023).

White, G. (2021). The Lazarus heist: how North Korea almost pulled off a billion-dollar hack. *BBC News* (21 June). www.bbc.co.uk/news/stories-57520169 (accessed 13 January 2023).

Williams, H.J. and Blum, I. (2018). *Defining Second Generation Open Source Intelligence (OSINT) for the Defense Enterprise.* RAND Corporation. https://apps.dtic.mil/sti/pdfs/AD1053555.pdf https://apps.dtic.mil/sti/pdfs/AD1053555.pdf (accessed 28 March 2023).

4

Collecting Intelligence

Intelligence can be collected from many sources. Indeed, many sources freely offer intelligence to anyone who desires to consume it. However, too much intelligence is counterproductive, and may simply cloud the picture, while applying incorrect intelligence, or maliciously false intelligence can only lead to making bad decisions.

No threat intelligence data can provide a crystal ball to see into the future and predict with perfect precision the attacks that will occur. Nevertheless, threat intelligence can be incredibly useful in providing forward looking statements based on observation and professional opinion.

Chapter 4 considers the issues that affect the suitability of sources of intelligence for inclusion in a threat intelligence programme.

4.1 Hierarchy of Evidence

Within any cyber incident nobody has a complete understanding of the full picture. The threat actor will hopefully be aware of their actions and the systems that they have compromised. Nevertheless, much information will remain unknown. The threat actor is unlikely to be aware of the entire IT estate of their victim, they will be unaware of the level of awareness of the attack by the victim, and cannot know the precise future actions of the victim.

Similarly, the victim may be aware of parts of an attack they have discovered, but will remain ignorant of the full extent of the threat actor's actions, their exact motivations, future actions, and exactly which systems (if any) that the threat actor has compromised. The victim will know what pieces of the attack that they have uncovered, but will remain unaware of that which they have not spotted.

Cyber Threat Intelligence, First Edition. Martin Lee.
© 2023 John Wiley & Sons, Inc. Published 2023 by John Wiley & Sons, Inc.

As wider campaigns of threat actors affecting many victims are discovered and described, patterns and similarities in these attacks can be identified and attributed to specific groups. Clearly, not every attack conducted by a single threat actor will be identified or correctly attributed. There will be many false negatives where attacks or evidence of attacks have been missed, and many false positives where attacks have been falsely attributed to a group or where innocuous activity has been incorrectly classified as malicious.

Even more insidiously, an attacker may purposefully leave clues that lead investigators to an incorrect conclusion regarding the origin or nature of an attack. These false flags further complicate analysis.

Within this mix of incomplete and possibly incorrect information what evidence can be believed?

Beyond all reasonable doubt is the level of proof that a jury in a criminal trial in a common law country must require in order to secure a conviction (Macmillan Dictionary 2022; Waldman 1959). To reach such a conclusion requires that the facts of the event under scrutiny are researched in detail, presented along with the necessary context by experts, and overseen by an impartial judge.

Although there have been many highly publicised cases where juries have reached a decision that has subsequently been shown to be incorrect, the conclusion of a criminal court is our highest standard of evidence.

Civil courts are held to a lower standard of proof. In these cases, a ruling is made *on the balance of probabilities*. That is to say, that on considering the evidence presented and the related arguments, it is more likely than not that the event took place as the prosecution described (Davies 2009).

These are large oversimplifications of due legal process that are unique to each jurisdiction. Nevertheless, legal rulings have the advantage that they are conducted after an incident has taken place, following investigation, and after analysis of the facts where competing hypotheses relating to the facts can be raised and considered.

The field of medicine has long pondered the issue of how to judge the reliability of evidence. Choosing the wrong treatment for patients, or persisting with a treatment that is less effective than others costs lives. The pharmaceutical industry invests large sums of money in conducting clinical trials to test if potential medications are actually effective, or if early success was nothing more than a statistical flaw, or possibly the result of wishful thinking.

Medical researchers have defined a hierarchy of reliability of evidence upon which clinical decisions should be made based on proven statistical analysis of data derived from well-designed trials (Burns et al. 2011). The exact hierarchy of evidence and the relative merits of evidence collecting methodology are still subject to review (Murad et al. 2016). Broadly speaking the hierarchy from the strongest to the weakest evidence is shown in Table 4.1.

Table 4.1   Hierarchy of evidence in medicine.

Strength of evidence	Type of Study	Description
Strongest evidence	Systematic Reviews and Meta Analyses	Combining many studies to calculate the effect of an intervention or a characteristic of an outcome.
	Randomised Clinical Trials	Testing if an intervention affects an outcome by randomly dividing a similar group into two. One group receives the intervention under test, the other receives a mock intervention (a placebo). The two groups are tested to see if there is a different outcome between the two.
	Cohort Studies	Analysing a specific characteristic within a group and how this affects the development of an outcome over time.
	Case Control Studies	Analysing the differences between similar cases with different outcomes to identify potential factors that led to (or protected against) the outcome under consideration.
Weakest evidence	Case Studies and Reports	Anecdotal reports of observations of single cases, or a collection of unstructured observations made over an extended time.

4.1.1   Example – Smoking Tobacco Risk

At the end of the nineteenth century, lung cancer was an extremely rare disease. Through the first half of the twentieth century physicians reported that the incidence of lung cancer appeared to be increasing. Case control studies identified that tobacco use correlated strongly with the development of lung cancer. This observation was confirmed by cohort studies examining the different rates of lung cancer development between non-smoking and smoking populations (Proctor 2012).

The cyber threat intelligence domain has yet to develop an accepted hierarchy of evidence for cyber threat intelligence reports. The following hierarchy is proposed (Table 4.2).

Table 4.2 A hierarchy of evidence for cyber security.

Strength of evidence	Type of report	Description
Strongest evidence	Legal investigations	Findings and outcomes of legal trials where large amounts of data have been collected, analysed by experts, and impartially examined.
	Analyses of many cases	Observations and analyses derived from the investigation of many incidents.
	Single case studies	Detailed descriptions of single incidents, such as forensic reports.
Weakest evidence	Anecdotal reports and Opinion	Unsubstantiated observations as well as opinion pieces.

By these measures strategic intelligence reports made from the analysis of many incidents are likely to provide stronger evidence than operational intelligence derived from a smaller set of incidents. In turn, this will be stronger evidence than tactical intelligence that can be derived from single studies or uncorroborated reports with little context.

This is not to say that the anecdotal evidence provided rapidly before the facts of a case are fully known is not of use. Similarly, the opinion of experienced practitioners is also highly valued. Value is always gleaned from timely intelligence from credible sources. However, stronger evidence is likely to emerge from identifying the consensus of opinion from many practitioners, or from identifying common features from large numbers of incidents.

4.2 Understanding Intelligence

No source of threat intelligence can fully understand the thought processes of a threat actor, their motivations, and their future actions. Similarly, no threat intelligence data can provide a crystal ball to see into the future and predict with perfect precision the attacks that will occur.

This does not prevent threat intelligence from looking forwards, making predictions about the future, or supplying analyses of the behaviour of threat actors. These predictions can be informative and greatly help in providing guidance, so long as the limitations of prediction are clearly explained and understood.

Threat intelligence is not a licenced profession. Anyone can call themselves a cyber threat intelligence analyst and publish threat intelligence reports for anyone who wishes to read them. Yet clearly, there are differences in the ability to generate intelligence between the intelligence agencies of a nation state, and an independent researcher. This is not to say that one is correct and the other is not, but the differences in reputation and dependability between the two need to be understood.

Navigating the nature of threat intelligence, and the raw data from which intelligence products are produced, requires notions of credibility and uncertainty to be correctly expressed so that consumers of intelligence can use their judgement appropriately.

4.2.1 Expressing Credibility

Not all sources of intelligence are equal. Intelligence may be published by entities with many years of experience and a strong reputation to uphold, or published by unknown entities with little more than a social handle as provenance.

Nevertheless, even the most reputable organisations sometimes get things wrong and publish information or conclusions that are incorrect. Similarly, previously unknown organisations can find themselves in the position to collect reliable intelligence from a source that is unavailable to other organisations.

The issue of expressing the reliability and credibility of intelligence sources taxed the Naval Intelligence Division of the British Admiralty during World War II. Reportedly, the Director of Naval Intelligence himself, Admiral John Henry Godfrey devised the solution (Wells 1972). The 'Admiralty Code' as it came to be called consisted of a two-dimensional scale with the reliability of the source of the intelligence ranked from A to F on one axis, and the credibility of the information ranked from 1 to 6 on the other.

Presumably, the scale was devised so that intelligence derived from Ultra intercepts could be circulated and identified as having come from an extremely reliable source without divulging further information that could lead to the identification of code cracking activities at Bletchley Park. Admiral Godfrey was Ian Fleming's superior during his war service in Naval Intelligence, and served as the inspiration for the fictional 'M' within Ian Fleming's James Bond series of books (Macintyre 2008).

The Admiralty Code is still widely used within militaries, intelligence agencies, and law enforcement today (Hanson 2015). The current NATO implementation of the code is as follows (Table 4.3).

Hence, credible information from a reliable source would be coded as A1, probably true information from a source that is not usually reliable, coded as D2. Organisations can define the intelligence they accept or reject based on the reliability and credibility score, and treat intelligence of dubious veracity or credibility appropriately.

Intelligence analysts should be mindful of the risks of discounting everything that does not fit with their preconceived ideas as doubtful or improbable, and ignoring it. Groupthink where analysts tend to accept one idea without

Table 4.3 The Admiralty Code.

Reliability of the collection capability		Credibility of the information	
A	Completely reliable	1	Completely credible
B	Usually reliable	2	Probably true
C	Fairly reliable	3	Possibly true
D	Not usually reliable	4	Doubtful
E	Unreliable	5	Improbable
F	Reliability cannot be judged	6	Truth cannot be judged

Source: Reproduced from Irwin and Mandel (2020).

considering alternative possibilities is a particular danger for the intelligence community. Many intelligence failures have been identified to have been due to groupthink emerging within the intelligence community with analysts toeing the line rather than critically evaluating evidence (Lassila 2008).

4.2.2 Expressing Confidence

Threat intelligence is not an exact science. We do not have a crystal ball to predict the future. We can never be sure to have uncovered every weakness. Nor can we profess to know everything about an attacker. Indeed, even the data we analyse may be tainted with intentional inaccuracies.

Nevertheless, we can make statements providing clarity on uncertain matters in order to help decision making provided we clearly state the level of certainty with which we make an assertion and the assumptions upon which they are based.

In knowledge management theory, knowledge is built from information combined with context. The foundation upon which knowledge is built is data, which consists of observables or facts (Headquarters, Department of the Army 2012) (Figure 4.1).

Data is processed into information. This is enriched with additional context by individual learning into knowledge. As others within a team share their knowledge, the individuals within the team learn together to develop a shared understanding. This develops through insight into wisdom.

As threat intelligence professionals we wish to cultivate wisdom within the consumers of our intelligence so that they are able to apply their wisdom in making good decisions. This wisdom develops over time through a steady stream of information from threat intelligence teams building knowledge within those who read intelligence reports. Nevertheless, all of this is rooted in the facts and observable features within data.

Within cyber threat intelligence, the data upon which we are basing our information is unlikely to constitute a complete representation of a situation. We can

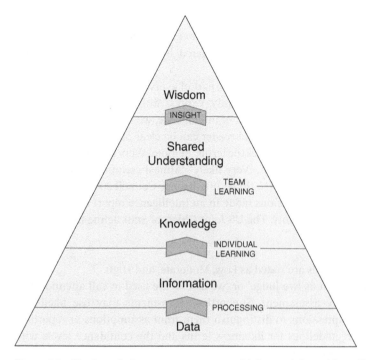

Figure 4.1 The knowledge management pyramid. *Source:* Adapted from Headquarters, Department of the Army (2012).

never expect to have all the necessary data; relevant data will always be missing. Indeed, some vital data may have been purposefully removed or hidden from us, and falsified incorrect data may have been added. Consequently, the information we are deriving from this data will omit important features, or may include features that are factually incorrect. No matter how hard we try, we will never be able to completely remove this taint.

The intelligence community expresses uncertainty using words of estimative probability (Kent 1964). The intelligence analyst must be aware of the gaps and errors in data and information, clearly indicate these to the reader, and apply their experience and professional knowledge to minimise the effect of these errors. The requirement to express uncertainty is explicitly included in the US Code of Laws as part of the subchapter describing, collection, analysis, and sharing of intelligence:

> include whether the product or products concerned were based on all sources of available intelligence, properly describe the quality and reliability of underlying sources, properly caveat and express uncertainties or confidence in analytic judgments. *(US Code)*

Analysts cannot avoid uncertainty by focusing only on the certain or most likely since this tends to omit presenting outcomes that although unlikely, nevertheless remain possibilities that should be considered by consumers of intelligence (Friedman and Zeckhauser 2012).

We're used to expressing uncertainty as part of everyday language. Words such as 'might', 'possibly', 'probably', 'certainly' express different levels of certainty regarding future events. In the context of intelligence, we need a standardised set of words so that both the analyst and reader can be clear on what is meant. The US National Intelligence Center uses the terms 'Remote', 'Very unlikely', 'Unlikely', 'Even chance', 'Probably / Likely', 'Very likely', 'Almost certainly', to denote certainty from least to most likely (National Intelligence Council 2007).

Often, assertions or conclusions made in an intelligence report are made with high, medium, or low certainty. The US Joint Chiefs of Staff define their levels of certainty as:

Confidence levels are stated as Low, Moderate, and High.

Phrases such as 'we judge' or 'we assess' are used to call attention to a product's key assessment. Supporting assessments may use likelihood terms or expressions to distinguish them from assumptions or reporting. Below are guidelines for likeliness terms and the confidence levels with which they correspond.

Low

- Uncorroborated information from good or marginal sources.
- Many assumptions.
- Mostly weak logical inferences, minimal methods application.
- Glaring intelligence gaps exist.

Terms used: Possible, could, may, might, cannot judge, unclear.

Moderate

- Partially corroborated information from good sources.
- Several assumptions.
- Mix of strong and weak inferences and methods.
- Minimum intelligence gaps exist.

Terms used: Likely, unlikely, probable, improbable, anticipate, appear.

High

- Well-corroborated information from proven sources.
- Minimal assumptions.

- Strong logical inferences and methods.
- No or minor intelligence gaps exist.

Terms used: Will, will not, almost certainly, remote, highly likely, highly unlikely, expect, assert, affirm.

Source: Reproduced from US JCS (2013).

There is no single consensus on which terms to use to denote certainty. Different agencies use different terms in different ways. The terms themselves are ambiguous, possessing different interpretations between analysts, and when translated into different languages. To help address this issue, terms of estimative probability are associated with numerical estimations of probability to assist in understanding the meaning of the terms (Ho et al. 2015).

The US Director of National Intelligence approves the terms shown in Table 4.4 for use in intelligence products, along with the indication of probability.

Nevertheless, there is a danger that referring to numerical probabilities implies a greater degree of precision of estimation than exists (Dhami and Mandel 2020). Analysts need to clarify their statements of probability with their level of confidence in the prediction. Confidence may be expressed as 'low', 'medium', or 'high' depending on the scope, quality, and sourcing of their information (National Intelligence Council 2007).

Agreeing on exactly what words to use and their exact meaning might be possible within an army under a single command structure. However, many different organisations use different criteria and different wording to denote their relative levels of certainty. This is especially true of cyber threat intelligence where many different entities from multiple countries seek to share intelligence (Kantor et al. 2017). In a world of uncertainty even the words used to describe that uncertainty are unclear. Ultimately the author of an intelligence report must make clear

Table 4.4 Estimative terms and their intended range of numerical probability.

Almost no chance	Remote	1–5%
Very unlikely	Highly improbable	5–20%
Unlikely	Improbable	20–45%
Roughly even chance	Roughly even odds	45–55%
Likely	Probable	55–80%
Very likely	Highly probable	80–95%
Almost certain	Nearly certain	95–99%

Source: ODNI (2016).

their assumptions and their levels of certainty, so that the consumer of that report can properly understand what the author meant.

Analysts need to be aware of what is not being said within reports. Information and context may be redacted due to national security or client confidentiality reasons. Organisations may be hesitant to publish intelligence reports that relate to the actions of their own or allied governments.

Analysts should be mindful that even the most credible of intelligence reports is unlikely to paint the full picture. Enrichment and verification of intelligence through additional sources is always a good idea, but beware of the dangers of circular reasoning.

4.2.3 Understanding Errors

Even the most credible of organisations can get things wrong. Or putting things more sympathetically, everyone is prone to interpreting information through their own lens, which tends to distort according to our own experience and expectations.

An error to be aware of within intelligence reports is that of circular reporting. One source reports something incorrect or as conjecture, a second source repeats the assertion as fact, which is then repeated by a third source, and so forth. Eventually, the original incorrect information is accepted as fact, simply because it has been cited so frequently (Joint Military Intelligence College 2001).

4.2.3.1 Example – the WannaCry Email

During the spread of the WannaCry worm in 2017 many reputable organisations incorrectly claimed that the worm was spread by email (Wong and Solon 2017). Indeed, on 12 May 2017 there were two novel ransomware variants in circulation. One, named WannaCry, was a worm that spread autonomously across the Internet before an independent researcher identified and took control of the 'kill switch' domain halting its spread (Greenberg 2020). The other, named Jaff did not spread autonomously, but was distributed over email (Tierney 2017).

Understandably, the two completely separate ransomware campaigns became conflated. It was very easy to imagine that the novel ransomware observed in email inboxes was responsible for the multiple reports of ransomware infection. However, this was not the case.

4.2.3.2 Example – the Olympic Destroyer False Flags

False flags are a perpetual hazard of intelligence collection. A threat actor may purposefully seed misinformation designed to mislead or frustrate analysis. False information taken at face value can be included in intelligence reports and ultimately stated as fact.

For example, the Olympic Destroyer malware contained indicators within the code that could be linked to four separate threat actors associated with three different countries. It is highly unlikely that the attack was a collaboration between the three countries, far more likely is that the threat actor included the indicators as a false flag operation in order to frustrate attribution (Mercer and Rascagneres 2018). Ultimately, six Russian military intelligence officers were indicted in connection with the attack (US Department of Justice, Office of Public Affairs 2020).

4.3 Third Party Intelligence Reports

Many organisations make available intelligence reports either for free, as part of a membership group, or as part of a paid for service. These organisations range from national intelligence agencies, national cyber security agencies, commercial cyber security companies, industry peers, to individual researchers.

These reports are written to be used. Understandably, authors or publishing organisations may wish to limit the distribution of reports in order to maintain confidentiality, and not disclose unnecessary information to a potential threat actor. In order to promote collaboration and the flow of intelligence, the Traffic Light Protocol (TLP) was created to provide simple to understand instructions regarding how the information may be shared (CISA 2022) (Table 4.5).

Documents distributed under the TLP are classed under one of four colours, however, the TLP is not without criticisms. There is no single standardised set of definitions for what the TLP indicators mean, nor is there any enforcement or legal basis for restricting sharing. Once information has been released the publisher is relying on the meaning of their restrictions to be understood and respected

Table 4.5 The traffic light protocol.

Colour	Meaning
White	No restrictions on distribution or usage, other than copyright laws.
Green	Recipients may use the information and distribute the document within the community in which it is shared. The information and document are not to be shared publicly.
Amber	Only to be used and distributed within the organisation to which the document has been distributed. Sharing may be allowed with clients and suppliers who may have a need to know the contents of the report.
Red	Information not to be shared or used outside of the meeting or conversation where the information is disclosed.

by the recipient. If in doubt, the recipient of the information should check with the issuer for use, but ultimately this depends on an honour system (ENISA 2021a).

Nevertheless, the TLP protocol has been widely adopted by the cyber threat intelligence community. There is a broad understanding of what each colour represents, and the markings help facilitate the sharing of intelligence that otherwise would not be distributed.

Sharing sensitive intelligence is often performed as part of a mutually beneficial relationship based on trust. As information is shared and boundaries are respected, participants often feel more inclined to share further intelligence with increasing benefits for all (Luiijf and Kernkamp 2015).

National governments are a useful source of intelligence, but sharing information between the public and private sectors, although beneficial, can be hindered by regulations and doubts over how the information will be used or protected (GAO 2010).

The sharing of state and military information is regulated and subject to additional restrictions. Classified information may not be shared with anyone without due authorisation (Luiijf and Kernkamp 2015). Understandably, intelligence agencies and law enforcement may wish to keep their methods and sources secret and not accidentally disclose their capabilities through releasing intelligence. Similarly, private industry may also not be in a position to share intelligence due to commercial confidentiality concerns, or regulations that prevent private information being shared without permission.

Within the US, various attempts have been made to facilitate public–private information sharing. The presidential executive order of 2013 mandated that the Director of National Intelligence and Secretary of Homeland Security should take steps to share intelligence with private sector providers of critical national infrastructure. In return, the Chief Privacy Officer and the Officer for Civil Rights and Civil Liberties of the Department of Homeland Security were mandated to seek methods to remove barriers for the private sector to share intelligence with public agencies (The White House 2013).

The resulting Cybersecurity Information Sharing Act provides the frameworks by which public and private sector entities could freely exchange cyber threat intelligence and defensive measures in a timely manner (ODNI 2016). Agencies are more open to sharing intelligence with the private sector, but meeting the needs and requirements of the various stakeholders involved has yet to be resolved (Miller 2020).

4.3.1 Tactical and Operational Reports

The information contained within these intelligence reports helps direct security teams against current threats. One form of information often included in these reports are Indicators of Compromise (IoCs). These indicators of IP addresses, domains, or the hash values of malware or malicious documents can be fed into threat management systems in order to block the communication with domains and IP addresses, the ingress of malicious files, and discover if the organisation is already affected by the threat.

Threats may be multifaceted with intelligence reports only showing one side of the threat. For instance, the change of a single byte within a malware file will result in a completely different hash value for the malware compared with the original, but the functionality may be identical. Similarly, an attacker may rotate through many domain names or use different IP addresses to conduct attacks against different targets. Hence, two different organisations may be faced with the same threat, but encounter completely different sets of IoCs.

IoCs indicating a current attack that have been shared by credible sources of intelligence should be taken seriously. Nevertheless, organisations need to remain aware of the limitations of intelligence. Tactical reports give visibility of threats impacting somewhere, but the same threat might not exhibit the same IoCs elsewhere.

Operational intelligence reports give additional context regarding threats. This added context allows intelligence teams to consider how the threat may impact the systems they protect, and how this might be discovered, even if the IoCs of the threat were different from those reported.

Intelligence describing software vulnerabilities may be less straightforward than first appears. Patching software installed throughout an organisation and ensuring that every copy of the software is updated is never easy. However, the software in question may have been integrated into third party products, which themselves require updating. This requires a patch from the third party vendor that may take significant time to be released.

Threat intelligence teams have an important role to play in identifying which patches should be prioritised for patching, and how these priorities may change. The release of proof of concept exploit code, or the widespread exploitation of a software vulnerability increases the urgency for software updates to be installed. Threat intelligence teams can also advise on which other software packages may be affected by a vulnerability.

4.3.1.1 Example – Heartbleed

Heartbleed (CVE-2014-0160) was a software vulnerability in the OpenSSL cryptographic library. Sending a malicious network packet to an affected network service caused the response to leak the contents of the memory used by OpenSSL. Potentially, this memory leak would include usernames and passwords as well as cryptographic keys or certificates that had been presented to, or used by the affected system (NIST 2014; Synopsis Inc. n.d.).

Security teams needed to upgrade not only every instance of the vulnerable OpenSSL implementation but every software package and network device that had been compiled using the vulnerable libraries.

The website devoted to the vulnerability noted:

> OpenSSL is the most popular open-source cryptographic library and TLS (transport layer security) implementation used to encrypt traffic on the Internet. Your popular social site, your company's site, commerce site, hobby site, site you install software from or even sites run by your government might be using vulnerable OpenSSL. Many online services use TLS to both to identify themselves to you and to protect your privacy and transactions. You might have networked appliances with logins secured by this buggy implementation of the TLS. Furthermore, you might have client-side software on your computer that could expose the data from your computer if you connect to compromised services (Synopsis Inc. n.d.).

Hence, even if you patched all your vulnerable copies of the software, you were still at risk from the vulnerability because you may unwittingly connect to vulnerable systems outside of your control that could be exploited to leak your credentials.

4.3.2 Strategic Threat Reports

National cyber security agencies and industry regulators are excellent sources of information regarding long term threats or specific threat actors. Analysis of many incidents may be necessary to identify long term trends within attacks. This data may only be available to bodies with responsibility for cyber security within countries or industry sectors.

Cyber security industry vendors write reports on threat actors or specific threats and frequently make these available for download. Similarly, international bodies such as Europol produce regular strategic reports on the nature of organised crime on the Internet (Europol 2021). ENISA publishes an annual report on the threat landscape, which describes how threats are changing from year to year, and the major threats affecting businesses (ENISA 2021b).

4.4 Internal Incident Reports

Resolved cyber security incidents are an opportunity to identify what went well during the response, to understand the goals of the threat actor and how they went about achieving these. The result of this reflection should be the identification of steps that can be taken to improve the security posture of the organisation so that such an incident will not reoccur. Or if it does reoccur, that the incident is dealt with faster and with less impact.

From an intelligence point of view, we wish to understand the *what, where, why, how, who,* and *when* of the incident. Incident reports typically focus on how the threat actor conducted their attack and what systems were affected at what point.

Through establishing a timeline we can examine how the attack unfolded and translate the steps taken as part of the attack into the procedures applied by the threat actor and document the techniques and tactics applied.

With a timeline in place, no matter how fragmentary and incomplete, we can begin to see the steps that the attacker took to conduct the attack. Applying kill chain analysis can help us understand how the threat actor was able to evade detection, achieve their goals, and why they were not thwarted in their attack.

We can represent the entire attack using the kill chain model and examine at each step of the kill chain how the attacker was able to progress the attack. Gaps within this analysis hint at evidence that has yet to be uncovered or a misunderstanding of the attack. Each action undertaken by the threat actor can also be considered as a mini-kill chain and used to build the picture of the tactics and techniques used by the threat actor.

With a better understanding of the tactics and techniques of the threat actor, we can use these to identify the procedures applied within the attack. At this point, we can begin to build a profile of the threat actor, comparing what is known about the actor from the attack with profiles of known threat actors and make estimations regarding the identity of the attacker.

The more that we learn about the attacker, how they went about their attack, and what they were attempting to achieve, the more that we can hunt for evidence to fill the gaps in the timeline. Even if we're unable to completely understand and fill all the gaps of the attack, we can hypothesise regarding how the attacker may have conceived and conducted it.

Through profiling the attacker and identifying how they went about the attack, we can examine how the attacker was able to evade detection, how existing defences failed, and make suggestions regarding what changes need to be made to defences to prevent similar attacks in the future.

4.5 Root Cause Analysis

The reasons defences fail and are able to be breached by attackers are rarely simple. Root cause analysis is a collection of techniques that can be used to uncover the active factors that cause a protection to fail and any latent factors that also may have contributed to the incident.

Table 4.6 Questions and reflections as part of root cause analysis.

Why?	Reflection
1) Why did the attacker successfully compromise the system?	The attacker was able to execute malicious code on a remote system to establish a network connection with the compromised system.
2) Why did the exploit code work?	An unpatched vulnerability existed on the system.
3) Why did the vulnerability exist on the system?	A vendor patch for the software had not been applied.
4) Why had the patch not been applied?	The system was deemed critical to business operations and unable to be taken out of production in order to patch.
5) Why was the system deemed too critical to patch?	The lack of failover system to allow systems to be taken offline for maintenance prevented the patch from being applied.

Continuing business operations without interruption is deemed a far higher priority than patching. |

First, the incident under analysis must be defined and described. In a complex investigation, this is likely to be a single step undertaken by the attacker, or a single protection that failed to operate as expected. The timeline of actions leading to the failure should be established and the factors leading to these actions (or omissions of actions) identified.

A common technique in finding the factors that led to a failure is to ask why something happened? And then ask why that happened until the 'why' question has been posed five times. This technique of five 'why's' is commonly used within engineering to uncover faults and improve efficiencies.

For example, if an attacker gained access to a system, the root cause analysis may comprise the steps outlined in Table 4.6.

Intelligence teams can help identify the reasons why attacks were successful and raise these with leadership so that weaknesses are addressed, and the security posture of the organisation improved.

4.6 Active Intelligence Gathering

Intelligence teams should not be content to simply collect intelligence from third parties, or from events in the past, but seek to actively collect information and data to support their intelligence goals.

Threat actors may give indications that an attack is imminent. Hacktivist threat actors may openly share the organisations that they wish their members and fellow travellers to attack. Potentially hostile nation states may start using increasingly bellicose language that is reported in the press, signalling that associated threat actors may begin hostile operations. Criminal threat actors may discuss which organisations they intend to target within criminal forums in order to gather resources for an attack.

All of these can be uncovered by threat intelligence teams through their own efforts or in collaboration with specialist intelligence suppliers to give advance warning of an impending attack. Knowing that an attack is imminent, and armed with some information regarding the possible identity of the attacker, intelligence teams can predict the TTPs that may be used as part of an attack and alert operational teams to potential indicators to watch for, or advise what defences need to be strengthened.

Within organisations, threat intelligence teams can deploy honeypots that appear to be an enticing target for a threat actor, but which have no legitimate function. The goal is to deploy a system that looks like a fully functional system, but which serves no other purpose than to be the target of attacks.

Ideally, there should be no engagement with the honeypot without malicious intent. Once a connection with the system is established and the actor engages with the system, the intelligence team can gather information regarding the infrastructure used by the attacker to conduct their attack as well as their TTPs. This information can be used to strengthen defences, to conduct threat hunting activities to see if the threat actor has penetrated the organisation, and to alert security operations teams to indicators to look for.

Honeypots can range from a username for a fictitious user where the username and password pair has been publicly disclosed or leaked, to entire systems masquerading as an unpatched server. Indeed, a honeypot could comprise networks of systems masquerading as a fully functioning factory or industrial plant. In all cases, the idea is to trick the attacker into conducting an attack against a system where they cannot do harm, but can be observed and strategies to defeat them devised.

Unlike honeypots, canary systems are not designed to attract malicious activity but to disclose the presence of malicious activity within active systems. Canaries may be systems, users, or even files. The goal is to alert security teams to the presence of an attacker, rather than to engage with the attacker and to learn more information about them.

Watermarked files are placed on file servers acting as canaries to identify unauthorised access, copying, or transfer of the file. If the file is transferred across the network or is found in an unexpected location, such as on the file system of an unauthorised device, an alert is raised with security teams to signal the potential data loss of data exfiltration.

In practice the distinction between honeypots and canaries is blurred. Honeypots are designed to interact with attackers in order to glean information and to distract the attacker from genuine systems. Canaries exist simply to alert security teams to suspicious behaviour.

Canary files are particularly useful for the identification of malicious insiders who are accessing or exfiltrating data to which they are not authorised to access. Evidently, being in unauthorised possession of a canary file is not proof of guilt. There may be perfectly legitimate reasons why a non-malicious user gains access to a canary file. For example, they may have failed to execute a task correctly and accidentally copied canary data. In which case, canary files can be helpful in identifying tasks where incorrect execution may lead to a data breach, by allowing users access to files and data that they do not need.

Considering what attackers might seek to achieve, how they might go about conducting their attack, and how this might be detected allows intelligence teams to devise traps for the attacker by which their presence and identity might be disclosed.

4.6.1   Example – the Nightingale Floor

Castles in mediaeval Japan were built with wooden floorboards that purposefully squeaked when walked upon. The emitted sounds resembled the song of the bush warbler bird, often translated into English as 'nightingale'. The sound betrayed the presence of anyone creeping around the castle at night, no matter how stealthy they tried to be. To distinguish friend from foe, allies were taught to walk with a specific rhythm that could be detected by the 'singing' of the floor as they walked (Baseel 2015).

4.6.2   Example – the Macron Leaks

During the French presidential elections of 2017, the campaign staff of candidate Emmanuel Macron were subject to attack by allegedly Russian state-sponsored threat actors. The attacker succeeded in stealing 15 GB of data including more than 21 000 emails from Macron's political party, *En Marche* (Vilmer 2019).

However, the campaign staff had prepared for such an eventuality and had seeded information within their data that led the attacker to honeypots to frustrate them. As this data was acquired and used by the attackers, it acted to divert the attackers' resources to useless systems and slow down the conduct of the attack.

Additionally, decoy information that was not only false, but ridiculously so, had been hidden within genuine information. When these documents and emails were released by the attackers as part of the attack, the campaign staff could use the presence of this ludicrous information to discredit the cache of stolen data (Gallagher 2017; Vilmer 2019).

This breach is examined in more detail in Chapter 9.

Summary

Intelligence can be gathered from many different sources. However, intelligence is different from evidence, it may contain errors or be derived from sources of varying quality. Intelligence analysts must be clear about the credibility of their sources, the confidence by which they make conclusions, and their permission to use information shared by others.

References

Baseel, C. (2015). Nightingale floors: the samurai intruder alarm system Japan's had for centuries. *SoraNews24* (17 April). https://soranews24.com/2015/04/17/nightingale-floors-the-samurai-intruder-alarm-system-japans-had-for-centuries (accessed 13 January 2023).

Burns, P.B., Rohrich, R.J., and Chung, K.C. (2011). The levels of evidence and their role in evidence-based medicine. *Plastic and Reconstructive Surgery* 128 (1): 305–310. https://doi.org/10.1097/PRS.0b013e318219c171.

Davies, S.H.H.J. (2009). *Proof on the Balance of Probabilities: What this Means in Practice*. Thomson Reuters Practical Law. https://uk.practicallaw.thomsonreuters.com/2-500-6576.

Dhami, M.K. and Mandel, D.R. (2020). UK and US policies for communication probability in intelligence analysis: a review. In: *Assessment and Communication of Uncertainty in Intelligence to Support Decision-Making*, Chapter 17, 17-1–17-9. North Atlantic Treaty Organization, Science and Technology Organization.

ENISA European Union Agency for Cybersecurity (2021a). *Considerations on the Traffic Light Protocol*. ENISA European Union Agency for Cybersecurity. https://www.enisa.europa.eu/topics/csirts-in-europe/glossary/considerations-on-the-traffic-light-protocol (accessed 13 January 2023).

ENISA European Union Agency for Cybersecurity (2021b). *ENISA Threat Landscape 2021*. European Union Agency for Cybersecurity (ENISA). https://www.enisa.europa.eu/publications/enisa-threat-landscape-2021 (accessed 13 January 2023).

Europol (2021). *Internet Organised Crime Threat Assessment (IOCTA) 2021*. Publications Office of the European Union. https://www.europol.europa.eu/cms/sites/default/files/documents/internet_organised_crime_threat_assessment_iocta_2021.pdf (accessed 13 January 2023).

Friedman, J.A. and Zeckhauser, R. (2012). Assessing uncertainty in intelligence. *Intelligence and National Security* 27 (6): 824–847.

Gallagher, S. (2017). Macron campaign team used honeypot accounts to fake out Fancy Bear. https://arstechnica.com/information-technology/2017/05/macron-campaign-team-used-honeypot-accounts-to-fake-out-fancy-bear (accessed 13 January 2023).

GAO (2010). *Critical Infrastructure Protection: Key Private and Public Cyber Expectations Need to Be Consistently Addressed*. US Government Accountability Office. https://www.gao.gov/products/gao-10-628 (accessed 6 March 2023).

Greenberg, A. (2020). The confessions of Marcus Hutchins, the hacker who saved the Internet. *Wired* (5 December). https://www.wired.com/story/confessions-marcus-hutchins-hacker-who-saved-the-internet (accessed 13 January 2023).

Hanson, J.M. (2015). The Admiralty Code: a cognitive tool for self-directed learning. *International Journal of Learning, Teaching and Educational Research* 14 (1): 97–115.

Headquarters, Department of the Army (2012). Knowledge management operations (FM 6-01.1). https://fas.org/irp/doddir/army/fm6-01-1.pdf (accessed 13 January 2023).

Ho, E.H., Budescu, D.V., Dhami, M.K., and Mandel, D.R. (2015). Improving the communication of uncertainty in climate science and intelligence analysis. *Behavioral Science & Policy* 1 (2): 43–65.

Irwin, D. and Mandel, D.R. (2020). Standard for evaluating source reliability and information credibility in intelligence production. In: *Assessment and Communication of Uncertainty in Intelligence to Support Decision-Making*, Chapter 7, 7-1–7.13. North Atlantic Treaty Organization, Science and Technology Organization.

Joint Military Intelligence College (2001). Intelligence warning terminology. https://www.hsdl.org/?view&did=7443 (accessed 13 January 2023).

Kantor, P.B., Egan, D.E., Bullinger, J. et al. (2017). Confidence assertions in cyber-security for an information-sharing environment. CCICADA-TR/2017-001. Command, Control and Interoperability Center for Advanced Data Analysis.

Kent, S. (1964). Words of estimative probability. *Studies in Intelligence* 8 (4): 49–65.

Lassila, K. (2008). A brief history of groupthink. *Yale Alumni Magazine*, January. https://yalealumnimagazine.com/articles/1947-a-brief-history-of-groupthink (accessed 13 January 2023).

Luiijf, H.A.M. and Kernkamp, A.C. (2015). Sharing cyber security information: good practice stemming from the Dutch public–private-participation approach. *Global Conference on Cyber Space (GCCS)*. http://dx.doi.org/10.13140/RG.2.1.4321.7442.

Macintyre, B. (2008). *For Your Eyes Only: Ian Fleming & James Bond*. Bloomsbury.

Macmillan Dictionary (2022). Beyond (a/all) reasonable doubt. https://www.macmillandictionary.com/dictionary/british/beyond-a-all-reasonable-doubt (accessed 13 January 2023).

Mercer, W. and Rascagneres, P. (2018). Who wasn't responsible for Olympic Destroyer. *Proceedings of VB 2018*, Montreal. https://www.virusbulletin.com/uploads/pdf/magazine/2018/VB2018-Rascagneres-Mercer.pdf (accessed 13 January 2023).

Miller, J. (2020). CISA's still overcoming challenges 5 years after Cybersecurity Information Sharing Act became law. *Federal News Network* (6 October).

https://federalnewsnetwork.com/reporters-notebook-jason-miller/2020/10/cisas-still-overcoming-challenges-5-years-after-cybersecurity-information-sharing-act-became-law (accessed 13 January 2023).

Murad, M.H., Asi, N., and Alsawas, M. (2016). New evidence pyramid. *BMJ Evidence-Based Medicine* 21 (4): 125–127. https://doi.org/10.1136/ebmed-2016-110401.

National Institute of Standards and Technology (2014). *CVE-2014-0160 Detail.* National Vulnerability Database. https://nvd.nist.gov/vuln/detail/cve-2014-0160 (accessed 13 January 2023).

National Intelligence Council (2007). *National Intelligence Estimate – Iran: Nuclear Intentions and Capabilities.* https://www.dni.gov/files/documents/Newsroom/Reports%20and%20Pubs/20071203_release.pdf (accessed 13 January 2023).

ODNI (2015). *Intelligence Community Directive 203.* Office of the Director of National Intelligence. https://irp.fas.org/dni/icd/icd-203.pdf (accessed 13 January 2023).

ODNI (2016). *Sharing of Cyber Threat Indicators and Defensive Measures by the Federal Government under the Cybersecurity Information Sharing Act of 2015.* The Office of the Director of National Intelligence, The Department of Homeland Security, The Department of Defense and The Department of Justice. https://www.cisa.gov/sites/default/files/publications/Federal%20Government%20Sharing%20Guidance%20under%20the%20Cybersecurity%20Information%20Sharing%20Act%20of%202015_1.pdf (accessed 13 January 2023).

Proctor, R.N. (2012). The history of the discovery of the cigarette–lung cancer link: evidentiary traditions, corporate denial, global toll. *Tobacco Control* 21 (2): 87–91. https://doi.org/10.1136/tobaccocontrol-2011.050338.

Synopsis Inc. (n.d.). *The Heartbleed Bug.* https://heartbleed.com (accessed 13 January 2023).

The White House (2013). *Executive Order – Improving Critical Infrastructure Cybersecurity.* The White House, Office of the Press Secretary. https://obamawhitehouse.archives.gov/the-press-office/2013/02/12/executive-order-improving-critical-infrastructure-cybersecurity (accessed 13 January 2023).

Tierney, S. (2017). WannaCry and Jaff: Two different ransomware attacks with a common goal. *Infoblox* (17 May). https://blogs.infoblox.com/company/wannacry-and-jaff-two-different-ransomware-attacks-with-a-common (accessed 13 January 2023).

United States Code (2019). United States Code, 2018 Edition, Supplement 1, Title 50 – WAR AND NATIONAL DEFENSE CHAPTER 45 – MISCELLANEOUS INTELLIGENCE COMMUNITY AUTHORITIES SUBCHAPTER IV – COLLECTION, ANALYSIS, AND SHARING OF INTELLIGENCE §3364. Assignment of responsibilities relating to analytic integrity. (b.2.A). US Government Publishing Office.

US Cybersecurity & Infrastructure Security Agency (2022). *Traffic Light Protocol (TLP) Definitions and Usage Cybersecurity & Infrastructure Security Agency.* https://www.cisa.gov/tlp (accessed 13 January 2023).

US Department of Justice, Office of Public Affairs (2020). Six Russian GRU officers charged in connection with worldwide deployment of destructive malware and other disruptive actions in cyberspace. https://www.justice.gov/opa/pr/six-russian-gru-officers-charged-connection-worldwide-deployment-destructive-malware-and (accessed 13 January 2023).

US Joint Chiefs of Staff (2013). JP 2–0, Joint Intelligence. https://irp.fas.org/doddir/dod/jp2_0.pdf (accessed 13 January 2023).

Vilmer, J.B.J. (2019). *The 'Macron Leaks' Operation: A Post-Mortem*. Atlantic Council & Institute for Strategic Research. https://www.atlanticcouncil.org/wp-content/uploads/2019/06/The_Macron_Leaks_Operation-A_Post-Mortem.pdf (accessed 13 January 2023).

Waldman, T. (1959). Origins of the legal doctrine of reasonable doubt. *Journal of the History of Ideas* 20 (3): 299–316. https://doi.org/10.2307/2708111.

Wells, A.R. (1972). *Studies in British Naval Intelligence, 1880–1945*. Kings College, University of London. https://kclpure.kcl.ac.uk/portal/files/2926735/294575.pdf (accessed 13 January 2023).

Wong, J.C. and Solon, O. (2017). Massive ransomware cyber-attack hits nearly 100 countries around the world. *The Guardian* (12 May). https://www.theguardian.com/technology/2017/may/12/global-cyber-attack-ransomware-nsa-uk-nhs (accessed 13 January 2023).

5

Generating Intelligence

Intelligence teams are well placed to understand their consumers' needs. Armed with this awareness, teams can synthesise intelligence and information into tailored reports that satisfy their customers, and contribute to improving the security posture. Similarly, teams that understand the operating environment of their organisation, and have access to data that is unavailable to others, are in an ideal situation to transform that data into intelligence reports.

Such intelligence is not only useful within our own organisations to guide decision makers, but also useful to external entities. Sharing intelligence is not just an altruistic act destined to strengthen and protect the 'herd' against attack. External entities can provide valuable feedback or enrich reports with additional context and details not available to the original authors. At the very least, creating a culture of share and share alike provides long term benefits for everyone.

Nevertheless, not all intelligence is equal. Teams need to be aware of the nature of their audience, their needs and expectations. Equally, produced intelligence needs to be clear. Strategic intelligence reports are written for senior decision makers to help make long term decisions. Operational intelligence reports are written for operational decision makers, providing information regarding the current environment for the near to medium future. Tactical reports describe the current situation and are often written to be ingested and read by machine.

Put simply, know your audience and provide them with what they need and expect. Don't play punk music to an audience expecting an opera, and don't provide opera to an audience expecting punk. Focus on providing the right information in the right format to the right audience.

Whatever the format of intelligence you intend to provide, ensure that you are making a meaningful contribution and that you have something to say that will provide clarity. The cyber threat landscape is complex, the world does not necessarily need another voice that will provide little more than noise in an already

Cyber Threat Intelligence, First Edition. Martin Lee.
© 2023 John Wiley & Sons, Inc. Published 2023 by John Wiley & Sons, Inc.

noisy situation. A clear voice that cuts through the hubbub, or that provides new observations that are urgently required is of great benefit.

This chapter considers the practice of transforming information into intelligence.

5.1   The Intelligence Cycle in Practice

The intelligence cycle as described in Chapter 3 of this book is the most widely known and accepted model for the production of intelligence. However, it is not the only model, nor is it necessarily the best model to apply to every situation.

There are a number of different intelligence production models that may be more appropriate for the needs of the consumer or be a better match for the capability of the intelligence team.

5.1.1   See it, Sense it, Share it, Use it

This recent model published by the office of the US Director of National Intelligence in 2018 provides a simple overview for conceptualising intelligence productions, and how the private sector can assist public sector authorities (ODNI 2018).

See it – The first step in collecting intelligence is having access to data in which the activities of threat actors can be identified. No single organisation either within the public or private sector can expect to have full visibility of every action conducted by threat actors. Instead, each organisation is affected by specific threats that leave traces within data.

Identifying these traces and describing the threat that affected the organisation allows the pooling of data and intelligence from many organisations. Together these shared reports produced from many different sources provide much greater situational awareness of threats than any single organisation could expect to obtain on their own.

The same is true for the discovery of vulnerabilities. Any vulnerabilities discovered by researchers within the private sector can be responsibly disclosed so that a patch can be developed, and then shared within the wider community for the benefit of everyone.

Sense it – Raw data must be processed in order to make sense, and enriched with context so that it can be interpreted by others and applied to their own situation. Threat intelligence must help others in understanding the threat so that they can understand the nature of the threat and take necessary action.

Intelligence must be actionable. The reader should be provided with clear instructions regarding how they should react, the actions they should take in order to mitigate it, or reduce their exposure to the threat.

Share it – Intelligence needs to reach those that need it. Decision makers need to be informed of the choices that they must make. Security operations teams need to be aware of the situations that they are likely to encounter. Sharing may take place within an organisation, with a community of peers, with external agencies who can put the intelligence to good use, or with a much wider audience who may not share the same background and understanding as those who have produced the intelligence.

Use it – Intelligence is only useful if it is read by others outside of the intelligence team, and helps them in guiding their actions to achieve better outcomes. It is important to validate that intelligence products have satisfied the requirements and needs of the audience. Demonstrating that the production of intelligence assists an organisation in improving the security posture is vital if the intelligence function is to continue to be funded. Constant feedback from consumers of intelligence allows intelligence teams to refine their intelligence production to ensure the quality of their reports.

Sometimes intelligence consumers don't put intelligence to good use. Reasons for poor utilisation of intelligence reports may be due to factors outside the control of the intelligence team. For instance, operational teams may lack the resources to read operational reports. In which case, switching to developing tactical reports that can be ingested by machine rather than requiring operations teams to read them may better meet their needs, despite the reduction of content and the omission of context. If intelligence products are not helping improve the organisation's security posture, intelligence teams should investigate the reasons and modify their products accordingly.

Ultimately, the 'See it, Sense it, Share it, Use it' model shares many concepts with the classical Intelligence Cycle, including the notions of collection, analysis, dissemination, and feedback.

5.1.2 F3EAD Cycle

One criticism that has been levied against the Intelligence Cycle is that the model is a passive system. The intelligence team waits for questions to be asked of them before gathering and preparing the intelligence, which is then disseminated. Once complete, the team investigates the utility of the intelligence produced, considers if the execution of the cycle can be prepared, then the cycle resets and awaits the next input.

The Intelligence Cycle model suggests that if no further questions are asked of the intelligence team, then the intelligence team sits and waits for the next request. Clearly, this does not reflect reality. Intelligence teams are not passive entities. Cyber threat intelligence teams are actively involved in working with operational teams in resolving potential or active incursions and constantly evaluating and prioritising threats. But this activity is not well represented by the Intelligence Cycle.

Within military field operations, a different operation model for intelligence is applied. Although the classical Intelligence Cycle is still applied for the production of strategic intelligence, a model based on Find, Fix, Finish, Exploit, Analyse, and Disseminate or F3EAD is often used within tactical situations (JWC 2011) (Figure 5.1).

Within this model decision makers set priorities for the integrated intelligence and operation teams. The intelligence teams work to identify where interventions are required. This intelligence is passed to operational teams who intervene to resolve the issue (Faint and Harris 2012). Thus, operational teams focus on the highest priority issues as identified by the intelligence teams in accordance with the terms decided by senior decision makers.

The first step within the process is 'Find'. This step can be undertaken simultaneously by intelligence and operational teams to identify potential targets for intervention. In a cyber threat intelligence context, these may be systems associated with a known indicator of compromise, systems that are missing a vital patch, or demonstrating some form of anomaly that warrants investigation.

The next phase is 'Fix'. This involves applying the intelligence gathering apparatus to understand the nature of the target under investigation, to supply all the intelligence necessary to proceed to the next phase, and to check if further investigation is required, or is the best use of resources to fulfil the teams' objectives.

The teams then proceed to 'Finish'. In this phase the operations team acts on the target to resolve the threat. In practice, this may imply simply applying a patch,

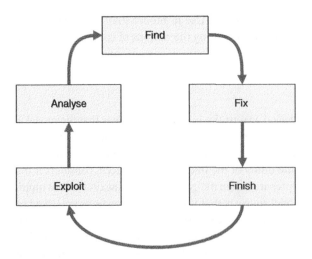

Figure 5.1 The F3EAD cycle. *Source:* adapted from JWC (2011).

or isolating a breached system before definitively removing threat actor access to the system and restoring normal operation.

The next step is to 'Exploit' the resolved target. At this point the forensic evidence from the threat is gathered, and the steps that led to the threat impacting on the system are identified. This may involve commissioning further intelligence gathering exercises to enrich the intelligence gathered so far.

Following evidence gathering we move to the 'Analyse' phase. At this point the evidence is analysed to understand how the threat occurred, the root cause of the event, what conclusions can be drawn, and lessons learned.

The final phase is 'Dissemination'. The intelligence produced from the 'Analyse' phase is shared with others, both within the organisation and potentially with external partners too. The goal is for the wider community to learn from the issue so that fewer similar events are encountered, and subsequent events can be detected and remediated faster (Faint and Harris 2012; FIRST 2021).

The F3EAD cycle does not necessarily operate as a linear sequential set of steps. Teams can execute steps as necessary, or kick off additional F3EAD cycles as needed. Ultimately the goal is to resolve threats as effectively, efficiently, and quickly as possible (Faint and Harris 2012).

5.1.3 D3A Process

The F3EAD process is not without criticism, notably that there is little scope for decision making (Gomez 2011). The D3A process: Decide, Detect, Deliver, Assess is analogous to F3EAD, but places more emphasis on planning and decision making.

During the first phase 'Decide', teams determine the various types of possible targets for intervention, their priorities, and how these might be detected. Before moving to the next phase, teams have clear descriptions of priority targets, how they will be identified, and how they will be addressed.

Teams then move to the 'Detect' phase where priority threats are identified using the material developed earlier. Once located, the 'Deliver' phase is invoked where the target threat is remediated according to the plan.

The final phase is to 'Assess' the actions to determine if these were indeed the correct targets to remediate, and that the operation proceeded smoothly and accurately. Any feedback is then integrated into the next 'Decide' phase of the operation (NATO 2021).

Although this model has been developed for the targeting of military objectives rather than intelligence production and utilisation, it is applicable to the production of tactical intelligence. In the case where intelligence on current threats needs to be rapidly delivered and acted upon, the D3A model may be particularly pertinent and useful.

5.1.4 Applying the Intelligence Cycle

The Intelligence Cycle and variants have different emphases and steps, but nevertheless share common concepts. There are notions of direction and planning as the first step, followed by the collection of data in order to identify pertinent information, before transforming this information into an intelligence product and delivering it where it is needed.

Although these steps refer specifically to the phases of the Intelligence Cycle, which is the most well-known and described of the variant approaches, they are applicable to the concepts and phases of every model.

5.1.4.1 Planning and Requirements

The cycle should begin with a well-articulated question and set of requirements from a senior decision maker, which can then be translated into a plan for gathering and producing the necessary intelligence. In reality, decision makers may not know what intelligence they require, may be unable to articulate their needs into suitable questions to direct the team, or be unaware of the intelligence team's capabilities.

Part of the role of the threat intelligence team is working together with intelligence consumers to understand their needs, helping to phrase questions that can be answered, and suggesting how intelligence capabilities can support the wider cyber security team. In the absence of effective direction or requirements, experienced threat intelligence professionals may have to adopt the role of a senior manager to ensure that the threat intelligence team is put to good use in supporting the security goals of the organisation.

Even the best phrased intelligence request may be impossible to fulfil if the intelligence team does not have access to the data necessary to provide the response. Intelligence teams should be aware of the data sources to which they have access, the sources that are easy to query, and those that are not. If potentially useful data is not able to be accessed, or is not in a state that is usable, the case can be made to gain access or transform the data so that it can be utilised.

The first steps of the Intelligence Cycle can become an iterative process where a question is asked of the intelligence team, but during the planning or collection phase it becomes apparent that it is not possible to provide an answer. A poorly phrased question can be refined by working together with the requestor. A question that cannot be answered due to lack of data can become a project to gain access to vital data.

Intelligence requirements, available resources, and allocated budget may be mutually incompatible. The requirements made of the intelligence team and the constraints put upon it may make it impossible for the team to comply. This situation may not be understood or recognised by anyone outside of the immediate team.

In these cases, identifying the various requirements and constraints, highlighting the incompatibilities and the trade-offs necessary in order to fulfil the requests is required. Even so, the various stakeholders may still not agree. Applying the MoSCoW prioritisation technique helps stakeholders focus on what is most important.

The mnemonic MoSCoW is used to describe and rank requirements according to the following criteria:

> M – Must Have – absolutely necessary requirements for the system.
> S – Should Have – important requirements that will add value to the system.
> C – Could Have – useful requirements, but will have little impact if omitted.
> W – Will Not Have – requirements that will not be implemented.
>
> *(Hatton 2008)*

Coming to agreement with multiple stakeholders regarding the best course of action is never easy. Different stakeholders may have radically different views regarding priorities for intelligence gathering and production, and the data sources necessary to support this. To complicate matters, many priorities may be assumed to be implicit by stakeholders and not expressed as a critical requirement during discussions.

Nevertheless, at the end of this phase, the intelligence team should have a set of coherent requirements, a well phrased question to answer, and a plan to gather the necessary data and the resources in order to accomplish this task.

5.1.4.2 Collection, Analysis, and Processing

Understandably, the data to be collected depends on the nature of the enquiry, and the requirements. The data necessary to fulfil a strategic intelligence request on the long term objectives of a threat actor is very different from that required to respond to an urgent request for tactical intelligence.

In any case, the analyst collecting the data must clearly record how the data was obtained. The steps necessary to obtain the data should be recorded so that the data collection is repeatable. A different analyst following the same steps should obtain the same set of data. Noting the exact query terms will be very useful if the same or similar requests are made in the future.

Raw data must be transformed and combined together with context to form information. The raw data itself is rarely useful to the end user. The analyst must extract the value from the data by summarising it or combining it with other information so that it conveys what the end user needs to know.

The analyst must understand the needs of the end user, as well as the requirements stated as part of the request. Remember, intelligence delivered too late is of no use, and that too much information hinders decision making. Yet at the same time, data gathering must be systematic with rigorous and objective analysis. There is no easy way to meet these sometimes conflicting constraints. Close dialogue with end users to understand their needs is key to producing useful intelligence and satisfying their demands.

Do not expect to get it right the first time. The Intelligence Cycle is a loop. Lessons are learnt as the final step of the cycle and applied to the next iteration. If the first attempt at producing intelligence does not meet the requestor or end user's needs, learn from the experience, make changes, and the next iteration will be a closer map. As teams work together more, an innate understanding of respective needs and capabilities will develop, but it takes time to reach this point.

5.1.4.3 Production and Dissemination

To be useful, intelligence must be delivered to the people who require the intelligence in the format that they can consume. The exact format will have been defined as part of the intelligence request and planning activities.

There is no single format for writing intelligence reports. There is no right or wrong way, but there are good practices that will help the consumers of the report in making best use of the intelligence.

Provide the summary first – include the summary of your analysis as the first section of the report so that people who are hurried or distracted can easily access the main findings. The mnemonic BLUF (Bottom Line Up Front) is a good way to remember this.

Separate facts from analysis – clearly differentiate information that is factual or that describes the situation from content that is analysis or conjecture. It is good practice to keep sections within a document where the facts of a situation are stated distinctly and separately from the sections where the analyst provides interpretation and conclusions.

Be actionable – make it easy for the reader to put information to good use by making the intelligence actionable. Provide instructions or further steps that a consumer of the report can do in order to implement any conclusions. Clear guidance helps the reader make the right decisions and carry out the correct actions.

Ensure traceability – the date, source and version of the report should be clearly stated so that the report can be cited by others and allow any feedback to be supplied to the correct team. Similarly, any references to other documents within the text should be appropriately cited. The sources of stated facts and any data presented should also be clearly referenced. Ideally, given an intelligence report and access to the same source data and documents, another analyst should be able to repeat the process to derive the same conclusions.

Keep it brief – there is no need to provide unnecessary detail. Through good referencing and record keeping, extraneous information need not be included within the report while maintaining traceability. Graphs and diagrams can help convey complex information succinctly. In writing intelligence reports, remember the adages: half as long is twice as good, and a picture paints a thousand words.

Provide any indicators of compromise (IoCs) in a format that is easily accessible or machine readable. In addition to any mention of IoCs in the text, include a separate section containing IoCs so that operational teams can readily extract this data.

Indicate distribution – clearly mark for whom the report is intended and any constraints for the distribution. The traffic light protocol (TLP) is useful in indicating how the report should be circulated (or not), but if restrictions on distribution are required make sure that the nature of these restrictions is stated.

Intelligence is only useful if it is delivered where it is needed. Ensure that the dissemination process meets the requestor's needs, and is what they expect. It is usually more effective to 'push' a completed intelligence report to the source, than to expect them to 'pull' it from the intelligence team.

5.1.4.4 Feedback and Improvement

As a final step in the intelligence cycle, collect feedback from consumers of the intelligence, and review the process used to generate the intelligence. Identify what worked well, and what was useful to the end user. Positive feedback to team members helps reinforce good practices and behaviours. Identify any issues or processes that worked less well than expected. Take steps to address any inefficiencies so that the intelligence team can progress and improve capabilities.

5.1.4.5 The Intelligence Cycle in Reverse

The process of intelligence production should not be a one-way street. The steps of the intelligence cycle should not necessarily be strictly followed in sequential order. Maintaining flexibility allows the intelligence production capability to improve during execution, and not just following a review at the end of the cycle.

For instance, during the data gathering phase, it may become apparent that more or better data is available than was first envisaged and that this may provide answers to more pertinent intelligence questions. Even though this intelligence was not specifically requested during the planning phase, the analyst may judge that this would support the mission of the cyber security department. In which case, while continuing with the production of the original intelligence, provide feedback to the requestor of any additional useful intelligence that may be easy to generate.

As intelligence analysts become acquainted with the data sources and telemetry available to them, as well as the needs of the teams to which they are delivering intelligence, analysts may identify opportunities for the production of useful intelligence. The intelligence team may act as trusted advisors instructing decision makers about the utility and possibilities of intelligence. Decision makers can then allocate resources appropriately based on cost–benefit analysis. If the costs of collecting and producing the intelligence are low, and the benefits to the wider organisation of the generated intelligence are high, then this should be highlighted.

5.2   Sources of Data

The nature of the data source that analysts will use as part of their data collection activities will depend on the nature of the request for intelligence. Providing a relevant response to the question posed of the team requires identifying the relevant data in which the answer is likely to be found.

The dataset must be relevant to the specific query, and may be derived from internal or external sources. Information relating to the number of systems within an organisation that are affected by a specific vulnerability is unlikely to be found within the firewall logs. Information relating to an external denial of service attack is unlikely to be found in the results of an internal network scan. And neither firewall logs nor a network scan will provide information about the long term goals of a state-sponsored threat actor.

The data source must also be amenable to a search within an appropriate time frame. Vast sets of data that describe every event that has occurred within an organisation for extended time periods may provide a complete view of activity within an organisation, but prove less useful than data summaries, which will provide rapid answers to a query.

The ideal data source is reliable, credible, offers complete visibility of an issue, is easy to access, and easy to query. In reality, trade-offs need to be made in order to work with data sources that are 'good enough'. Trading off the reliability or credibility of a source for ease of query is unlikely to be satisfactory. Poor quality or unreliable data invariably leads to poor analyses and conclusions.

Frequently, intelligence teams are tasked to generate operational intelligence from analysing security events or system logs. Although such telemetry is being collected, intelligence teams may find that the data which is vital to respond to an intelligence request is unusable. Telemetry that is not stored, unavailable to search, or simply contains too much data to reasonably process is useless to intelligence analysts.

The intelligence team can work with engineering teams to draw up and cost a project plan describing how systems that currently do not support the needs of the intelligence team can be amended or developed to meet intelligence needs. But it is for senior decision makers to decide on the priorities for resources. Even if such a project is approved, the development cycles necessary to bring the project to fruition may be long.

Intelligence teams are faced with a choice: working with engineering teams to ensure that relevant data is captured in an accessible and usable location and format, which can be a lengthy and expensive process, or working with the data that is available. Often less than ideal data sources can provide partial answers to questions, or provide answers to related questions.

The exact course of action is determined through dialogue with stakeholders seeking to optimise the trade-off between the rapidity of the response with the accuracy of the response and the cost of providing the response. If the rapid delivery of operational intelligence is a high priority requirement for an organisation, then the investment in systems to support this is necessary.

Intelligence teams should make good use of their advisory capacity and their ability to provide respected, objective analyses of a situation in order to research the benefits and costs of appropriate solutions for their data management and data access needs.

5.3 Searching Data

A common question asked of cyber threat intelligence teams is to identify if an organisation has been affected by an attack described in a third party report. Responding to such a question depends on the capability of the intelligence function and the utility of the data to which they have access.

Considering the ideal situation where the cyber intelligence team has access to a Security information and event management (SIEM) solution where all security and system events are logged, aggregated, and searchable, how would a team go about responding to such a request?

Searching within the logs for the presence of any IoCs described in the report would be a good first step. Network or firewall logs will be expected to contain evidence if any systems have made network connections to malicious IP addresses described in the report. Querying system logs for the presence of the published file hash values of any malicious software or tools used in the attack will clearly identify traces of the attack.

The presence of a known malicious IP address, or a known malicious file hash value within logs will warrant investigation. This may be an indication of an attack, evidence of a test, or the traces left by a curious user. In any case, the analyst will need to delve further to identify the nature of the activity that led to the log entry and to discount the possibility of a false positive or false alarm. If the trace is due to a successful attack, the analyst will need to escalate the issue and consider initiating an incident response process.

However, a negative result does not prove the absence of the attack. The same attacker may have launched an almost identical attack against the organisation, but using slightly different IP addresses, or subtly different malicious files that have radically different file hash values.

The report may include further IoCs, which can be searched for, such as file names or file paths used by the attacker, or changes made to affected systems. The presence of these may provide evidence of an attack.

If none of these are present, we must enlarge our search and apply our knowledge of the attacker. The attacker may have used an IP address proximate to one described in the report. Searching for the presence of addresses within the same CIDR (Classless Inter-Domain Routing) range, where feasible, may give an indication of the attack.

Querying passive DNS databases can uncover additional attacker resources. These systems identify domain names that are associated with specified IP addresses, or IP addresses that are, or have previously been, associated with specified domain names.

The attacker may have used an unreported domain name as part of the attack that passive DNS may uncover due to its association with the known malicious IP address. Alternatively, the passive DNS system may uncover additional malicious IP addresses that have been previously associated with known malicious domains. In this way, elements of the attacker's infrastructure and resources can be elucidated, along with clues as to other IP addresses or ranges that might have been used in an attack.

The TTPs used as part of the attack can be used to model the attack and to direct threat hunting activities. For example, if the attack was reported as using compromised credentials, then the system logs may contain evidence of a user account being used at an unusual time, or accessed from an unusual location. Exfiltration of large amounts of data is likely to leave traces in network logs. Searching for unusual data transfers or network activity can uncover evidence of the attack.

Ultimately the analyst must make the call regarding how much time and resources they devote to hunting for indicators that may have been left by a threat actor. There is little to be gained in searching for the presence of phantoms that may not exist. However, uncovering new indicators associated with an attack, or further data regarding an adversary's resources is a great help in the detection of further attacks and in turn can assist other cyber threat intelligence teams in their hunts for attacks.

5.4 Threat Hunting

In the absence of a specific request to investigate a threat, intelligence teams may be engaged in the self-directed search for evidence of threats. This threat hunting seeks to distil the unmanageable number of events recorded in logs to a manageable handful of traces that warrant active investigation. Investigation and enrichment with other sources of intelligence further reduces these cases to a handful that require escalation to other teams for remediation or immediate incident response.

Hunting for threats is achieved through the application of an analyst's professional knowledge, a sense of curiosity, awareness of the data and systems within the environment as well as data science.

5.4.1 Models of Threat Hunting

Reportedly, many hunting activities are ad hoc, taking place without applying any documented methodology despite the existence of conceptual models (Daszczyszak et al. 2019). The Sqrrl Hunting Loop describes threat hunting as consisting of four phases (Figure 5.2).

Hunting activities begin with a hypothesis regarding evidence that might be discovered to uncover malicious activity. The hypothesis is investigated using tools and techniques to refute or confirm the original hypothesis. This investigation may uncover new patterns or potential evidence of TTPs. These traces can be further investigated and enriched to identify if malicious activity has occurred.

Tools and techniques that prove successful in identifying maliciousness can be automated to provide regular threat hunts taking place in the background. Any indication of attacks can be highlighted and routed to operational teams for further triage and investigation.

This basic framework has subsequently been extended by the UK government to include various exit points from the loop where the investigation phase may result in a hypothesis being unproven, uncovering suspicious behaviour, or the

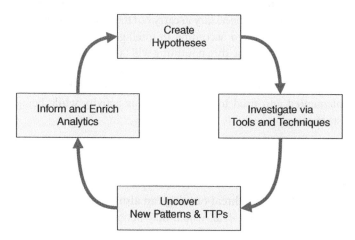

Figure 5.2 The Hunting Loop. *Source:* Adapted from Sqrrl (2016).

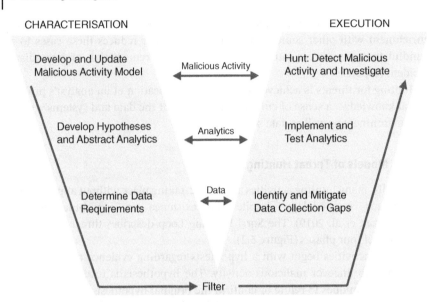

CHARACTERISATION   EXECUTION

Figure 5.3 The 'V' diagram of TTP hunting. *Source:* Adapted from Daszczyszak et al. (2019).

presence of malicious behaviour initiating an incident response process (Digital Data and Technology 2019).

The Hunting Loop is not the only threat hunting model. Daszczyszak et al. propose the 'V' diagram model (Daszczyszak et al. 2019) (Figure 5.3).

In this model, during the characterisation phase, the various TTPs under consideration are defined and used to formulate hypotheses regarding how these TTPs may be uncovered within the environment. These hypotheses are expressed as analytic tests, for which the data requirements necessary to carry out the tests are identified.

The tests are filtered and prioritised according to intelligence needs and the nature of the environment in which the threat hunting will take place. During the execution phase, the necessary data requirements are verified against the data collection capabilities. Any gaps in data collection are then mitigated. The analytic tests are then implemented and used to detect malicious activity while being tuned and refined as required.

5.4.2 Analysing Data

Structured hunting activities search for the presence of specific indicators, such as IoCs or evidence of TTPs. However, threat hunting can also be an unstructured activity looking for anomalies within data, which may betray evidence of malicious behaviour.

One of the simplest methods for unstructured hunting is 'stacking'. In this approach, tools developed by the analyst count the occurrence of features within a dataset and stack them according to their frequency of occurrence. This simple ranked list of features can be anything that can be counted, such as recorded user-agent identification strings, or the different IP addresses that have connected to a system, etc.

Anomalous features are those that appear to be different from the others within the dataset. This may be because they are the most frequent, the least frequent, or simply because they stand out from the other members of the dataset for some reason. To an experienced analyst, some features stand out as simply being 'wrong'. The trick for successful threat hunting is to express these intuitions and hunches as algorithmic tests that can be automated. Analysts can't hope to view all system logs all the time, but automated tests can constantly scan for things that look 'wrong'.

Changes in the frequency of occurrence of a feature can indicate anomalies. If a feature is consistently encountered at a low level, but one day jumps to be one of the most frequently encountered then this should be investigated to understand why this is the case.

We may not be able to predict exactly the frequency of an observation for a given time period, but with enough data we can model the frequency of occurrence, and use this model to identify anomalous behaviour. Frequency of occurrence data often follows a predictable distribution of values; one such distribution is referred to as Gaussian or normal distribution. When graphed, this distribution pattern is sometimes referred to as the bell curve, due to the graph resembling the shape of a bell (Figure 5.4).

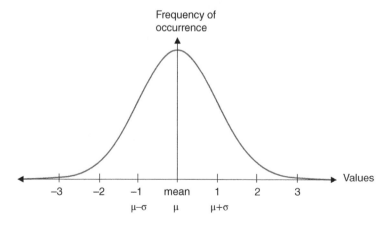

Figure 5.4 Normal Gaussian distribution.

Within this distribution, values are centred around the mean (average) value, often referred to using the Greek letter μ. The 'width' of the spread of values around the mean is measured with the standard deviation, referred to with the Greek letter σ. Approximately 68% of the expected values will fall within one standard deviation from the mean; 95% fall within twice the standard deviation either side of the mean; and 99.7% of values will be within three times the standard deviation (Wikipedia 2022). This implies that anything that is more than three times the standard deviation away from the mean is an anomalous value. In the context of threat hunting, this is a very interesting observation, which should be escalated for inspection.

Calculating the values of the mean and standard deviation for datasets are easy to achieve using statistical libraries of computing languages. Cut-off values for the lowest and highest expected values can be calculated as:

Low value $= \mu - z\sigma$

High value $= \mu + z\sigma$

Where: $z = 2$, to select for approximately 95% of expected values, or $z = 3$, to select for approximately 99.7% of expected values. μ is the mean of the sample, and σ the standard deviation of the sample.

Any observed value that is below the low cut-off value, or above the high cut-off value indicates an anomaly. Within any given environment, tweaking and experimentation can be expected. It may be that three times the standard deviation ($z = 3$) results in too many anomalous values to investigate, possibly four or five times the standard deviation will reduce the number of anomalies to manageable quantities.

Not all values follow a bell curve distribution. If a value can never be less than zero, but the upper value is unbounded, then the log-normal distribution is a useful model to consider (Figure 5.5).

In this distribution, the natural logarithm values of the tested variable are distributed normally, not the variable itself. Data following this distribution may have a mean value is quite different from the mode (most frequent) value, with a long tail of upper values.

To identify anomalous values, we still need to calculate cut-off values for the variable, beyond which we wish to escalate for investigation. However, the calculations for these cut-off values are different from those for the normal distribution. Approximate values for these can be calculated using the large sample theory method, if a large enough number of samples have been collected and studied.

Low value $= \mu - z\,\mathrm{sqrt}(\sigma^2 / n)$

High value $= \mu + z\,\mathrm{sqrt}(\sigma^2 / n)$

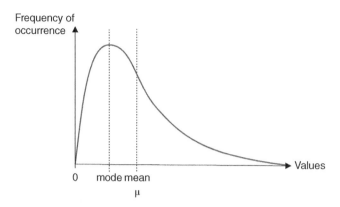

Figure 5.5 Log-normal distribution.

Where: z = 2, to select for approximately 95% of expected values, or z = 3, to select for approximately 99.7% of expected values. μ is the mean of the sample, σ the standard deviation of the sample, and n is the number of items sampled (Olsson 2005).

Again, some tweaking of values is to be expected. The goal is not to calculate exact probabilities, but to derive a metric that can be used to recognise anomalous values, however we wish to define the term 'anomalous'. Defining mathematical models of expected or usual behaviour allows us to compare the 'here and now' with 'normality'. If current observations are different from what is expected, then it is time to investigate and find out why this is the case.

5.4.3 Entity Behaviour Analytics

User and Entity Behaviour Analytics (UEBA) is an application of machine learning and artificial intelligence where the behaviour of users and entities, such as systems or computers, is modelled to identify the 'normal' state of the entity. The current state of behaviour of the entity is compared with its own normal state, or the usual state of similar entities. If the entity is behaving differently, then an alert is generated and the reasons for the difference explored.

UEBA collects large amounts of data to construct a set of features that describe the entity's behaviour. These features can include:

Logon and logoff events.
Use of removable devices, including the device name and type.
File access events, such as the creation of a file, copying a file, deleting a file, etc.
HTTP access events, including the URL and the browser type.
Email sending, including the subject line and any recipients.

(Eldardiry et al. 2014)

These features can be used to calculate a weighted vector with many dimensions. Clustering algorithms can group together similar entity behaviour vectors to spot outliers, or calculate the relative deviation in behaviour between usual and current behaviour. In either case, if the current observations are too different from those expected, then the entity's behaviour is anomalous and should be investigated further.

5.5 Transforming Data into Intelligence

'Data' consists of verifiable facts and observations. Collecting many data points together and presenting this coherently forms 'information'. In the context of threat intelligence, Intelligence is simply information. In its simplest form, tactical intelligence can be little more than sets of indicators of compromise accompanied by some context, which may be just a few words of description.

Intelligence also consists of analysis: data enriched with context and the further information necessary to increase the understanding and raising knowledge of the consumer. An informed and knowledgeable intelligence consumer is empowered to make better decisions. Nevertheless, providing analysis is a dangerous thing. It is all too easy to provide biased rather than objective analysis, or simply to come to the wrong conclusions, and enable poor decision making by the consumer.

Analysts may be faced with large volumes of data, some of it contradictory, and certainly none of it painting a complete picture of the situation. This data can be interpreted in many different ways. To present a picture of what is happening and likely to happen, analysts must make sense of the data interpreting it to form a conceptual model of the situation that can be shared and communicated.

Coming to conclusions requires a reasoning process, and the creation of various hypotheses that may explain the situation. Hypothesis generation is one of the key skills of the intelligence analyst. The human mind tends to see the patterns that it expects to see within data. Accordingly, conclusions tend to be drawn towards those that fit the experiences and cultural background of the analyst.

Removing all potential bias is an impossible task. However, analysts can seek many different hypotheses, testing if the data fits the model and making clear the various assumptions inherent to the hypothesis so that others can test and challenge the hypothesis themselves.

5.5.1 Structured Geospatial Analytical Method

The Structured Geospatial Analytical Method (SGAM) describes how an intelligence analyst can develop hypotheses and come to a conclusion through foraging

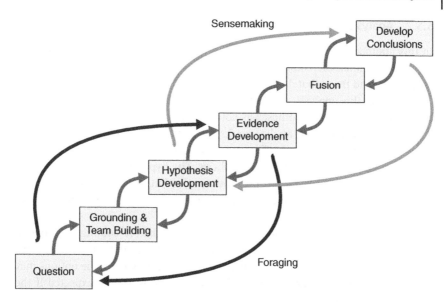

Figure 5.6 The Structured Geospatial Analytical Model. *Source:* Adapted from Wikimedia (2022) based on Pirolli and Card (2005).

for information and using this in sensemaking. The hypotheses developed can be supported or discounted through further foraging for information, in turn building and developing hypotheses into conclusions (Bacastow 2020) (Figure 5.6).

As with the intelligence cycle, the process begins with a question followed by data gathering (grounding) and the forming of a team in order to gather further evidence and provide analysis. Hypotheses are generated that explain and fit the evidence. Further data is gathered to support or refute the evidence, and is fused with further intelligence or information to determine the consistency of the hypothesis with what is known. Conclusions are drawn regarding the available evidence and the strength of the hypothesis, which can then be presented as intelligence.

The process can also be reversed. Starting with a conclusion, this can be compared with additional intelligence to determine its consistency with current understanding of the situation. Further evidence to support or discount the conclusion is gathered before further hypotheses that may better fit the evidence can be proposed. These can then form the basis for further data gathering and hypothesis building (Bacastow 2020).

Hypotheses and accepted conclusions can be continuously tested against information, strengthening or disproving them. Where an accepted conclusion is in opposition to new data, either the conclusion or the data is wrong. In either case, the reason for the discrepancy needs investigating.

5.5.2 Analysis of Competing Hypotheses

In this approach, the analyst identifies all the reasonable hypotheses and compares them against each other simultaneously to identify the hypotheses that best fit the data, and those that do not.

To perform this analysis, the analyst lists the salient points of the evidence as rows, and the various hypotheses as columns to form a matrix. Where the evidence fits the evidence, the analyst marks this positively on the matrix, and where it does not, marks it negatively. The scores within the columns indicate where the data supports or detracts from the hypothesis. The hypothesis that fits best is not necessarily the one with the most positive marks, but more likely to be the one with the fewest negatives, since this hypothesis is the least refuted by the evidence (Heuer 1999a).

Some refinement and iterations may be necessary before coming to a conclusion. Some data may not be helpful to distinguish between options because it fits with too many or too few of the studied hypotheses. Similarly, some options may be disproved by the absence of critical evidence that would be expected if the hypothesis were true.

Searching for evidence that would disprove hypotheses is more useful than searching for supporting evidence, due to our inherent tendency for conformational bias. Typically, people will tend to select data that fits with existing mental models. Consciously reversing this tendency and actively looking for refuting evidence helps neutralise this bias.

The process of analysing competing hypotheses is no panacea for ensuring good reasoning. Analysts may still reach poor conclusions or find it difficult to overcome biases despite training in the technique (Dhami et al. 2019).

5.5.3 Poor Practices

Alexander George identifies five poor practices in decision making:

Satisficing – selecting the first option which seems 'good enough' instead of systematically analysing the best option.

Incrementalism – selecting options that require little change, rather than considering that major change might be necessary.

Consensus – selecting the option that peers or the customer are most likely to agree with, as opposed to options that may be correct but unpopular.

Reasoning by analogy – selecting options based solely on prior experience with other options. Seeking to replicate successes or avoid failures without fully evaluating the options.

Decision by principles or maxims – selecting options by applying a rule of thumb.

George (1980) quoted in Heuer (1999b).

To these we can add:

Selective perception – selecting evidence that fits a favourite hypothesis or idea.

Failure to generate appropriate hypotheses – inability to consider the wider range of possible hypotheses, but instead settling for a smaller number that fits preconceptions.

Failure To Consider Diagnosticity of Evidence – not identifying that evidence fails to distinguish between many hypotheses and as such serves no purpose in identifying the best option.

Failure To Reject Hypotheses – omitting to discount and no longer consider hypotheses that have been proven to be incorrect.

(Heuer 1999b).

Within any discussion of data analysis and production of intelligence, we must also consider apophenia – the ability to discern patterns and connections where none exist (Carroll 2016). Many of the patterns and evidence we discern in data may not exist, or may simply be random occurrences. Although we may search for purpose in events and seek to explain them as part of some grand plan, we must remain open to the possibility that stuff happens and frequently happens for no reason at all.

In every case, a hypothesis to consider is that the evidence is just a random occurrence. In statistics, this is known as the 'null hypothesis', that there is no relationship between two sets of data. Professional statisticians, as with good intelligence analysts, will only suggest that a connection may exist if it can be proved to a level of certainty that the apparent connection is not due to a quirk of randomness.

5.6   Sharing Intelligence

Intelligence is only useful if it is put to use where it is needed. Any intelligence report must meet the needs of the intended audience. As previously stated, there is no right or wrong format, if the customer is satisfied with the format of the report, that is all that is needed.

Although a report may be developed for a specific customer, the report may also be useful to others in understanding the threats that they face. The wider cyber security community is united in a common goal in securing systems and fighting against threats. Sharing information with similar organisations can only be expected to improve security and benefit the community overall.

The UK government identifies six benefits of intelligence sharing:

Awareness of current cyber threats affecting various sectors – organisations can improve their own understanding of threats through learning via perspectives of peer organisations other than their own.

Understanding of attackers' tactics, techniques, and procedures – in order to mount an effective defence against threats, organisations must be aware of the nature of the threats that are likely to impact upon them.

Acquisition of information that would otherwise be unavailable/inefficiently available through public sources or security vendor reporting – the nature of the intelligence shared between peers is likely to be different from that obtained from other sources.

Decision making regarding technology, controls, and resources allocation and escalation – real life experiences of responding to threats and the mechanics of how other organisations respond can be very useful in directing and improving in-house capabilities.

Detection capabilities on networks – the experiences of other organisations in their capabilities to detect threats may be radically different (for better or worse) from their peers. Knowing where your detection capabilities stand in comparison with others helps in the prioritisation of resources.

Mitigation and responses prior to an actual event – real life experiences may be very different from what might be expected, and may identify areas for improvement that hadn't previously been anticipated.

(FCDO 2021)

However, there are many issues to consider before sharing intelligence. Despite indicating sharing restrictions there is no absolute certainty that an intelligence report won't be circulated further than desired. Sharing may take place as part of a trusted relationship between entities, within a group where there are clear rules as to how reports may be used and circulated, or with a statutory or regulatory body that has clear rules as to the use and republication of information. Alternatively, intelligence may be openly published and widely shared without restriction. Each model has its own risks and benefits which should be carefully considered.

In any case, sharing requires a commitment from senior management that sharing intelligence is something that the organisation will engage in, to set the parameters in which the sharing will take place, and to establish the mechanics of with whom and how intelligence will be shared.

Intelligence is produced and shared within a regulatory and legal environment. Organisations seeking to share intelligence should be aware of, and happy to accept, any legal risk associated with the dissemination and publication of their intelligence reports.

Internal rules should make it clear what information can and cannot be shared, and in what context. All organisations operate subject to national law and additional regulations to which they are subject, no information should be shared that would jeopardise legal or regulatory compliance.

Organisations should consider if their intelligence reports contain any of the following:

Nationally sensitive information – including any classified information, or information derived from classified information. Information that may be prejudicial to the interests of the nation state, or relate to military matters. Every jurisdiction has its own regulations regarding the sharing or publication of sensitive information, and a level of tolerance in these matters. Consequences can be severe for individuals who fail to appropriately protect such information.

Legally protected information – personally identifiable information that could identify individuals including any victims, perpetrators, or third parties who have been spoofed or involved in some way. Laws vary between jurisdictions, but as a rule of thumb don't disclose any personal information. If the nature of the victim is a vital part of the description of the attack, such as with a spear phishing campaign, refer to the victim using a description of the job role such as 'a senior financial executive' instead. This conveys vital information that others can use to protect potential victims, but does not disclose an identity. If sharing examples of spam or phishing attack emails be sure to redact email addresses that can inadvertently identify the victim or a spoofed third party.

Regulatory protected information – organisations operating in certain sectors, such as health care or financial services, etc., may be subject to additional regulations regarding information or even descriptions of operating environments that cannot be disclosed.

Commercially sensitive information – be careful not to accidentally trade secrets or commercial or operational plans when sharing intelligence.

Damaging information – it is easy to share information that could aid an attacker. Avoid disclosing details of operational environments that could be used by an attacker to compromise systems. Details of the cyber security posture or security responses do not need to be disclosed. Although feedback relating to practices that were successful or that worked less well than anticipated is always useful to improve the capabilities of security teams.

Occasionally, it is impossible not to name an organisation as part of the report, such as when warning of a phishing attack where the reputation of an organisation is being spoofed. In which case, make the report clear that the named organisation was not compromised, but their good name and reputation was maliciously abused.

It is not uncommon for the public relations team of intelligence publishers to inform counterparts in an organisation that is to be named in a forthcoming report soon to be published. This allows the named organisation to prepare their own response to the publication, or to politely request for their name to be removed. Consider how you would wish your own organisation to be treated if it was to be named in such a report, and treat all other organisations accordingly.

There is little to be gained in naming organisations affected by an attack unless they themselves choose to do so. An indication of the victim's industrial sector is often enough detail to put the intelligence to good use. Public relations departments and corporate lawyers may be unwelcoming to any potentially negative report that overtly names their organisation.

Threat actors themselves are unlikely to welcome reports detailing their activities. The security industry has developed a wide variety of pseudonyms so that malicious activity can be ascribed to specific entities without the real world identity of those entities, or the nation state by whom they are employed, needing to be disclosed. There is always some degree of doubt in attributing attacks to a specific group, and the groups themselves go to great lengths to hide their true identities. Identifying the exact organisation or specific individuals behind an attack is the remit of law enforcement rather than cyber threat intelligence professionals in the private sector. Attribution is discussed in more detail in Chapter 6.

5.6.1 Machine Readable Intelligence

Sharing intelligence reports in a structured machine readable format allows the report to be ingested into operational systems so that threat hunting can be conducted automatically, and context given to already identified threats. This ensures that the provenance of the intelligence is tracked, and the integrity of the report is maintained since there is no opportunity for a mis-keying error when copying indicators.

Tactical intelligence reports are frequently shared in machine readable formats. This allows pertinent information regarding threats to be rapidly distributed and consumed, minimising analyst time in preparing or reading the reports.

A number of formats for sharing reports have been published, including those shown in Table 5.1.

The European information security agency, ENISA, identified 53 different information sharing standards relevant to cyber threat intelligence (Kaiafas 2017). Specific standards are useful for expressing specific information in a format well suited to the task, such as Malware Attribute Enumeration and Characterization (MAEC) for describing malware (The MITRE Corporation 2020), or Vocabulary for Event Recording and Incident Sharing (VERIS) for recording incidents (VERIS 2022). However, not only must you be able to express the information that you wish to include in an intelligence report in a machine readable format, but everyone to whom you distribute the report must possess software to be able to parse and make use of the report.

As with all intelligence reports, understand the needs of the consumer and the machine readable formats of intelligence that they are able to access. An important and timely intelligence brief delivered in an unreadable format will be of little use.

Table 5.1 Types of machine readable cyber threat intelligence formats.

Name	Description	Reference
Structured Threat Information eXpression (STIX)	JavaScript Object Notation (JSON)-based format for expressing cyber threat intelligence.	Barnum (2014), OASIS (2022a)
Trusted Automated eXchange of Indicator Information (TAXII)	A HTTP/HTTPS framework for sharing intelligence in STIX (or other) format.	Connolly et al. (2012), OASIS (2022b)
MISP Standards	A family of standards describing JSON files used for sharing intelligence.	MISP (2022)
Incident Object Description Exchange Format (IODEF)	An XML format for exchanging information relating to threats.	Danyliw (2016), Kampanakis and Suzuki (2017)

5.7 Measuring the Effectiveness of Generated Intelligence

Metrics for intelligence are discussed in Chapter 3. For reports that have been created internally, we wish to demonstrate that generating intelligence is a good use of resources, and has advanced the security posture. If the intelligence has been shared, then we wish to show how sharing has advanced the security posture of the wider community, and the benefits that this has brought to the organisation. This may be in the form of new intelligence reports that have been supplied by third parties as part of an intelligence sharing partnership, or simply an increase in esteem and recognition of the prowess of the security function.

Nevertheless, going to the trouble of generating intelligence reports is likely to add to the understanding of threats within the organisation and will create a library of reports and recommendations against which the incremental progress of the security function can be measured. Therefore, the number of security improvements that were made due to the findings of a threat intelligence report would be a suitable metric to demonstrate the utility of the activity.

Sharing intelligence in turn begets sharing. If the threat intelligence team is producing intelligence to share, with how many organisations is this intelligence being shared? What is the feedback from these organisations? Is the intelligence produced useful within their respective cyber security functions? From these organisations, how many intelligence reports were shared back? Was this intelligence useful?

Ultimately, we wish to know if generating and sharing intelligence is a helpful and useful activity that is contributing to the security posture of the organisation, and which is meeting requirements. We should approach these questions with the same analytical rigour as we approach any analysis. The hypothesis that resources may be better utilised elsewhere, for example to the prompt installation of patches, should not be rejected out of hand, but investigated and decided upon based on justifiable data and facts.

Summary

Telemetry and internal data are a rich source of information, which can be transformed into intelligence. In practice, the intelligence cycle is only one of many different frameworks by which intelligence can be generated.

Identifying and investigating anomalous signals or hunting threats within data sources can uncover evidence of attacks. However, there may be other reasons for the existence of these traces, all hypotheses should be carefully considered. We must also consider the format of the intelligence we supply, and any restrictions that we might need to place on our reports.

References

Bacastow, T. (2020). *Structured Geospatial Analytic Method (SGAM) in Geog 885*. Advanced Analytic Methods in Geospacial Intelligence. https://www.e-education. psu.edu/geog885/l3_p3.html (accessed 13 January 2023).

Barnum, S. (2014). *Standardizing Cyber Threat Intelligence Information with the Structured Threat Information eXpression (STIX™)*. The Mitre Corporation. http://stixproject.github.io/about/STIX_Whitepaper_v1.1.pdf (accessed 6 March 2023).

Carroll, R.T. (2016). *Apophenia*. The Skeptics Dictionary. http://skepdic.com/ apophenia.html (accessed 13 January 2023).

Connolly, J., Davidson, M., Richard, M., and Skorupka, C. (2012). *The Trusted Automated eXchange of Indicator Information (TAXII™)*. The Mitre Corporation. https://www.mitre.org/sites/default/files/publications/taxii.pdf (accessed 28 March 2023).

Danyliw, R. (2016). *The Incident Object Description Exchange Format Version 2. RFC 7970*. Internet Engineering Task Force (IETF). https://datatracker.ietf.org/doc/ html/rfc7970 (accessed 13 January 2023).

Daszczyszak, R., Ellis, D., Luke, S., and Whitley, S. (2019). *TTP-Based Hunting*. MITRE Corporation. https://www.mitre.org/sites/default/files/publications/ pr-19-3892-ttp-based-hunting.pdf (accessed 28 March 2023).

Dhami, M.K., Belton, I.K., and Mandel, D.R. (2019). The 'analysis of competing hypotheses' in intelligence analysis. *Applied Cognitive Psychology* 33 (6): 1080–1090. https://doi.org/10.1002/acp.3550.

Digital Data & Technology. Cyber Security Programme (2019). *Detecting the Unknown: A Guide to Threat Hunting. v.2.0.* https://hodigital.blog.gov.uk/wp-content/uploads/sites/161/2020/03/Detecting-the-Unknown-A-Guide-to-Threat-Hunting-v2.0.pdf (accessed 13 January 2023).

Eldardiry, H., Sricharan, K., Liu, J. et al. (2014). Multi-source fusion for anomaly detection: using across-domain and across-time peer-group consistency checks. *International Journal of Wireless Mobile Networks, Ubiquitous Computing and Dependable Applications* 5 (2): 39–58.

Faint, C. and Harris, M. (2012). F3EAD: OPS/intel fusion 'feeds' the SOF targeting process. *Small Wars Journal* 31 (7). https://smallwarsjournal.com/jrnl/art/f3ead-opsintel-fusion-"feeds"-the-sof-targeting-process (accessed 28 March 2023).

FIRST, Cyber Threat Intelligence SIG (2021). *Cyber Threat Intelligence SIG, Methods and Methodology.* Forum of Incident Response and Security Teams. https://www.first.org/global/sigs/cti/curriculum/methods-methodology (accessed 13 January 2023).

Foreign Commonwealth & Development Office (2021). *Cyber Threat Intelligence Information Sharing Guide.* https://www.gov.uk/government/publications/cyber-threat-intelligence-information-sharing/cyber-threat-intelligence-information-sharing-guide (accessed 13 January 2023).

George, A. (1980). *Presidential Decision Making in Foreign Policy: The Effective Use of Information and Advice.* Routledge.

Gomez, J.A. (2011). The Targeting Process: D3A and F3EAD. *Small War Journal.* https://apps.dtic.mil/sti/pdfs/ADA547092.pdf (accessed 13 January 2023).

Hatton, S. (2008). Choosing the right prioritisation method. *19th Australian Conference on Software Engineering*, 517–526. IEEE.

Heuer, R.J. Jr. (1999a). Analysis of competing hypotheses. In: *Psychology of Intelligence Analysis*, Chapter 8, 95–110. https://www.e-education.psu.edu/geog885/sites/www.e-education.psu.edu.geog885/files/geog885q/file/Lesson_08/PsychofIntelNew.pdf (accessed 28 March 2023).

Heuer, R.J. Jr. (1999b). Strategies for analytical judgment: transcending the limits of incomplete information. In: *Psychology of Intelligence Analysis*, Chapter 4, 31–50. https://www.e-education.psu.edu/geog885/sites/www.e-education.psu.edu.geog885/files/geog885q/file/Lesson_08/PsychofIntelNew.pdf (accessed 28 March 2023).

Joint Warfighting Center, Joint Training Division (2011). *Insights & Best Practices: Intelligence Operations at the Operational Level.* US Joint Forces Command. https://nllp.jallc.nato.int/iks/sharing%20public/intel.pdf (accessed 13 January 2023).

Kaiafas, G. (ed.) (2017). *Proactive Risk Management through Improved Cyber Situational Awareness: D5.1 Threat Intelligence Sharing: State of the Art and Requirements.* https://ec.europa.eu/research/participants/documents/downloadPublic?documentIds=080166e5b2a13ee7&appId=PPGMS (accessed 13 January 2023).

Kampanakis, P. and Suzuki, M. (2017). *Incident Object Description Exchange Format Usage Guidance. RFC 8274.* Internet Engineering Task Force (IETF). https://datatracker.ietf.org/doc/html/rfc8274 (accessed 13 January 2023).

MISP Published Standards (2022). https://www.misp-standard.org/standards (accessed 13 January 2023).

NATO, Allied Joint Publication (2021). *NATO Standard AJP-3.9. Allied Joint Doctrine for Joint Targeting.* NATO Standardization Office. https://nso.nato.int/nso/nsdd/main/standards (accessed 28 March 2023).

OASIS Cyber Threat Intelligence (2022a). *Introduction to STIX.* https://oasis-open.github.io/cti-documentation/stix/intro (accessed 13 January 2023).

OASIS Cyber Threat Intelligence (2022b). *Introduction to TAXII.* https://oasis-open.github.io/cti-documentation/taxii/intro (accessed 13 January 2023).

Office of the Director of National Intelligence (2018). *A White Paper on the Key Challenges in Cyber Threat Intelligence: Explaining the 'See it, Sense it, Share it, Use it' Approach to Thinking about Cyber Intelligence.* https://www.hsdl.org/?abstract&did=819359 (accessed 13 January 2023).

Olsson, U. (2005). Confidence intervals for the mean of a log-normal distribution. *Journal of Statistics Education* 13 (1). https://doi.org/10.1080/10691898.2005.11910638.

Pirolli, P. and Card, S.K. (2005). The sensemaking process and leverage points for analyst technology as identified through cognitive task analysis. *Proceedings of International Conference on Intelligence Analysis.* https://www.e-education.psu.edu/geog885/sites/www.e-education.psu.edu.geog885/files/geog885q/file/Lesson_02/Sense_Making_206_Camera_Ready_Paper.pdf (accessed 28 March 2023).

Sqrrl (2016). *A Framework for Cyber Threat Hunting.* https://www.threathunting.net/files/framework-for-threat-hunting-whitepaper.pdf (accessed 13 January 2023).

The MITRE Corporation (2020). *Malware Attribute Enumeration and Characterization (MAEC™).* https://maecproject.github.io/about-maec (accessed 13 January 2023).

VERIS Community (2022). VERIS: the vocabulary for event recording and incident sharing. http://veriscommunity.net/index.html (accessed 13 January 2023).

Wikimedia Commons contributors, File:Sgam.png (2022). Wikimedia commons, the free media repository. https://commons.wikimedia.org/w/index.php?title=File:Sgam.png&oldid=497984215 (accessed 13 January 2023).

Wikipedia (2022). *68–95–99.7 rule.* https://en.wikipedia.org/wiki/68%E2%80%9395%E2%80%9399.7_rule (accessed 13 January 2023).

6

Attribution

Attribution is the art and science of linking a cyber incident to a specific threat actor. At the scene of every crime, perpetrators leave behind evidence that can be used to prove their association with the crime. In this respect, cyber security is no different from physical crime.

Instead of searching for DNA evidence or fingerprints at the scene of the crime, we must search for the similarities between attacks, especially the repeated use of specific tools or infrastructure, to link known threat actors with their crimes. Used effectively, attribution can be a powerful deterrent to threat actors, and help uncover patterns that can be used to detect and predict subsequent attacks.

Chapter 6 presents why attribution is important, and the points to consider when attributing an attack.

6.1 Holding Perpetrators to Account

Norms of behaviour are maintained within our societies via systems of rewards and punishments. Rewards range from informal words of praise, through recognition of esteem and status, to formal awards of honours or medals. Punishments range from words of admonishment, restitution to victims, through to prolonged loss of liberty or even forfeiture of life.

The cyber domain is no different. National and international laws apply to actions conducted in cyberspace, in addition to recognised norms of behaviour, that regulate and control the actions of participants. Anyone transgressing these rules should expect appropriate sanctions.

In practice, the nature of the Internet and the cyber domain provides opportunities for transgressors to hide their identity and frustrate responses to hold them to account. Worse, a perpetrator may reside in a jurisdiction where their malicious actions are tolerated or even encouraged.

Cyber Threat Intelligence, First Edition. Martin Lee.
© 2023 John Wiley & Sons, Inc. Published 2023 by John Wiley & Sons, Inc.

6.1.1 Punishment

Justifications for punishment are based on the concepts of retribution and the utilitarian principles of incapacitation, deterrence, rehabilitation, and restoration (Carlsmith 2006).

The principle of retribution is that wrongdoing merits sanctioning, and that the sanctions should be in proportion to the transgression. This is the basis of the Judeo-Christian tradition of an 'eye for an eye', that an offender should receive their just desserts for their offences (Miethe and Lu 2004).

The utility principle is based on the concept that punishment is able to limit future transgressions. Punishment deters the transgressor, and others from future offending. Incapacitating the transgressor by removing them from society through incarceration, or restricting access to the tools or locations necessary for them to offend, prevents the offender from committing further crimes.

Punishment also offers a chance of rehabilitation where the offender may reflect on their behaviour, or be actively reformed so that they can change their ways and participate in society. Restorative punishment seeks to put right the wrongs caused by the transgression. The offender must provide some form of restitution to seek to restore the effects of their transgression.

Denunciation combines both utilitarian and retribution theories. Being recognised as a transgressor is a punishment in itself and allows for society to cast judgement on the offender. Additionally, the consequences of denunciation exert a deterrent effect on potential offenders who wish to avoid public identification (Wringe 2017).

Hence, punishment of cyber crime offenders can satisfy a desire for justice to be performed, prevent further crimes being committed, provide restitution for victims, and act to deter future crimes.

6.1.2 Legal Frameworks

Before transgressions can be identified, we must have codes of conduct against which behaviour can be measured to locate actions that step outside of acceptable conduct. Many cyber crimes are cyber-enabled, that is to say that they are crimes that can be committed with or without the assistance of computer systems. These crimes including fraud, harassment, etc., and are typically already illegal and covered by existing legislation.

Other crimes are cyber-dependent. That is to say that networked computer systems are a prerequisite for the crime to take place. These crimes include activities such as denial of service attacks or unauthorised computer access (McGuire and Dowling 2013).

As technology progresses and creates unforeseen side effects such as cyber-dependent crime, so society and legislation must keep pace; however, these will necessarily lag behind the conduct of new forms of criminal behaviour. Attempting to prosecute cyber-dependent crimes using pre-computer era laws risked cases foundering due to the inapplicability of legislation to these new crimes (Smith et al. 2004a).

6.1.3 Cyber Crime Legislation

With the advent of computer crime, new laws were required to regulate anti-social behaviour. However, the implementation and wording of laws differs between jurisdictions. One of the peculiarities of cyber crime is that the victim and perpetrator of a crime may be in completely different jurisdictions with different considerations of what constitutes cyber crime.

One example of these discrepancies was the identification of the suspect believed to be responsible for writing the 'ILOVEYOU' email worm. The worm spread widely in May 2000. Users were fooled by the social engineering of receiving a message from an unknown admirer and opened the 'love letter' malicious email. On opening the email attachment, malicious Visual Basic script sent a copy of itself to every entry in the local Windows Address Book (Sharma 2011). The number of messages sent brought down many email servers and is estimated to have resulted in costs of up to $10 billion (Winder 2020).

The individual suspected of being responsible for the worm was identified in the Philippines. Nevertheless, the relevant Philippine law only applied where there were fraudulent purposes, which didn't apply to this case. Therefore, as far as the Philippine law was concerned, no crime had been committed (Smith et al. 2004b).

International efforts to harmonise laws relating to computer systems and data processing date to the mid-1980s with the adoption of Council of Europe's (COE) Convention for the Protection of Privacy of Individuals with regard to Automatic Processing of Personal Data in 1985 (COE 1981). This convention recognised the increasing transnational flow of personal data and the necessity of protecting the privacy of that data.

Shortly afterwards in 1986, the Organisation for Economic Co-operation and Development (OECD) published the report *Computer-Related Crime: Analysis of Legal Policy* outlining a 'minimum list' of computer crimes that should be proscribed internationally (OECD 1986).

Ultimately, these activities led to the adoption of the COE's Convention on Cybercrime from November 2001 (COE 2001a). Signed by over 65 nation states including many non-COE members, this is the first multilateral legally binding treaty to address cyber crime. Importantly, the treaty not only outlaws specific activities, but also requires signatories to implement investigative procedures and partake in international cooperation with regard to investigating crimes (Smith et al. 2004c).

6.1.4   International Law

In parallel to work on harmonising criminal law between jurisdictions, research continued on the applicability of international law to cyber operations in the context of armed conflict between nation states and to the conduct of cyber operations during peacetime. These findings regarding how existing international laws apply to cyber security were published by the NATO Cooperative Cyber Defence Centre of Excellence as the Tallinn Manual (Schmitt 2013, 2017).

This publication clarified that the physical and logical infrastructure that contribute to the cyberspace domain located within a nation state are sovereign to that nation state. This means that the nation state is able to regulate its own sovereign cyberspace domain, conduct cyber operations within its own cyberspace domain, but not conduct operations that infringe on the sovereign cyberspace of another nation.

Operations that infringe on a nation's cyberspace include any actions that cause physical damage, the loss of functionality that infringes on the ability of the state to exercise governmental functions, or that infringes on the sovereignty of the state itself.

6.1.5   Crime and Punishment

Together these conventions and clarifications of international law provide a widely accepted international legal framework by which actions that interfere with computer systems, and the data that they process, are forbidden. This framework also offers a mechanism through which offences against these laws can be prosecuted and transgressors punished.

Even if legal prosecution and punishments are not possible, we are still able to sanction offenders through denunciation. This in itself can act as an effective punishment.

Table 6.1 contains a summary of offences against the confidentiality, integrity and availability of computer data and systems as defined by the COE Convention on Cybercrime.

6.2   Standards of Proof

The aim of cyber threat intelligence is to gather and analyse information in order to support decision making. This is distinct from the role of the digital forensic investigator who must secure and analyse evidence to a standard that is acceptable in a court of law.

There is much overlap between the two approaches, including the desire to gain understanding from data, however there are some major differences. Intelligence is concerned with the present and future, what is happening now and what is

Table 6.1 Offences defined by the COE convention on cybercrime.

Offence	Explication
Illegal access	The unauthorised intrusion into computer systems, or unauthorised access to data. This excludes access 'with right' such as access by the system owner, or access to a public open access system such as a web server.
Illegal interception	The unauthorised intentional interception of non-public data.
Data interference	The unauthorised intentional interference in the proper functioning of computer programs and data. This covers anything that damages processing or deletes data including malicious code, but does not include the installation or configuration of software by the owner or operator of the system.
System interference	The intentional hindering of operation of computer systems such by denial of service attacks or malware that substantially slows the operation of the system.
Misuse of devices	The commission of illegal acts against systems and data. Additionally covers the distribution of tools designed to facilitate illegal acts against systems. Although tools for the authorised legitimate testing of systems are not covered.

Source: Adapted from COE (2001b).

likely to happen. Forensics is solely concerned with the past and what has happened. Both disciplines seek to be objective and correct in their analyses, but to be useful intelligence must be 'timely'. Forensic analysis does not share the 'shelf-life' time constraints of intelligence reports. A thorough forensic analysis is likely to remain as useful as the day it was written many years into the future.

6.2.1 Forensic Evidence

The UK Association of Chief Police Officers set out four principles to govern the handling of digital forensic evidence:

Principle 1: No action taken by law enforcement agencies, persons employed within those agencies, or their agents should change data, which may subsequently be relied upon in court.

Principle 2: In circumstances where a person finds it necessary to access original data, that person must be competent to do so and be able to give evidence explaining the relevance and the implications of their actions.

Principle 3: An audit trail or other record of all processes applied to digital evidence should be created and preserved. An independent third party should be able to examine those processes and achieve the same result.

Principle 4: The person in charge of the investigation has overall responsibility for ensuring that the law and these principles are adhered to.

(ACPO 2012)

These principles and other best practices form the basis of ISO/IEC 27037, the international standard describing the collection, acquisition, and preservation of digital evidence (ISO 2012). The forensic practitioner must establish the chain of custody for the digital evidence documenting the source of the evidence, how it has been obtained, and the steps taken to analyse the data.

Ultimately, forensic analysis is seeking to come to a decision regarding what has happened to a legal standard of proof based on the evidence of a case. Although forensic information regarding attacks is of great use to threat intelligence analysts, lengthy custody of evidence procedures are not.

Threat intelligence analysts are typically not seeking to present evidence at a court of law, but to compile a report that is 'good enough' to satisfy requirements and that can be delivered as soon as possible. Additionally, threat intelligence reports expect and embrace doubt and uncertainty without trying to remove these.

Intelligence is not evidence. Intelligence is not produced to meet a legal standard of evidence, nor to convict, but with the purpose of supporting decision making. The production of intelligence must manage the uncertainty of potentially unreliable, incomplete, conflicting information, and convey this uncertainty while providing useful conclusions; see Section 4.2.2 on Expressing Confidence in Chapter 4.

Intelligence analysts should be able to not only present likely outcomes with a high degree of confidence, but also unlikely outcomes with high confidence, and those outcomes that are likely but with a low degree of confidence.

6.3 Mechanisms of Attribution

The goal of attribution within cyber threat intelligence is to associate an attack (or event) with a wider pattern of activity, which in turn is associated with a specific threat actor.

Occasionally this task is facilitated when threat actors attribute their own attacks to themselves. The hacktivist group LulzSec openly and publicly claimed the credit for hacking a variety of organisations, stealing information, and conducting denial of service attacks (Pendergrass 2012). Their high profile campaign of activity ultimately came to an end with the arrest of many members of the group (Arthur 2013).

Threat actors may indirectly attribute an attack to themselves through the reuse of personal identifiers such as usernames or emails. These identifiers may be used as part of an attack or in the procurement of resources for the attack, but can also be used in other contexts such as on social media or online forums.

Threat actors with poor awareness of operational security can reuse nicknames or social media handles in personal and malicious contexts and consequently divulge information that can be used for identification. Similarly, nicknames or handles with minor modifications such as additional characters or incremented numbers can be used to link malicious and non-malicious activities to an individual.

Nevertheless, even with what appears to be a clear purposeful or accidental admission of an attack by a threat actor, there is always a possibility that this information has been planted as a 'false flag' in order to disguise the true identity of the perpetrator. Threat intelligence analysts should always look at the wider context of an attack and consider if it is consistent with previous activity and whether it is consistent with the presumed goals of the threat actor. If this is not the case, the analyst should seek to understand why this is so while remaining mindful of the possibility that a third party is seeking to provide evidence that frames an innocent party.

6.3.1   Attack Attributes

Every attack is unique. The set of features that describe the attack, the systems that were compromised, the techniques used by the attacker, the time of day of the attack, etc., are specific to that particular attack. Although these attack attributes are unique, each piece of information tells us something about the threat actor.

Together these pieces of information help form a profile of the threat actor. Very rarely does a single attribute uniquely identify a threat actor, but they can be used as the basis for building hypotheses regarding which threat actor was responsible for an attack. Or, at the very least, suggesting which threat actors were unlikely to have been responsible.

6.3.1.1   Attacker TTPs

We are all creatures of habit. We tend to reuse the skills and tools with which we are familiar. Developing new tools, or becoming proficient in new skills takes time, resources, and effort, which we are loath to do.

Threat actors are no different. Behind every attack is an individual with goals to achieve and a set of skills and tools with which to conduct their business. Although their skill set and repertoire of tools at their disposal may evolve over time, threat actors will mostly seek to achieve their aims by using the same skills and tools that they have used before.

The habits, familiarities, and resistance to change of the threat actors are to the advantage of the threat intelligence analyst, since these patterns of activity allow us to characterise threat actor groups.

The tactics, techniques, and procedures used in an attack are also known as the attacker's tradecraft. Those observed in an attack can be compared with the profiles of known threat actors to form hypotheses regarding who might or might not be responsible for an attack (ODNI 2018). This is discussed in greater detail in Chapter 2.

Bespoke tools such as exploit code, and the vulnerabilities that the attacker chooses to exploit are very much part of the threat actor's tradecraft. Some threat actors use specific remote access trojans (RATs) to provide long term access to compromised systems. Finding one of these RATs used in an attack provides strong evidence indicating the identity of the threat actor.

Similarly, research into vulnerabilities and the development of exploit code is resource intensive, the exploitation of a specific vulnerability or the code used in the exploitation may also provide strong clues as to the threat actor.

6.3.1.2   Example – HAFNIUM

In March 2021, a previously unknown threat actor name HAFNIUM was identified as exploiting zero-day vulnerabilities in on-premise Exchange servers (MSTIC 2021). At the time of discovery, the pattern of activity indicated that the attacks were being perpetuated by a single threat actor. However, there was little or no overlap with other known threat actor groups. Therefore, the activity was attributed to a new, previously unknown threat actor given the name HAFNIUM.

Further analysis showed that the threat actor was installing a particular RAT named China Chopper on compromised systems (White 2021). This RAT was first identified in 2013, and is known to be used by a small group of threat actors (MITRE 2017a). Hence, we have a strong indication that the HAFNIUM threat actor has associations with this family of threat actors. Potentially, HAFNIUM is one of the existing threat actors known to use China Chopper, or a new group that shares tooling with these existing threat actors.

6.3.1.3   Attacker Infrastructure

As described in the Diamond Model, the attacker exposes not only their capabilities but also part of their infrastructure when they conduct attacks. Attacks that originate from the same IP address or that share command and control could be assumed to be related to the same threat actor if the attacks were happening at the same time.

Not all Internet Service Providers (ISPs) are equal. Some may be very diligent in identifying and removing customers who indulge in malicious activity. Others actively market their services to threat actors by providing bulletproof hosting, i.e. offering network infrastructure while ignoring take-down requests for hosting malicious activity (Konte et al. 2015).

Some attackers prefer to abuse legitimate services such as online code repositories to host malware or command and control facilities (Kovacs 2017; Trend Micro 2017). Or they might also hide their actual IP address behind the services of a Content Delivery Network (Raghuprasad et al. 2021).

The distributed nature of the Internet and the ease with which services can be procured means that threat actors are not limited to service providers within their country of residence. Nevertheless, the choices made in the provision of infrastructure and how it is deployed tells us something about the threat actor's preferences, and how these differ from other threat actors.

6.3.1.4 Victimology

The final step in the kill chain is 'action on objectives', where the attacker completes their objectives for the attack. These objectives may be abrupt such as the execution of ransomware or the exfiltration of data, where there is a clear moment where the objective is complete. Or the attacker may be conducting a long term attack where the objective is open-ended, such as achieving persistent access to a system, potentially to conduct future attacks, or to install crypto-mining malware destined to steal Central Processing Unit (CPU) cycles over a long period of time.

Occasionally, the objectives of the attacker appear unclear. Potentially, attackers may choose not to conclude an attack, possibly because they feared that they were discovered, or the goal of the attack was simply to demonstrate prowess to an unknown third party. Furthermore, the actual objectives of the attack may have been disguised and obscured by the execution of ransomware or wiper malware.

In any case, the nature of the victim and how they were selected by the threat actor as well as what we observe as the final steps of the attack tells us something about the attacker's motivations and capabilities. Patterns may not be discernible from single attacks, but over time clear patterns in the selection of victims may become apparent.

The attacker may select their victims according to geopolitical ambitions, or carefully select victims due to the vertical industry sector in which they operate (Chon and Clover 2015). It is even possible to identify patterns in the job roles targeted by threat actors within organisations (Le Borgne 2019).

6.3.1.5 Malicious Code

Not every cyber attack uses malicious code or tools. Many financial scams rely on nothing more complex than using email or a messaging application to request the victim to make a bank transfer to send money to the attacker. However, numerous attacks do rely on some form of tooling to initiate the attack, to establish and maintain a presence on affected devices, or to keep track and manage successful attacks.

Threat actors can choose to abuse legitimate software, putting it to uses never envisaged by the creator, use dual-use tools that can be put to legitimate or illegitimate use, use malicious tools used by a variety of threat actors, or develop their own bespoke malicious tools.

From the attacker's perspective whatever tools they use must be effective and represent good use of the attacker's resources. Each approach has relative advantages and disadvantages. Abusing legitimate tools and services may lead to the attacker being locked out by the provider and no longer able to use the tool.

Dual-use tools may not have the exact functionality desired, however, they may not be detected as malicious by defenders. Bespoke tools may fulfil requirements, but once detected can be blocklisted across the entire industry, rendering them unable to be used again.

The selection of a tool represents an investment by the attacker in terms of familiarity and training. Changing tooling is disruptive, and initially likely to be less efficient as the team becomes used to the new tool. Hence, attackers tend to stick with tried and tested tooling, and this choice becomes a characteristic by which we can distinguish threat actors.

No matter how esoteric, writing malware is a form of software engineering. Software development is difficult to get right, and represents a significant use of resources for the attacker. Although the software development process of the threat actors is often hidden from us, we can expect that they are applying industry best practices for which we may find evidence.

One such best practice is to outsource development. Threat actors are observed to abuse commercially available red team penetration testing tools. Such software is professionally developed to a high standard and readily available. Despite malicious use being against the terms and conditions of the software, the attacker can be assured of acquiring a high quality, functional tool set.

Similarly, open-source community developed software projects are also used. Although software quality may vary between projects, multiple engineers can collaborate on a project. This community involvement potentially permits malicious developers to contribute to otherwise legitimate projects for their own ends.

Alternatively, threat actors may develop their malicious code in-house using their own code base and engineering techniques. Occasionally, threat actors may choose to publish the source code of their malicious tools (Rokon et al. 2020). In encouraging others to use their tools, or reuse the code in other malicious software it becomes more difficult to tie the malicious software to any single group (Hutchings and Clayton 2017).

Identifying that a particular tool has been used in an attack allows threat intelligence teams to narrow attribution. Certain RAT, used to maintain access and execute commands on compromised systems, are unique to specific groups, or only used within a small set of threat actors. For example, MarkiRAT is used by the Ferocious Kitten threat actor group to target Persian speakers in Iran (Global Research & Analysis Team, Kaspersky Lab 2021); ViperRAT is used by an as yet unidentified threat actor group against the Israeli defence forces (Palmer 2017); whereas PoisonIvy is widely used by a number of threat actors (MITRE 2017b).

An attack that involves a malicious tool that has not been observed elsewhere can still betray information about the nature of the attacker. Reusing software components and libraries is a common technique of software engineering. Although the majority of the code base of a bespoke malicious tool may be unique, commonalities may be identified with other tools. This may be evidence of a shared code base used by a group of threat actors to develop tools.

For example, a number of suspected Chinese threat actors have shared similarities in their tools, pointing to the existence of a hypothetical quartermaster providing software development resources and infrastructure to the groups (FireEye 2014). Occasionally, errors in the code base point to a common origin. The BlackEnergy 2 trojan possessed a unique implementation of the RC4 cypher that differed from the accepted standard (Stewart 2010). This same implementation technique was reused in the later VPNFilter malware (Shevchenko 2018). On its own, this is not proof that the two malware originated from the same code base, anyone could have implemented the cypher using the incorrect published technique, but it is an indication to be considered with the ensemble of evidence.

6.3.2 Asserting Attribution

After defining the various attributes of an attack, and considering which of these are informative, the threat analyst can compare these with the tradecraft of known threat actors. In some cases, there will be little or no overlap between the attributes of the attack under scrutiny and the attributes of attacks conducted by particular threat actors.

In these circumstances, in the absence of further information, the threat intelligence analyst may determine with high confidence that the threat actor was not responsible for an attack. In cases where there is a strong overlap between the features of an attack and those previously encountered in attacks conducted by a specific threat actor, the analyst may conclude that the threat actor is responsible.

Often there will not be a clear match for a threat actor. The analyst should consider the strengths and weaknesses of the various options as to the identity of the threat actor. An alert analyst may identify that although many features of the attack tend to point to a particular threat actor, some key features of that actor are absent. This may be an indication that the key feature may be present, but not yet identified, or that the conclusion is incorrect.

Analysts must consider all the evidence, and their level of certainty and confidence in reaching their conclusion. Clearly stating the evidence that led to their conclusion, and reasons for doubt helps additional analysts refine the conclusion if further evidence becomes available, or will help with their own analysis.

6.4   Anti-Attribution Techniques

It would be naive to expect that threat actors are unaware of the techniques used for attribution. Awareness of how attribution is achieved allows threat actors to frustrate these techniques to disguise their identity.

6.4.1   Infrastructure

Threat actors may choose to use a service provider that has been known to be associated with other threat actors. Analysts may identify that another threat actor has used the same IP address or IP range and come to an incorrect conclusion regarding the attribution of subsequent attacks.

Alternatively, threat actors may choose to abuse the services of the most commonly used service providers in the knowledge that many threat actors are using the same services. In such cases, the use of the particular service is no longer a distinguishing feature between threat actors, but a common feature of many actors.

6.4.2   Malicious Tools

I've already discussed the possibilities of dual-use tools, and open-source projects for frustrating or mis-directing attributions, but there are other techniques available as well.

Threat actors can plant false flags within their code in order to frustrate attribution. The Olympic Destroyer malware that caused disruption during the opening of the 2018 Winter Olympic Games contained features within the code, which were characteristic of four different threat actors from three different countries (Rascagneres and Lee 2018).

Within the malware the threat actor included references to a file naming system and included wiper functionality that were both similar to those used by the Lazarus Group threat actor. A code similarity with APT3, and a function only previously used by APT10 were present. And code artefacts similar to those found in NotPetya attributed to APT28 were also present (Burgess 2018). Ultimately, the attack was attributed by the British and US authorities to the Sandworm Team threat actor believed to be associated with Russian military intelligence (Raab 2020; USDOJ 2020).

Threat actors may use obfuscation techniques or polymorphic engines to change the nature of the malware. Obfuscating variable names, introducing code, which is never executed, or that has no effect on execution, encoding routines as data to be executed following decoding are all techniques used to hide the effects of the malware and actor behind it (Szor and Ferrie 2001).

Conversely, the techniques used to frustrate attribution themselves can become an indication of the threat actor. Simply using such techniques becomes part of the evidence associated with an attack that an analyst must consider.

6.4.3 False Attribution

If attribution attacks help defenders in uncovering more information regarding the nature, goals, and TTPs of a threat actor, then false attribution can only help attackers.

Demonstrably incorrect attack attributions reduce confidence in correct attributions. Threat actors can cast doubt on attributions by pointing out how a similar attribution has been incorrect in the past, thus confusing analysis and helping to escape being held responsible for their actions.

Incorrect attribution adds incorrect data to the corpus of attacks believed to have been carried out by a threat actor, polluting and confusing correct data, and potentially leading to further incorrect attributions.

6.4.4 Chains of Attribution

Our ability to attribute attacks is built upon years of research into the threat actor groups. Analysts have built up information regarding the infrastructure, capabilities, and objectives of threat actor groups. Each new data point relating to a group adds to our understanding and better allows the identification of further attacks and their attribution.

However, within these datasets, we must be aware that there may have been incorrectly attributed attacks that have tainted the data. Analysts should be mindful of the actual reliability of the data upon which they make their assertions. Equally, we should be careful not to pollute these chains with weak or incorrectly attributed information. Attribution is not an easy task.

6.5 Third Party Attribution

The role of the cyber threat intelligence analyst within the private sector is distinct from that of an investigator working within law enforcement or an analyst working within a national intelligence agency. The public sector has investigatory capabilities and access to information that are unavailable to the private sector.

Occasionally, these capabilities come to light. In 2014, the Dutch intelligence services reportedly compromised the systems of the Russian intelligence group known as 'Cozy Bear' or APT29. The system penetration included the security camera giving the Dutch intelligence services visual confirmation of the members of the Russian group as they arrived or left from work, as well as their computer systems (van Rosenthal 2018).

This incursion allowed the Dutch intelligence services to identify that the group was responsible for the compromise of the Democratic National Congress and the release of stolen documents as part of a campaign of interference in the 2016 US presidential election (Nakashima and Harris 2018; Crowdstrike 2020; Select Committee on Intelligence, US Senate 2020).

When a national agency makes a public statement of attribution, it is staking both its own, and its country's, reputation on the line. Although the corroborating evidence that has led to the attribution may not be made public and open to scrutiny, it is highly unlikely that the publication has been made on a whim. Nevertheless, such statements are necessarily shaped within the context of the country's own internal and foreign politics. It should be remembered that public denunciation is a tool of political policy (Egloff 2020).

Organisations that choose to make public their conclusion's attribution should be applauded for contributing to the rich mix of intelligence information and sharing their expertise. As with all sources of intelligence, the analyst must carefully evaluate the reliability of the source and come to their own conclusion in the context of the broader set of information available.

6.6 Using Attribution

Cyber attacks do not happen by accident. Behind every cyber attack is a perpetrator, a threat actor who has carried out the attack for a reason. However, the complex nature of the Internet and software characteristics combined with the ability to hide behind proxy actors, stolen credentials, or shared systems means that it is often difficult to come to a clear verdict for the guilty party.

Nevertheless, similarities to previous attacks, and especially the reuse of techniques and procedures combined with an understanding of the attacker's apparent objectives and their choice of victims, gives clear indications as to the responsible party. Threat intelligence analysts must accept and adapt to uncertainty. This is not to say that nothing can be done.

Rid and Buchanan propose the 'Q Model', where attribution is made according to tactical, technical, operational, and strategic indicators, and the outcome is communication (Rid and Buchanan 2014) (Figure 6.1).

The communications tail is an integral part of the model. Not only must the nuances and estimative probability of the attribution be communicated, but also

Figure 6.1 The Q model of attribution. *Source:* Adapted from Rid and Buchanan (2014).

the means of transforming the attribution to action. On its own, communicating attribution can be an effective tool. Threat actors may abort operations, change tactics, or be forced to publicly react to the attribution (Rid and Buchanan 2014).

Internal communication is also effective. Attribution can lead to a great situational awareness of threats, a better understanding of the strategic threat landscape, and at an operational level help understand and predict future attacks.

The characterisation and attribution sequence published by Carnegie Endowment follows these steps (Figure 6.2).

This model takes into consideration if the incident was deliberate, the motive of the actor, and the gravity of the incident. The notion of gravity is decided by these criteria:

- The adversary's aim(s) and intended effect(s).
- The actual effects of the action (which might be bigger, smaller, more localised, more widespread, more enduring, or more fleeting than the perpetrators may have intended).
- The targets engaged (such as whether critical infrastructure was attacked).
- The modalities employed in the attack.
- The extent to which the operation violated agreed-upon (or, at the very least, desired) norms and other obligations undertaken by the perpetrator.
- Whether the action represents (or is, at least, likely to become) a broader/bolder pattern of behaviour or is merely a one-off action.

(Levite and Lee 2022)

Follow-up actions are decided based on the gravity of the action, the confidence of the attribution and the various benefits and potential consequences of considered actions.

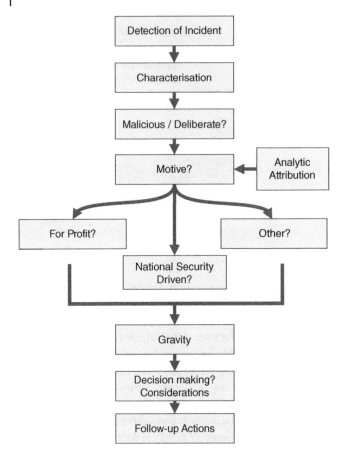

Figure 6.2 Characterisation and attribution sequence (*Source:* Adapted from Levite 2022).

Summary

Attribution is the art and science of linking malicious activity to a threat actor. This is achieved by comparing the evidence collected from an attack with that collected from previous attacks. A significant overlap in the conduct of an attack with a previous attack suggests that they might have been carried out by the same actor.

Identifying who is responsible for attacks helps in understanding the threat landscape. Holding perpetrators to account for their actions and obtaining appropriate retribution to atone for previous attacks and deter future malicious acts should be the ultimate goal of attribution. Nevertheless, attribution is often clouded in uncertainty, and public denunciation risks disclosing operation details of how attacks have been detected and characterised.

References

Arthur, C. (2013). LulzSec: what they did, who they were and how they were caught. *The Guardian* (16 May). https://www.theguardian.com/technology/2013/may/16/lulzsec-hacking-fbi-jail (accessed 13 January 2023).

Association of Chief Police Officers (2012). *ACPO Good Practice Guide for Digital Evidence, version 5.* https://www.npcc.police.uk/documents/FoI%20publication/Disclosure%20Logs/Information%20Management%20FOI/2013/031%2013%20Att%2001%20of%201%20ACPO%20Good%20Practice%20Guide%20for%20Digital%20Evidence%20March%202012.pdf (accessed 13 January 2023).

Burgess, M. (2018). The UK just blamed Russia for four major cyberattacks. That's huge. *Wired* (4 October). www.wired.co.uk/article/uk-russia-cyberattack-hack-blame (accessed 13 January 2023).

Carlsmith, K.M. (2006). The roles of retribution and utility in determining punishment. *Journal of Experimental Social Psychology* 42 (4): 437–451. https://doi.org/10.1016/j.jesp.2005.06.007.

Chon, G. and Clover, C. (2015). US spooks scour China's 5-year plan for hacking clues. *Financial Times* (25 November). https://www.ft.com/content/40dc895a-92c6-11e5-94e6-c5413829caa5 (accessed 13 January 2023).

Council of Europe (1981). Convention for the Protection of Individuals with regard to Automatic Processing of Personal Data. https://rm.coe.int/1680078b37 (accessed 13 January 2023).

Council of Europe (2001a). Convention on Cybercrime. https://www.coe.int/en/web/conventions/full-list?module=treaty-detail&treatynum=185 (accessed 13 January 2023).

Council of Europe (2001b). Explanatory report to the Convention on Cybercrime. https://rm.coe.int/16800cce5b (accessed 13 January 2023).

Crowdstrike Blog (2020). CrowdStrike's work with the Democratic National Committee: setting the record straight. *From the Front Lines* (5 June). https://www.crowdstrike.com/blog/bears-midst-intrusion-democratic-national-committee (accessed 13 January 2023).

Egloff, F.J. (2020). Public attribution of cyber intrusions. *Journal of Cybersecurity* 6 (1). https://doi.org/10.1093/cybsec/tyaa012.

FireEye (2014). Supply chain analysis: from quartermaster to SunshopFireEye. *Mandiant.* https://www.fireeye.com/content/dam/fireeye-www/global/en/current-threats/pdfs/rpt-malware-supply-chain.pdf (accessed 13 January 2023).

Global Research & Analysis Team, Kaspersky Lab (2021). Ferocious Kitten: 6 years of covert surveillance in Iran, 16 June. https://securelist.com/ferocious-kitten-6-years-of-covert-surveillance-in-iran/102806 (accessed 13 January 2023).

Hutchings, A. and Clayton, R. (2017). Configuring Zeus: a case study of online crime target selection and knowledge transmission. *2017 APWG Symposium on Electronic Crime Research (eCrime)*, 33–40. IEEE.

ISO/IEC 27037:2012 (2012). *Information Technology – Security Techniques – Guidelines for Identification, Collection, Acquisition and Preservation of Digital Evidence.* International Standards Organization. https://www.iso.org/standard/44381.html (accessed 13 January 2023).

Konte, M., Perdisci, R., and Feamster, N. (2015). ASwatch: An AS reputation system to expose bulletproof hosting ASes. *Proceedings of the 2015 ACM Conference on Special Interest Group on Data Communication*, 625–638.

Kovacs, E. (2017). Hackers can use git repos for stealthy attack on developers. *Security Week* (4 August). https://www.securityweek.com/hackers-can-use-git-repos-stealthy-attack-developers (accessed 13 January 2023).

Le Borgne, Y. (2019). Victimology: in the shoes of a cybersecurity analyst. https://www.threatq.com/victimology-cybersecurity-analyst (accessed 13 January 2023).

Levite, A. and Lee, J. (2022). *Attribution and Characterization of Cyber Attacks.* Carnegie Endowment for International Peace. https://carnegieendowment. org/2022/03/28/attribution-and-characterization-of-cyber-attacks-pub-86698 (accessed 13 January 2023).

McGuire, M. and Dowling, S. (2013). *Cyber Crime: A Review of the Evidence. Summary of Key Findings and Implications.* Home Office Research Report 75. https://assets. publishing.service.gov.uk/government/uploads/system/uploads/attachment_data/ file/246749/horr75-summary.pdf (accessed 13 January 2023).

Microsoft Threat Intelligence Center (2021). HAFNIUM targeting Exchange Servers with 0-day exploits. https://www.microsoft.com/security/blog/2021/03/02/ hafnium-targeting-exchange-servers (accessed 13 January 2023).

Miethe, T. and Lu, H. (2004). Punishment philosophies and types of sanctions. In: *Punishment: A Comparative Historical Perspective*, 15–49. Cambridge University Press. https://doi.org/10.1017/CBO9780511813801.003.

MITRE Corporation (2017a). China Chopper. https://attack.mitre.org/software/S0020 (accessed 13 January 2023).

MITRE Corporation (2017b). PoisonIvy. https://attack.mitre.org/software/S0012 (accessed 13 January 2023).

Nakashima, E. and Harris, S. (2018). How the Russians hacked the DNC and passed its emails to WikiLeaks. *The Washington Post* (13 July). https://www. washingtonpost.com/world/national-security/how-the-russians-hacked-the-dnc-and-passed-its-emails-to-wikileaks/2018/07/13/af19a828-86c3-11e8-8553-a3ce89036c78_story.html (accessed 13 January 2023).

Office of the Director of National Intelligence (2018). A guide to cyber attribution. https://www.dni.gov/files/CTIIC/documents/ODNI_A_Guide_to_Cyber_ Attribution.pdf (accessed 13 January 2023).

Organisation for Economic Co-operation and Development (1986). Computer-related crime: analysis of legal policy.

Palmer, D. (2017). Hackers are using this Android malware to spy on Israeli soldiers. *ZDNet* (17 February). https://www.zdnet.com/article/hackers-are-using-this-android-malware-to-spy-on-israeli-soldiers (accessed 13 January 2023).

Pendergrass, S. (2012). Hackers gone wild: the 2011 spring break of LulzSec. *Issues in Information Systems* 13 (1): 133–143.

Raab, D. (2020). UK exposes series of Russian cyber attacks against Olympic and Paralympic Games. UK Foreign, Commonwealth & Development Office. https://www.gov.uk/government/news/uk-exposes-series-of-russian-cyber-attacks-against-olympic-and-paralympic-games (accessed 13 January 2023).

Raghuprasad, C., Svajcer, V., and Malhotra, A. (2021). Attackers use domain fronting technique to target Myanmar with Cobalt Strike, 16 November. https://blog.talosintelligence.com/2021/11/attackers-use-domain-fronting-technique.html (accessed 7 March 2023).

Rascagneres, P. and Lee, M. (2018). Who wasn't responsible for Olympic Destroyer? *Talos Intelligence* (26 February). https://blog.talosintelligence.com/2018/02/who-wasnt-responsible-for-olympic.html (accessed 13 January 2023).

Rid, T. and Buchanan, B. (2014). Attributing cyber attacks. *Journal of Strategic Studies* 1 (2): 4–37. https://doi.org/10.1080/01402390.2014.977382.

Rokon, M.O.F., Islam, R., Darki, A. et al. (2020). Sourcefinder: finding malware source-code from publicly available repositories in github. *23rd International Symposium on Research in Attacks, Intrusions and Defenses. RAID 202*. https://www.usenix.org/system/files/raid20-rokon.pdf (accessed 13 January 2023).

van Rosenthal, E.B. (2018). Dutch intelligence first to alert U.S. about Russian hack of Democratic Party, 25 January. https://nos.nl/nieuwsuur/artikel/2213767-dutch-intelligence-first-to-alert-u-s-about-russian-hack-of-democratic-party (accessed 13 January 2023).

Schmitt, M. (2013). *Tallinn Manual on the International Law Applicable to Cyber Warfare*. Cambridge University Press. https://doi.org/10.1017/CBO9781139169288.

Schmitt, M. (2017). *Tallinn Manual on the International Law Applicable to Cyber Warfare*, 2e. Cambridge University Press. https://doi.org/10.1017/9781316822524.

Select Committee on Intelligence, United State Senate (2020). *Report of the Select Committee on Intelligence, United State Senate on Russian Active Measures Campaigns and Interference in the 2016 U.S. Election. Volume 4: Review of the Intelligence Community Assessment.* https://www.intelligence.senate.gov/sites/default/files/documents/Report_Volume4.pdf (accessed 13 January 2023).

Sharma, V. (2011). An analytical survey of recent worm attacks. *International Journal of Computer Science and Network Security* 11 (11): 99–103.

Shevchenko, S. (2018). 'VPNFilter' botnet: a SophosLabs analysis. SophosLaps. https://www.sophos.com/de-de/medialibrary/PDFs/technical-papers/sophos-VPN-Filter-analysis-v2.pdf (accessed 13 January 2023).

Smith, R., Grabosky, P., and Urbas, G. (2004a). The prosecutor as gatekeeper. In: *Cyber Criminals on Trial*, 31–47. Cambridge University Press. https://doi.org/10.1017/CBO9780511481604.005.

Smith, R., Grabosky, P., and Urbas, G. (2004b). Cross-border issues. In: *Cyber Criminals on Trial*, 48–60. Cambridge University Press.

Smith, R., Grabosky, P., and Urbas, G. (2004c). The quest for harmonisation of cyber crime laws. In: *Cyber Criminals on Trial*, 86–105. Cambridge University Press. https://doi.org/10.1017/CBO9780511481604.008.

Stewart, J. (2010). *BlackEnergy Version 2 Threat Analysis*. Secureworks Threat Intelligence Research. https://www.secureworks.com/research/blackenergy2 (accessed 13 January 2023).

Szor, P. and Ferrie, P. (2001). Hunting for metamorphic. *Virus Bulletin Conference*.

Trend Micro (2017). Winnti abuses GitHub for C&C communications. https://www.trendmicro.com/en_us/research/17/c/winnti-abuses-github.html (accessed 13 January 2023).

US Department of Justice, Office of Public Affairs (2020). Six Russian GRU officers charged in connection with worldwide deployment of destructive malware and other disruptive actions in cyberspace. https://www.justice.gov/opa/pr/six-russian-gru-officers-charged-connection-worldwide-deployment-destructive-malware-and (accessed 13 January 2023).

White, J. (2021). Analyzing attacks against microsoft exchange server with China chopper webshells. *Palo Alto Unit 42* (8 March). https://unit42.paloaltonetworks.com/china-chopper-webshell (accessed 13 January 2023).

Winder, D. (2020). This 20-year-old virus infected 50 million Windows computers in 10 days: why the ILOVEYOU pandemic matters in 2020. *Forbes* (4 May). https://www.forbes.com/sites/daveywinder/2020/05/04/this-20-year-old-virus-infected-50-million-windows-computers-in-10-days-why-the-iloveyou-pandemic-matters-in-2020 (accessed 13 January 2023).

Wringe, B. (2017). Rethinking expressive theories of punishment: why denunciation is a better bet than communication or pure expression. *Philosophical Studies* 174 (3): 681–708.

7

Professionalism

Threat intelligence has a long pedigree dating back to antiquity. As warfare became more complex and armies grew in size from the nineteenth century onwards, so military intelligence grew in importance (Wheeler 2012). The Duke of Wellington (1769–1852), famed as a general during the Napoleonic Wars, recognised the significance of intelligence, remarking that all the business of war was *'guessing what was at the other side of the hill'* (Ratcliffe 2017). As the years progressed, so the size of the 'hill' that needed to be peered over has grown in size, requiring better intelligence and ultimately leading to the development of national intelligence agencies during the second half of the twentieth century.

Since the 1990s the Internet has developed largely within the private sector. The connected autonomous networks that comprise the Internet are, for the vast majority, held and controlled privately (Arnold et al. 2020). The data traversing these networks, the systems receiving and processing these data, and the resulting logs are majoritively held by the private sector.

Cyber threats conducted over the Internet have consequences for national security (Isenberg et al. 2021). Yet it is within the logs and data held privately that much of the evidence of these attacks are located. Hence, the emerging requirement for cyber threat intelligence (CTI) professionals to gather and analyse this information.

The recency of CTI as a notion is illustrated by the fact that the first searches for the term on Google's search engine date from September 2007 (Google Trends n.d.). From the mid-2000s onwards, governments began to recognise the value of the information and intelligence within the private sector. Consequently, governments sought to establish information exchanges to facilitate the exchange of intelligence and boost the resilience of organisations to cyber attack, especially those operating critical national infrastructure (Chambers and Gallegos 2006; ENISA et al. 2009).

Although threat intelligence is an ancient concept, there has been a relatively short space of time for the private sector to develop a CTI capability. At the same time, the rapid evolution of threats has changed the nature of threat analysis. As a result, CTI is developing into a distinct but emerging profession.

Established professions such as medicine or law trace their lineage back to the middle ages or earlier, and have long established pathways to qualification. Aspirants to the profession must demonstrate that they have completed the required years of education and training, as well as swearing to abide by the prescribed standards of conduct.

For CTI to become widely respected and recognised as a profession, practitioners within the domain must demonstrate the same levels of training and conduct as expected of any other profession. Chapter 7 considers what it means to be a professional, and what can be learnt from existing professions and applied to CTI.

7.1 Notions of Professionalism

To understand what is meant by professionalism, and update the concept, we must consider the origins of the notion. Medieval professions and guilds controlled the practice and practitioners of trades. They provided a brethren of fellow practitioners with whom to exchange ideas and knowledge, required training for new members, and excluded outsiders from exercising their activity.

The professions differentiated themselves from other trades by requiring theoretical knowledge as well as practical skill. Entry to a profession was reserved to the literate who had received a university education and had the social standing of the gentility (Carr-Saunders and Wilson 1933).

As the Industrial Revolution progressed new professions based on the application of theoretical knowledge emerged; these included mechanical engineers, civil engineers, accountants, opticians, etc. (Carr-Saunders and Wilson 1933).

The assistant secretary of the General Education Board of New York City in 1915 succinctly summarised six criteria for recognising if an activity constituted a profession:

Intellectual operations with large individual responsibility – professionals apply their intelligence to problems seeking to understand and master them. Professionals take personal responsibility for their work.

Derive their raw material from science and learning – the profession is advanced through theoretical and practical research, and the exchange of ideas.

Have an absolutely definite and practical object – professions are not theoretical but work to achieve defined objectives.

Possess an educationally communicable technique – professions have a shared notion of a common body of knowledge and skills that must be mastered in order to conduct professional practice.

Tendency to self-organisation – professionals gravitate together to form professional associations. These associations perform regulatory and social roles as well as organising the profession to act towards the common good.

Devotion to well-doing – professionals are not primarily motivated by financial gain but work towards an altruistic notion of improvement.

(Flexner 1915)

These are only one example of criteria by which professions and professionals may be recognised. Typically, professionals are identified by their knowledge, skill, and consequent high esteem within the communities in which they apply their skills.

The concept of a profession is not always positive. Professions are also characterised by their ability to restrict and control access to work, often through a state granted monopoly. Those who have not followed the prescribed training cursus and joined the professional body may be prevented from carrying out work that is within their capabilities, or must subordinate their work to a regulated professional.

Professions act as a guarantee of quality for the public. The training and certification of members of a profession reassures lay people that the professional can be trusted to offer expert knowledge and skill on complex matters where mistakes can have major consequences.

7.1.1 Professional Ethics

Being a professional is more than sharing an occupation with others. Within the notion of professionalism is the concept of serving a higher purpose. The physician, lawyer, and engineer do more than turn up, do their job, and collect their fee. The physician heals the sick and gives comfort to the dying, the lawyer provides access to justice for those who most need it, the engineer develops the machines and systems that keep society functioning (Davis 2003).

This moral purpose of the professional brings esteem to the profession in wider society. Maintaining this moral purpose requires consistently acting to do the 'right thing'. What constitutes the 'right thing' is not always obvious or clear. Professional codes of ethics govern and guide decision making so that actions can be shown to be ethical in nature (Bird 1998). An ethical action is one that can be considered '*on reasonable reflection, [one that] promises to maximise benefits for the moral community and distribute them fairly*' (Kultgen 1988).

That professionals will act ethically forms the basis of trust between a profession and society. Trustworthy professions are trusted to apply their esoteric knowledge appropriately, their services and counsel are trusted, and they are trusted to regulate their behaviour and actions through their own behavioural codes (Brien 1998).

These codes set out how members of the profession are expected to behave. Members that do not abide by these rules are subject to sanction, and potential exclusion from the profession, ultimately forbidden from exercising an activity.

7.2 Developing a New Profession

Does CTI meet the criteria of a profession?

CTI is an intellectual activity that requires understanding complex problems. Practitioners certainly should take responsibility for and pride in their work. The profession is advanced through the publication of reports, practical research, and the exchange of ideas both in online forums and in-person symposia.

It is a very practical activity oriented to the production of threat intelligence reports. There is a notion of a higher purpose, our work helps to protect networked computer systems from attack and to hold those conducting such attacks to account. However, there is no widely accepted existent code of conduct or ethics.

There are no barriers to carrying out threat intelligence; it is a democratic activity. Anyone can call themselves a threat intelligence analyst. There are no exams to pass, no licence to achieve, no state sanctioned monopoly.

Although many CTI practitioners may belong to professional associations such as the International Information System Security Certification Consortium (ISC)^2 or the Institute of Electrical and Electronics Engineers (IEEE), etc. there is no widely accepted single body acting as a professional association for CTI.

7.2.1 Professional Education

There is an emerging common body of knowledge relating to CTI. Universities offer degrees in CTI at undergraduate and postgraduate levels, or offer it as a module as part of a broader cyber security degree course.

Many non-university bodies offer training, examination, and certification in CTI (Table 7.1).

Online education organisations such as Cybrary, Udemy, Coursera, etc., also offer threat intelligence training.

Although there may be no single organisation dictating the composition of a common body of knowledge for CTI, the ensemble of the curricula offered by universities and certification bodies can be considered to comprise the various terms and concepts with which an aspiring CTI profession should be familiar.

Table 7.1 Examples of professional certificates.

Certifying body	Certification	Reference
CREST	Practitioner Threat Intelligence Analyst	CREST (2021a)
	Registered Threat Intelligence Analyst	CREST (2021b)
	Certified Threat Intelligence Manager	CREST (2021b)
EC-Council	Certified Threat Intelligence Analyst	EC Council (2021)
GIAC	Cyber Threat Intelligence (GCTI)	GIAC (2021a)
SANS	FOR578: Cyber Threat Intelligence	SANS (2021)
McAfee Institute	Certified Cyber Intelligence Investigator (CCII)	McAfee Institute (2021b)
	Certified Cyber Intelligence Professional (CCIP)	McAfee Institute (2021a)

7.2.2 Professional Behaviour and Ethics

Professionalism is distinct from ethics. The former describes the skills, competences, and conduct that are expected from professionals, the latter describes guidelines for determining the correct course of action. However, there are many overlaps between the two concepts. In essence, a code of ethics governs decision making, and a code of conduct governs actions (Nieweler 2014).

A professional is expected to behave professionally towards themselves and others. Even without further definition we can recognise 'professional behaviour' as the opposite of acting 'unprofessionally'.

Examining how other professions define professional standards and their required behaviour allows us to identify the conduct that should be expected of CTI professionals.

7.2.2.1 Professionalism in Medicine

Medicine has a long tradition of requiring professional behaviour from physicians. The Greek physician Hippocrates is credited as having written in the fourth century BCE the earliest surviving medical oath requiring that physicians adhere to certain norms of behaviour. In various forms, the oath is still taken by graduating medical students to this day (Hulkower 2016).

The original Hippocratic oath covers a variety of points of professionalism which are summarised in Table 7.2.

Professionalism remains an integral part of the medical curriculum. The Hippocratic oath remains remarkably relevant in the twenty-first century, although the exact tenets of professionalism included in medical curricula have

Table 7.2 Summary of the Hippocratic oath.

Faithfulness	I swear ... that, according to my ability and judgement, I will keep this Oath and this contract
Duty to teachers	To hold him who taught me this art equally dear to me as my parents
Duty to teach others	I will impart a knowledge of the art to my own sons, and those of my teachers, and to students bound by this contract
Duty to patients	I will do no harm or injustice to them
Ethical limits on behaviour	I will not give a lethal drug to anyone ... I will not ... cause an abortion
Recognition of own competence	I will leave this to those who are trained in this craft
Duty of proprietary behaviour	avoiding any voluntary act of impropriety or corruption
Duty of confidentiality	Whatever I see or hear in the lives of my patients, ... which ought not to be spoken of outside, I will keep secret
Accountability	So long as I maintain this Oath faithfully and without corruption, may it be granted to me to partake of life fully ... However, should I transgress this Oath and violate it, may the opposite be my fate

Source: Adapted from Hulkower (2016).

Table 7.3 Items of modern medical professional behaviour.

Relating to others	quality of interaction with peers, staff, patients
Self-awareness	dealing with critique, self-criticism
Communication skills	giving and asking information, listening to others
Personal qualities	tolerance, empathy, leadership, respect for others, active performance, and efficient task performance

Source: Adapted from van Mook (2009).

evolved to be more relevant to modern medicine. Typical items taught in medical schools cover the following points: reliability and responsibility, honesty and integrity, maturity, self-critique, absence of impairment, communication skills (Arnold 2002). Indeed, the professional behaviour of medical students is assessed against frameworks such as those shown in Table 7.3.

Physicians must work effectively with professionals from other medical disciplines, recognising and respecting their specialisms and differences of opinion. Doctors must also convey complex information to a variety of different audiences. Predictably, doctors with better communication skills achieve improved health care outcomes from their patients and deliver better quality of care (Rider and Keefer 2006).

These are relevant to CTI. As professionals, we must be able to communicate effectively with fellow professionals, and in terms that are understood by our clients. We must be able to work together as a team with other disciplines while remaining focused on our clients' best interests.

7.2.2.1.1 Medical Ethics

'*Medicine used to be simple, ineffective and relatively safe. It is now complex, effective and potentially dangerous*' wrote the eminent medical authority Sir Cyril Chantler on modern medicine (Chantler 1998). As technical progress advances medicine, the physician is frequently confronted with decisions that must be made, but for which moral concerns or priorities conflict (BMA 2012).

Such decisions can be resolved through reflecting on the notions of what is right and wrong, what ought to be done or not, with respect to the laws in vigour and according to the principles of medical ethics (Table 7.4).

Medical ethics is a core part of the medical curriculum. All medical decision making has an ethical component (Fox et al. 1995).

The close integration of professionalism and ethics into everyday professional practice is something to which the nascent CTI profession should pay close attention.

7.2.2.2 Professionalism in Accountancy

Accountancy is a very different profession from medicine, nevertheless accountants are expected to abide by relevant standards of professionalism.

The International Ethics Standards Board for Accountants (IESBA) sets the ethical standards for professional accounts. They require accountants to adhere to five fundamental principles (Table 7.5).

The accountancy profession is not immune from lapses in professional and ethical behaviour.

Table 7.4 Principles of medical ethics.

Self-determination or autonomy	Individuals are free to decide treatment or to decline treatment, so long as such a decision does not harm others.
Honesty or integrity	Doctors must communicate effectively so that the patient is not deceived or misled.
Confidentiality	Patients have a right to confidentiality unless there is a risk of harm or overriding public interest.
Fairness or equity	Decisions must be made in respect of the wider picture and if a choice may be detrimental to others.
Harm and benefit	Doctors should seek to maximise benefit and minimise harm.

Source: Adapted from BMA (2012).

Table 7.5 Principles of accountancy ethics.

Integrity	An accountant is straightforward and honest in their professional relationships.
Objectivity	An accountant is not affected by bias, conflicts of interest, or undue influence in their professional work.
Professional competence and due care	An accountant acts diligently in accordance with the relevant standards in their work, and will maintain their professional knowledge.
Confidentiality	An accountant respects the confidentiality of information gained during their work.
Professional behaviour	Accountants comply with relevant law and do not indulge in behaviour that discredits the profession.

Source: Adapted from IESBA (2019).

Enron was a leading energy, communications, and paper supply. Founded in 1985, annual revenue grew to $9 billion in 1995 and to over $100 billion in 2000. In 2001 the company's share price crashed, causing shareholder losses of nearly $11 billion following restatement of the company's income and allegations of accounting irregularities (Li 2010).

The investigation following the collapse of Enron in 2001 suggested that the auditor Arthur Andersen *'did not fulfil its professional responsibilities in connection with its audits of Enron's financial statements, or its obligation to bring to the attention of Enron's Board (or the Audit and Compliance Committee) concerns about Enron's internal contracts'* (Powers et al. 2002).

Arthur Andersen, at the time one of the world's largest accountancy firms, had a dual role as auditor to Enron, but also as a consultant selling services to Enron. Less than 30% of the fees that Andersen received from Enron came from audits, the remainder came from consulting. The audit team was evaluated as not having undertaken their obligations with the diligence and objectivity of a truly independent objective auditor and failing to appropriately investigate or highlight weakness in Enron's accounts (Cunningham and Harris 2006). Ultimately the scandal caused the demise of Arthur Andersen, and resulted in criminal convictions for several of Enron's former executives (McBarnet 2005; Segal 2021).

Contributing to this failure of professional values was the conflict between two different notions of professionalism. One concept is that of the professional as the guardian of public interest, as someone less concerned about commercial interests, but seeking to serve a higher social function. The other is the separate concept of the professional as a commercial entity seeking to generate revenue from selling their services (Suddaby et al. 2009).

The conflict between doing public good, and commercial pressure is relevant to cyber threat professionals. We should be mindful of the lessons learnt by the accountancy profession following the scandals of the early 2000s. Most notably, professionals must have an objective stance, and hold the integrity of their profession higher than the financial pressures of commercialism or the efficiency drives of managerialism (Lea 2012).

The five IESBA principles are proposed to be strengthened with the addition of moral courage (Mintz 2020). This is the willingness to persevere in exerting professional scepticism, and choosing to act when something is wrong (Burden 2018). The notion is similar to the Greek concept of *parrhesia*, a fundamental tenet of ancient democracy, the ability, and the obligation, to speak frankly and to express the truth as one sees it (Saxonhouse 2005).

Such courage is necessary to state and stand by an informed professional opinion regarding a threat or the evolution of a threat, no matter how unpopular or negative the consequences.

Moral courage provides the imperative to stand up and call out behaviour that is wrong. In a speech denouncing sexism and misogyny, Lt. Gen. David Morrison, then chief of the Australian Army, coined the phrase, '*the standard you walk past is the standard you accept*' (Wikiquote 2022). That is to say, if you witness behaviour that falls below the standards of conduct that you expect, if you fail to act or speak out to stop that behaviour, then that is the level of behaviour you find acceptable.

7.2.2.3 Professionalism in Engineering

Finally, let us consider professionalism in engineering. Broadly speaking, and depending on the jurisdiction, there are three categories of engineers. People whose job title includes the term 'engineer', qualified engineers who have completed a training or education in an engineering subject, and licenced engineers who have been granted a licence to practise by a recognised engineering registration body (Dexter 2020).

In jurisdictions where it is enforced, certain rights are reserved for licenced engineers, such as the ability to use the title 'engineer', to be able to offer engineering services to the public, or to certify engineering specifications.

Licenced engineers are certified as having demonstrated mastery of the common body of knowledge for their specialisation through education, training, and examination. They also demonstrate their professionalism through adhering to professional behaviour and ethics.

The US National Society of Professional Engineers expects engineers to dedicate their professional knowledge to the advancement and betterment of public health, safety, and welfare,

Pledging:

To give the utmost of performance;
To participate in none but honest enterprise;
To live and work according to the highest standards of professional conduct;
To place service before profit, the honour and standing of my profession before personal advantage, and the public welfare above all other considerations.

(NSPE 2021)

The European Federation of National Engineering Associations requires that individual engineers have a personal obligation to act with integrity, in the public interest, and to exercise all reasonable skill and care in carrying out their work. In so doing engineers:

Shall maintain their relevant competences at the necessary level and only undertake tasks for which they are competent
Shall not misrepresent their educational qualifications or professional titles
Shall provide impartial analysis and judgement to employer or clients, avoid conflicts of interest, and observe proper duties of confidentiality
Shall carry out their tasks so as to prevent avoidable danger to health and safety, and prevent avoidable adverse impact on the environment
Shall accept appropriate responsibility for their work and that carried out under their supervision
Shall respect the personal rights of people with whom they work and the legal and cultural values of the societies in which they carry out assignments
Shall be prepared to contribute to public debate on matters of technical understanding in fields in which they are competent to comment.

(FEANI 2006)

Despite both organisations regulating the behaviour of professionals of the same discipline, the codes are subtly different. This underlines that although professionals are expected to adhere to the standards of behaviour required by relevant bodies, professionalism is not a set of absolute rules, but about how we conduct our behaviour, how we relate to others, and what is expected of us by the wider public.

7.2.2.3.1 Engineering Ethics

The ability to recognise ethical and professional responsibilities is a required outcome of accredited engineering degrees (ABET 2019). One way of studying and understanding the importance of ethics and the consequences of ethical failings is through the study of accidents where failures in professional ethics led to harm (Harris Jr et al. 1996).

The *Challenger* space shuttle accident is a well-known but complex case study for engineering ethics. The NASA space shuttle *Challenger* exploded shortly after take-off leading to the death of the seven astronauts on board. The immediate cause was a failure of a seal in one of the solid booster rockets. The failed seal led to the release of burning gases resulting in the loss of the spacecraft (USGPO 1986).

The O-ring seal had been designed as a pair of seals to provide redundancy in case one failed. However, during previous launches some seals had been observed as having nearly burnt through entirely. This evidence of near-failure was referred to as 'anomalous', yet because the seals had not failed, but operated as required, these incidences of near-failure became accepted as evidence of acceptable risks rather than as a safety problem (Murata 2006).

Engineers within the manufacturer of the seals were concerned at the risk of failure of the seal, and particularly concerned of the effect of the low air temperature forecast for the day of the launch on the resilience of the seals. Despite strong convictions that the launch should be delayed, engineers lacked the technical data necessary to fully support their argument and failed to convince management to halt the launch (Rossow 2012).

However, we risk analysing the accident with the bias of hindsight. Up to the point of launch the engineering consensus was that the known issues with the O-ring seals were an acceptable risk. Nobody knew for certain that a seal would fail, if this had been the case and communicated, then the launch surely would not have taken place (Rossow 2012).

Subsequent analysis has highlighted the importance of organisational culture as a contributing factor to the accident. Instead of engineers being required to prove flightworthiness to management before a flight could take place, the issue was reversed. Management required engineers to prove that the shuttle was not flightworthy. This was not a situation for which the engineers were prepared (Dombrowski 2007). Engineers had doubts, but prior to take-off, had no proof that a failure would occur.

This case study is particularly pertinent to CTI. A major contributing factor to the disaster was the failure to perceive and communicate risk. This is a key role of threat intelligence professionals: correctly communicating threats and risk so that they are understood by decision makers to facilitate good decision making.

Professionalism includes the notion of serving the wider interest, and of having the moral courage to stand for what is right. It is worth reflecting before the event what we would do as CTI professionals if our concerns regarding a major threat with severe consequences were dismissed out of hand. What would we need to have done to assuage our consciences, or better, avert a catastrophe from happening?

The real world is full of complexity and the conflicting demands of schedule and cost (Murata 2006). Those of us engaged in communicating risk and the consequences of vulnerabilities must be diligent not only in uncovering threats, but also in developing our communication skills so that information is properly understood and acted upon.

7.2.3 Certifications and Codes of Ethics

The bodies offering certification in CTI enforce their own codes of ethics as part of ensuring that certified people maintain the necessary standard.

The Council of Registered Ethical Security Testers (CREST) requires both certified individuals and member companies to abide by their code of ethics. Their code of ethics takes the form of general concepts with explanations and details of the behaviour expected or proscribed. These are summarised below (Tables 7.6 and 7.7).

The EC-Council's code of ethics consists of 19 points, which consist of instructions to obey rather than principles of behaviour to follow. These instructions include requirements to respect confidentiality, protect intellectual property, disclose dangers, act within competence, not use illegally obtained software, not engage in improper financial practices, only use authorised systems, disclose conflicts of interest, manage projects well, share knowledge, behave ethically when soliciting services, act ethically, do not engage in illegal hacking or associate with malicious hackers, don't abuse certificates or logos, not convicted of a felony (EC Council n.d.).

Ethical codes expressed as instructions of proscribed or mandatory behaviours are problematic since there is an implication that if a behaviour is not listed as

Table 7.6 Ethical standards required of individuals by CREST.

Honesty	Members follow applicable laws and regulations, conducting themselves with honesty and integrity.
Bribery, corruption, and extortion	Members must not offer or receive bribes, or other forms of unethical behaviour.
Competition	Members must compete fairly and not conduct anti-competitive behaviour.
Integrity	Members must not act in detriment to their client or act to give rise to conflicts of interest.
Professionalism	Members will keep their skills and knowledge up to date.
Personal example	Members will act as role models giving assistance and credit where due and accepting responsibility for their work.
Application and compliance	Members will respect others and not accept instruction that breaks laws, regulations of professional standards.

Source: Adapted from CREST (2019).

Table 7.7 Additional ethical standard required by CREST of member companies.

Credibility	Members will be objective in the assessments applying systematic and verifiable processes in their work.
	Members will safeguard confidential information and behave legally and ethically.
Integrity	Members must follow applicable laws and regulations and ensure that their staff and subcontractors do the same.
Responsibility and respect	Members take responsibility for their actions performing their work with diligence and integrity. Ensuring that their work is justifiable and defendable.
Sense of mission	Members will promote the public understanding of cyber security, rebut false statements regarding the profession, and share knowledge with other members.

Source: Adapted from CREST (2019).

forbidden then it is permitted. Codes may go to great lengths to list specified proscribed behaviour that an individual must not do. However, if unethical behaviour such as indulging in sexual harassment or uttering hate speech, for example, are omitted from the list, does that mean that individuals engaging in such behaviour do not break the code or deserve sanction?

Overly prescriptive codes risk a lack of proportionality. A code of ethics forbidding professionals from 'breaking any law' may appear as an effective means of ensuring that a professional community is free from criminals. However, the clause implies that receiving a parking ticket or speeding fine would be a violation of the code. Few members would remain within the profession if the clause was enforced, and if the clause was not enforced, what purpose does it serve?

Ethical codes are best expressed as guidelines that can be interpreted and applied with proportionality and context. Rather than forbidding law breaking, the spirit of such a clause could be better expressed as: 'do not engage in criminal behaviour', or simply 'maintain good public morals'.

Ideally, codes of ethics should clarify an organisation's values in order to empower those who are subject to the code to resolve ethical conundrums in their day-to-day work, allowing new situations and issues to be considered ethically and developing moral judgement (ECT Ethics and Compliance Initiative 2021; Sekerka 2009).

The Global Information Assurance Certification (GIAC) code of ethics is based around the principles outlined in Table 7.8.

The four principles are easy to remember, proportionate, and with the accompanying text easy to comprehend as well.

Table 7.8   The GIAC code of ethics.

Respect for the public	I will accept responsibility in making decisions with consideration for the security and welfare of the community.
	I will not engage in or be a party to unethical or unlawful acts that negatively affect the community, my professional reputation, or the information security discipline.
Respect for the certification	I will not share, disseminate, or otherwise distribute confidential or proprietary information pertaining to the GIAC certification process.
	I will not use my certification, or objects or information associated with my certification (such as certificates or logos) to represent any individual or entity other than myself as being certified by GIAC.
Respect for the employer	I will deliver capable service that is consistent with the expectations of my certification and position.
	I will protect confidential and proprietary information with which I come into contact.
	I will minimise risks to the confidentiality, integrity, or availability of an information technology solution, consistent with risk management practice.
Respect for myself	I will avoid conflicts of interest.
	I will not misuse any information or privileges I am afforded as part of my responsibilities.
	I will not misrepresent my abilities or my work to the community, my employer, or my peers.

Source: Adapted from GIAC (2021b).

7.3   Behaving Ethically

In the absence of a specific code of ethics that regulates the nascent profession of CTI, CTI professionals must apply their own judgement and strive to do the right thing within the wider context of working to benefit society, and choose to do the right thing. There are a variety of models and workflows that can be followed when faced with an ethical problem that can help resolve the issue, or identify the best course of action.

7.3.1   The Five Philosophical Approaches

Philosophers have developed five different approaches to consider ethical issues (Velasquez et al. 2015).

The utilitarian approach considers the various courses of action available, seeking to understand who will benefit and who will be harmed from each course of action. The ethical action is the one that provides the greatest benefits for the greatest number of people with the least harm.

The rights approach considers the rights of those affected by an action. An action that infringes on the rights of others, such as their right to privacy, their right not to be injured, and their right to self-determination, is harmful. The ethical action is that which best respects the rights of those involved.

The fairness approach considers that everyone should be treated equitably. Favouritism that gives unjustifiable benefit to some people, or discrimination that gives unjustifiable burdens on some people are both wrong. The ethical action is that which does not promote favouritism or discrimination on anyone.

The common-good approach considers that we are all part of a wider community that is bound together by common values and goals. The ethical actions are those that promote the good of the community as a whole.

The virtue approach considers that some ideals are inherently virtuous and that we should strive to be a virtuous person. In considering possible actions, we should consider what kind of person would carry out such an action. The ethical action is that which would be chosen by the most virtuous individual.

We can approach an ethical dilemma through applying each of the five principles to potential courses of outcome. Any option that does not fit with any of the principles is unlikely to be ethical. The option that fits best with the principles is likely to be the most ethical, but any option that satisfies at least one of the principles can be considered ethical to some degree. No matter the outcome, through applying the five principles technique a decision maker can demonstrate that a decision was made by applying a process to arrive at an ethical outcome, and document the ethical points of each course of action considered.

7.3.2 The Josephson Model

The Josephson Institute of Ethics publishes a seven step model to resolve ethical problems, summarised below:

1. Stop and Think – calmly analyse the situation.
2. Clarify Goals – clarify long term and short term goals.
3. Determine Facts – identify what you know and what you need to know. Consider all perspectives but omit unreliable information such as gossip. Seek the opinions of people whose judgement you respect.
4. Develop Options – make a list of possible options.
5. Consider Consequences – examine each option according to: trustworthiness, respect, responsibility, fairness, caring, and citizenship. Discard options that violate any of these principles. Consider your choices from the point of view of other stakeholders, identify who will be helped and who will be hurt.
6. Choose – seek the counsel of people you respect, think what the most ethical person you know would do, and do unto others as you would have them do to you.

7. Monitor and Modify – monitor the outcome and be prepared to revisit and modify decisions if they are causing unintended and undesired effects.

(Josephson Institute n.d.)

This clear process is very easy to follow and apply to work situations. The first two instructions to stop, calmly assess the situation, and consider what it is that we are trying to achieve are particularly important to remember in pressured, stressful situations where the importance of ethics may be overlooked.

7.3.3 PMI Ethical Decision Making Framework

An analogous ethical step-by-step process is published by the Project Management Institute (PMI) to guide project managers in resolving ethical dilemmas (Ethics Member Advisory Group 2013).

1. Assessment – make sure that you are in possession of the facts and consider the following points:
   a. Is this legal?
   b. Is this in alignment with the professional code of ethics?
   c. Is this in agreement with the employer's code of ethics?
   d. Does this meet your own personal ethics and those of your peers?
2. Alternatives – have you considered all the options?
   a. Are there alternative choices?
   b. Are the pros and cons of each choice understood?
3. Analysis – identify candidate options and test their validity.
   a. Will this option have a benefit or be to the detriment of stakeholders?
   b. Does this option consider cultural differences?
   c. Will this still seem a good option one year from now?
   d. Is this a free choice?
   e. Are you calm and not stressed?
4. Application – apply ethical principles.
   a. Would this choice be to the greater good?
   b. Does this choice treat others as you would wish to be treated?
   c. Is this a fair and beneficial choice?
5. Action – make a decision.
   a. Are you happy to take responsibility for this decision?
   b. If your decision was made public, would you still feel this was the right choice?
   c. Are you ready to take action?

This is also an easy process to implement within a busy work environment. Importantly, the first point is to consider if the course of action is legal. If the answer to any of the points in the assessment step is 'no', then almost certainly this is not the course of action to take.

An additional point worth considering is would you be happy if your name was reported alongside your intended course in the press? If you would rather that your decision was not made part of the public record, then it may not be ethically justifiable.

7.4 Legal and Ethical Environment

CTI does take place within a legal and ethical vacuum. Every step in the intelligence cycle faces ethical and legal hazards. However, armed with an ethical framework and through exercising due diligence, these hazards can be navigated.

As honourable members of society we should abide by the laws of the jurisdiction in which we live and work. Obviously, the exact legislation and the jurisprudence under which these laws are applied depends on the jurisdiction. For the purposes of this chapter, legal consideration is limited to the Council of Europe Convention on Cybercrime (Council of Europe 2001). However, in practice signatory countries to the Convention may have implemented the articles of the convention differently, or not at all.

As ethical professionals, in addition to abiding by the law, we shall also seek to maximise the benefit of our work and avoid or minimise doing harm.

In passing we shall remind ourselves that the definition of CTI is:

> The process and outcome of gathering and analysing information relating to the people or things that may cause damage to electronic networked devices, in order to assist decision making.

And, that the phases of the intelligence cycle are planning, collection, analysis and processing, production, and dissemination.

Where threat intelligence activities may adversely impact others, or there is any doubt as to the ethics or legality of an operation, the threat intelligence team should follow a defined process and document how decisions were considered according to ethics and potential legal hazards. At some point it may be necessary to justify a decision that has been taken. Even if the decision ultimately proved to be poor, the team that can show that this was a considered decision, arrived at through considering other options, and provide the evidence of the ethical reasoning behind the decision, is likely to be treated much less harshly than the team that can show no such thing.

We cannot know the future, we cannot foresee all the potential outcomes of our decisions, nor will every decision that we make turn out for the best. However, we can prepare to defend the decisions that we make, and show that they were made in good faith with the evidence that was available at the time.

7.4.1 Planning

Threat intelligence products should bring benefit. This may be a benefit to a client or employer, to advance personal interests, or for the benefit of the wider community. There is little point in producing something that will be of no benefit to anyone.

Conversely, threat intelligence will almost certainly be of detriment to someone. Threat intelligence may frustrate the goals of threat actors. However, the individuals or groups that in our eyes are threat actors, and by consequence 'bad guys', may not share this opinion of themselves.

Threat actors may consider themselves as patriotic warriors, people setting right an injustice, or providing for their family and loved ones who would otherwise go without. Importantly, the threat actor's actions may not be illegal in their own jurisdiction.

For example, the individual suspected of developing the Love Bug worm, which damaged 50 million computers worldwide, reportedly did not commit a crime in their own jurisdiction. At the time of the incident there was no legislation covering computer crime in their home country (Landler 2000; Winder 2020).

In this case, we can argue that although the individual had not broken any laws in their own jurisdiction, their actions caused harm elsewhere. Therefore, although our intelligence reports may be to the detriment of the suspected threat actor, our work does help to protect many systems across the globe from harm. On balance we can argue that our intelligence is beneficial to society.

However, consider the case where a threat actor is a national government conducting a hostile offensive cyber operation against a third party. The action may be sanctioned and legal within the perpetrator's country. Should we publicly release intelligence regarding the attack so that it can be stopped to minimise harm to the target, to the detriment of the attacker? Is the identity of the target of the attack important? Does it matter if the perpetrator or target of the attack is our own nation, or a nation to which we feel kinship or hostility?

As CTI professionals, we must remain objective and focus on our role of impartially gathering and analysing information in order to inform and assist decision making. Conflicts of interest, such as nationality, or feelings of kinship with third parties, which may affect judgement or impinge on objectivity should be declared within analyses, or better, if a conflict of interest is identified, the analyst should recuse themselves from the investigation.

7.4.1.1 Responsible Vulnerability Disclosure

Disclosing vulnerabilities is ethically hazardous. In disclosing the presence of a vulnerability, we are providing benefit to those who are affected by the vulnerability through awareness so that they can take steps to mitigate the risk, or apply a patch to resolve the vulnerability. However, we may also cause harm by alerting attackers to the presence of a vulnerability that they can choose to exploit.

Choosing to do nothing is an option. But closing our eyes and shutting our mouths does not make the risk go away. The risk of exploitation would still exist if we disclosed the existence of the vulnerability or not. Responsible vulnerability disclosure seeks to maintain the benefit to society in disclosing the vulnerability while minimising the risks that disclosure will alert threat actors.

The OWASP vulnerability cheat sheet describes a process through which researchers may disclose a vulnerability responsibly (OWASP 2021). In summary, researchers should take steps to report the vulnerability to an appropriate person within the affected organisation, and explain the vulnerability in a way that can be understood and replicated, while respecting the privacy of others, and without demanding payment.

Threatening extortion in relation to a vulnerability is clearly unethical. Receiving payment in return for responsible disclosure as a bug bounty is not uncommon, but should not be expected. Professionals are motivated by a higher purpose rather than commercial concerns, but nevertheless need to earn a living. Receiving bug bounty payments is normally considered ethical unless there is a reason to the contrary.

If the researcher is unable to make contact with an appropriate person, make progress with the disclosure, or wishes to disclose the issue anonymously, many national Computer Emergency Response Teams (CERTs) are willing and able to act as a third party to coordinate vulnerability disclosure on behalf of researchers. Disclosing via a national CERT allows the researcher to request that their anonymity is maintained.

Doing the right thing and responsibly disclosing vulnerabilities is not without legal risk. Recipients of a well-intentioned disclosure may not welcome the contact and respond with legal threats (Haworth 2021; Immanni 2021).

The identification of vulnerability within computer code or systems may be forbidden by the CoE Convention on Cybercrime. Article 2 forbids the access to the whole or any part of a computer system without right. A vendor may consider accessing proprietary information, such as computer code, even if it resides on a computer owned by the researcher as accessing 'without right' that information (Council of Europe 2001).

The researcher may fall foul of Article 6b, which forbids possession of items, including software, which facilitates an infraction as defined in Article 2. Alternatively, the vendor may consider unauthorised access of their computer code as an infringement of their copyright covered under Article 10 of the Convention (Council of Europe 2001).

7.4.1.2 Vulnerability Hoarding

The issue of nation states hoarding otherwise undiscovered zero-day vulnerabilities is an interesting ethical issue. Nation states may research zero-day vulnerabilities and develop exploit code to exploit the vulnerability but omit to inform the vendor so that the vulnerability remains unpatched (Schneier 2014).

A corpus ('hoard') of these vulnerabilities and associated exploit code can be built up by agencies within the nation state in order to compromise computer systems so that they can further their objectives. These objectives may be related to military operations, intelligence gathering, or conducting law enforcement investigations. Alternatively, the nation state may choose to disclose the vulnerability to the vendor so that the issue may be fixed (White House 2017).

To retain a vulnerability for their own use, rather than choose to disclose it to the vendor, the nation state must logically conclude that the benefits gained from their own use of an undisclosed vulnerability outweigh the potential negative consequences if the vulnerability were to be discovered or abused by a hostile threat actor (Armerding 2017a).

Unfortunately, a cache of likely nation state developed exploit code was stolen and made publicly available in 2016 (Armerding 2017b; Morse and Jackman 2019). Within this cache was the exploit code that was ultimately integrated into the destructive worm WannaCry and used to wreak havoc across the Internet. Ultimately the worm is estimated to have caused $4 billion in damages (Gregory 2021). Hopefully, such estimates of potential damage will feature in future cost–benefit analyses when the decision to disclose or not disclose a vulnerability is being considered.

Hoarding of vulnerabilities by nation states has been resoundingly condemned by companies within the technology industry (Smith 2017; Tech Accord 2018). Nevertheless, the practice continues with formal oversight of risks and benefits by government bodies (Caulfield et al. 2017; GCHQ 2018).

Is this activity ethical? Do the benefits of the activity outweigh the negatives and are the risks of conducting the activity properly understood and managed? Clearly there are two sides to this debate. Although one side is vocal in opposition, the other is silent due to confidentiality requirements, leading to an unbalanced discussion of the issue.

7.4.2 Collection, Analysis, and Processing

CTI requires sifting large amounts of data. This may include logging data from a variety of systems in order to understand the actions of a threat actor. Within this data may be personal or sensitive information. Indeed, through accessing multiple systems and multiple logs, threat analysis professionals may be able to combine data to identify additional private information that otherwise would not be available.

Necessity and proportionality are fundamental principles of data protection (European Data Protection Supervisor 2020). We should be able to demonstrate that such processing of data is necessary in order to carry out our mission to protect systems and data from harm. If the data we are processing is not necessary or useful to our purpose what is the point of spending time analysing it?

However, is the amount of processing of potentially personal data proportionate? Proportionality requires that only that personal data which is adequate and relevant for the purposes of the processing is collected and processed (European Data Protection Supervisor 2020).

A relevant example is discovering a dump of stolen personal information on a server. Downloading the data through idle curiosity is unethical, since there is no possible benefit. Such an action would be against data protection legislation because there is no purpose for the processing of the data (Mondschein and Monda 2019).

However, downloading in order to investigate if the breached data originated from your own systems, or to secure the data dump before involving law enforcement could be argued as being beneficial. The EU General Data Protection Regulations (GDPR) provide for processing personal data under the legitimate interest of preventing fraud, ensuring network and information security, or reporting possible criminal acts to a relevant authority (GDPR 2016).

7.4.2.1 PRISM Programme

In 2013, *The Guardian* and *The Washington Post* disclosed the details of the PRISM programme's ability to intercept, store, and analyse electronic communications that pass through the US (Greenwald and MacAskill 2013; Gellman and Poitras 2013). The presence of the programme and capabilities were subsequently confirmed by the US government (DNI 2013; PCLOB 2014).

The nature and scope of the surveillance quickly raised ethical questions about the programme, which was described by a former lieutenant colonel within the notorious East German Stasi as '*a dream come true*' (Macnish 2018; Schofield 2013). Yet the programme has been implicated in preventing at least 50 terrorist attacks (Madison 2013).

Do the benefits of mass interception of electronic communications in detecting and preventing terrorist attacks outweigh the loss of privacy? Is such interception necessary and proportional for the purposes of detecting and preventing crime? In analysing large amounts of combined data sources in order to produce CTI are we creating a similar programme but on a smaller scale?

None of these are necessarily easy questions to answer. We should be prepared to justify our own work, show that we have considered ethics, and not be afraid to modify working practices or to deploy additional safeguards when necessary.

7.4.2.2 Open and Closed Doors

A server accepting TCP connections on port 80 for which the IP address has a published DNS record for a domain name can reasonably be expected to be granting permission for people to access it as a web server. However, what if the web server software has been placed on the system and opened to the world without the consent of the system owner, and is providing the command and control panel for a botnet?

Ethically, we can argue that the benefit of researching and understanding the botnet to prevent crime, outweighs any detriment to the privacy of the threat actor or disruption to their business. However, do the ethics change when instead of a botnet command and control panel, we identify the industrial control system for a dam or other piece of critical national infrastructure?

Two German researchers were able to identify four water control systems and seven remote heating systems that had control systems entirely open to the Internet (Internetwache 2016; Millman 2016). They disclosed the vulnerabilities responsibly and helped to remove the vulnerable systems from the Internet. Choosing to investigate the effects of changing settings within the panels would have been unethical due to the foreseeable risk of harmful consequences for such an action.

Is this situation different from investigating the uncovered control panel of a botnet by randomly pressing buttons? Although there may be benefits from understanding the action and scope of the botnet, the unforeseen negative effects due to accidentally triggering actions by the botnet may massively outweigh any benefits.

The Convention on Cybercrime forbids access to '*any part of a computer system without right*'. Can the CTI researcher argue that they have a right to access a botnet control panel? The threat actor may not publicly object to the unauthorised access, but the owner of a compromised system on which the control panel is located might identify the researcher and mistake them for the threat actor.

Such a case of mistaken identity may be more likely if the researcher has identified and used the credentials necessary to access a secured botnet control panel. Even the most cautious researcher may find themselves leaving forensic traces of their actions at the scene of a crime.

7.4.3 Dissemination

After production we must disseminate our threat intelligence and share it with others so that it may be consumed and used.

We should carefully consider the restrictions on the distribution of our intelligence by choosing an appropriate traffic light protocol marking. Labelling an intelligence briefing as green or white and publishing without restriction maximises the potential recipients and hence maximises the benefit. But if the report reaches the hands of the threat actor and allows them to change their actions and avoid subsequent detection, does this mean that the intelligence report has caused harm?

Marking such a report as orange and distributing it to those who are known to be affected by the threat restricts distribution. In doing so, we're restricting those who can benefit from the report. Restricted distribution will certainly be less beneficial than open publication. However, if by doing so we prevent the threat actor from being tipped off, then we also minimise potential harm.

There are no hard rules, or easy choices in deciding the distribution model. In some cases, the benefit of wide publication may outweigh any harm due to tipping off the threat actor that they have been uncovered. In other cases, keeping information on a strict need-to-know basis with tightly controlled distribution of intelligence to keep techniques and sources of information secret may be the best option.

We have duties to those who share information with us. If someone has taken us into their confidence and given us information, we should not abuse that trust and subsequently share that information beyond the intentions of the originator. If their intentions for the limits of sharing are not immediately clear, clarification should be sought from the originator.

7.4.3.1 Doxxing

Doxxing or doxing, is the publishing of private information about someone without their permission (Cambridge English Dictionary n.d.). Researchers may uncover significant personal information regarding the identities of threat actors and their victims. Publishing this information may not provide any additional benefit to an intelligence report. Indeed, it may cause harm, in that it allows a genuine threat actor to portray themselves as a victim of harassment or a personal attack following the publication of their own personal data.

There is also the risk that the researcher has incorrectly identified a threat actor, or that the threat actor has stolen the identity of an innocent third party. In which case the researcher would risk accusing an innocent individual who themselves has been the victim of a crime.

Laws relating to libel, where someone has written something false or negative about a third party, are different in every jurisdiction. Laws may include private messages as a source of libel, or even a fact that can be proven to be true, but which insults the honour of someone as being libel (Clyde and Co 2019).

Cyber intelligence reports typically attribute attacks to aliases of threat actors even if the actual identity of the threat actor is strongly suspected (MITRE 2022).

These aliases are widely known and recognised, but perform a useful function in allowing researchers to refer to threat actors under a pseudonym, thus reducing the risk of libel.

Victims of attacks deserve privacy. Identifying them is unlikely to provide additional benefit beyond describing the nature of their business and location. In 2014, a steel works in Germany was reported as suffering extensive damage due to a cyber attack. The German authorities publicly reported the attack, allowing similar heavy industries across the world to be alerted to the possibility and consequences of the attack, but did not disclose the identity of the victim (BBC 2014). To have done so would not have added additional benefit to the report, but may have harmed the victim.

7.5   Managing the Unexpected

Even the best prepared intelligence programme can encounter surprises, especially when external entities are involved. Intelligence sharing partnerships may involve multiple partners, who may have different or conflicting objectives compared with others. The discovery of intelligence that affects a partner may result in them behaving unexpectedly and seeking to suppress intelligence, which otherwise they would have encouraged to be shared.

Vulnerability disclosure is particularly susceptible to partners changing their mind on the wisdom of publication when a vulnerability directly affects them. Similarly, commercial or nation state partners may find the publication of an intelligence report problematic and seek to suppress disclosure. Potentially a report may disclose confidential information or depict one of their own partners in a negative light.

In such instances it is useful to recall the goal of a threat intelligence function – to inform decision makers so that they can make better decisions. The ramifications of a course of action that causes significant upset or harm to a partner may be severe, and the wider consequences may be unknown to the threat intelligence team. The ethical dimension of a course of action is likely to form part of the briefing that an intelligence team presents to decision makers, but it is for decision makers to make decisions.

Nevertheless, the threat intelligence landscape is fluid and populated by many different entities. A tricky ethical dilemma on whether to publish or not may be rendered moot by a third party disclosing the contentious issue independently.

If a decision is to be made, the ethical frameworks presented earlier in this chapter are there to assist decision making. Although behaving ethically is a choice, occasionally there are no good outcomes to be found, and a decision maker must choose the least bad option and accept the consequences.

Behaviour that breaks ethical norms or that damages the trust upon which relationships and partnerships are based should not go unchallenged. Sanctioning unethical behaviour conveys that such behaviour is not accepted and helps reinforce community norms (Mulder 2016). However, the effects of sanctioning are complex. Sanctions can reduce trust and lead to less co-operation. Regimes where positive behaviour is rewarded, and transgressors are punished fairly tends to lead to reinforcement of community norms (van Dijk et al. 2014).

7.6   Continuous Improvement

Continuous improvement in resolving ethical issues, minimising risks, adhering to laws and regulations requires commitment, and an organisation that can learn from previous mistakes.

Procedures and policies should be documented so that they can be amended as moral hazards are encountered and addressed. Clearly documented procedures can be taught to new members of staff, so that analysts know how to perform their role correctly. Outlining where hazards and risks have been identified and how they have been addressed prevents the same mistakes being duplicated.

Above all, ethical decisions should be documented and discussed. Ethics is a practical discipline, like all skills ethical decision making would be expected to improve with practice. Actively demonstrating to colleagues that ethics is a key part of intelligence activities and decision making helps promote moral development and develop moral courage so that when faced with a difficult decision, we do the right thing.

Summary

Professionalism is an ancient concept relating to the conduct of technically sophisticated activities. Professionals are expected to have completed adequate training and education to be acquainted with their profession's accepted common body of knowledge, and to behave ethically and appropriately in their activities. Significantly, professionals are expected to have a higher purpose beyond commercial consideration in their activities.

CTI does not have a single regulatory body overseeing the training and conduct within the domain. Nevertheless, people working within the discipline should seek to behave professionally, with integrity, and to apply ethics to their decision making.

References

ABET (2019). Criteria for accrediting engineering programs, 2020–2021. https://www.abet.org/accreditation/accreditation-criteria/criteria-for-accrediting-engineering-programs-2020-2021 (accessed 13 January 2023).

Armerding, T. (2017a). Should governments keep vulnerabilities secret? *Naked Security* (1 August). https://nakedsecurity.sophos.com/2017/08/01/should-governments-keep-vulnerabilities-secret (accessed 13 January 2023).

Armerding, T. (2017b). Shadow Brokers cause ongoing headache for NSA. *Naked Security* (15 November). https://nakedsecurity.sophos.com/2017/11/15/shadow-brokers-cause-ongoing-headache-for-nsa (accessed 13 January 2023).

Arnold, L. (2002). Assessing professional behavior: yesterday, today, and tomorrow. *Academic Medicine* 77 (6): 502–514.

Arnold, T., He, J., Jiang, W. et al. (2020). Cloud provider connectivity in the flat internet. *Proceedings of the ACM Internet Measurement Conference*, 230–246.

BBC News (2014). Hack attack causes 'massive damage' at steel works, 22 December. https://www.bbc.com/news/technology-30575104 (accessed 13 January 2023).

Bird, S.J. (1998). The role of professional societies: codes of conduct and their enforcement. *Science and Engineering Ethics* 4 (3): 315–320.

Brien, A. (1998). Professional ethics and the culture of trust. *Journal of Business Ethics* 17 (4): 391–409.

British Medical Association (2012). Bridging the gap between theory and practice: the BMA's approach to medical ethics. In: *Medical Ethics Today: The BMA's Handbook of Ethics and Law*, 3e, 1–19. https://doi.org/10.1002/9781444355666.ch.

Burden, A. (2018). What is moral courage? Institute of Chartered Accountants of Scotland. https://www.icas.com/members/professional-development/what-is-moral-courage (accessed 13 January 2023).

Cambridge English Dictionary (n.d.). Doxing. https://dictionary.cambridge.org/dictionary/english/doxing (accessed 13 January 2023).

Carr-Saunders, A.M. and Wilson, P.A. (1933). Professions before the industrial revolution. In: *The Professions*, 289–294. Oxford University Press.

Caulfield, T., Ioannidis, C., and Pym, D. (2017). The U.S. vulnerabilities equities process: an economic perspective. In: *GameSec 2017: Decision and Game Theory for Security*, 131–150. Springer. https://doi.org/10.1007/978-3-319-68711-7_8.

Chambers, J.T. and Gallegos, G.G. (2006). *Public–Private Sector Intelligence Coordination, Final Report and Recommendations by the Council*. National Infrastructure Advisory Council. https://www.cisa.gov/sites/default/files/publications/niac-intelligence-coordination-final-report-07-11-06-508.pdf (accessed 7 March 2023).

Chantler, C. (1998). Soundbites. *British Medical Journal* 317 (7173): 1666.

Clyde & Co (2019). *Defamation and Social Media in the UAE.* Clyde & Co Insights. https://www.clydeco.com/en/insights/2019/04/defamation-and-social-media-in-the-uae (accessed 13 January 2023).

Council of Europe (2001). Convention on Cybercrime. https://www.coe.int/en/web/conventions/full-list?module=treaty-detail&treatynum=185 (accessed 13 January 2023).

CREST (2019). Code of ethics for suppliers of cyber security services v3.

CREST (2021a). CREST practitioner threat intelligence analyst. https://www.crest-approved.org/certification-careers/crest-certifications/crest-practitioner-threat-intelligence-analyst/ (accessed 13 January 2023).

CREST (2021b). CREST registered threat intelligence analyst. https://www.crest-approved.org/certification-careers/crest-certifications/crest-registered-threat-intelligence-analyst/ (accessed 13 January 2023).

Cunningham, G.M. and Harris, J.E. (2006). Enron and Arthur Andersen: the case of the crooked E and the fallen a. *Global Perspectives on Accounting Education* 3 (1): 27–48.

Davis, M. (2003). What can we learn by looking for the first code of professional ethics? *Theoretical Medicine and Bioethics* 24 (5): 433–454.

Dexter, D. (2020). *The Difference Between Professional Engineers, Engineering and Certifications.* ASPE Pipeline. https://www.aspe.org/pipeline/pipeline-exclusive-the-difference-between-professional-engineering-engineering-and-certifications (accessed 13 January 2023).

van Dijk, E., Mulder, L.B., and de Kwaadsteniet, E.W. (2014). For the common good? The use of sanctions in social dilemmas. In: *Reward and Punishment in Social Dilemmas* (ed. P.A.M. Van Lange, B. Rockenbach and T. Yamagishi), 70–84. Oxford University Press. https://doi.org/10.1093/acprof:oso/9780199300730.003.0005.

Directory of National Intelligence (2013). *Facts on the Collection of Intelligence Pursuant to Section 702 of the Foreign Intelligence Surveillance Act.* http://online.wsj.com/public/resources/documents/prismfactsheet0608.pdf (accessed 13 January 2023).

Dombrowski, P.M. (2007). The evolving face of ethics in technical and professional communication: *Challenger* to *Columbia*. *IEEE Transactions on Professional Communication* 50 (4): 306–319.

EC Council (2021). Certified threat intelligence analyst. https://www.eccouncil.org/programs/threat-intelligence-training (accessed 13 January 2023).

EC Council (n.d.). *Code of Ethics.* https://www.eccouncil.org/code-of-ethics (accessed 13 January 2023).

ECT Ethics & Compliance Initiative (2021). Developing an organizational code of conduct. https://www.ethics.org/resources/free-toolkit/code-of-conduct (accessed 13 January 2023).

ENISA, Symantec Inc., and Landitd Ltd. (2009). *Good Practice Guide, Network Security Information Exchanges*. ENISA European Union Agency for Cybersecurity. https://www.enisa.europa.eu/publications/good-practice-guide (accessed 7 March 2023).

Ethics Member Advisory Group (2013). The leader's choice: five steps to ethical decision making. *PMI® Global Congress 2013—EMEA*. https://www.pmi.org/learning/library/ethical-decision-making-trend-5788 (accessed 13 January 2023).

European Data Protection Supervisor (2020). Necessity & Proportionality. https://edps.europa.eu/data-protection/our-work/subjects/necessity-proportionality_en (accessed 13 January 2023).

Fédération Européenne d'Associations Nationales d'Ingénieurs (2006). FEANI position paper on Code of Conduct: Ethics and Conduct of Professional Engineers. https://www.feani.org/sites/default/files/Position%20Paper%20Code%20of%20Conduct%20Ethics.pdf (accessed 13 January 2023).

Flexner, A. (1915). Is social work a profession? *The 42nd Annual Session of the National Conference of Charities and Correction*, Baltimore, Maryland. https://socialwelfare.library.vcu.edu/social-work/is-social-work-a-profession-1915 (accessed 13 January 2023).

Fox, E., Arnold, R.M., and Brody, B. (1995). Medical ethics education: past, present, and future. *Academic Medicine* 70 (9): 761–769. https://doi.org/10.1097/00001888-199509000-00011.

GCHQ (2018). The equities process. https://www.gchq.gov.uk/information/equities-process (accessed 13 January 2023).

GDPR (2016). Regulation (EU) 2016/679 of the European Parliament and of the Council of 27 April 2017 on the protection of natural persons with regard to the processing of personal data and on the free movement of such data, and repealing Directive 95/46/EC (General Data Protection Regulation). *Official Journal of the European Union*. https://eur-lex.europa.eu/legal-content/EN/TXT/HTML/?uri=CELEX:32016R0679&from=EN#d1e40-1-1 (accessed 13 January 2023).

Gellman, B. and Poitras, L. (2013). U.S., British intelligence mining data from nine U.S. Internet companies in broad secret program. *The Washington Post* (7 June). https://www.washingtonpost.com/investigations/us-intelligence-mining-data-from-nine-us-internet-companies-in-broad-secret-program/2013/06/06/3a0c0da8-cebf-11e2-8845-d970ccb04497_story.html (accessed 13 January 2023).

GIAC (2021a). GIAC cyber threat intelligence (GCTI). https://www.giac.org/certifications/cyber-threat-intelligence-gcti (accessed 13 January 2023).

GIAC (2021b). GIAC advisory board and GIAC management. *Code of Ethics*. https://www.giac.org/policies/ethics (accessed 13 January 2023).

Google Trends (n.d.). https://trends.google.com/trends/explore?date=all&q="cyber%20threat%20intelligence" (accessed 13 January 2023).

Greenwald, G. and MacAskill, E. (2013) NSA Prism program taps in to user data of Apple, Google and others. https://www.theguardian.com/world/2013/jun/06/us-tech-giants-nsa-data (accessed 13 January 2023).

Gregory, J. (2021). What has changed since the 2017 WannaCry ransomware attack? *Security Intelligence* (1 September). https://securityintelligence.com/articles/what-has-changed-since-wannacry-ransomware-attack (accessed 13 January 2023).

Harris, C.E. Jr., Davis, M., Pritchard, M.S., and Rabins, J. (1996). Engineering ethics: what? why? how? and when? *Journal of Engineering Education* 85 (2): 93–96. https://doi.org/10.1002/j.2168-9830.1996.tb00216.x.

Haworth, J. (2021). When vulnerability disclosure goes sour: new GitHub repo details legal threats and risks faced by ethical hackers. *The Daily Swig* (15 April). https://portswigger.net/daily-swig/when-vulnerability-disclosure-goes-sour-github-repo-details-legal-threats-and-risks-faced-by-ethical-hackers (accessed 13 January 2023).

Hulkower, R. (2016). The history of the Hippocratic Oath: outdated, inauthentic, and yet still relevant. *Einstein Journal of Biology and Medicine* 25 (1): 41–44.

IESBA (2019). International ethics standards board for accountants fact sheet. https://www.ethicsboard.org/system/files/uploads/IESBA/IESBA-Fact-Sheet.pdf (accessed 13 January 2023).

Immanni, M. (2021). Security researcher sued for a bug disclosure, raises funds for legal fight. https://techdator.net/security-researcher-sued-for-a-bug-disclosure-raises-funds-for-legal-fight (accessed 13 January 2023).

Internetwache.org (2016). How we pwned your ICS or why you should not put your HMI on the internet. https://en.internetwache.org/how-we-pwned-your-ics-or-why-you-should-not-put-your-hmi-on-the-internet-18-08-2016 (accessed 13 January 2023).

Isenberg, R., Kristensen, I., Mysore, M., and Weinstein, D. (2021). *Building Cyber Resilience in National Critical Infrastructure*. McKinsey & Company. https://www.mckinsey.com/business-functions/risk-and-resilience/our-insights/building-cyber-resilience-in-national-critical-infrastructure (accessed 7 March 2023).

Josephson Institute (n.d.). The seven-step path to better decisions. https://josephsoninstitute.org/med-4sevensteppath (accessed 13 January 2023).

Kultgen, J.H. (1988). Introduction, professionalism and morality. In: *Ethics and Professionalism*, 3–18. University of Pennsylvania Press.

Landler, M. (2000). A Filipino linked to 'love bug' talks about his license to hack. *The New York Times* (21 October). https://www.nytimes.com/2000/10/21/business/a-filipino-linked-to-love-bug-talks-about-his-license-to-hack.html (accessed 13 January 2023).

Lea, D. (2012). Professionalism in an age of financialization and managerialism. *Business & Professional Ethics Journal* 31 (1): 25–50.

Li, Y. (2010). The case analysis of the scandal of Enron. *International Journal of Business and Management* 5 (10): 37–41.

Macnish, K. (2018). *The Ethics of Surveillance: An Introduction*. Routledge.

Madison, L. (2013). Obama defends 'narrow' surveillance programs. *CBS News* (19 July). https://web.archive.org/web/20130627182800/http://www.cbsnews.

com/8301-250_162-57590025/obama-defends-narrow-surveillance-programs (accessed 13 January 2023).

McAfee Institute (2021a). Certified cyber intelligence investigator (CCII). https://www.mcafeeinstitute.com/products/certified-cyber-intelligence-investigator-ccii (accessed 13 January 2023).

McAfee Institute (2021b). Certified cyber intelligence professional (CCIP). https://www.mcafeeinstitute.com/products/certified-cyber-intelligence-professional-ccip (accessed 13 January 2023).

McBarnet, D. (2005). 'Perfectly legal': a sociological approach to auditing. In: *Ethics and Auditing*, Chapter 2 (ed. T. Campbell and K. Houghton), 25–77. ANU E Press. https://library.oapen.org/bitstream/handle/20.500.12657/33759/459097.pdf?sequence=1#page=193.

Millman, R. (2016). Critical infrastructure in Europe exposed to hackers. https://www.scmagazine.com/news/security-news/critical-infrastructure-in-europe-exposed-to-hackers (accessed 13 January 2023).

Mintz, S. (2020). Codifying the fundamental principles of 'professional behavior': strengthening professionalism by enhancing moral conduct. *CPA Journal*. https://www.cpajournal.com/2020/03/30/codifying-the-fundamental-principles-of-professional-behavior (accessed 13 January 2023).

MITRE Corporation (2022). Groups. https://attack.mitre.org/groups (accessed 13 January 2023).

Mondschein, C.F. and Monda, C. (2019). The EU's general data protection regulation (GDPR) in a research context. In: *Fundamentals of Clinical Data Science* (ed. P. Kubben, M. Dumontier and A. Dekker), 55–71. Springer Open. https://library.oapen.org/bitstream/handle/20.500.12657/22918/1007243.pdf?sequence=1#page=59 (accessed 7 March 2023).

van Mook, W.N., Gorter, S.L., O'Sullivan, H. et al. (2009). Approaches to professional behaviour assessment: tools in the professionalism toolbox. *European Journal of Internal Medicine* 20 (8): e153–e157.

Morse, D. and Jackman, T. (2019). NSA contractor sentenced to nine years in theft of massive amounts of classified material. *The Washington Post* (19 July). https://www.washingtonpost.com/local/public-safety/nsa-contractor-who-stole-massive-amounts-of-classified-material-set-for-sentencing-friday/2019/07/18/83f1bf96-a995-11e9-9214-246e594de5d5_story.html (accessed 13 January 2023).

Mulder, L.B. (2016). When sanctions convey moral norms. *European Journal of Law and Economics* 46: 331–342. https://doi.org/10.1007/s10657-016-9532-5.

Murata, J. (2006). From *Challenger* to *Columbia*: what lessons can we learn from the report of the *Columbia* accident investigation board for engineering ethics? *Techné: Research in Philosophy and Technology* 10 (1): 30–44.

National Society of Professional Engineers (2021). Engineers Creed. https://www.nspe.org/resources/ethics/code-ethics/engineers-creed (accessed 13 January 2023).

Nieweler, A. (2014). Code of ethics and code of conduct – what's the difference? *WhistleBlower Security* (23 June). https://blog.whistleblowersecurity.com/blog/code-of-ethics-and-code-of-conduct-whats-the-difference (accessed 13 January 2023).

OWASP (2021). Vulnerability disclosure cheat sheet. https://cheatsheetseries.owasp.org/cheatsheets/Vulnerability_Disclosure_Cheat_Sheet.html (accessed 13 January 2023).

Powers, W.C., Troubh, R.S., and Winokur, H.S. Jr. (2002). *Report of Investigation, Special Investigative Committee of the Board of Directors of Enron Corp.* https://www.sec.gov/Archives/edgar/data/1024401/000090951802000089/big.txt (accessed 13 January 2023).

Privacy and Civil Liberties Oversight Board (2014). *Report on the Surveillance Program Operated Pursuant to Section 702 of the Foreign Intelligence Surveillance Act.* https://web.archive.org/web/20150218223115/http://www.pclob.gov/library/702-Report.pdf (accessed 13 January 2023).

Ratcliffe, S. (2017). Duke of Wellington 1769–1852: British soldier and statesman. In: *Oxford Essential Quotations*, 5e (ed. S. Ratcliffe). Oxford University Press. https://doi.org/10.1093/acref/9780191843730.001.0001.

Rider, E.A. and Keefer, C.H. (2006). Communication skills competencies: definitions and a teaching toolbox. *Medical Education* 40 (7): 624–629.

Rossow, M. (2012). Engineering ethics case study: the *Challenger* disaster. https://www.online-pdh.com/file.php/288/Ethics_Challenger_Disaster_2nd_Edition.pdf (accessed 13 January 2023).

SANS (2021). FOR578: cyber threat intelligence. https://www.sans.org/cyber-security-courses/cyber-threat-intelligence (accessed 13 January 2023).

Saxonhouse, A.W. (2005). The practice of parrhesia. In: *Free Speech and Democracy in Ancient Athens*, 85–99. Cambridge University Press. https://doi.org/10.1017/CBO9780511616068.006.

Schneier, B. (2014). Disclosing vs. Hoarding vulnerabilities. *Schneier on Security* (22 March). https://www.schneier.com/blog/archives/2014/05/disclosing_vs_h.html (accessed 13 January 2023).

Schofield, M. (2013). Memories of Stasi color Germans' view of U.S. surveillance programs. *McClatchy Washington Bureau* (10 July). https://www.mcclatchydc.com/news/nation-world/national/article24750439.html (accessed 13 January 2023).

Segal, T. (2021). *Enron Scandal: The Fall of a Wall Street Darling.* Investopedia. https://www.investopedia.com/updates/enron-scandal-summary (accessed 13 January 2023).

Sekerka, L.E. (2009). Organizational ethics education and training: a review of best practices and their application. *International Journal of Training and Development* 13 (2): 77–95.

Smith, B. (2017). The need for urgent collective action to keep people safe online: lessons from last week's cyberattack. *Microsoft on the Issues* (14 March). https://blogs.microsoft.com/on-the-issues/2017/05/14/need-urgent-collective-action-keep-people-safe-online-lessons-last-weeks-cyberattack (accessed 13 January 2023).

Suddaby, R., Gendron, Y., and Lam, H. (2009). The organizational context of professionalism in accounting. *Accounting, Organizations and Society* 34 (3–4): 409–427.

Tech Accord (2018). Governments need to do more, and say more, on vulnerability handling. https://cybertechaccord.org/government-vulnerability-handling (accessed 13 January 2023).

US Government Printing Office (1986). *Investigation of the* Challenger *Accident. Report of the Committee on Science and Technology House of Representatives.* US Government Printing Office. https://www.govinfo.gov/content/pkg/GPO-CRPT-99hrpt1016/pdf/GPO-CRPT-99hrpt1016.pdf (accessed 13 January 2023).

Velasquez, M., Velasquez, M., Andre, C. et al. (2015). Thinking ethically. *Markkula Center for Applied Ethics* (1 August). https://www.scu.edu/ethics/ethics-resources/ethical-decision-making/thinking-ethically (accessed 13 January 2023).

Wheeler, D.L. (2012). A guide to the history of intelligence 1800–1918. *Intelligencer: Journal of U.S. Intelligence Studies* 19 (1): 47–50.

White House. Whitehouse.gov (2017). Vulnerabilities equities policy and process for the United States Government. https://trumpwhitehouse.archives.gov/sites/whitehouse.gov/files/images/External%20-%20Unclassified%20VEP%20Charter%20FINAL.PDF (accessed 13 January 2023).

Wikiquote (2022). David Morrison. https://en.wikiquote.org/wiki/David_Morrison (accessed 13 January 2023).

Winder, D. (2020). This 20-year-old virus infected 50 million Windows computers in 10 days: why the ILOVEYOU pandemic matters in 2020. *Forbes* (4 May). https://www.forbes.com/sites/daveywinder/2020/05/04/this-20-year-old-virus-infected-50-million-windows-computers-in-10-days-why-the-iloveyou-pandemic-matters-in-2020 (accessed 13 January 2023).

8

Future Threats and Conclusion

Nobody has a crystal ball with which to view the future. Nevertheless, we can look at prior trends and extrapolate these moving forward into the near future to estimate what might happen. Any predictions regarding future technology are necessarily going to be made with medium confidence at best.

The very concept of cyber threat intelligence is relatively recent, and has changed rapidly over the past few years. The threats against computer systems, the nature of the systems themselves, and the tools at the disposal of cyber threat analysts are different today than they were 15 years ago, so we can envisage that these items will be different again in another 15 years' time.

As technology develops, new applications become apparent. New systems can be developed to support and improve our professional and personal lives. This new technology also provides new opportunities for threat actors to subvert these systems. In turn, cyber threat professionals are required to understand these new threats, understand the motivations and capabilities of threat actors, and to protect and mitigate against these. No matter what the future holds, there will be a need for threat intelligence professionals to understand the threat landscape and to brief decision makers.

8.1 Emerging Technologies

We can make broad predictions regarding the size, processing power, and cost of computer systems. Moore's Law, an observation that the density of transistors able to be placed on silicon chips doubles approximately every two years, has described and shaped the development of integrated circuits since the mid-1960s. Chip development is now approaching fundamental physical limits meaning that Moore's Law is no longer likely to hold true. It is becoming more difficult to find ways by which more transistors can be fitted on silicon wafers, meaning that

Cyber Threat Intelligence, First Edition. Martin Lee.

improvements in transistor density will take longer to achieve (Theis and Wong 2017).

This is not to say that computer chip development is at an end. On the contrary, chip development will likely produce chips that consume less power, cost less per unit, and that are tightly coupled with the essential components of a computer such as memory, storage, graphics processing, and networking. These new systems manage to deploy an entire computer system onto a single chip (Vellante and Floyer 2021).

These small, cheap, yet single-performant chip systems will be networked and connected to local networks as well as the Internet. It is likely that current distinctions between wireless and cellular communications will blur. Systems will make autonomous decisions as to what protocol and signal strength is necessary to communicate with a desired system (Akyildiz et al. 2020).

Proximate systems communicate most efficiently using low signal strength, and high frequency band protocols. These allow large amounts of data to be exchanged quickly without the signal travelling farther than necessary. Connections to distant or cloud-based systems are best made using cellular networks, where systems communicate with an access point, which requires a higher signal strength and lower frequency band to travel to an access point serving many systems (Akyildiz et al. 2020).

Small, connected devices will allow data processing systems to be located close to the environments where data is being created. This paradigm of edge computing means that data can be collected and processed rapidly in place, allowing decisions to be made quickly through artificial intelligence (AI).

Local servers will manage local devices, offering services that can't be performed on the stand-alone systems, such as additional data processing or storage. Data summaries and metrics relating to the local environment can be shared with the next level of supervisory servers, probably provided as remote cloud computing systems (Xiao et al. 2019; Zhou et al. 2019).

These systems will enable many new use cases; although which applications will succeed commercially has yet to be discovered. Despite not knowing the nature of these applications, we can envisage that there will be many of these small, networked computer systems deployed looking after the needs of local environments. We can also envisage some of the threats that these systems will face. The building management, health care, and transport sectors are likely sectors where these systems will be deployed, and can act as example case studies.

8.1.1 Smart Buildings

The built environment consists of the infrastructure, the buildings, and services necessary for people to work and live. Technology will permit these to perform more efficiently providing a better experience for people and economising energy.

Buildings are responsible for approximately 40% of energy consumption and 36% of CO_2 emissions in the EU (Lazarova-Molnar and Mohamed 2019). If we are to reduce power consumption and CO_2 emissions, then optimising energy use in buildings must be a priority.

Smart buildings use integrated sensors and actuators to power down electricity consuming systems when they are not required, and anticipate when systems will be needed so that they are ready in advance for people to use. Upgrading existing buildings to a smart building reduces energy consumption by 30–50%, even upgrading a single building management system can result in energy savings of 5–15% (King and Perry 2017).

These sensors and actuators are frequently referred to as the Internet of Things (IoT). These small computing devices sense the use of areas and facilities, and this data is interpreted with contextual information in order to make changes to the environment through actuators controlling the provision of heat/cooling, light, ventilation, and power (Soudan et al. 2018).

For example, a smart building can surmise that on weekends and public holidays there is no need to provide lighting or anything other than minimal heating and cooling to office areas because nobody is present. The building may know or discover that one floor contains a 24/7 operations team, which does require full service, allowing services to be diverted to areas where they are needed and conserved where they are not.

Ultimately, smart buildings can help achieve net-zero carbon emissions while providing improved security and well being for occupants, and at the same time reducing maintenance costs for operators through identifying when maintenance is required early (Nesler et al. 2021).

These IoT systems will be nothing more than small computer systems sensing and interacting with the environment. Their functionality will be provided by software and network access. However, we know from prior experience that software will contain vulnerabilities, and networked systems are subject to attacks.

8.1.1.1 Software Errors

When software is developed by humans, errors will be found within the code. The frequency of errors within software can be predicted mathematically, and the same classes of errors tend to recur time and time again (Bhatt et al. 2017). One common error within software engineering is neglecting to verify user supplied data to prevent buffer overflow errors (CWE 2021). Despite this class of vulnerability being described since 1972, it remains one of the most frequent vulnerabilities of IoT devices (Al-Boghdady et al. 2021; Anderson 1972).

Automated testing of software code during development will help identify vulnerabilities before they are published in production code. AI assistants incorporated into integrated development environments (IDEs) will help programmers identify how code can be improved or areas where vulnerabilities may be encountered.

However, even the most effective automated checking and supervision is unlikely to help if the specification for a software engineering project is incorrect. Software engineers will be perfectly capable of developing systems of very high quality, which are completely inappropriate for the task required because the requirements were wrong.

Even if we can hope for improvements in software quality, an increased reliance on AI brings its own risks.

The reasoning by which AI comes to a decision is opaque. Models trained on one set of data may come to incorrect decisions when applied to a real world situation. If the AI is processing large amounts of data, incidents where incorrect decisions are being made may be missed.

The Sybil attack takes advantage of AI decision making by spoofing data to appear to originate from many trusted systems, but instead, the data has been supplied by a threat actor (Douceur 2002). Hence, the AI system analyses the data it has available and comes to an incorrect decision based on the fake data it has been supplied.

Smart buildings will present opportunities for threat actors to compromise the confidentiality, integrity, and availability of both the building systems as well as the data they generate and rely on for operation. Attacks against systems that interact with the physical world can have physical consequences too.

Cyber threat intelligence professionals will be required to model the threats against such systems, advise on protections, and ensure that the owners and operators of these systems are aware of the threats they face.

8.1.1.2 Example – Maroochy Shire Incident

Maroochy Shire township in Queensland, Australia, upgraded the local wastewater processing systems. New supervisory control and data acquisition (SCADA) systems were installed in 142 pumping stations across the area. Soon after installation, problems began occurring. Pumps did not run when they should have run, alarms were not reported to the central computer, communications between the central computer and the pumping stations were lost, system parameters were altered without authorisation (Abrams and Weiss 2008).

Before the cause was rectified, millions of litres of raw sewage flowed into the environment. In the words of an Australian Environmental Protection Agency representative, '*Marine life died, the creek water turned black and the stench was unbearable for residents*' (Smith 2001).

The cause was ultimately identified to be a malicious insider. An individual who had worked on the installation of the system, but subsequently denied further employment at the locality, drove around the township issuing radio commands to the system from computer equipment installed in his car. These unauthorised instructions ultimately resulted in the sewage spill. The perpetrator was sentenced to two years in prison (Smith 2001; Abrams and Weiss 2008).

This incident demonstrates the potential consequences of cyber attacks against IoT systems that interact with the environment. Malicious disruption or control of these systems can have dire consequences on the environment and human health.

8.1.2 Health Care

Another application for the sensors and actuators of the IoT is in health care. If sensors can measure the physical environment in a building, then it follows that tiny sensors can measure the biometrics of the body. Already consumer grade sensors are able to measure physical activity, heart rate, blood pressure, blood glucose levels, and blood oxygen levels. Patients are able to monitor their own health, and share their data with their physician over the Internet (Mamdiwar et al. 2021; Vegesna et al. 2017).

There will always be a place for in-person visits and discussion with a personal physician. However, tele-medicine where medical consultations are conducted remotely by video is often simpler, quicker, and more efficient for both doctors and patients, resulting in a better quality of health care, and patient satisfaction while controlling costs (Deloitte Insights 2021).

These innovations will also provide opportunities for cyber criminals. Already the health care industry is a major target for ransomware threat actors (ITPro 2022). The untargeted destructive WannaCry worm hit the UK's health system severely, causing the cancellation of approximately 7 000 patient visits in England alone (Smart 2018).

Despite the raised profile of cyber attacks against the health care sector due to the damage caused by WannaCry, much remains to be done to secure systems. Four years after WannaCry, one study found that 81% of UK health care organisations suffered a ransomware attack in the previous year with 64% having to cancel appointments due to cyber attack (Coker 2021).

Health care is likely to remain an attractive target for threat actors. The sector increasingly relies on electronic data and multiple systems. This is only likely to increase in the future. The patient records, and data generated from health systems is highly confidential and has high availability requirements as well.

Disruption of health care systems leading to the unavailability of data results in critical situations. Without access to the appropriate data and systems, medical appointments cannot be fulfilled, treatments cannot be safely delivered, and lives are put at risk. These heightened stakes presumably mean that leaders are more likely to acquiesce to the demands of an attacker. Hence, the sector may become more attractive for attackers.

As medical devices become more widespread and increasingly used outside health care facilities, the threats to these devices and the systems with which they communicate will change. Cyber threat intelligence professionals have a key part to play in shaping the regulations and standards with which these devices will need to comply. Without the engagement of the threat intelligence community explaining the threats and how threat actors are likely to attack these systems, so that the medical community can take action, this sector is likely to remain at heightened risk of attack.

8.1.2.1 Example – Conti Attack Against Irish Health Sector

Health Services Executive (HSE) is the public body providing health care and social services within Ireland. In May 2021, the organisation was hit by Conti ransomware, which caused widespread disruption to health care across the nation (Cullen 2021).

On 18 March, a single workstation was compromised via an email with a malicious Excel document, by 23 March the attacker had achieved persistence on the affected system. On 31 March, anti-virus software in monitor only mode identified malicious software on the affected system (HSE Board and PWC 2021).

During 7 to 13 May, starting from the affected system, the attacker used the point of ingress to attack and successfully compromise many systems within a variety of hospitals and the HSE itself. At 01:00 on 14 May, the attacker executed ransomware installed on the compromised systems. Ultimately recovery took four months even with the aid of the decryption key (HSE Board and PWC 2021).

Systems that had not been directly affected by the ransomware were taken offline in order to protect them. This resulted in key systems being unavailable. The normal workflow for requesting and receiving diagnostic radiology reports was severely affected (Anderson and Torreggiani 2021).

Due to the disruption, staff had to revert to manual processing of patient information with access to basic diagnostic information such as lab results and images curtailed. Services that were previously automated, such as accessing blood stocks for transfusions, had to readopt long superseded methods (Stritch et al. 2021). At times, electronic data for patient appointments was unavailable, therefore patients could only be processed if they presented with their appointment letter in hand. Radiotherapy treatments for cancer could not be delivered because the patient's treatment plans were unavailable (HSE Board and PWC 2021).

Despite previous incidents, the cyber security posture of health systems in Ireland was inadequate at the time of the attack. Cyber threat intelligence can help prevent similar incidents by highlighting the nature of the threat, the opportunity for threat actors, and the consequent damage.

Health care provision is undergoing rapid change. Naysayers are rarely welcome when new technology is being planned, or worse, already deployed without input from cyber security professionals. However, innovations that bring new efficiencies, cost savings, and new functionality, as well as incrementally improved systems, require adequate cyber security protection if such incidents are not to be repeated.

8.1.3 Transport Systems

Sensors, actuators, and the ability for autonomous systems to process data locally before making decisions regarding the best course of action is leading widespread change in the transport industry. Autonomous transport systems will be able to navigate from point to point, picking up the correct cargo, or passengers, delivering their payload to the destination via the most efficient route.

This autonomous transport will take place over sea and river, rail and rivers (Fiedler et al. 2019). Drivers of vehicles are already increasingly supported by computer systems. ABS brakes sense if the application of the brakes by the driver is causing the wheel to skid, and apply effective breaking automatically. Sat-nav systems already route drivers to their destination taking into consideration traffic levels (Cusack 2021). These systems will increase in sophistication assisting drivers with the tasks of driving and improving safety until they are able to take full control.

In parallel, the move to autonomous transport will also require improvements in infrastructure so that ports, roads, and rail infrastructure are able to communicate with vehicles informing them of any conditions, limitations, or restrictions that will affect their journey (Duval et al. 2019).

Smart infrastructure indirectly enables scams. Vehicles may be charged for entering the congested centres of cities, charged tolls for crossing bridges, or for using highways. These tolls are enforced through automated number plate recognition, with fines sent to drivers who have not already paid the relevant charge. Scammers can piggyback on awareness of these charges by sending fraudulent demands for payment to vehicle owners for fictitious use of infrastructure, or by offering fake payment collection systems (Fox 2020; Transport for London n.d.; Warrington Guardian 2019).

The transport industry relies on a complex web of interconnecting systems. Interrupting any one of these systems can have far reaching and unpredictable consequences. As transport and the supply chains reliant on transport become increasingly integrated and reliant on technology, risks to this sector will become more prominent.

A number of recent attacks demonstrate potential weaknesses within transport. A presumed ransomware attack against a company known for consumer sport devices, reportedly affected their professional range of products preventing pilots from submitting flight plans, or downloading mandatory navigational data (Hay Newman 2020).

A series of cyber attacks in February 2022 disrupted fuel distribution in Europe. It is far from clear if these attacks were part of a coordinated plan of disruption or an unlucky co-incidence. The operations of two German fuel storage and distribution companies were disrupted by cyber attack leading to difficulties for the organisations to distribute fuel to tankers for delivery to retail fuel pumps (Wittels et al. 2022).

Concomitantly, oil terminal facilities reportedly located at Antwerp and Ghent were disrupted due to cyber attacks leading to difficulties in loading and unloading fuel-carrying barges (Muncaster 2022). A few months earlier a cyber attack against the Colonial pipeline in the US led to disruption of the fuel supply causing price increases at pumps, long queues at retail pumps, and localised shortages (Tsvetanov and Slaria 2021; Turton and Mehrotra 2021).

Complex innovations such as autonomous vehicles can be expected to be exposed to complex risks due to the failure or compromise of the many systems that will enable their function. Cyber threat intelligence professionals have a key role to play in the development of such systems by applying their experience to consider how such systems may be attacked, or disrupted through attacks against disparate systems.

8.2 Emerging Attacks

Bad guys do not get any dumber. We can only expect threat actors to improve their capabilities. On the other hand, the motivations of threat actors, theft, fraud, self-gratification, espionage, furthering geopolitical ambitions, etc., are as old as humanity itself. While the motivations of threat actors are unlikely to change the means by which the attacks are conducted will evolve.

8.2.1 Threat Actor Evolutions

8.2.1.1 Criminal Threat Actors

The hallmark of the criminal threat actor is the aim to achieve illicit financial gain. Criminals have been adept at adapting 'traditional' criminal business models to the online environment and conducting their operations at a distance from their intended victims.

We can certainly envisage that current attacks against current systems will continue. As financial services are increasingly delivered over the Internet, it is extremely unlikely that attackers will cease in their efforts to gain access to financial accounts through phishing attacks or by developing malware. Similarly, dating scams or advance fee fraud that prey on human weaknesses are unlikely to ever become extinct.

8.2.1.1.1 *Crimes of Persuasion*

Any system that involves people will be vulnerable to crimes of persuasion, where a threat actor uses social engineering in order to convince a victim to work against their best interests. Even if it would be possible to create a technically flawless system that is resistant to any software or hardware exploitation, such a system would still be vulnerable to human error.

The business email compromise scam involves an attacker masquerading as a supplier or senior manager requesting that a fictitious urgent invoice is paid (FBI 2021). As business is increasingly conducted virtually without face-to-face contact, we can envisage that criminals will seek to exploit communication to conduct similar frauds.

We can imagine that the operation of smart buildings and smart health care will involve the provision of services from many different providers. A building manager overseeing many different smart buildings while having inherited a portfolio of maintenance contracts from various different suppliers may struggle with distinguishing genuine from fake invoices for services. This would be a prime target for business email compromise scammers.

8.2.1.1.2 *Crimes of Compromise*

Once an attacker has access to a system and is able to execute arbitrary code on the system, the attacker can decide what functions they would like the system to perform. Importantly, the attacker doesn't necessarily need full administrator access to a system in order to profit. User-level access is often sufficient for an attacker to make illicit gain from a compromised system.

Ransomware has proved to be a profitable business for criminals. In essence, ransomware applies the criminal business model of kidnap to data; taking something of value from the victim and offering to return it if paid. The criminal encrypts the system data rendering the data, and frequently the system platform too, unavailable to the legitimate owner.

In order to regain access to the data, the victim is requested to pay a ransom. If the ransom is paid, the criminal releases the cryptographic key necessary to decrypt the data. The average ransom paid in a ransomware attack has been measured to be US $170 404 (Sophos 2021).

The health care industry is particularly targeted by ransomware (Coker 2021; Warfield 2021). If patient care records are hit with ransomware and encrypted lives are at risk, this provides a strong pressure on decision makers to pay the ransom and restore services. It's easy to imagine that future connected health care devices and health management systems will also be tempting targets for attackers.

Hitting individual systems with ransomware is one strategy, however causing widespread disruption by hitting an entire organisation or facility with ransomware causes more pain for the victim, and presumably a greater propensity to pay the ransom. Accordingly, transport hubs such as ports can be envisaged as a lucrative opportunity to cause major disruption (Gallagher and Brukhardt 2021; The Maritime Executive 2020).

Similarly, a ransomware attack against a smart building could result in the entire building becoming dysfunctional with users of the building unable to enter or possibly leave. Again, the amount of disruption resulting from such an attack would be a strong incentive for the building operator to pay the ransom.

The resources of compromised systems can be stolen instead of encrypted. Ransomware is an extremely abrupt attack that is intended to be impossible to ignore. As computing devices become cheaper and ubiquitous, if a device becomes affected by ransomware, the victim may not notice, or may choose to replace the device as dysfunctional.

In these cases, the attacker may prefer to persist undetected on the device and steal computing resources by diverting processor cycles to solve cryptographic challenges in order to mine cryptocurrency (Nadeau 2021).

The network connectivity can also be appropriated by an attacker, and used as part of a denial of service attack. In these attacks, akin to extortion, an attacker demands payment from a target. If payment is not forthcoming, the attacker commands their compromised systems to clog the network of the victim.

However, with improvements in networking and the use of AI to optimise network selection, we can envisage that denial of service (DoS) attacks will be mitigated automatically and become a less effective attack.

Attacks on smart buildings could be used as a diversionary attack. Denial of service attacks have been launched in order to divert the time and attention of security teams away from more serious attacks. Already threat actors have used DoS attacks as a smokescreen in order to steal $900 000 from a financial institution (Krebs 2013), and this is not the only time that such an attack has occurred (Musli 2013).

8.2.1.2 Nation State Threat Actors

Nation state threat actors advance the geopolitical interests of their masters. Typically, this is achieved through espionage, stealing confidential information, or disruption of the critical national infrastructure or societies of rival states.

Certainly, offensive cyber operations will be part of overt warfare. The Russo–Georgia conflict in 2008 combined a coordinated attack against Georgian government websites, banks, transport, and telecommunications companies with a large-scale land, sea, and air invasion of conventional forces (Connell and Volger 2017). As critical national infrastructure becomes completely automated, cyber attacks that disable infrastructure are likely to be deployed in a way similar to the strategic bombing campaigns of World War II to disable industrial production and the ability to effectively conduct warfare (Beagle 2001).

The 2022 invasion of Ukraine similarly engaged a major cyber capability. Prior to the invasion, espionage campaigns sought intelligence on Ukrainian international relations and defensive capabilities, and secured access to key infrastructure. Immediately following the invasion, destructive wiper malware and denial of service attacks attempted to disable infrastructure and systems (Microsoft DSU 2022).

Establishing toeholds, or identifying vulnerabilities, within national infrastructure, which can be utilised in case of offensive action is likely to be a priority during future conflicts. As vulnerabilities are fixed and latent persistence is removed, this will become an ongoing activity with threat actors constantly probing for weaknesses and defenders constantly blocking and resolving attacks.

This is likely to create a constant, chronic, low-level conflict (Connell and Volger 2017; Pawlak et al. 2020). This conflict will be largely conducted by proxy agents, working at arm's length from the state they serve (Liles 2010; Maurer 2018). In essence, this arena will resemble the sixteenth century model of conducting proxy naval conflict by privateers; self-financing criminal gangs given state protection in return for some degree of state direction (Egloff 2017).

8.2.1.2.1 Quantum Threats

Current computer systems operate with the notion of 'bits', registers that can exist in a state representing '1' or '0'. This model for computing has served us well, facilitating the many advances in information technology. Switching between these two states takes a certain amount of time. Although this time may be very small, and has tended to decrease with each new generation of computer chips, this presents a limit for computing capacity.

Quantum computers offer an analogous but different model. Instead of operating with 'bits' of information, quantum systems operate with 'qubits'. These 'qubits' can exist in a state representing '1' or '0' as well as a mixed state representing both '1' and '0' at the same time. They only exist in a fixed state when they are measured.

This feature allows quantum computers to make calculations far faster than current computing systems. Although such systems can't perform calculations that current systems are unable to, they allow certain calculations, which would take an unfeasibly long time using current architectures (Rincon 2019). Despite large amounts of research, and the development of proof of concept systems, making a functional, working quantum computer system is not straightforward (Pakin 2019).

Many current encryption techniques rely on the fact that it is impractical to calculate the prime factors of large numbers with current computers. However, although Shor's algorithm can only be executed on a suitably powerful quantum computer, it can rapidly identify such prime numbers (Ugwuishiwu et al. 2020).

Hence, whoever develops a fully functional quantum computer with adequate processing capacity will be able to decrypt data in transit and at rest that has been encrypted using algorithms that are not resistant to quantum decryption (NSA 2021).

The development of a quantum computer within a nation state intelligence agency is unlikely to be announced with great fanfare, but to be used in secret. It is highly unlikely that any state possessing such a capability will resist the temptation to use it. Astute cyber threat intelligence professionals may be able to discern evidence that such a device has been developed. An increase in APT activity compromising systems that process data in transit, or discovering breaches of backed-up and encrypted data for example, may be the types of clues left by a state eager to use its new capability. There are already those who believe that encrypted data is being collected in anticipation of quantum technology becoming available (Sparkes 2021).

If a powerful quantum computer system is possible, eventually, the private sector will develop similar capabilities. At this point, decryption of non-quantum secure encryption algorithms will be within the reach of all threat actors. In anticipation of the demise of current encryption algorithms, standards bodies are evaluating encryption techniques that will resist attacks by quantum computers (NIST 2022). Cyber threat intelligence professionals must be sure to advise decision makers on when it will be necessary to depreciate older encryption algorithms and move to modern alternatives.

8.2.1.2.2 Hybrid Threats

Hybrid threats refers to '[a country] *using multiple instruments of power and influence, with an emphasis on nonmilitary tools, to pursue its national interests outside its borders*' (Treverton et al. 2018). The nature of modern communications technology provides threat actors with the possibility of achieving geopolitical influence and gains without needing to resort to physical warfare. Propaganda, disinformation, and economic tools such as funding lobbying organisations or political parties allows a hostile state to extend their influence beyond their borders.

Russian military doctrine combines offensive cyber capability with propaganda and psychological manipulation within the concept of 'information warfare' (Devali 2020). Embedded within the notion of 'information warfare' is the idea of manipulating an opponent, destabilising and disorienting them while supplying controlled information and a narrative that induces them to adopt decisions and behaviour decided by the initiator of the action (Thomas 2004).

Information can be used to manipulate by many means (Table 8.1).

Current cyber threats frequently centre on the 'hacking' and compromise of networked systems with the aim of causing them to function in a way not desired

Table 8.1 Techniques for using information to manipulate adversaries.

Distraction	Creating a real or imaginary threat to one of the enemy's most vital locations (flanks, rear, etc.) during the preparatory stages of combat operations, thereby forcing him to reconsider the wisdom of his decisions to operate along an axis.
Overload	Frequently sending the enemy a large amount of conflicting information.
Paralysis	Creating the perception of a specific threat to a vital interest or weak spot.
Exhaustion	Compelling the enemy to carry out useless operations, thereby entering combat with reduced resources.
Deception	Forcing the enemy to reallocate forces to a threatened region during the preparatory stages of combat operations.
Division	Convincing the enemy that they must operate in opposition to coalition interests.
Pacification	Leading the enemy to believe that pre-planned operational training is occurring rather than offensive preparations, thus reducing his vigilance.
Deterrence	Creating the perception of insurmountable superiority.
Provocation	Force them into taking action advantageous to your side.
Overload	Dispatching an excessively large number of messages to the enemy during the preparatory period.
Suggestion	Offering information that affects the enemy legally, morally, ideologically, or in other areas.
Pressure	Offering information that discredits the government in the eyes of its population.

Source: Komov (1997) as reported in Thomas (2004).

by the owner. Future threats may focus on abusing networked systems, allowing them to function legitimately as envisaged by the operator, but using them to manipulate populations and achieve outcomes that were never considered by the system owner as a risk.

Manipulating public opinion during elections can help elect a candidate favoured by a malicious entity, or provoke a landslide election with a large margin with the potential to suppress (or oppress) the opposition (Simpser 2013). The US presidential election of 2016 was considered by many as almost certainly influenced by foreign interests seeking to sway public opinion through social media, and the targeting, hacking, and release of information to damage unfavoured candidates (Abrams 2019; Mueller 2019). The compromise and leaking of information during the French presidential election of 2017 is discussed in Chapter 9.

Defeating information warfare campaigns is not a simple matter. Free speech and open debate are hallmarks of a democracy. Identifying when the debate is not open, but being manipulated with opposing voices crowded out of the discussion is not an easy matter. Intervening to prevent such manipulation and holding perpetrators to account is even more complex (Sander 2019).

Cyber threat intelligence analysts will need to understand this emerging threat and ensure that decision makers are aware of the consequences of such a threat. Similarly, we can envision an emerging branch of cyber threat intelligence concerned with the detection of malicious attempts at swaying public opinion through the abuse of communication systems.

8.2.1.3 Other Threat Actors

As a rule of thumb, criminal threat actors are responsible for the vast majority of cyber attacks. Nation state threat actors are the cause of far fewer attacks, but are responsible for the most sophisticated attacks. Other threat actors such as hacktivists or terrorists are much less active and less sophisticated than criminal or nation state threat actors.

The hacktivist groups of the early to mid-2010s declined almost certainly due to the efforts of law enforcement and a series of high profile arrests. This is not to say that hacktivism has gone away. Hacktivists continue to release archives of data obtained from public and illegally accessed sources (Schaffer 2021).

Hacktivism as an activity is uniquely vulnerable when compared with criminal or state-sponsored threat actors. The latter seek to avoid attention and conduct their operations with as little publicity as possible. Conversely, hacktivists often conduct their operations with a view to courting publicity for their cause. Their visibility attracts law enforcement attention, and their nature as a group of like-minded people leaves them open to infiltration.

We can envisage offensive cyber skills being used by terrorist organisations (Goodwin 2021). Extremists are adept at using social media and the online environment as a means of spreading their message and attracting recruits to their cause (Winter et al. 2020). There is no reason why skilled cyber security operatives should be resistant to radicalisation, and directed to launch attacks in support of an extreme ideology.

The ideological rallying call may come from states themselves. During the invasion of Ukraine in 2022, the Ukrainian deputy prime minister announced the formation of the IT Army of Ukraine, a volunteer effort where participants were encouraged to conduct denial of service attacks against specified websites (Burgess 2022; Schenchner 2022). Anyone who wished to participate in conducting offensive cyber operations in support of Ukraine could participate.

In parallel, the Anonymous hacktivist collective also launched an operation against Russian organisations, and entities operating in Russia (Milmo 2022). Associated entities and their attacks have compromised many organisations and released vast amounts of stolen data (Faife 2022).

Despite successes, at this point it is unclear if the activity has assisted in the efforts against the invasion, serves to escalate tensions, or merely acts as a distraction. It is possible that popular, open-season hacking activities may serve as a smoke-screen for the activities of nation state threat actors in compromising systems, or indeed criminal entities seeking to gain access to systems for future use.

At the very least, we can expect to see similar activities as a part of future conflicts.

8.3 Emerging Workforce

As an emerging profession, there are few candidates with many years of experience in the domain for a hiring manager to recruit. Hiring for any role within cyber security is fraught with difficulty; there is more demand for recruits than applicants to fill the roles. The $(ISC)^2$ estimates that the global cyber security workforce will need to grow 65% in order to meet needs (ISC2 2021). Clearly this is an unattainable goal.

In order to recruit, hiring managers must think creatively and look for staff from non-traditional backgrounds who will bring valuable skills and experience from other professions and be trained to perform a role. The European security agency, ENISA, sees training provided by employers as key to helping recruits gain the necessary skills (ENISA 2019).

Employers need to be realistic regarding their hiring goals. Expecting to hire fully qualified and competent staff who will be able to hit the ground running in threat intelligence is unlikely. Hiring someone who has potential and is likely to gain the necessary skills with support and training is a feasible goal.

8.3.1 Job Roles and Skills

Defining the functions performed by a threat intelligence team, and the skills required to fulfil these functions is a difficult task. The demands made on cyber threat intelligence teams will evolve over the coming years, as will the various roles that comprise the team.

Threat actors continuously develop their skills and evolve their attacks. In return, the skills and knowledge of the people within the threat intelligence team must also evolve. Some job roles will become more specialised over time, such as those that focus on specific facets of attacks or threat actor behaviour. Other job roles may become more prominent and important, such as communication skills including the ability to convey complex information succinctly.

Skills frameworks allow the evolving mix of aptitude, training, and knowledge that are required for the roles within a team, and those acquired by team members to be enumerated, defined, and documented. Where there are gaps between the skills required and those offered by team members, training or further experience can fill discrepancies. Similarly, when hiring, the requirements for skills and knowledge necessary to fulfil the job role can be compared by those offered by candidates (Figure 8.1).

The NICE framework provides a mechanism by which employers can describe knowledge, skills, tasks, and competencies necessary for cyber security roles (NIST 2020). Those seeking to join the cyber security workforce can discover the skills and knowledge necessary for different job roles (NIST 2021). Candidates can identify the types of roles that best fit their current profile, and spot which skills they need to acquire to apply for other roles.

The Skills Framework for the Information Age (SFIA) is widely used to model skills, expertise, and requirements across digital industries. This framework defines 120 skills categorised into the seven high-level categories of: strategy and architecture, change and transformation, development and implementation, delivery and operation, people and skills, relationships, and engagement (SFIA 2021a).

Threat intelligence is included within the set of described skills, defined as:

Developing and sharing actionable insights on current and potential security threats to the success of integrity of an organisation.

(SFIA 2021b)

Job role

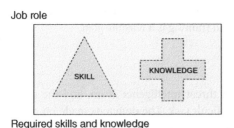

Required skills and knowledge

Figure 8.1 Illustration of how candidate skills and knowledge maps to the needs of a defined job role. *Source:* Adapted from NIST SP 800-181 (Peterson et al. 2020).

Candidate

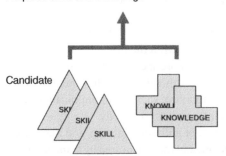

Offered skills and knowledge

It goes on to state that threat intelligence activities include tasks such as:

Gathering data from a variety of open or proprietary intelligence sources.
Processing and classifying threat data to make it useful and actionable by others.
Packaging the data for use by consumers of the information.
Enabling the use of the data automatically by security tools.
Providing threat intelligence to help others mitigate vulnerabilities or to respond to security incidents.

(SFIA 2021b)

SFIA defines seven levels of responsibility for each skill. These responsibilities can be thought of as levels of mastery or competency for a specific skill. These are defined in Table 8.2.

Each level of responsibility applies to the five attributes of skills as shown in Table 8.3.

Table 8.2 The seven levels of responsibility, from SFIA.

Level 1	Follow	Performs routine tasks under direction.
Level 2	Assist	Performs a range of activities under routine direction.
Level 3	Apply	Performs a range of activities, sometimes complex, under general direction.
Level 4	Enable	Performs a broad range of complex activities under general direction with accountability.
Level 5	Ensure, advise	Implements and executes policies, responsible for meeting objectives.
Level 6	Initiate, influence	Contributes to developing policies and strategy with defined authority and accountability.
Level 7	Set strategy, inspire, mobilise	Leads formulation of strategy with full accountability for self and those to whom responsibilities have been assigned.

Source: Adapted from SFIA (2021b).

Table 8.3 The five key attributes of skills, as defined in SFIA.

Autonomy	The degree of supervision, accountability, or authority.
Influence	The amount of influence over peers, customers, suppliers, or degree of inspiration given.
Complexity	The complexity of work tasks from routine to complex, through to development of policy and strategy.
Business skills	The amount of awareness and influence over other parts of the business including risk management, legal compliance, innovation as well as communication skill ability.
Knowledge	The amount of domain knowledge and scope of knowledge regarding other domains.

Source: Adapted from SFIA (2021b).

Hence, the competencies necessary for roles within cyber threat intelligence teams can be described by listing the various skills required such as: threat intelligence, digital forensics, providing specialist advice, etc., along with the relevant level of responsibility.

The US National Initiative for Cybersecurity Careers and Studies has already mapped many cyber security jobs to the NICE framework. Within the domain of cyber threat intelligence, the roles are defined as shown in Table 8.4.

Table 8.4 Different roles within the domain of threat intelligence as described in NICCS.

All-source collection manager	Identifies collection authorities and environment; incorporates priority information requirements into collection management; develops concepts to meet leadership's intent. Determines capabilities of available collection assets, identifies new collection capabilities; and constructs and disseminates collection plans. Monitors execution of tasked collection to ensure effective execution of the collection plan.
	Defines 5 required abilities, 82 knowledge items, 23 skills, and 46 tasks to perform.
All-source collection requirements manager	Evaluates collection operations and develops effects-based collection requirements strategies using available sources and methods to improve collection. Develops, processes, validates, and coordinates submission of collection requirements. Evaluates performance of collection assets and collection operations.
	Defines 3 required abilities, 74 knowledge items, 19 skills, and 33 tasks to perform.
All-source analyst	Analyses data/information from one or multiple sources to conduct preparation of the environment, respond to requests for information, and submit intelligence collection and production requirements in support of planning and operations.
	Defines 18 required abilities, 56 knowledge items, 18 skills, and 42 tasks to perform.
Cyber Intel planner	Develops detailed intelligence plans to satisfy cyber operations requirements. Collaborates with cyber operations planners to identify, validate, and levy requirements for collection and analysis. Participates in targeting selection, validation, synchronisation, and execution of cyber actions. Synchronises intelligence activities to support organisation objectives in cyberspace.
	Defines 17 required abilities, 89 knowledge items, 36 skills, and 45 tasks to perform.

Cyber operator	Conducts collection, processing, and/or geolocation of systems to exploit, locate, and/or track targets of interest. Performs network navigation, tactical forensic analysis, and, when directed, executes on-net operations.
	Defines 4 required abilities, 44 knowledge items, 26 skills, and 26 tasks to perform.
Cyber Ops planner	Develops detailed plans for the conduct or support of the applicable range of cyber operations through collaboration with other planners, operators, and/or analysts. Participates in targeting selection, validation, synchronisation, and enables integration during the execution of cyber actions.
	Defines required 16 abilities, 77 knowledge items, 18 skills, and 43 tasks to perform.
Threat/Warning analyst	Identifies collection authorities and environment; incorporates priority information requirements into collection management; develops concepts to meet leadership's intent. Determines capabilities of available collection assets; identifies new collection capabilities; and constructs and disseminates collection plans. Monitors execution of tasked collection to ensure effective execution of the collection plan.
	Defines required 5 abilities, 82 knowledge items, 23 skills, and 46 tasks to perform.
Multi-disciplined language analyst	Applies language and culture expertise with target/threat and technical knowledge to process, analyse, and/or disseminate intelligence information derived from language, voice, and/or graphic material. Creates and maintains language-specific databases and working aids to support cyber action execution and ensure critical knowledge sharing. Provides subject matter expertise in foreign language-intensive or interdisciplinary projects.
	Defines required 4 abilities, 47 knowledge items, 28 skills, and 29 tasks to perform.

Source: Adapted from NICSS (2021).

Hiring managers should be aware that the ideal candidate that exactly matches the skill profile that they have defined probably doesn't exist. Team members are individuals with a mix of formal and informal training and experience coupled with the aptitude for a role. Hiring someone who has a similar experience, training, and outlook to other members of the team may not be the best option.

8.3.2 Diversity in Hiring

Drawing correct conclusions in threat intelligence is a matter of drawing on many different sources of information and considering the various hypotheses that the information may support. Restricting sources of intelligence to a particular type or source would clearly be counterproductive. Similarly, failing to consider various hypotheses or dismissing some out of hand would also be less than effective.

We are all products of our upbringing, education, training, and the environment in which we live and work. These factors necessarily influence our thought processes. No matter how logical and open minded we believe ourselves to be, we all possess various cognitive biases that adversely affect how we process memory, attention, and information (Haselton and Nettle 2006; Ruhl 2021).

Teams in which members share similar backgrounds and training, or teams that are highly cohesive are prone to develop the cognitive bias known as groupthink. In these cases, members feel a strong affinity to the group; opinions and decisions are made not necessarily according to merit, but how they fit with the group beliefs and norms (Janis 1982).

Such groups tend towards self-censorship where members do not want to rock the boat by challenging decisions, offering dissenting opinions, or not asking difficult questions for fear of seeming foolish or not a 'team player'. The group will arrive at the decision which individual members think most other members will agree with, rather than the decision which most individual members think is correct (Sunstein and Hastie 2015).

Groupthink errors have been implicated in intelligence failures including the fall of France in 1940, the search for non-existent weapons of mass destruction, and the subsequent invasion of Iraq in 2003 (Ahlstrom and Wang 2009; Select Committee on Intelligence 2006). Indeed, the term groupthink was coined in response to considering the intelligence and decision errors that led to the Bay of Pigs failed invasion of Cuba in 1961 (Lassila 2008).

To counter the risk of groupthink, it is important to hire diverse teams with a broad set of backgrounds and perspectives. Heterogeneous teams are known to produce more innovative and unique solutions to problems (Jackson et al. 1995). Diverse teams seem to flourish partly because people with different backgrounds approach problems in different ways, and also because team members put more effort into explaining their points of view when they perceive that others may not share their opinions (Philips et al. 2014).

An interesting opinion on the importance of diversity in intelligence is that the reportedly, largely white, middle class, protestant intelligence staff of the CIA didn't recognise the threat posed by Osama bin Laden in the mid to late 1990s. To the CIA his communications were easy to dismiss as those of an eccentric living in a cave who posed no threat. Whereas to potential recruits to bin Laden's cause, the same messages could be interpreted as portraying him as a pious leader of a rightful war (Syed 2019).

Ultimately, reflection on missed intelligence opportunities and the recognition that diversity could be used as an intelligence advantage led to a concerted effort by the CIA to diversify their workforce (Jamali and O'Connor 2021; Rhodan 2015).

Establishing and growing the cyber threat intelligence profession requires more than hiring a diverse workforce. The cyber security workforce has much to do to increase sex equality; only 25% of cyber security practitioners are women (ISC2 2021), although employment of minorities in the US cyber workforce at 25% is higher than the general US employment rate of minorities (21%) (Reed and Acota-Rubio 2018).

The future cyber threat intelligence workforce must be much more diverse in background and have a higher proportion of women than at present. Homogeneity leads to missed intelligence opportunities and overlooked hypotheses.

8.3.3 Growing the Profession

The demand for fully trained and experienced cyber threat intelligence professionals is likely to exceed supply for the foreseeable future. In order to staff cyber threat intelligence teams, we must be creative and look to integrate people with transferable skills into the domain, as well as spotting talent to develop within early career individuals.

The traits that we should look for within the people we wish to develop are:

Systemic thinkers – Being able to consider the bigger picture of day-to-day work.

Team players – Being able to work effectively within a team, and with other teams that may have different objectives and priorities.

Technical and social skills – Being able to understand cyber security issues from various different perspectives, especially those of the users.

Civic duty – A sense of responsibility to wider society and pride in 'doing the right thing'.

Continued learning – Actively learning and staying abreast of technological changes throughout a career.

Communication – Being able to convey complex information in a manner that is relatable by an audience.

(Henry 2021)

Building a fluid career path where people are able to join the cyber intelligence profession at various stages of their career is vital to welcome external talent and their respective skills. Also, this facilitates the ability of trained intelligence professionals to spend time working outside of cyber threat intelligence teams, both to increase awareness of the benefits of threat intelligence within other functions, and to gain experience of the needs of other teams.

Achieving this will require providing the necessary training material so that people can reach the required level of knowledge necessary for each career stage. Current threat intelligence professionals can help by publishing their successes, sharing best practices, tips and tricks for others to learn from, in addition to helping to train and mentor others.

Openly sharing techniques risks exposing our tradecraft with threat actors, so that they can improve their techniques to avoid detection. However, if we are to expand the profession and the workforce, we must provide information for people to train themselves, especially during their early careers. Possibly, by providing engaging content, tutorials, and support, we can entice those who are fascinated by the opportunities of cyber security to pursue a career in cyber threat intelligence rather than as a threat actor.

8.4 Conclusion

At every moment during history, there has been a need for people who seek out and understand the threats that we face. Effective response requires knowledge and wisdom developed through consistently observing and reacting to those which risk causing harm.

Throughout history, criminals have proved adept at exploiting mankind's innovations, identifying ways of making illicit profit or furthering their own agendas. Hostile nation states, and those who seek to undermine our way of life have also used technologies and inventions to harm our societies.

With the advent of 'cyberspace', that is to say the development of computer systems connected via communication networks, it is unfortunately no surprise that these same entities have turned their efforts to subverting these systems. As so much of our personal and professional lives are reliant on networked systems, understanding the risks and threats to these systems has become vital.

The history of electronic computers is tightly coupled with the use of these systems to subvert or to gain advantage of others. Initially shrouded in great secrecy and tightly restricted to the public sector, the emerging profession of cyber threat intelligence has developed as a distinct entity within the private sector.

As a developing profession within a rapidly changing environment, the skills, knowledge, and best practices it is necessary to perform are in flux. Hence, the importance of establishing a common body of knowledge upon which cyber threat intelligence professionals can build. As a profession united against a common enemy, cyber threat intelligence professionals have proved to be remarkably open in sharing tips, information, and allowing others to benefit from their research.

Technology will continue to develop, and threats will continue to evolve. If we are to put new technology to good use in benefitting our societies and enriching our lives, we must ensure that those who are developing these new applications are well informed about potential threats. As long as there is cyber technology, there will be a need for cyber threat intelligence to keep abreast of the threats and to ensure that good decisions are made to keep these new technologies operating for the benefit of mankind.

References

Abrams, A. (2019). Here's what we know so far about Russia's 2016 meddling. *Time* (18 April). https://time.com/5565991/russia-influence-2016-election (accessed 13 January 2023).

Abrams, M. and Weiss, J. (2008). *Malicious Control System Cyber Security Attack Case Study – Maroochy Water Services, Australia*. The Mitre Corporation. https://apps. dtic.mil/sti/pdfs/AD1107275.pdf (accessed 28 March 2023).

Ahlstrom, D. and Wang, L.C. (2009). Groupthink and France's defeat in the 1940 campaign. *Journal of Management History* 15 (2): 159–177. https://doi. org/10.1108/17511340910943804.

Akyildiz, I.F., Kak, A., and Nie, S. (2020). 6G and beyond: the future of wireless communications systems. *IEEE Access* 8: 133995–134030. https://doi.org/10.1109/ ACCESS.2020.3010896.

Al-Boghdady, A., Wassif, K., and El-Ramly, M. (2021). The presence, trends, and causes of security vulnerabilities in operating systems of IoT's low-end devices. *Sensors* 21 (7): 2329.

Anderson, J.P. (1972). *Computer Security Technology Planning Study. Report to USAF Deputy for Command and Management Systems, HQ Electronic Systems Division*. https://csrc.nist.gov/csrc/media/publications/conference-paper/1998/10/08/ proceedings-of-the-21st-nissc-1998/documents/early-cs-papers/ande72a.pdf (accessed 13 January 2023).

Anderson, T. and Torreggiani, W.C. (2021). The impact of the cyberattack on radiology systems in Ireland. *Irish Medical Journal* 114 (5): 347.

Beagle, T.W. (2001). *Operation Pointblank in Effects-Based Targeting: Another Empty Promise?* Air University Maxwell AFB. http://www.jstor.org/stable/ resrep13830.10.

Bhatt, N., Arnand, A., Yadavalli, V.S.S., and Kumar, V. (2017). Modeling and characterizing software vulnerabilities. *International Journal of Mathematical, Engineering and Management Sciences* 2 (4): 288–299.

Burgess, M. (2022). Ukraine's volunteer 'IT Army' is hacking in uncharted territory. *Wired* (27 February). https://www.wired.com/story/ukraine-it-army-russia-war-cyberattacks-ddos (accessed 13 January 2023).

Coker, J. (2021). 81% of UK healthcare organizations hit by ransomware in last year. https://www.infosecurity-magazine.com/news/healthcare-ransomware-last-year (accessed 13 January 2023).

Connell, M. and Volger, S. (2017). *Russia's Approach to Cyber Warfare*. Center for Naval Analyses. https://www.cna.org/cna_files/pdf/DOP-2016-U-014231-1 Rev.pdf (accessed 28 March 2023).

Cullen, P. (2021). Cyberattack on HSE systems prompts cancellation of key medical procedures. *The Irish Times* (15 May). https://www.irishtimes.com/news/health/

cyberattack-on-hse-systems-prompts-cancellation-of-key-medical-procedures-1.4565631 (accessed 13 January 2023).

Cusack, J. (2021). How driverless cars will change our world. *BBC Future* (30 November). https://www.bbc.com/future/article/20211126-how-driverless-cars-will-change-our-world (accessed 13 January 2023).

CWE Common Weakness Enumeration (2021). *CWE-120: Buffer Copy without Checking Size of Input ('Classic Buffer Overflow')*. The Mitre Corporation. https://cwe.mitre.org/data/definitions/120.html (accessed 28 March 2023).

Deloitte Insights (2021). *2021 Global Health Care Outlook. Accelerating Industry Change*. Deloitte Touche Tohmatsu Limited. https://documents.deloitte.com/insights/Globalhealthcareoutlook (accessed 28 March 2023).

Devali, D. (2020). An overview of the development of the Russian information warfare concept: part 1. *Hadtudományi Szemle* 13 (1): 27–35. https://doi.org/10.32563/hsz.2020.1.2 .

Douceur, J.R. (2002). The sybil attack. In: *International Workshop on Peer-to-Peer Systems* (ed. P. Druschel, F. Kaashoek and A. Rowstron), 251–260. Springer. https://www.microsoft.com/en-us/research/wp-content/uploads/2002/01/IPTPS2002.pdf (accessed 28 March 2023).

Duval, T., Hannon, E., Katseff, J. et al. (2019). *A New Look at Autonomous-Vehicle Infrastructure*. McKinsey & Company. https://www.mckinsey.com/industries/travel-logistics-and-infrastructure/our-insights/a-new-look-at-autonomous-vehicle-infrastructure (accessed 28 March 2023).

Egloff, F. (2017). Cybersecurity and the age of privateering. In: *Understanding Cyber Conflict. Fourteen Analogies* (ed. G. Perkovich and A.E. Levite), 231–247. Georgetown University Press. https://carnegieendowment.org/2017/10/16/cybersecurity-and-age-of-privateering-pub-73418 (accessed 28 March 2023).

ENISA European Union Agency for Cybersecurity (2019). Cybersecurity skills development in the EU. https://www.enisa.europa.eu/publications/the-status-of-cyber-security-education-in-the-european-union (accessed 13 January 2023).

Faife, C. (2022). They've leaked terabytes of Russian emails, but who's reading? *The Verge* (22 April). https://www.theverge.com/2022/4/22/23036079/russian-emails-leaked-ddosecrets (accessed 13 January 2023).

Federal Bureau of Investigation (2021). Business email compromise. https://www.fbi.gov/scams-and-safety/common-scams-and-crimes/business-email-compromise (accessed 13 January 2023).

Fiedler, R., Bosse, C., Gehlken, D. et al. (2019). *Autonomous Vehicles' Impact on Port Infrastructure Requirements*. Fraunhofer Center for Maritime Logistics and Services CML. https://safety4sea.com/wp-content/uploads/2019/06/IAPHPort-of-Hamburg-Autonomous-vehicles-impact-on-port-infrastructure-requirements-2019_06.pdf (accessed 28 March 2023).

Fox, A. (2020). Vigilance urged after police reports of car congestion fine scam. *The Northern Echo.* https://www.thenorthernecho.co.uk/news/18731130.vigilance-urged-police-reports-car-congestion-fine-scam (accessed 13 January 2023).

Gallagher, R. and Brukhardt, P. (2021). 'Death Kitty' ransomware linked to South African port attack. https://www.bloomberg.com/news/articles/2021-07-29/-death-kitty-ransomware-linked-to-attack-on-south-african-ports (accessed 13 January 2023).

Goodwin, C. (2021). Fighting cyberweapons built by private businesses. *Microsoft on the Issues* (15 July). https://blogs.microsoft.com/on-the-issues/2021/07/15/cyberweapons-cybersecurity-sourgum-malware (accessed 13 January 2023).

Haselton, M.G. and Nettle, D. (2006). The paranoid optimist: an integrative evolutionary model of cognitive biases. *Personality and Social Psychology Review* 10 (1): 47–66.

Hay Newman, L. (2020). A cyberattack on Garmin disrupted more than workouts. *Wired* (27 July). https://www.wired.com/story/garmin-outage-ransomware-attack-workouts-aviation (accessed 13 January 2023).

Henry, C. (2021). Cybersecurity workforce diversity – including cultures, personalities and neurodiversity. *ISACA Journal* 5: 1–5.

HSE Board and PWC (2021). Conti cyber attack on the HSE independent post incident review. https://www.hse.ie/eng/services/publications/conti-cyber-attack-on-the-hse-full-report.pdf (accessed 13 January 2023).

ISC2 (2021). A resilient cybersecurity profession charts the path forward. Cybersecurity workforce study, 2021. https://www.isc2.org/Research/Workforce-Study# (accessed 13 January 2023).

ITPro (2022). Why is the healthcare industry so vulnerable to ransomware? https://www.itpro.co.uk/security/ransomware/362981/why-is-the-healthcare-industry-so-vulnerable-to-ransomware (accessed 13 January 2023).

Jackson, S.E., May, K.E., and Whintey, K. (1995). Understanding the dynamics of diversity in decision-making teams. In: *Team Effectiveness and Decision Making in Organizations*, 204–261. Jossey-Bass.

Jamali, N. and O'Connor, T. (2021). CIA sees diversity as weapon against changing threats from China, Russia. *Newsweek* (5 March). https://www.newsweek.com/cia-diversity-weapon-changing-threat-china-russia-1574167 (accessed 13 January 2023).

Janis, I.L. (1982). *Groupthink: Psychological Studies of Policy Decisions and Fiascoes.* Houghton Mifflin Company.

King, J. and Perry, C. (2017). *Smart Buildings: Using Smart Technology to Save Energy in Existing Buildings.* American Council for an Energy-Efficient Economy. https://www.aceee.org/sites/default/files/publications/researchreports/a1701.pdf (accessed 28 March 2023).

Komov, S.A. (1997). About methods and forms of conducting information warfare. *Military Thought (English Edition)* 4: 18–22.

Krebs, B. (2013). DDoS attack on bank hid $900,000 cyberheist. *Krebs on Security* (19 February). https://krebsonsecurity.com/2013/02/ddos-attack-on-bank-hid-900000-cyberheist (accessed 13 January 2023).

Lassila, K. (2008). A brief history of groupthink. *Yale Alumni Magazine*. https://yalealumnimagazine.com/articles/1947-a-brief-history-of-groupthink (accessed 13 January 2023).

Lazarova-Molnar, S. and Mohamed, N. (2019). Collaborative data analytics for smart buildings: opportunities and models. *Cluster Computing* 22 (1): 1065–1077.

Liles, S. (2010). Cyber warfare: as a form of low-intensity conflicy and insurgency. *Conference on Cyber Conflict*, 47–57. CCD COE Publications.

Mamdiwar, S.D., Shakruwala, Z., Chadha, U. et al. (2021). Recent advances on IoT-assisted wearable sensor systems for healthcare monitoring. *Biosensors* 11 (10): 372.

Maurer, T. (2018). Cyber proxies: an introduction. In: *Cyber Mercenaries: The State, Hackers, and Power*, 3–28. Cambridge University Press. http://dx.doi.org/10.1017/9781316422724.002.

Microsoft Digital Security Unit (2022). Special Report: Ukraine. An overview of Russia's cyberattack activity in Ukraine. Microsoft. https://aka.ms/ukrainespecialreport (accessed 13 January 2023).

Milmo, D. (2022). Anonymous: the hacker collective that has declared cyberwar on Russia. *The Guardian* (27 February). https://www.theguardian.com/world/2022/feb/27/anonymous-the-hacker-collective-that-has-declared-cyberwar-on-russia (accessed 13 January 2023).

Mueller, R.S. (2019). *Report on the Investigation into Russian Interference in the 2016 Presidential Election*, vol. 1. US Department of Justice. https://www.justice.gov/archives/sco/file/1373816 (accessed 28 March 2023).

Muncaster, P. (2022). Cyber-attacks hobble some of Europe's largest ports. *Infosecurity Magazine* (4 February). https://www.infosecurity-magazine.com/news/cyberattacks-hobble-europe-ports/ (accessed 13 January 2023).

Musli, S. (2013). Cybercrooks use DDoS attacks to mask theft of banks' millions. *CNet Tech* (21 August). https://www.cnet.com/tech/services-and-software/cybercrooks-use-ddos-attacks-to-mask-theft-of-banks-millions (accessed 13 January 2023).

Nadeau, M. (2021). Cryptojacking explained: How to prevent, detect, and recover from it. https://www.csoonline.com/article/3253572/what-is-cryptojacking-how-to-prevent-detect-and-recover-from-it.html (accessed 13 January 2023).

National Initiative for Cybersecurity Careers and Studies (NICCS) (2021). NICE cybersecurity workforce framework work roles. https://niccs.cisa.gov/workforce-development/cyber-security-workforce-framework/workroles (accessed 13 January 2023).

National Institute of Standards and Technology (2020). Employer resources. https://www.nist.gov/itl/applied-cybersecurity/nice/nice-framework-resource-center/employer-resources (accessed 13 January 2023).

National Institute of Standards and Technology (2021). Learner resources. https://
www.nist.gov/itl/applied-cybersecurity/nice/nice-framework-resource-center/
learner-resources (accessed 13 January 2023).

National Institute of Standards and Technology, US Department of Commerce
(2022). Post-quantum cryptography. https://csrc.nist.gov/Projects/post-quantum-
cryptography (accessed 13 January 2023).

National Security Agency (2021). Quantum computing and post-quantum cryptography.
https://media.defense.gov/2021/Aug/04/2002821837/-1/-1/1/Quantum_FAQs_
20210804.PDF (accessed 13 January 2023).

Nesler, C., Lam, K.P., and Lasternas, B. (2021). *How to Build Smart, Zero
Carbon Buildings – and Why it Matters*. World Economic Forum. https://
www.weforum.org/agenda/2021/09/how-to-build-zero-
carbon-buildings (accessed 28 March 2023).

Pakin, S. (2019). The problem with quantum computers. *Scientific American*
(10 June). https://blogs.scientificamerican.com/observations/the-problem-
with-quantum-computers (accessed 13 January 2023).

Pawlak, P., Tikk, E., and Kertunen, M. (2020). *Cyber Conflict Uncoded. The EU and
Conflict Prevention in Cyberspace*. European Union Institute for Security Studies.
https://www.iss.europa.eu/content/cyber-conflict-uncoded (accessed 28 March 2023).

Peterson, R., Santos, D., Smith, M.C. et al. (2020). *Workforce Framework for Cybersecurity
(NICE Framework). NIST Special Publication 800-181 rev 1*. National Institute of
Standards and Technology NIST. http://dx.doi.org/10.6028/NIST.SP.800-181r1.

Philips, K.W., Medin, D., Lee, C.D. et al. (2014). How diversity works. *Scientific
American* 311 (4): 42–47.

Reed, J. and Acota-Rubio, J. (2018). *Innovation through Inclusion: The Multicultural
Cybersecurity Workforce, an (ISC)2 Global Information Security Workforce Study*.
Frost and Sullivan. https://www.isc2.org/-/media/Files/Research/Innovation-
Through-Inclusion-Report.ashx (accessed 28 March 2023).

Rhodan, M. (2015). CIA lags in recruiting diverse workforce, reports finds. *Time*
(30 June). https://time.com/3941782/cia-diversity-recruitment-report (accessed
13 January 2023).

Rincon, P. (2019). Google claims 'quantum supremacy' for computer. *BBC News*
(23 October). https://www.bbc.com/news/science-environment-50154993
(accessed 13 January 2023).

Ruhl, C. (2021). What is cognitive bias. *Simply Psychology* (4 May). https://www.
simplypsychology.org/cognitive-bias.html (accessed 13 January 2023).

Sander, B. (2019). Democracy under the influence: paradigms of state responsibility
for cyber influence operations on elections. *Chinese Journal of International Law*
18 (1): 1–56. https://doi.org/10.1093/chinesejil/jmz003.

Schaffer, A. (2021). Hacktivists are back. *Washington Post* (11 October). https://www.
washingtonpost.com/politics/2021/10/11/hacktivists-are-back (accessed
13 January 2023).

Schenchner, S. (2022). Ukraine's 'IT Army' has hundreds of thousands of hackers, Kyiv says. *Wall Street Journal* (4 March). https://www.wsj.com/livecoverage/russia-ukraine-latest-news-2022-03-04/card/ukraine-s-it-army-has-hundreds-of-thousands-of-hackers-kyiv-says-RfpGa5zmLtavrot27OWX (accessed 13 January 2023).

Select Committee on Intelligence (2006). *Senate Report 109–360*. U.S. Government Printing Office. https://www.intelligence.senate.gov/publications/committee-activities-2003-2004-november-16-2006 (accessed 13 January 2023).

SFIA (2021a). SFIA version 8. https://sfia-online.org/en/sfia-8 (accessed 13 January 2023).

SFIA (2021b). Threat intelligence. https://sfia-online.org/en/sfia-8/skills/threat-intelligence (accessed 13 January 2023).

Simpser, A. (2013). *Why Governments and Parties Manipulate Elections: Theory, Practice, and Implications*. Cambridge University Press. https://doi.org/10.1017/CBO9781139343824.

Smart, W. (2018). *Lessons Learned: Review of the WannaCry Ransomware Cyber Attack*. Chief Information Officer for the Health and Social Care System. https://www.england.nhs.uk/wp-content/uploads/2018/02/lessons-learned-review-wannacry-ransomware-cyber-attack-cio-review.pdf (accessed 28 March 2023).

Smith, T. (2001). Hacker jailed for revenge sewage attacks. *The Register* (31 October). https://www.theregister.com/2001/10/31/hacker_jailed_for_revenge_sewage (accessed 13 January 2023).

Sophos (2021). The state of ransomware 2021. https://secure2.sophos.com/en-us/medialibrary/pdfs/whitepaper/sophos-state-of-ransomware-2021-wp.pdf (accessed 13 January 2023).

Soudan, M.B., Al Rifaie, H.M., Asmar, T.M., and Majzoub, S. (2018). Smart home energy management system: an exploration of IoT use cases. *2018 Advances in Science and Engineering Technology International Conferences (ASET)*, 1–5.

Sparkes, M. (2021). Spies may be storing data to decrypt with a future quantum computer. *New Scientist* (12 October). https://www.newscientist.com/article/2293341-spies-may-be-storing-data-to-decrypt-with-a-future-quantum-computer (accessed 13 January 2023).

Stritch, M.M., Winterburn, M., and Houghton, F. (2021). The Conti ransomware attack on healthcare in Ireland: exploring the impacts of a cybersecurity breach from a nursing perspective. *Canadian Journal of Nursing Informatics* 16: 3–4.

Sunstein, C.R. and Hastie, R. (2015). From high hopes to fiascos. In: *Wiser: Getting Beyond Groupthink to Make Groups Smarter*, 21–42. Harvard Business School Publishing.

Syed, M. (2019). Viewpoint: was CIA 'too white' to spot 9/11 clues? https://www.bbc.com/news/world-us-canada-49582852 (accessed 13 January 2023).

The Maritime Executive (2020). Ransomware cripples IT systems of inland port in Washington State, 19 November. https://www.maritime-executive.com/article/

ransomware-attack-cripples-systems-of-inland-port-in-washington-state (accessed 13 January 2023).

Theis, T.N. and Wong, H.S.P. (2017). The end of Moore's Law: a new beginning for information technology. *Computing in Science & Engineering* 19 (2): 41–50.

Thomas, T.L. (2004). Russia's reflexive control theory and the military. *Journal of Slavic Military Studies* 17: 237–256. https://doi.org/10.1080/13518040490450529.

Transport for London (n.d.). Unofficial selling websites – transport for London. https://tfl.gov.uk/modes/driving/congestion-charge/unofficial-selling-websites (accessed 13 January 2023).

Treverton, G.F., Thvedt, A., Chen, A.R. et al. (2018). *Addressing Hybrid Threats*. Swedish Defence University. https://www.diva-portal.org/smash/record.jsf?dswi d=5222&pid=diva2:1219292 (accessed 7 March 2023).

Tsvetanov, T. and Slaria, S. (2021). The effect of the colonial pipeline shutdown on gasoline prices. *Economic Letters* 209: 110133. http://dx.doi.org/10.1016/j.econlet.2021.110122.

Turton, W. and Mehrotra, K. (2021). Hackers breached colonial pipeline using compromised password. *Bloomberg* (4 June). https://www.bloomberg.com/news/articles/2021-06-04/hackers-breached-colonial-pipeline-using-compromised-password (accessed 13 January 2023).

Ugwuishiwu, C.H., Orji, U.E., and Asogwa, C.N. (2020). An overview of quantum cryptography and Shor's algorithm. *International Journal of Advanced Trends in Computer Science and Engineering* 9 (5): 7487–7495.

Vegesna, A., Tran, M., Angelaccio, M., and Arcona, S. (2017). Remote patient monitoring via non-invasive digital technologies: a systematic review. *Telemedicine and e-Health* 23 (1): 3–17.

Vellante, D. and Floyer, D. (2021). A new era of innovation: Moore's Law is not dead and AI is ready to explode. *Silicon Angle* (10 April). https://siliconangle.com/2021/04/10/new-era-innovation-moores-law-not-dead-ai-ready-explode (accessed 13 January 2023).

Warfield, N. (2021). Why healthcare keeps falling prey to ransomware and other cyberattacks. *Threat Post* (2 July). https://threatpost.com/healthcare-prey-ransomware-cyberattacks/167525 (accessed 13 January 2023).

Warrington Guardian (2019). LETTER: 'Scam Mersey Gateway Bride toll site should be taken down', 22 August. www.warringtonguardian.co.uk/yoursay/letters/17854007.letter-scam-mersey-gateway-bride-toll-site-taken-down (accessed 13 January 2023).

Winter, C., Neumann, P., Meleagrou-Hitechns, A. et al. (2020). Online extremism: research trends in internet activism, radicalization, and counter-strategies. *International Journal of Conflict and Violence* 14 (2): 1–20. https://doi.org/10.4119/ijcv-3809.

Wittels, J., Graham, R., and Gallagher, R. (2022). Cyberattackers target key fuel-distribution firms in Europe. *Bloomberg* (2 February). https://www.bloomberg.com/news/articles/2022-02-02/cyberattack-on-europe-s-fuel-network-hits-germany-and-trade-hub (accessed 13 January 2023).

Xiao, Y. et al. (2019). Edge computing security: state of the art and challenges. *Proceedings of the IEEE* 107 (8): 1608–1631.

Zhou, Z. et al. (2019). Edge intelligence: paving the last mile of artificial intelligence with edge computing. *Proceedings of the IEEE* 107 (8): 1738–1762.

9

Case Studies

Cyber threat intelligence is not a perfect discipline. It is impossible to foresee every eventuality or to provide the ideal guidance in time to prevent every incident. The threat landscape is chaotic and dynamic; threat actors actively seek to bypass defences and take advantage of security weaknesses.

Case studies provide an opportunity to reflect on real world incidents, on the timeline of how the incident unfurled, and on the opportunities presented to threat intelligence teams. Looking back over past experiences allows intelligence teams to consider how they would behave in the same situation, and identify potential gaps in current intelligence provisions.

At the very least, we should be keen to learn from past events, to consider adopting practices that have proved successful elsewhere and seek to avoid previous failures. Asking the question, 'at what point would I have identified this threat, and how would I have responded?' is an excellent starting point for improving intelligence capabilities.

This chapter presents a selection of high profile case studies including examples of intelligence failures and successes. These are presented to assist the teaching of cyber threat intelligence, and as a learning tool for practitioners.

We should not harshly judge organisations that share information regarding a breach. Sharing information allows others to learn and gives the opportunity to augment defences. Case studies are a vital part of evolving cyber threat intelligence, and organisations that share detailed information regarding a breach should be applauded.

Case studies are necessarily illuminated by the bright light of hindsight. Rarely is there a smoking gun of a single failed or omitted control. The causes of breaches and the steps that lead to compromise are complex.

Even the best cyber security teams do not reach the correct conclusion or react optimally or appropriately all of the time. Decisions that in retrospect do not

Cyber Threat Intelligence, First Edition. Martin Lee.
© 2023 John Wiley & Sons, Inc. Published 2023 by John Wiley & Sons, Inc.

appear appropriate are almost certainly chosen as being the most obvious course of action with the information available at the time.

Case studies are never a full picture of what happened, and should not be considered as a forensic analysis of an incident; information may have been omitted or amended for reasons of data or operational confidentiality. As with any incident, the only person who knows what exactly happened is the threat actor, and they are unlikely to point out any mistakes in our analysis. We must base our analyses on that which is publicly available while recognising that this may be incomplete.

The best studies provide a narrative structure and enough information so that we can consider and learn from the incident. The coherent narrative of an incident report does not necessarily reflect how information was received or understood at the time. During incidents, information is almost always partial, frequently conflicting, and sometimes wrong.

These case studies have been selected as being well known and well described. They are certainly not representative of day-to-day threats. However, routine operations are typically well handled because they are frequent and hence, well rehearsed. Significant attacks are rare; consequently, they tend to be well documented and therefore qualify as suitable case studies.

9.1 Target Compromise 2013

On 18 December 2013, news broke that Target, a major US retailer, was investigating a potential data breach involving millions of customer credit cards that had occurred around the period of Black Friday 2013, the busiest shopping day of the year in the US (Krebs 2013a).

Ultimately, Target reached a $18.5 million voluntary agreement with the Attorneys General of US states to settle the civil claims that the Attorneys General could have brought against Target (Schneiderman 2017). In total, Target was reported as having incurred $292 million of cumulative expenses in relation to the data breach (Target Corporation 2017). In the aftermath of the attack the Chief Information Officer resigned (Shrivastava and Thomas 2014). Within six months of the breach, the Chief Executive Officer resigned, ending a 35-year career with the firm (Hadley 2014).

9.1.1 Background

In the years preceding the 2013 breach, Target emerged as a leader in using customer data to identify their customers' shopping habits, and how they might be able to influence these (Duhigg 2012; Pole 2010). Investments included the

American retailer creating an organisation based in India partly to drive business intelligence systems initiatives (Jacob 2010). The importance of the application of technology, and by inference data, to the company's strategy was underlined in the chairman's report to the shareholders.

> In 2013, we'll continue to pursue a strategy that is being shaped by our guests' expectations for more shopping flexibility and price transparency, and the rapid pace of change in technology. To ensure that we continue to strengthen our guests' love for our brand and deliver the surprise and delight they have come to expect, we'll leverage our greatest asset, our stores, in combination with increased investment in our digital platforms, to create a seamless, relevant and personalized experience.
>
> *(Target Corporation 2013)*

So effective was customer data analysis, that Target was able to determine purchasing patterns that identified pregnant customers and allowed the due date to be estimated (Hill 2012). Predicting purchases and the circumstances of the purchase allowed the company to pre-empt sales to customers by offering coupons to help ensure that these purchases would be made within Target's stores.

Target's statistician noted:

> We have the capacity to send every customer an ad booklet, specifically designed for them that says, 'Here's everything you bought last week and a coupon for it.'
>
> Just wait. We'll be sending you coupons for things you want before you even know you want them.
>
> *(Duhigg 2012)*

Apocryphally, Target was able to correctly deduce that a teenage woman was pregnant, sending her pregnancy-related coupons, which enraged her father since he was unaware of the situation (Hill 2012). As part of these efforts, Target was very clear that they were in compliance with all federal and state laws, including those related to protected health information. By their own admission they were '*very conservative about compliance with all privacy laws*' (Duhigg 2012).

In the preceding years, organised crime gangs had increasingly turned towards stealing personal data including credit card numbers (Krebs 2009). In 2009, a card payment processing company suffered what was at the time believed to be the largest data breach ever (Messmer 2009).

The processor was certified as compliant with Payment Card Industry (PCI) standards at the time of the breach, however despite best efforts a SQL injection vulnerability had been overlooked. Exploitation of the vulnerability allowed criminals to compromise the processor's corporate network (Cheney 2010). Once within the corporate network, the attackers spent almost six months evading detection and attempting to access the card processing network. The attackers installed packet sniffing malware to capture payment card data while the data was in transit rather than compromising data-at-rest databases of card data (Cheney 2010).

To facilitate the exchange between criminals that specialised in stealing credit card data, and those that specialised in monetising the data, criminal forums sprung up where stolen data could be bought and sold (Paretti 2008). One way in which criminals could monetise credit card data was using it to create fake credit cards, which are then used to make fraudulent purchases (Crail and Adams 2021).

Restaurants and retailers were recognised as being particular targets for criminals seeking to steal credit card details (Oremus 2012). Presumably this was due to criminals identifying that these organisations would process large volumes of credit cards that could be stolen. At the same time, malware writers were developing malware specifically designed to operate within point of sale systems in order to identify and exfiltrate credit card data within Random Access Memory (RAM) (Rodriguez 2017).

Target was not complacent. Risks due to disruption to their computer systems were recognised and clearly stated in the annual report:

> A significant disruption in our computer systems could adversely affect our operations. If our efforts to protect the security of personal information about our guests and team members are unsuccessful, we could be subject to costly government enforcement actions and private litigation and our reputation could suffer.
>
> *(Target Corporation 2013)*

The consequences of an attack were recognised:

> Our systems are subject to damage or interruption from power outages, telecommunications failures, computer viruses and malicious attacks, security breaches and catastrophic events. If our systems are damaged or fail to function properly, we may incur substantial costs to repair or replace them...
>
> *(Target Corporation 2013)*

Risk management and threat mitigation in addition to incident response and reporting programmes were in place:

> We have a program in place to detect and respond to data security incidents. To date, all incidents we have experienced have been insignificant.
>
> *(Target Corporation 2013)*

The nature of Target's security investments were further clarified by the Chief Financial Officer in a deposition following the breach.

> For many years, Target has invested significant capital and resources in security technology, personnel and processes, including firewalls, malware detection software, intrusion detection and prevention capabilities and data loss prevention tools. We perform internal and external validation and benchmarking assessments. Target's last assessment for compliance with the Payment Card Industry Data Security Standards (PCI DSS) was completed on September 20, 2013, by Trustwave. On that date, Trustwave certified Target as compliant with PCI DSS.
>
> *(Mulligan 2014a)*

9.1.2 The Attack

The attack did not start with Target, but was reported as affecting their refrigeration and heating, ventilation, and air conditioning (HVAC) supplier (SC Staff 2014). The company specialised as a refrigeration contractor for supermarkets and had access to Target's systems for the purposes of electronic billing, contract submission, and project management (Majority Staff Report for Chairman Rockefeller 2014). Credentials to access Target's systems were reportedly compromised by the attacker (Krebs 2014a).

Exactly how the attacker compromised these credentials from the HVAC supplier is unclear. Reports claim that the credentials were obtained through the use of a password stealing trojan (Krebs 2014b). The supplier referred to the attack as 'a sophisticated attack', which suggests that the attack wasn't as simple as a phishing email (SC Staff 2014).

It is unclear if the attack on the HVAC supplier was part of a widespread credential harvesting attack, which led the attacker to Target, or if the attacker had undertaken reconnaissance regarding suppliers to Target as part of a specific campaign against the retailer.

However, reportedly at the time of the breach, documents were available on the web that detailed Target's facilities management, supplied resources for HVAC and refrigeration companies, and provided a case study which detailed information relating to Target's network (Krebs 2014b; Radichel 2014).

Given the context of the attack and the reported availability of such information, it is likely that the attack on the HVAC supplier was a part of a specific campaign against Target, but in the absence of any confirmatory information this remains uncertain.

Armed with the HVAC supplier's credentials to a supplier portal, the attacker was potentially able to gain access to Target's internal network. No information relating to how that was achieved has been published. It is likely that the attacker discovered a vulnerability within the supplier's portal, and used that to gain access to the operating system of the server that housed the portal. The attacker likely exploited another vulnerability to escalate their privileges, and then explore the network before compromising additional systems.

The attacker is believed to have obtained the credentials at least two months before the attacker gained access to Target's systems. The mechanism by which the attacker spread across the network and reached the point of sale environment has not been released, although a report suggests that penetration testers were able to reach the point of sale environment from the core network when they were engaged following the breach (Krebs 2015).

In any case, the attacker gained access to Target's systems possibly as early as 12 November. Within a few days the attacker was able to deploy malware on the point of sale systems possibly as early as 15 November (Jarvis and Milletary 2014; Majority Staff Report for Chairman Rockefeller 2014). The malware installed is believed to have been a variant of BlackPOS, a memory scraping malware that retrieves credit card details from the RAM of point of sale systems (Krebs 2014c; Zetter 2014).

Stolen data was transferred to a central repository on a compromised internal machine. This device exfiltrated the data to an external system that was presumably under the control of the attackers using the FTP protocol (Jarvis and Milletary 2014). Reportedly, 11 GB of data relating to 110 million customer records was exfiltrated (Fisher 2014; Majority Staff Report for Chairman Rockefeller 2014).

The stolen card data was soon made available for purchase on criminal markets selling in batches of one million cards priced at between $20 and $100 per card (Krebs 2013b). The cards had reportedly all been used at Target between 27 November and 15 December.

Stolen credit cards vary in price according to the amount of data included in the dump. For example, card data including the card verification code sells for a higher price than those without. Fresh stolen data sells at a premium, since the issuing bank may not have had time to cancel the card. And, as with any market, oversupply of stolen data depresses prices as supply outstrips demand (Ablon et al. 2014).

Importantly, the malicious activity on Target's systems had apparently not been missed. Malware detection systems within Target had detected the presence of Malware on 30 November, a second security system alerted on suspicious activity at the same time (Infosecurity Magazine 2014; Riley et al. 2014).

Although BlackPOS, the malware family used in the attack, was known at the time, the particular modified variant used was not. The malware detection system identified the presence of malicious functionality within the unknown file, but did not identify the association with BlackPOS, reporting the unknown file as '*malware.binary*' (Finkle and Heavey 2014).

The security specialist team in Bangalore identified the threat and reported it to the security operations team in Minneapolis who reportedly chose not to react (Finkle and Heavey 2014; Riley et al. 2014). We can hypothesise that the operations team were overwhelmed with alerts and were not provided with the information necessary to prioritise this particular alert (Finkle and Heavey 2014).

On 12 December Target was informed by officials from the Department of Justice that they had been breached. This was confirmed on 15 December and the vast majority of the malware removed; by 18 December all the malware had been removed from the point of sale systems. The breach was made public on 19 December (Mulligan 2014b).

The success of this attack appears to be a threat intelligence failure. Information without context is of little use to those who must make decisions. It is inconceivable that an operations centre would have failed to take action if the context of the alert had been supplied: unknown malware with similarities to credit card stealers has been discovered on point of sale systems.

9.2   WannaCry 2017

At, or shortly before, 07:24 UTC on the morning of Friday 12 May 2017, a self-propagating worm that encrypted the files systems of the computers it infected first spread on to the Internet (Lee et al. 2017). Within two days at least 200 000 systems in 150 countries had been affected (Reuters Staff 2017).

The attack disrupted factories, railways, telecoms, credit card payments, and health services across the planet. The UK National Health Service was particularly affected. In excess of 19 000 patient appointments were cancelled due to the attack with health care providers reduced to using pen and paper because electronic systems were unavailable (Morse 2018).

The attack has been attributed to North Korean state threat actors, with one named individual indicted for the attack (Bossert 2017; Lord Ahmad of Wimbledon 2017; US Department of Justice, Office of Public Affairs 2018a). The motivation for the attack is unclear, but almost certainly linked to the geopolitical situation of North Korea.

Intelligence assessments of North Korean threat actors note that they are reckless and unpredictable, prepared to use '*capabilities without any concern for attribution, and for ideological motives which are alien to other countries*' (Grieve 2017). Possibly, WannaCry is the first example of a global cyber weapon, or it may have been a clumsy attempt at ransomware, which got out of hand.

North Korea denies the allegation that they were behind WannaCry and calls such an accusation '*a wicked attempt*' to tighten international sanctions on the country (BBC 2017a).

9.2.1 Background

9.2.1.1 Guardians of Peace

The genesis of WannaCry is a complex entanglement of geopolitics and victimology. We are unlikely to ever know the exact motivation behind the attack, but we can trace threads of the attack to the Sony Pictures hack of 2014.

Preproduction of the comedy film, *The Interview*, was announced in March 2013 (Siegel 2013). The plot of the film revolves around assassinating the leader of North Korea. The theme of the film was not well received within the country. The Korean Central News Agency declared:

> The act of making and screening such a movie that portrays an attack on our top leadership … is a most wanton act of terror and act of war, and is absolutely intolerable. *(McCurry 2014)*

Complaints about the film were made by the North Korean ambassador to the Secretary-General of the United Nations (Reuters Staff 2014). Sony Pictures reportedly delayed the release of the film and made some changes to tone down the content (Siegel 2014).

One month before the scheduled release of the film on 24 November, Sony Pictures suffered the effects of a threat actor referring to themselves as '*The Guardians of Peace*' who released a destructive wiper malware within the organisation and stole a considerable amount of confidential data (The Associated Press 2014).

The Destover malware used in the attack spread autonomously between systems using Windows shares and the Server Message Block (SMB) protocol before persisting on infected devices and accepting commands from the command and control infrastructure. Among the capabilities of the malware is the ability to render devices inoperable and wipe disk drives (Cha 2018; CISA 2014).

The stolen data was reported to include company emails, employees' personal information, and unreleased film scripts, ultimately 38 million files full of stolen data were released. The disruption to the IT estate caused great disruption, as did the fall-out from the breached confidential data (Seal 2015).

North Korea denied responsibility for the attack, but suggested, '*the hacking into Sony Pictures Entertainment might be a righteous deed of the supporters and sympathisers with the DPRK*' (Financial Times 2014). The FBI disagreed, publishing their assessment that the North Korean government was responsible for the attack (FBI 2014). This attribution was reiterated by President Obama the same day:

> The FBI announced today, and we can confirm that North Korea engaged in this attack. I think it says something interesting about North Korea that

they decided to have the state mount an all-out assault on a movie studio because of a satirical movie. *(Brady 2014)*

Not every security expert was convinced by the attribution (DeSimone and Horton 2017). However, if the goal of the offensive operation was to prevent the release of the film, then it had some success. Following threats by the attackers against movie theatres that showed the film, the theatrical release was cancelled. The studio stated:

> Sony Pictures has been the victim of an unprecedented criminal assault against our employees, our customers, and our business. Those who attacked us stole our intellectual property, private emails, and sensitive and proprietary material, and sought to destroy our spirit and our morale – all apparently to thwart the release of a movie they did not like. We are deeply saddened at this brazen effort to suppress the distribution of a movie, and in the process do damage to our company, our employees, and the American public. We stand by our filmmakers and their right to free expression and are extremely disappointed by this outcome.
>
> *(Fleming 2014)*

The film went on to have a very successful online and digital distribution, becoming the top-selling film of 2014 for on-demand movie services (Bacle 2014; Lang 2015).

Nevertheless, North Korea had achieved an objective, to prevent the cinema release of *The Interview*, by means of a cyber attack where other efforts had failed, thus illustrating the effectiveness of cyber attacks to achieve wider objectives.

9.2.1.2 The Shadow Brokers

The establishment of the Comprehensive National Cybersecurity Initiative by the US government in January 2008 established the requirement to coordinate offensive and defensive cyber research, at the same time requiring '*the coordination and application of offensive capabilities to defend US information systems*' (The White House 2008).

These requirements led to the development of a vulnerabilities equities process by which the relative merits of disclosing or retaining a newly discovered vulnerability could be considered (Jaikaran 2017). Governments are faced with a dilemma when a previously unknown vulnerability is discovered by a governmental researcher. The vulnerability can be disclosed to the vendor to be fixed, thus improving the security of the nation as a whole, or the vulnerability can be exploited for national security purposes, improving the security of the nation through investigative, intelligence, or offensive operatives.

The vast majority of vulnerabilities identified by the US government are reportedly disclosed, with a minority being retained for national security use (Jaikaran 2017). The exact criteria used for determining if a vulnerability is disclosed or retained are unknown, but an outline of some of the questions asked in evaluating vulnerabilities were published by the cyber security coordinator to the White House in 2014:

> How much is the vulnerable system used in the core internet infrastructure, in other critical infrastructure systems, in the U.S. economy, and/or in national security systems?
>
> Does the vulnerability, if left unpatched, impose significant risk?
>
> How much harm could an adversary nation or criminal group do with knowledge of this vulnerability?
>
> How likely is it that we would know if someone else was exploiting it?
>
> How badly do we need the intelligence we think we can get from exploiting the vulnerability?
>
> Are there other ways we can get it?
>
> Could we utilize the vulnerability for a short period of time before we disclose it?
>
> How likely is it that someone else will discover the vulnerability?
>
> Can the vulnerability be patched or otherwise mitigated?
>
> *(Daniel 2014)*

In August 2016, a previously unknown and still unidentified threat actor naming themselves the Shadow Brokers offered a cache of files for auction claiming that the data consisted of cyber weapons obtained from the Equation Group (Solon 2016). The threat actor known as the Equation Group is believed by many to be part of the US National Security Agency (NSA) (ThaiCERT 2021).

Apparently unable to attract suitable bids for their cache, the Shadow Brokers released their files to the world in two lots on 8 and 14 April. The second of these two releases contained the EternalBlue tool, which exploited a vulnerability (CVE-2017-0144) in the implementation of the Server Message Block version 1 (SMBv1). This exploit allows an attacker to send a specially crafted network packet to vulnerable systems and execute arbitrary code (Brange 2017).

The Shadow Brokers' release also included the backdoor tool DoublePulsar. Used in conjunction with the EternalBlue exploit, the DoublePulsar implant can be installed as a memory resident kernel-level backdoor waiting for SMB network packets containing further instructions, or code to execute (Mimoso 2017).

The vulnerabilities exploited by the tools in the dump of code were patched as critical updates by Microsoft in their March patch Tuesday security bulletin MS17-010 (Microsoft Security Bulletins 2017). However, although patching is recognised as important, it isn't always straightforward for organisations to swiftly apply patches, even those marked as critical (Emma W. 2019).

9.2.1.3 Threat Landscape – Worms and Ransomware

The first decade of the twenty-first century was characterised by a number of worms. Malware such as Nimda, Code Red, SQL Slammer, and Conficker spread autonomously across the Internet infecting systems without any human intervention (Sharma 2011). However, the last major worm outbreak due to Conficker had peaked in 2010, and by 2013 the worm was in decline (Asghari et al. 2014). By 2017, worms were in danger of being considered as malware of the past.

During the same period, ransomware was developing as a criminal business model. The GPCode malware of 2005 was the first modern malware where a criminal encrypted files demanding payment for decryption. However, it was the success of CryptoLocker in 2013 that requested payment in cryptocurrency that led to a jump in the number of ransomware families (Fiscutean 2020).

In the year preceding WannaCry, researchers predicted that the future of ransomware was cryptoworms that combined the encryption and ransom model from ransomware with the autonomous propagation model of the worm. In such a scenario, ransomware would spread from computer to computer, infecting and encrypting systems (Francis 2016; Spring 2016).

The first tentative examples of autonomously propagating ransomware were discovered, as was the first ransomware observed to spread by writing itself to network drives and removable media so that it could spread from machine to machine (Aurangzeb et al. 2017). Soon after, Spora ransomware was observed spreading in a similar manner (Lemmou and Souidi 2017; Microsoft Defender Security Research Team 2017a).

9.2.2 The Attack

9.2.2.1 Prelude

The tools released by the Shadow Brokers on 14 April were simple and easy to use. The EternalBlue exploit gave ring-0 kernel access to compromised computers. However, patches to resolve the vulnerabilities had already been released.

In a blog published on 14 April, a manager of the Microsoft Security Response Center wrote:

> Today, Microsoft triaged a large release of exploits made publicly available by Shadow Brokers. Understandingly, customers have expressed concerns around the risk this disclosure potentially creates. Our engineers have investigated the disclosed exploits, and most of the exploits are already patched.
>
> *(Misner 2017)*

A Rapid7 blog declared:

> A trove of nation state-level exploits being released for anyone to use is certainly not a good thing, particularly when they relate to the most widely-used software in the world, but the situation is not as dire as it originally seemed. There are patches available for all of the vulnerabilities, so a very good starting point is to verify that your systems are up to date on patches.

Before jokingly finishing with:

> wait for the next inevitable bunker-level catastrophe to hit, because this isn't it.
>
> *(Brown 2017)*

Nevertheless, Rapid7 had identified the major threat:

> For most organizations the larger threat is that of attackers co-opting these very sophisticated and now public exploits and other post-exploitation tools and using them to achieve their own goals. It will not be long before we will start to see more widespread attacks using these tools.
>
> *(Brown 2017)*

By 21 April, the number of systems compromised with DoublePulsar was measured to be in excess of 41 000, and rising. Six days later, on 27 April more than 400 000 systems were infected with DoublePulsar (Binaryedge 2017).

One industry expert was quoted describing the situation as:

> The polite term for what's happening is a bloodbath. The impolite version is dumpster fire clown shoes shit show ... I'm hopeful this is the wakeup moment for people over patching Windows machines.
>
> *(Thomson 2017a)*

By the end of April malware including ransomware and cryptominers had been discovered that had implemented EternalBlue as a method for spreading (ESET 2017; Trend Micro 2017).

At the beginning of May 2017, the threat intelligence outlook was dire. Despite patches being available, computers across the planet were being compromised with the recently released DoublePulsar backdoor, presumably with the aid of the similarly recently released exploit code. Threat actors were beginning to integrate the same or similar exploit code in their malware.

9.2.2.2 Malware

The innovation of WannaCry was to combine autonomous propagation worm functionality with ransomware. The malware attempts to connect over TCP port 445 to each IP address on the same subnet and to randomly generated public IP addresses. When the malware successfully connects to a device, it checks for the absence of DoublePulsar, and if the device supports SMBv1 protocol. If both of these checks are true, the malware exploits the vulnerability abused by EternalBlue, installs DoublePulsar and uses this backdoor to transfer and execute the payload.

The attempts at exploiting systems over internal and external IP addresses allowed the malware to spread efficiently across the Internet and within private networks. The malware sent back metadata regarding the infection over Tor to a command and control server. This metadata consists of the host and username allowing the attacker to track the spread of the malware, but nothing more (Akbanov et al. 2019).

Early reports of the spread of WannaCry erroneously stated that the malware was spread by email (Brenner 2019). Almost certainly, these incorrectly identified emails contained the Jaff ransomware, which was first sent in the hours before WannaCry infections started (Biasini et al. 2017; Tierney 2017).

These incorrect intelligence reports hampered the response against WannaCry. Security teams devoted resources to identifying WannaCry emails within their IT infrastructure, and some disconnected email servers to prevent subsequent infection, which in turn further impeded the response against WannaCry and the flow of correct information (Smart 2018).

The malware itself is modular in nature. The SMB worm functionality, the persistence mechanism, the file encryption routines, and ransom note are all contained within separate executable files. This architecture permits a different payload to be deployed by the worm functionality instead of ransomware, although this was never observed. The nature of the code suggested that different individuals had developed the separate components (Lee et al. 2017).

The ransom note displayed by an executable file was not a feature observed within other samples of ransomware at the time (Lee et al. 2017). Contemporaneous ransomware usually required ransoms to be paid to unique cryptocurrency wallets. This allowed attackers to verify that the ransom for a specific victim had been paid. WannaCry requested payment to be made to one of three bitcoin wallets. These wallets were common to the entire set of victims hit by WannaCry (Kan 2017).

Common wallets to which ransoms are paid would imply that reconciliation of payment would need to be performed manually by the threat actors, potentially an enormous task given the scope of the infection (Glance 2017). Additionally, the mechanism of encryption destroyed the private key necessary to decrypt the files. This means that apart from a subset of files encrypted using a separate mechanism, it would be impossible for the attackers to supply the key required to restore affected systems (Check Point 2017; Symantec 2017).

A further distinguishing feature of the malware was the presence of a 'kill switch'. Following infection, the malware makes a HTTP request to a domain, if the connection is successful, the malware does not execute further. The form of the domain name is consistent with someone mashing keys on a QWERTY keyboard (McBride 2017).

At the time of release of the malware, the kill switch domain was unregistered. The registration and sinkholing of the domain by a researcher prevented the malware from spreading further (MalwareTech 2017).

These features distinguish WannaCry from other malware, clearly this was a new participant to the field of ransomware, but what were the goals of the threat actor? If the goal was to perpetrate the criminal business model of ransomware, then the malware had a number of failings.

The criminal could not easily keep track of which victims had paid the ransom. The criminal was not in possession of the main private key, so could not decrypt files. The criminal included a kill switch in their attack, but did not register the kill switch domain so that a third party could halt the attack. These failings are not consistent with a serious attempt at criminal ransomware. Despite the scale of the attack, only $140 000 worth of ransom was paid (BBC 2017c).

Possibly WannaCry was an experiment that 'escaped' accidentally. In which case, the threat actor could have registered the kill switch domain and halted the attack. That this did not happen suggests that the release of the malware was voluntary.

Was WannaCry a purely destructive worm that was released in order to further geopolitics or to convey a message? In which case, this was an indiscriminate attack against every country connected to the Internet. Potentially, this was a message in order to demonstrate capability and intent. In any case, there was no revendication or further indication of what the attack was intended to achieve.

Similarities in the code of WannaCry and previous attacks attributed to North Korea quickly led to allegations that the North Korean threat actor, Lazarus Group was involved in some way (Solon 2017). Further intelligence and investigation led to the naming of one of the individuals suspected as having been involved in creating the malware and being a member of Lazarus Group (Cimpanu 2018a).

Prior to the attack, there was no indication that malware as destructive and as fast spreading as WannaCry was imminent. However, since the release of attack code by Shadow Brokers, the disclosure of the mechanism of exploitation of CVE-2017-0144, and the rapid increase in the number of systems compromised with DoublePulsar, it was clear that there was active exploitation happening in the wild.

Diligent threat intelligence professionals should have been highlighting the risk of exposing unpatched SMBv1 ports to the Internet, questioning the wisdom of supporting the obsolete SMBv1 protocol, and pressing for rapid application of the

March patch Tuesday security bulletin MS17-010. If such recommendations were made, in too many cases they went unheeded resulting in the most destructive cyber incident yet encountered at the time.

9.3 NotPetya 2017

WannaCry illustrated that destructive autonomously spreading worms were not threats from the past, but very much a current risk. The success of WannaCry coupled with extensive press coverage could be expected to inspire threat actors to create further worms.

The question was not if there was to be a new worm, but how soon the next would arrive. The response was 27 June 2017, just over six weeks since the advent of WannaCry. If WannaCry was a clumsy attempt at ransomware, or a cyber weapon camouflaged as ransomware, there was no doubt with NotPetya. This was a destructive cyber weapon targeted at Ukraine, which caused massive international collateral damage.

The 'Five Eyes' group of countries of the US, the UK, Australia, Canada, and New Zealand attributed the attack as having been conducted by the Russian military (Muncaster 2018; UK National Cyber Security Centre 2018). The US press statement on the matter was blunt:

> In June 2017, the Russian military launched the most destructive and costly cyber-attack in history. The attack, dubbed 'NotPetya', quickly spread worldwide, causing billions of dollars in damage across Europe, Asia, and the Americas. It was part of the Kremlin's ongoing effort to destabilize Ukraine and demonstrates ever more clearly Russia's involvement in the ongoing conflict. This was also a reckless and indiscriminate cyber-attack that will be met with international consequences.
>
> *(The White House 2018)*

Subsequently, the US Department of Justice has indicted four Russian military intelligence officers as having been involved in the development of NotPetya (US Department of Justice, Office of Public Affairs 2020). Russia denies involvement calling the allegations groundless and Russophobic (Reuters Staff 2018).

9.3.1 Background

The geopolitics of Kyiv and Moscow have been linked since the early middle ages. The dissolution of the Soviet Union led to the reestablishment of Ukraine as an independent state in 1991 (Gerhard 2002). Since the pro-European Union protests and unrest, known as Euromaidan, and the subsequent Ukrainian revolution of 2014, relations between Russia and Ukraine have been tense (Charron 2016; Umland and Kinder 2015).

In 2014, Russia annexed the Ukrainian territory of Crimea. The UN General Assembly condemned the move and called on nations not to recognise the annexation (UN 2014). Russia asserts that the accession of Crimea to the Russian Federation is thanks to the self-determination of the Crimean people (van den Driest 2015). The Donbas region of Ukraine was plagued by armed conflict between pro-Moscow and pro-Kyiv factions (ACLED 2020). In February 2022, Russian launched a full scale invasion of Ukraine (Kirby 2022).

In tandem with the degradation of political relations and the developing hostile military situation, during the mid-2010s Ukraine suffered cyber attacks that were attributed to pro-Russian and suspected Russian state threat actors (Baezner 2018; Cunningham 2020). Notably, the BlackEnergy attack of 2015 briefly interrupted electricity supplies to a region in Western Ukraine, the first time a threat actor had succeeded in disrupting power supplies (Cherepanov and Lipovsky 2016; Zetter 2016).

At the beginning of June 2017, the recent WannaCry worm should have given cause for network managers to reflect on the need for supporting deprecated network protocols, the dangers of opening network ports to the Internet, and the benefits of an appropriately segmented network architecture. However, it would have been very unlikely that network teams would have had the time to make more than minor changes, especially as there was no apparent urgency.

Organisations located in Ukraine, or with operations based in Ukraine would have been aware of the continuing risk of cyber attacks. But, again, there was no indication that an attack was imminent, or that such an attack would use worm functionality.

9.3.2 The Attack

NotPetya spread autonomously as a worm, but used a novel initial distribution technique: the supply chain, in order to widely infect organisations before spreading. This technique was not entirely unknown, the Havex malware was distributed through compromised legitimate software update systems (Rrushi 2015), and XcodeGhost was a trojanised compiler of dubious origin, which introduced malicious functionality into otherwise legitimate software at compile time (Xiao 2015). NotPetya was the first malware to be distributed while integrated into entirely legitimate software through the software update system.

9.3.2.1 Distribution

M.E.Doc is a legitimate accounting software package widely used within Ukraine. At some point M.E.Doc was compromised, resulting in versions of the accounting software containing a malicious backdoor to be distributed as an update on 14 April, 15 May, and 22 June 2017 (Cherepanov 2017a; Maynor et al. 2017).

The malicious code collects information including the Ukrainian legal entity identifier (EDRPOU), any proxy and email settings, including usernames and passwords, and every email address for the organisation contained within the accounting package database. These data are passed back to the legitimate update server, which is compromised to act as a command and control server (Cherepanov 2017a; Maynor et al. 2017).

The backdoor within the malicious code has six innate commands allowing the attacker to instruct the backdoor to download and upload files and execute supplied commands or files (Maynor et al. 2017). It is possible that the backdoor was used to download and execute additional payloads prior to the NotPetya worm. Intriguingly, the backdoor may have been used to download and execute the XData ransomware, possibly as a system test for the threat actors on 18 May (Cherepanov 2017b, 2017c).

In the minutes before 09:15 UTC on 27 June, the threat actor modified the legitimate update server to proxy to an additional server under the control of the attacker. It is presumed that by using this server the threat actor instructed the trojanised accounting software to download and execute the NotPetya worm (Maynor et al. 2017; Olenick 2017).

It is important to recognise and appreciate M.E.Doc for their openness and transparency in allowing others to learn from this incident. It is through under-standing incidents such as these that organisations can better protect themselves in the future.

9.3.2.2 Payload

The NotPetya payload contained a range of mechanisms for spreading. The malware attempted to gain credentials from the infected machine through Mimikatz-like functionality, and the *CredEnumerateW* function of the Windows Application Programming Interface (API) to steal credentials from system memory or the credential store, respectively (Microsoft Defender Security Research Team 2017b; Talos 2017).

The malware enumerates the local network and searches for devices with open TCP port 139 or port 445 and also uses Windows Management Instrumentation Command-line (WMIC) functionality in order to find remote file shares. When the malware has found a file share directory, it uses stolen credentials in conjunction with WMIC commands or the legitimate system tool PsExec to copy the malware to the file share and execute it (Microsoft Defender Security Research Team 2017b; Talos 2017).

The malware also used the EternalBlue and EternalRomance exploits for CVE-2017-0144 and CVE-2017-045 that had been disclosed by the Shadow Brokers in April 2017 (Brange 2017). In conjunction with these exploits, the malware used a modified version of the DoublePulsar backdoor, presumably to maintain the DoublePulsar backdoor functionality but with a different byte signature to evade anti-virus detection (Talos 2017).

Once the malware had spread to a system and was executed, the malware encrypted files, wiped logs, and would either overwrite the master boot sector, or the first 10 sectors of the disk drive depending on the system privileges the malware had acquired (Talos 2017). The result of this is to render the machine incapable of booting correctly.

One hour after initial infection, the compromised system will reboot (Talos 2017). The malware does not attempt to communicate the private key necessary to decrypt files to the threat actor. This observation and the fact that the malware discards the data that it overwrites strongly suggests that the malware is not ransomware but a destructive wiper. The threat actors had no intention or functionality to restore affected systems (CISA 2017).

9.3.2.3 Spread and Consequences

Using a Ukrainian accounting software package as a vector, and the timing of the attack on the day before the Constitution Day public holiday in Ukraine, suggests that the attack was targeted against the country (Secureworks Counter Threat Unit Research Team 2017).

Unlike WannaCry the malware did not attempt to spread to public IP addresses, but only over internal networks. However, many organisations had branch offices in Ukraine and Ukrainian firms had offices in other countries allowing the worm to spread outside of the country over corporate networks. Similarly, organisations in third countries may have had trusted connections with suppliers, customers, or partners in Ukraine. These exposed connections allowed the worm to spread globally through networks of trusted internal connections.

All industrial sectors were affected. The logistics sector was no exception. The shipping giant Maersk, responsible for 15% of the world's shipping network, has been particularly transparent in the impact the worm had on their systems (Hill 2019; Thomson 2017b).

Reportedly, the attack crippled the organisation's network within seven minutes, trashing approximately 50 000 laptops, disabling the company's VoIP phone system, and deleting all contacts from mobile phones (Bannister 2019; Ritchie 2019). Nevertheless, the organisation contained the infection within their container shipping operation, allowing six of their nine businesses to maintain normal operation (Tills 2018).

According to reports, during the attack staff were unable to print, all of the 1 200 applications used within the organisation were inaccessible, and of these 1 000 were destroyed. Of 6 200 servers, 3 500 were destroyed; although back-ups were available, the data couldn't be restored due to the likelihood of re-infection of the newly restored systems (Ritchie 2019). Staff had to process operations manually without the benefit of IT while IT teams rebuilt the IT estate. Over 10 days the IT department, '*had to install 4 000 new servers, 45 000 new PCs, 2 500 applications*' (Cimpanu 2018b). After two weeks, global applications had been restored, after four weeks, 49 000 laptops had been restored (Ritchie 2019).

The attack is estimated to have cost Maersk between \$250 and \$300 million (Ritchie 2019). According to one report, the damage was due to the targeted accounting software being installed on a single computer within the Ukraine branch office (Greenberg 2018).

Maersk was not alone in being subject to such damages. The pharmaceutical company Merck reportedly suffered \$870 million in damages with the loss of 30 000 end point computers as well as 7 500 servers (Voreacos et al. 2019). The TNT division of transport company FedEx reportedly incurred \$300 million in damages from the attack (BBC 2017b).

The lessons from this attack are many. Organisations that may not consider themselves as primary targets of a sophisticated nation state-sponsored attack may still suffer such an attack as 'collateral damage'. Security teams should plan accordingly, ensuring that similar attacks can be contained so that damage is limited, and that systems along with vital data can be restored from offline back-ups with minimum disruption to business operations.

9.4 VPNFilter 2018

On 23 May 2018, the US Department of Justice seized the domain used for the command and control of a botnet consisting of some 500 000 compromised systems that were being prepared for an attack. Due to the confiscation of the domain, the threat actor was unable to issue commands to the botnet, and consequently unable to pursue their objectives.

VPNFilter is an example of a cyber attack that was averted due to the application of cyber threat intelligence.

9.4.1 Background

The preceding section outlines the geopolitical situation in Ukraine. Following the extent and scope of the disruption caused by WannaCry and NotPetya in 2017, threat intelligence analysts were aware of the possibility of subsequent large-scale attacks.

During 2016 and 2017, reports surfaced regarding attacks against network infrastructure, the routers and switches that control network traffic and that connect systems to the Internet (CISA 2016; Cisco 2017; NCSC 2017). Network infrastructure is a tempting target for threat actors. Network traffic that passes through a compromised network device can be rerouted, blocked, intercepted and read, or modified.

Network infrastructure devices are small computers with a CPU, persistent storage, and an operating system. However, they very rarely have the security protections of end point systems or servers such as anti-virus software. Devices are often expected to run without interruption, which makes installing software updates to patch vulnerabilities difficult to schedule (Berres and Griffin 2012).

9.4.2 The Attack

VPNFilter used an unusual mechanism for communicating the IP address of the command and control server to the malware. The IP address was encoded within the metadata of images served from an image hosting service, or if this was unavailable from images hosted on the domain toknowall.com.

This domain had been registered in December 2015, but it wasn't until 4 May 2017 that it was changed to point to the IP address that it kept for the rest of the campaign (Talos 2018a). Presumably this date marks, or is very close to, the start of the campaign.

It was the need to download the image in order to connect to the command and control server that first allowed the malware to be identified. In August 2017, a router was observed connecting to the image hosting service without instruction (McKeown 2018). On further analysis, the router was found to be infected with the previously unencountered malware.

The malware primarily infected small office and home office routers as well as network storage devices. Although this initial infection vector remains unknown, all affected devices had known vulnerabilities. Once installed, the first stage downloaded the image to decode and call out to the command and control server in order to download and install the second stage payload (Talos 2018b).

The first stage was persistent on infected devices, but the second stage was not and needed to be redownloaded and installed following a reboot of the device. This second stage contained functionality including file collection, command execution, data exfiltration, and device management. Interestingly this stage contained a 'self-destruct' mechanism by which it could render the infected device inoperable by writing over part of the device's firmware (Symantec 2018).

The second stage also provided modular functionality for stage 3 plug-ins to provide additional services for the malware. Additional plug-ins included the ability to participate in denial of service attacks, mapping the internal network, which connects to the router, installing a proxy server, redirecting traffic crossing the router, capturing credentials in traffic traversing the router, and the identification of traffic using the widely used SCADA protocol, Modbus (Talos 2018a, 2018b).

The code within the malware contained an error within the implementation of the RC4 cypher stream algorithm. The exact same error was observed within the BlackEnergy malware suggesting that the two malware were developed by the same team, or shared a common code base (Talos 2018a).

Telemetry allowed the identification of the spread and localisation of the malware; 500 000 infected devices were identified, the vast majority of which were located in Ukraine. A large spike in the number of infections on 18 May was interpreted as heralding an imminent attack (Talos 2018a).

The US Department of Justice took the step of confiscating the toknowall.com domain (US Department of Justice, Office of Public Affairs 2018b). The security and technology industries acted together to coordinate the response against the malware (Daniel 2018). This resulted in the threat actor no longer being able to issue instructions to the infected devices (Talos 2018b).

The objectives of the threat actor remain unknown even after the capacities of the malware had been identified. The ability to identify Modbus traffic indicating the presence of industrial control systems, coupled with malware kill functionality that could permanently disable the router implies that the threat actor could seek to render remotely accessed control systems inoperable.

The Ukrainian authorities believed that an attack was being prepared to coincide with the UEFA Champions League football final, which was held in Kyiv on 26 May (Finkle and Polityuk 2018). Without additional intelligence, this remains conjecture. The Kremlin denies any involvement in the malware (Martin 2018).

This operation is an example of the successful application of threat intelligence to identify and understand an anomalous observation early in the conduct of a malicious campaign. The private sector was able to use their understanding and visibility of the threat environment to assist law enforcement in using their powers and remit to protect systems and our societies from attack. Ultimately, the threat actor was unable to progress their campaign due to private–public sector intelligence sharing and action.

9.5 SUNBURST and SUNSPOT 2020

NotPetya demonstrated the potential of distributing malware through supply chain attacks by hijacking the updated distribution process of legitimate software. This technique would be expected to only be accessible to the most sophisticated of threat actors, but would allow attackers to bypass perimeter security defences and deliver malicious code to the most valuable of targets.

During early September 2019, threat actors were reportedly able to penetrate the systems of SolarWinds, an American software company (Ramakrishna 2021). It is believed that the attackers were able to use this access to integrate malicious code into the build of the company's Orion product, an application providing IT inventory management monitoring to customers.

The trojanised versions of the software affected 18 000 organisations (Cimpanu 2020) including many governmental entities (Fey and Wiese 2020). The US and UK governments ultimately attributed the attack to Russia's Foreign Intelligence Service (aka APT29 or SVR) (Raab 2021; US Department of the Treasury 2021). The head of Russia's intelligence service denies being responsible for the attacks, calling the claims absurd, '*like a bad detective novel*' (Reuters 2021).

9.5.1 Background

Before releasing the NotPetya destructive payload, the threat actor was able to collect the Ukrainian legal entity identifier from every organisation infected with the trojanised accounting software package. We can assume that this informed the threat actor of the efficiency of distributing malware through the supply chain.

If further confirmation was required, the compromised version of the otherwise legitimate system management tool, CCleaner in September 2017 was downloaded over 2 million times (Avast Threat Intelligence Team 2018). The details of over 800 000 systems infected with the trojanised tool were stored in the attacker's database (Brumaghin et al. 2017). From these, the threat actor was able to select 40 for infecting with the second stage payload (Avast Threat Intelligence Team 2018).

As the main political and economic intelligence gathering agency of Russia, the '*Sluzhba vneshney razvedki Rossiyskoy Federatsii*' (SVR) or Foreign Intelligence Service would be expected to engage in espionage (Galeotti 2016). The SVR needs to innovate not only to defeat the anti-espionage efforts of foreign powers, but also to compete with other intelligence agencies within Russia (Soldatov and Borogan 2011).

In 2018, the head of the British intelligence service described the Russian government as the 'chief protagonist' in a campaign aimed at undermining the West (MacAskill 2018). The SVR operates as an arm of Russian foreign policy seeking intelligence to support strategic Russian businesses in securing foreign contacts, and to acquire details of technology that are currently not available within Russia (Galeotti 2016).

Although the dangers of Russia's muscular foreign policy were recognised in the West (Carter 2016), there was no specific warning of an increased risk of Russian espionage. One unnamed US official referred to Russian spying using prescient words: '*It's more complex now. The complexity comes in the techniques that can be used*' (Strobel and Walcott 2018).

Threat intelligence analysts were aware of the risks of supply chain attacks and the possibility of compromised legitimate software finding its way inside organisations. There was no intelligence to suggest that such an attack was imminent.

9.5.2 The Attack

From the attacker's point of view, the most useful legitimate software suites to compromise are those that are widely used within target organisations. Or, if the software used by the specific target is not known, software used by organisations with a similar profile to the target would also be a good choice. Ideally, the software should have low-level access to as many systems and networks as possible. This gives threat actors the most flexibility and broadest range of actions once an attack is successful.

As such, network and system management packages would appear to be a good choice for compromising. If a threat actor was looking to compromise networks of the US Federal Government, then it would be expected that the threat actor would seek out software known to be used within the Government (SolarWinds 2021).

From the many options available to attackers, we do not know the logic or process by which the highly reputed business SolarWinds was selected by the threat actor. We do know that by mid-September 2019, the threat actor had left traces that were subsequently identified within SolarWinds' systems (Ramakrishna 2021).

The first modification of the source of the Orion product was observed in October 2019 where an empty .NET class was added to the product build (Pericin 2020). The unobtrusive name of the class, *OrionImprovementBusinessLayer* was consistent with Orion's class naming patterns (Pericin 2020).

On 26 March, the malicious functionality, named SUNBURST was included within the Orion build and distributed to customers (Kovacs 2020; Ramakrishna 2021). The malicious functionality was particularly well camouflaged, containing multiple techniques to disguise its existence. Following an initial two weeks of dormancy, the malicious functionality ran as a new thread while the Orion software performed background inventory checks (FireEye 2020; Pericin 2020). The malicious network traffic was disguised as Orion Improvement Program protocol, and any reconnaissance information was stored within plug-in configuration files to hide its origin (FireEye 2020).

The malicious code was signed with the genuine certificate as part of the code build process, further complicating the task of identifying the malicious code (Pericin 2020). Indeed, a bespoke piece of malware named SUNSPOT was found infecting the build server, which modifies the source files when the Orion software package was being built (CrowdStrike 2021).

The SUNBURST backdoor included the functionality to execute instructions provided by the attackers via the command and control network, to transfer files, profile or reboot the system, as well as disabling system services (FireEye 2020). Backdoored systems were also associated with dropper malware named TEARDROP, which was able to install further malware (FireEye 2020).

The activity continued until SolarWinds was informed on 12 December 2020 (Ramakrishna 2021). During this time, at least 200 victims were targeted for additional compromise including various branches of the US government (Baker 2021; Turton 2020).

Detecting malicious code integrated within legitimate software is fiendishly difficult. Supply chain attacks such as this require significant resources and know-how. Microsoft estimates that the threat actor was likely to have deployed more than 1 000 engineers to work on the project (Tung 2021). To the eagle-eyed there were signs: the command and control traffic would have been visible, as would active network reconnaissance and any additional payloads downloaded as part of the attack. However, detecting these without prior knowledge would not have been an easy matter.

Before the discovery of the breach, there was little that threat intelligence could contribute. There was no indication that such activity was imminent, or that SolarWinds would be subject to such an attack. Once the attack was uncovered, threat intelligence could provide the necessary details to identify if an organisation had been affected by the attack, along with the necessary context for decision makers to understand the implications.

9.6 Macron Leaks 2017

In the final hours of the French presidential election of 2017, an archive of 15 gigabytes of data stolen from the campaign team of the candidate Emmanuel Macron were released on the Internet in an apparent attempt to sway voters. The release of the stolen data was only part of an extended malicious campaign against the candidate (Vilmer 2019). However, the apparent attempt at swaying the election failed with Macron winning 66.1% of the vote and becoming president of the French Republic.

This attack is particularly interesting partly because it shows the ambition of threat actors in their use of cyber attacks, but also because through the judicious use of threat intelligence, although the campaign team were unable to prevent the attack from occurring, they were able to neutralise the attack.

9.6.1 Background

Russian military doctrine and geopolitical ambition has evolved the notion of information warfare where military goals can be achieved without firing a shot. The concept of information warfare covers the use of offensive cyber actions as well as using psychology to trick an opponent into choosing actions that are detrimental to their own interests. The aim being to destabilise the society and government of a nation state without undertaking military action (Thomas 2019).

During the 2016 US presidential elections, Russian agents and interests are believed to have conducted a multifaceted campaign of propaganda and media manipulation to favour the candidate perceived as more friendly to Russia, Donald Trump, against the more hawkish candidate, Hilary Clinton (ODNI 2017). The campaign culminated with the release of emails and documents exfiltrated from the Democratic National Committee, the Democratic Congressional Campaign Committee, and emails from Clinton's campaign staff (Abrams 2019; CrowdStrike Blog 2020).

The French presidential campaign of 2017 offered an opportunity to conduct a repeat of this successful campaign.

9.6.2   The Attack

From December 2016, members of the Macron campaign team were subject to targeted phishing attacks, malicious emails. A campaign of fake news apparently to discredit Macron coincided with these attacks. In the run up to the election, further phishing sites were spotted being deployed (Auchard 2017). By 25 April, the campaign team reported having identified 2 000–3 000 hacking attacks, including denial of service attacks being targeted against them (Vilmer 2019).

Ultimately, the email accounts of five colleagues of Macron were compromised. This resulted in 15 GB of data including 21 075 emails being released on the evening of Friday 5 May 2017. The release was timed to occur only a few hours before the French media blackout preventing reporting on the election was due to begin before voting took place on 7 May (Vilmer 2019).

French authorities were clearly aware of the attacks from January 2017. The Minister of Defence warned of the use of false information to disrupt the presidential campaign; President Hollande requested specific measures to be in place to respond to cyber attacks affecting the campaign (L'Express 2017). By late April, the attacks against the campaign were reported internationally, and at some point, US Intelligence officials warned their counterparts in France about the attack (BBC 2017d; Jopling 2018). Macron's campaign team had ample time to prepare for an eventual breach.

Understanding that 100% protection against compromise was impossible, the team prepared a counter-campaign to derail the attack. Fake accounts containing fake information were created, and the attackers' phishing sites were flooded with fake credentials (Dickey 2017; Nossiter et al. 2017). When the leak was published, the campaign quickly took control of the narrative and released a press statement:

> The movement has been the victim of a massive and coordinated hacking operation giving rise tonight to the dissemination on social networks of internal information of various kinds (e-mails, accounting documents, contracts, etc.). The files, which are circulating, were obtained a few weeks

ago from a hack of the professional and personal email accounts of several staff members of the movement. Those who circulate these documents have added many fake documents to the collection of authentic ones in order to sow doubt and disinformation. By intervening in the last hour of the official campaign, this operation is clearly a matter of democratic desta-bilization, as was already witnessed in the United States during the last presidential campaign.

(as reported in Vilmer 2019)

The release largely contained genuine documents stolen from the campaign seeded with fake documents placed by the attackers containing discrediting infor-mation. However, the cache also contained the fake information placed by the campaign team, which could be pointed out as being ludicrously and obviously fake. Hence, discrediting the release and blurring the distinction between what was genuine and fake within the release (Nossiter et al. 2017).

In anticipation of a potential breach, campaign workers had been briefed to expect any email they sent to be leaked, and to think of their communica-tions this way. Emails were to be used for day-to-day communications, confidential information was only to be communicated over encrypted chat applications, and anything sensitive was reserved for face-to-face com-munication. *(Raulin and Gendron 2017)*

Although threat intelligence was unable to prevent the attack from occurring, good intelligence and understanding of the threat actors' goals did frustrate the attack. Even though the attacker was able to successfully conclude the cyber com-ponent of the attack and exfiltrate data, the apparent ultimate goal of influencing public opinion through releasing the data was unsuccessful thanks to the judi-cious use of threat intelligence.

The Kremlin denies any involvement (Wilsher 2017).

References

Ablon, L., Libicki, M.C., and Golay, A.A. (2014). *Markets for Cybercrime Tools and Stolen Data: Hackers' Bazaar*. RAND National Security Research Division. https://www.rand.org/content/dam/rand/pubs/research_reports/RR600/RR610/ RAND_RR610.pdf (accessed 10 March 2023).

Abrams, A. (2019). Here's what we know so far about Russia's 2016 meddling. *Time* (18 April). https://time.com/5565991/russia-influence-2016-election (accessed 13 January 2023).

ACLED Project (2020). Donbas: where the guns do not stay silent. Armed Conflict Location & Event Data Project. http://www.jstor.org/stable/resrep24686 (accessed 13 January 2023).

Akbanov, M., Vassilakis, V.G., and Logothetis, M.D. (2019). WannaCry ransomware: analysis of infection, persistence, recovery prevention and propagation mechanisms. *Journal of Telecommunications and Information Technology* 1: 113–124. https://doi.org/10.26636/jtit.2019.130218.

Asghari, H., Ciere, M., and van Eten, M.J.G. (2014). Post-mortem of a zombie: Conficker cleanup after six years. *Proceedings of the 24th USENIX Security Symposium*. https://www.usenix.org/system/files/sec15-paper-asghari.pdf (accessed 13 January 2023).

Auchard, E. (2017). Macron campaign was target of cyber attacks by spy-linked group. *Reuters* (24 April). https://www.reuters.com/article/us-france-election-macron-cyber/macron-campaign-was-target-of-cyber-attacks-by-spy-linked-group-idUSKBN17Q200 (accessed 13 January 2023).

Aurangzeb, S., Aleem, M., Iqbal, M.A., and Islam, M.A. (2017). Ransomware: a survey and trends. *Journal of Information Assurance & Security* 6 (2): 48–58.

Avast Threat Intelligence Team (2018). New investigations into the CCleaner incident point to a possible third stage that had keylogger capacities. *Avast* (8 March). https://blog.avast.com/new-investigations-in-ccleaner-incident-point-to-a-possible-third-stage-that-had-keylogger-capacities (accessed 13 January 2023).

Bacle, A. (2014). 'The Interview' is 2014's top-selling movie on YouTube, Google Play. *Entertainment Weekly* (30 December). https://ew.com/article/2014/12/30/the-interview-google-play-youtube (accessed 13 January 2023).

Baezner, M. (2018). *Cyber and Information Warfare in the Ukrainian Conflict*. ETH Zürich: Risk and Resilience Team, Center for Security Studies (CSS). http://dx.doi.org/10.3929/ethz-b-000321570.

Baker, P. (2021). The SolarWinds hack timeline: who knew what, and when? *CSO Online* (4 June). https://www.csoonline.com/article/3613571/the-solarwinds-hack-timeline-who-knew-what-and-when.html (accessed 13 January 2023).

Bannister, A. (2019). When the screens went black: how NotPetya taught Maersk to rely on resilience – not luck – to mitigate future cyber-attacks. *The Daily Swig* (9 December). https://portswigger.net/daily-swig/when-the-screens-went-black-how-notpetya-taught-maersk-to-rely-on-resilience-not-luck-to-mitigate-future-cyber-attacks (accessed 13 January 2023).

BBC (2017a). North Korea calls UK WannaCry accusations 'wicked'. *BBC News* (31 October). https://www.bbc.com/news/world-asia-41816958 (accessed 13 January 2023).

BBC (2017b). NotPetya cyber-attack cost TNT at least $300m. *BBC News* (20 September). https://www.bbc.com/news/technology-41336086 (accessed 13 January 2023).

BBC (2017c). WannaCry ransomware bitcoins move from online wallets. *BBC News* (3 August). https://www.bbc.com/news/technology-40811972 (accessed 13 January 2023).

BBC (2017d). Russian hackers 'target' presidential candidate Macron. *BBC News* (25 April). https://www.bbc.co.uk/news/technology-39705062 (accessed 13 January 2023).

Berres, Y. and Griffin, J. (2012). Optimizing network patching policy decisions. *27th Information Security and Privacy Conference (SEC)*, 424–442.

Biasini, N., Brumaghin, E., and Mercer, W. (2017). Jaff ransomware: player 2 has entered the game. *Talos Intelligence* (12 May). https://blog.talosintelligence.com/2017/05/jaff-ransomware.html (accessed 13 January 2023).

Binaryedge Blog (2017). DoublePulsar. https://blog.binaryedge.io/2017/04/21/doublepulsar (accessed 13 January 2023).

Bossert, T.P. (2017). It's official: North Korea is behind WannaCry. *Wall Street Journal* (18 December). https://www.wsj.com/articles/its-official-north-korea-is-behind-wannacry-1513642537 (accessed 13 January 2023).

Brady, J.S. (2014). *Remarks by the President in Year-End Press Conference*. The White House, Office of the Press Secretary. https://obamawhitehouse.archives.gov/the-press-office/2014/12/19/remarks-president-year-end-press-conference (accessed 10 March 2023).

Brange, V. (2017). Analysis of the Shadow Brokers release and mitigation with Windows 10 virtualization-based security. *Microsoft Security* (16 June). https://www.microsoft.com/security/blog/2017/06/16/analysis-of-the-shadow-brokers-release-and-mitigation-with-windows-10-virtualization-based-security (accessed 13 January 2023).

Brenner, B. (2019). WannaCry: the ransomware worm that didn't arrive on a phishing hook. *Naked Security* (17 May). https://nakedsecurity.sophos.com/2017/05/17/wannacry-the-ransomware-worm-that-didnt-arrive-on-a-phishing-hook (accessed 13 January 2023).

Brown, R. (2017). The Shadow Brokers leaked exploits explained. *Rapid7 Blog* (18 April). https://www.rapid7.com/blog/post/2017/04/18/the-shadow-brokers-leaked-exploits-faq (accessed 13 January 2023).

Brumaghin, E., Carter, E., Mercer, W. et al. (2017). CCleaner command and control causes concern. *Talos Intelligence* (20 September). https://blog.talosintelligence.com/2017/09/ccleaner-c2-concern.html (accessed 13 January 2023).

Carter, A. (2016). *Remarks by Secretary Carter on the Budget at the Economic Club of Washington, D.C.* US Department of Defense. https://www.defense.gov/News/Transcripts/Transcript/Article/648901/remarks-by-secretary-carter-on-the-budget-at-the-economic-club-of-washington-dc (accessed 28 March 2023).

Cha, M. (2018). Since the hacking of Sony Pictures. *VB2018*. https://www.virusbulletin.com/virusbulletin/2018/11/vb2018-paper-hacking-sony-pictures (accessed 13 January 2023).

Charron, A. (2016). Whose is Crimea? Contested sovereignty and regional identity. *The Region* 5 (2): 225–256.

Check Point (2017). WannaCry – paid time off? *Check Point Blog*. https://blog. checkpoint.com/2017/05/14/wannacry-paid-time-off (accessed 13 January 2023).

Cheney, J.S. (2010). Heartland payment systems: lessons learned from a data breach. *FRB of Philadelphia-Payment Cards Center Discussion Paper*. https://doi. org/10.2139/ssrn.1540143.

Cherepanov, A. (2017a). Analysis of TeleBots' cunning backdoor. *WeLiveSecurity by Eset*. https://www.welivesecurity.com/2017/07/04/analysis-of-telebots-cunning-backdoor (accessed 13 January 2023).

Cherepanov, A. (2017b). TeleBots are back: supply-chain attacks against Ukraine. *WeLiveSecurity by Eset* (30 June). https://www.welivesecurity.com/2017/06/30/ telebots-back-supply-chain-attacks-against-ukraine (accessed 13 January 2023).

Cherepanov, A. (2017c). XData ransomware making rounds amid global WannaCryptor scare. *WeLiveSecurity by Eset* (4 July). https://www.welivesecurity. com/2017/05/23/xdata-ransomware-making-rounds-amid-global-wannacryptor-scare (accessed 13 January 2023).

Cherepanov, A. and Lipovsky, R. (2016). BlackEnergy – what we really know about the notorious cyber attacks. *Virus Bulletin VB2016*. https://www.virusbulletin.com/ uploads/pdf/magazine/2016/VB2016-Cherepanov-Lipovsky.pdf (accessed 13 January 2023).

Cimpanu, C. (2018a). How US authorities tracked down the North Korean hacker behind WannaCry. *ZDNet* (6 September). https://www.zdnet.com/article/how-us-authorities-tracked-down-the-north-korean-hacker-behind-wannacry (accessed 13 January 2023).

Cimpanu, C. (2018b). Maersk reinstalled 45,000 PCs and 4,000 servers to recover from NotPetya attack. *Bleeping Computer* (25 January). https://www. bleepingcomputer.com/news/security/maersk-reinstalled-45-000-pcs-and-4-000-servers-to-recover-from-notpetya-attack (accessed 13 January 2023).

Cimpanu, C. (2020). SEC filings: SolarWinds says 18,000 customers were impacted by recent hack. *ZDNet*, Zero Day (14 December). https://www.zdnet.com/article/ sec-filings-solarwinds-says-18000-customers-are-impacted-by-recent-hack (accessed 13 January 2023).

Cisco Security Advisory (2017). *Cisco Smart Install Protocol Misuse*. Cisco. https:// tools.cisco.com/security/center/content/CiscoSecurityAdvisory/cisco-sa-20170214-smi (accessed 28 March 2023).

Crail, C. and Adams, D. (2021). What happens to stolen credit card numbers? *Forbes Advisor* (9 August). https://www.forbes.com/advisor/credit-cards/what-happens-to-stolen-credit-card-numbers (accessed 13 January 2023).

CrowdStrike Blog (2020). CrowdStrike's work with the Democratic National Committee: setting the record straight. *From the Front Lines* (5 June). https://www.

crowdstrike.com/blog/bears-midst-intrusion-democratic-national-committee (accessed 13 January 2023).

CrowdStrike Intelligence Team (2021). *SUNSPOT: An Implant in the Build Process.* Crowdstrike Blog, Research & Theat Intel. https://www.crowdstrike.com/blog/sunspot-malware-technical-analysis (accessed 13 January 2023).

Cunningham, C. (2020). *A Russian Federation Information Warfare Primer.* Henry M. Jackson School of International Studies, University of Washington. https://jsis.washington.edu/news/a-russian-federation-information-warfare-primer (accessed 28 March 2023).

Daniel, M. (2014). Heartbleed: understanding when we disclose cyber vulnerabilities. *White House Blog* (28 April). https://obamawhitehouse.archives.gov/blog/2014/04/28/heartbleed-understanding-when-we-disclose-cyber-vulnerabilities (accessed 13 January 2023).

Daniel, M. (2018). CTA actions around VPNFilter. *Cyber Threat Alliance Blog* (23 May). https://www.cyberthreatalliance.org/cta-actions-around-vpnfilter (accessed 9 March 2023).

DeSimone, A. and Horton, N. (2017). *Sony's Nightmare before Christmas. The 2014 North Korean Cyber Attack on Sony and Lessons for US Government Actions in Cyberspace.* Johns Hopkins Applied Physics Laboratory. https://www.jhuapl.edu/Content/documents/SonyNightmareBeforeChristmas.pdf (accessed 28 March 2023).

Dickey, C. (2017). Did Macron outsmart campaign hackers? *The Daily Beast* (7 May). https://www.thedailybeast.com/did-macron-outsmart-campaign-hackers (accessed 13 January 2023).

van den Driest, S.F. (2015). Crimea's separation from Ukraine: an analysis of the right to self-determination and (remedial) secession in international law. *Netherlands International Law Review* 62: 329–363. https://doi.org/10.1007/s40802-015-0043-9.

Duhigg, C. (2012). How companies learn your secrets. *New York Times Magazine* (16 February). https://www.nytimes.com/2012/02/19/magazine/shopping-habits.html (accessed 13 January 2023).

Emma W. (2019). The problems with patching. *National Cyber Security Centre Blog* (10 July). https://www.ncsc.gov.uk/blog-post/the-problems-with-patching (accessed 13 January 2023).

ESET (2017). ESET : WannaCry n'est pas le seul à utiliser l'exploit EternalBlue. *Global Security Mag.* https://www.globalsecuritymag.fr/ESET-WannaCry-n-est-pas-le-seul-a,20170517,71168.html (accessed 13 January 2023).

FBI National Press Office (2014). *Update on Sony Investigation.* Federal Bureau of Investigation. https://www.fbi.gov/news/pressrel/press-releases/update-on-sony-investigation (accessed 28 March 2023).

Fey, L.C. and Wiese, S.D. (2020). America the vulnerable: the nation state hacking threat to our economy, our privacy, and our welfare. *Kansas Journal of Law & Public Policy* 30: 370–399.

Financial Times (2014). N Korea denies being behind Sony attack. https://www.ft.com/content/b02173d8-7e5f-11e4-b7c3-00144feabdc0 (accessed 13 January 2023).

Finkle, J. and Heavey, S. (2014). Target says it declined to act on early alert of cyber breach. *Reuters* (13 March). https://www.reuters.com/article/us-target-breach-idUSBREA2C14F20140313 (accessed 13 January 2023).

Finkle, J. and Polityuk, P. (2018). U.S. seeks to take control of infected routers from hackers. *Reuters* (23 May). https://www.reuters.com/article/us-cyber-routers-ukraine-idUSKCN1IO1U9 (accessed 13 January 2023).

FireEye (2020). Highly evasive attacker leverages SolarWinds supply chain to compromise multiple global victims with SUNBURST backdoor. *Mandiant Threat Research* (13 December). https://www.mandiant.com/resources/evasive-attacker-leverages-solarwinds-supply-chain-compromises-with-sunburst-backdoor (accessed 13 January 2023).

Fiscutean, A. (2020). A history of ransomware: the motives and methods behind these evolving attacks. *CSOOnline* (27 July). https://www.csoonline.com/article/3566886/a-history-of-ransomware-the-motives-and-methods-behind-these-evolving-attacks.html (accessed 13 January 2023).

Fisher, D. (2014). Target attackers took 11 GB of data, researchers say. *Threat Post* (17 January). https://threatpost.com/target-attackers-took-11-gb-of-data-researchers-say/103691 (accessed 13 January 2023).

Fleming, M. Jr. (2014). It's official: Sony scraps 'The Interview'. *Deadline* (17 December).

Francis, R. (2016). Ransomworm: the next level of cybersecurity nastiness. *CSO Online* (27 December). https://www.csoonline.com/article/3151964/ransomworm-the-next-level-of-cybersecurity-nastiness.html (accessed 13 January 2023).

Galeotti, M. (2016). *Putin's Hydra: Inside Russia's Intelligence Services.* European Council on Foreign Relations. https://ecfr.eu/wp-content/uploads/ECFR_169_-_INSIDE_RUSSIAS_INTELLIGENCE_SERVICES_WEB_AND_PRINT_2.pdf (accessed 28 March 2023).

Gerhard, S. (2002). Ukraine and Russia: two countries – one transformation. *Connections* 1 (2): 1–8.

Glance, D. (2017). WannaCry hackers had no intention of giving users their files back even if they paid. *The Conversation* (15 May). https://theconversation.com/wannacry-hackers-had-no-intention-of-giving-users-their-files-back-even-if-they-paid-77751 (accessed 13 January 2023).

Greenberg, A. (2018). The untold story of NotPetya, the most devastating cyberattack in history. *Wired* (22 August). https://www.wired.com/story/notpetya-cyberattack-ukraine-russia-code-crashed-the-world (accessed 13 January 2023).

Grieve, D. (2017). *Intelligence and Security Committee of Parliament Annual Report 2016–2017.*

Hadley, M. (2014). Target CEO out as data breach fallout goes on. https://eu.usatoday.com/story/money/business/2014/05/05/target-ceo-steps-down/8713847 (accessed 13 January 2023).

Hill, K. (2012). How Target figured out a teen girl was pregnant before her father did. *Forbes* (26 February). https://www.forbes.com/sites/kashmirhill/2012/02/16/

how-target-figured-out-a-teen-girl-was-pregnant-before-her-father-did (accessed 13 January 2023).

Hill, M. (2019). GartnerSEC: Maersk CISO outlines lessons learned from NotPetya attack. *Infosecurity Magazine* (10 September). https://www.infosecurity-magazine.com/news/maersk-ciso-lessons-notpetya (accessed 13 January 2023).

Infosecurity Magazine (2014). Target may have ignored pre-breach intrusion warning. https://www.infosecurity-magazine.com/news/target-may-have-ignored-pre-breach-intrusion (accessed 13 January 2023).

Jacob, S. (2010). Target India is a long-term strategic asset. *The Economic Times* (25 February). https://economictimes.indiatimes.com/opinion/interviews/target-india-is-a-long-term-strategic-asset/articleshow/5613476.cms (accessed 13 January 2023).

Jaikaran, C. (2017). *Vulnerabilities Equities Process*. Congressional Research Service. https://lieu.house.gov/sites/lieu.house.gov/files/CRS%20Memo%20-%20Vulnerabilities%20Equities%20Process.pdf (accessed 28 March 2023).

Jarvis, K. and Milletary, J. (2014). *Inside a Targeted Point-of-Sale Data Breach*. Dell SecureWorks. https://krebsonsecurity.com/wp-content/uploads/2014/01/Inside-a-Targeted-Point-of-Sale-Data-Breach.pdf (accessed 28 March 2023).

Jopling, L. (2018). *Countering Russia's Hybrid Threats: An Update*. NATO Parliamentary Assembly Committee on the Civil Dimension of Security (CDS). https://www.nato-pa.int/download-file?filename=sites/default/files/2018-12/166%20CDS%2018%20E%20fin%20-%20HYBRID%20THREATS%20-%20JOPLING_0.pdf (accessed 28 March 2023).

Kan, M. (2017). Paying the WannaCry ransom will probably get you nothing. Here's why. *PC World* (15 May). https://www.pcworld.com/article/406793/paying-the-wannacry-ransom-will-probably-get-you-nothing-heres-why.html (accessed 13 January 2023).

Kirby, P. (2022). Why has Russia invaded Ukraine and what does Putin want? *BBC News* (17 April). https://www.bbc.co.uk/news/world-europe-56720589 (accessed 13 January 2023).

Kovacs, E. (2020). SolarWinds likely hacked at least one year before breach discovery. *Seucrity Week* (18 December). https://www.securityweek.com/solarwinds-likely-hacked-least-one-year-breach-discovery (accessed 13 January 2023).

Krebs, B. (2009). Organized crime behind a majority of data breaches. *Washington Post* (15 April). https://www.washingtonpost.com/wp-dyn/content/article/2009/04/15/AR2009041501196.html (accessed 13 January 2023).

Krebs, B. (2013a). Sources: Target investigating data breach. *Krebs on Security* (18 December). https://krebsonsecurity.com/2013/12/sources-target-investigating-data-breach (accessed 13 January 2023).

Krebs, B. (2013b). Cards stolen in Target breach flood underground markets. *Krebs on Security* (20 December). https://krebsonsecurity.com/2013/12/cards-stolen-in-target-breach-flood-underground-markets (accessed 13 January 2023).

Krebs, B. (2014a). Email attack on vendor set up breach at Target. *Krebs on Security* (12 February). https://krebsonsecurity.com/2014/02/email-attack-on-vendor-set-up-breach-at-target (accessed 13 January 2023).

Krebs, B. (2014b). Target hackers broke in via HVAC company. *Krebs on Security* (5 February). https://krebsonsecurity.com/2014/02/target-hackers-broke-in-via-hvac-company (accessed 13 January 2023).

Krebs, B. (2014c). A first look at the Target intrusion, malware. *Krebs on Security* (15 January). https://krebsonsecurity.com/2014/01/a-first-look-at-the-target-intrusion-malware (accessed 28 March 2023).

Krebs, B. (2015). Inside Target Corp., days after 2013 breach. *Krebs on Security* (21 September). https://krebsonsecurity.com/2015/09/inside-target-corp-days-after-2013-breach/comment-page-1 (accessed 13 January 2023).

Lang, B. (2015). 'The Interview' makes $40 million online and on-demand. *Variety* (20 January). https://variety.com/2015/film/news/the-interview-makes-40-million-online-and-on-demand-1201409731 (accessed 13 January 2023).

Lee, M., Mercer, W., Rascagneres, P., and Williams, C. (2017). Player 3 has entered the game: say hello to 'WannaCry'. *Talos Intelligence* (12 May). https://blog.talosintelligence.com/2017/05/wannacry.html (accessed 13 January 2023).

Lemmou, Y. and Souidi, E.M. (2017). An overview on Spora ransomware. *International Symposium on Security in Computing and Communication*, 259–275. https://doi.org/10.1007/978-981-10-6898-0_22.pdf.

L'Express (2017). Présidentielle: Hollande demande des mesures contre les cyberattaques. https://www.lexpress.fr/actualite/politique/elections/presidentielle-hollande-demande-des-mesures-contre-les-cyberattaques_1879379.html (accessed 13 January 2023).

Lord Ahmad of Wimbledon (2017). *Foreign Office Minister Condemns North Korean Actor for WannaCry Attacks*. UK Foreign & Commonwealth Office. https://www.gov.uk/government/news/foreign-office-minister-condemns-north-korean-actor-for-wannacry-attacks (accessed 28 March 2023).

MacAskill, E. (2018). MI5 chief: Kremlin is 'chief protagonist' in campaign to undermine West. *The Guardian* (14 May). https://www.theguardian.com/uk-news/2018/may/14/mi5-chief-kremlin-russia-is-chief-protagonist-in-campaign-to-undermine-west (accessed 13 January 2023).

Majority Staff Report for Chairman Rockefeller (2014). *A 'Kill Chain' Analysis of the 2013 Target Data Breach*. United States Senate Committee on Commerce Science and Transportation. https://www.commerce.senate.gov/services/files/24d3c229-4f2f-405d-b8db-a3a67f183883 (accessed 28 March 2023).

MalwareTech (2017). Finding the kill switch to stop the spread of ransomware. *National Cyber Security Centre* Blog, 13 May.

Martin, A.J. (2018). Kremlin planning Champions League cyber attack, Ukrainian state agency claims. *Sky News* (23 May). https://news.sky.com/story/

kremlin-planning-champions-league-cyber-attack-ukrainian-state-agency-claims-11383050 (accessed 13 January 2023).

Maynor, D., Olney, M., and Younan, Y. (2017). The MeDoc connection. *Talos Intelligence*. https://blog.talosintelligence.com/the-medoc-connection/ (accessed 13 January 2023).

McBride, A. (2017). The hours of WannaCry. *Cisco Umbrella* (16 May). https://umbrella.cisco.com/blog/the-hours-of-wannacry (accessed 13 January 2023).

McCurry, J. (2014). North Korea threatens 'merciless' response over Seth Rogen film. *The Guardian* (25 June). https://www.theguardian.com/world/2014/jun/25/north-korea-merciless-response-us-kim-jong-un-film (accessed 13 January 2023).

McKeown, M. (2018). *Affidavit in Support of an Application for a Seizure Warrant*. US District Court for the Western District of Pennsylvania. https://www.justice.gov/opa/press-release/file/1066051/download (accessed 28 March 2023).

Messmer, E. (2009). Heartland: 'largest data breach ever'. *CSO Online* (20 January). https://www.csoonline.com/article/2123599/heartland—largest-data-breach-ever-.html (accessed 13 January 2023).

Microsoft Defender Security Research Team (2017a). Ransomware: a declining nuisance or an evolving menace? https://www.microsoft.com/security/blog/2017/02/14/ransomware-2016-threat-landscape-review (accessed 13 January 2023).

Microsoft Defender Security Research Team (2017b). New ransomware, old techniques: Petya adds worm capabilities. *Microsoft Security* (27 June). https://www.microsoft.com/security/blog/2017/06/27/new-ransomware-old-techniques-petya-adds-worm-capabilities (accessed 13 January 2023).

Microsoft Security Bulletins (2017). Microsoft security bulletin MS17-010 – critical. https://docs.microsoft.com/en-us/security-updates/SecurityBulletins/2017/ms17-010 (accessed 13 January 2023).

Mimoso, M. (2017). NSA's DoublePulsar kernel exploit in use internet-wide. *Threat Post* (24 April). https://threatpost.com/nsas-doublepulsar-kernel-exploit-in-use-internet-wide/125165 (accessed 13 January 2023).

Misner, P. (2017). Protecting customers and evaluating risk. *Microsoft Security Response Center* (14 April). https://msrc-blog.microsoft.com/2017/04/14/protecting-customers-and-evaluating-risk (accessed 13 January 2023).

Morse, A. (2018). Investigation: WannaCry cyber attack and the NHS. Report by the Comptroller and Auditor General, National Audit Office. https://www.nao.org.uk/wp-content/uploads/2017/10/Investigation-WannaCry-cyber-attack-and-the-NHS.pdf (accessed 13 January 2023).

Mulligan, J.J. (2014a). *Written Questions for the Record of Chairman Leahy for John J. Mulligan Executive Vice President and Chief Financial Officer Target Corporation*. https://www.judiciary.senate.gov/imo/media/doc/020414QFRs-Mulligan.pdf (accessed 28 March 2023).

Mulligan, J.J. (2014b). *Written Testimony Before the Senate Committee on the Judiciary Hearing on Privacy in the Digital Age: Preventing Data Breaches and Combating Cybercrime.* Testimony of John Mulligan Executive Vice President and Chief Financial Officer Target. https://corporate.target.com/_media/TargetCorp/global/PDF/Target-SJC-020414.pdf (accessed 13 January 2023).

Muncaster, P. (2018). Five eyes nations united in blaming Russia for NotPetya. https://www.infosecurity-magazine.com/news/five-eyes-united-blaming-russia (accessed 13 January 2023).

Nossiter, A., Sanger, D.E., and Perlroth, N. (2017). Hackers came, but the French were prepared. *The New York Times* (9 May). https://www.nytimes.com/2017/05/09/world/europe/hackers-came-but-the-french-were-prepared.html (accessed 13 January 2023).

Office of the Director of National Intelligence (2017). Russia's influence campaign targeting the 2016 US presidential election. https://www.dni.gov/files/documents/ICA_2017_01.pdf (accessed 13 January 2023).

Olenick, D. (2017). Cisco Talos NotPetya analysis: attacker could launch again. *SC Media* (6 July). https://www.scmagazine.com/news/security-news/ransomware/cisco-talos-notpetya-analysis-attacker-could-launch-again (accessed 13 January 2023).

Oremus, W. (2012). A burger, an order of fries, and your credit card number. Why it's so easy for hackers to steal financial information from restaurants. *Slate* (22 March). https://slate.com/technology/2012/03/verizons-data-breach-investigations-report-reveals-that-restaurants-are-the-easiest-target-for-hackers.html (accessed 13 January 2023).

Paretti, K.K. (2008). Data breaches: what the underground world of carding reveals. *Santa Clara High Technology Law Journal* 25 (2): 375–413.

Pericin, T. (2020). SunBurst: the next level of stealth. *ReversingLabs Blog* (16 December). https://blog.reversinglabs.com/blog/sunburst-the-next-level-of-stealth (accessed 13 January 2023).

Pole, A. (2010). How Target gets the most out of its guest data to improve marketing ROI. https://www.predictiveanalyticsworld.com/machinelearningtimes/how-target-gets-the-most-out-of-its-guest-data-to-improve-marketing-roi/6815 (accessed 13 January 2023).

Raab, D. (2021). *Russia: UK and US Expose Global Campaign of Malign Activity by Russian Intelligence Services.* UK Foreign, Commonwealth & Development Office. https://www.gov.uk/government/news/russia-uk-and-us-expose-global-campaigns-of-malign-activity-by-russian-intelligence-services (accessed 28 March 2023).

Radichel, T. (2014). Case study: critical controls that could have prevented Target breach. https://www.giac.org/paper/gsec/35355/case-study-critical-controls-prevented-target-breach/140127 (accessed 13 January 2023).

Ramakrishna, S. (2021). New findings from our investigation of SUNBURST. *Orangematter, SolarWinds* (11 January). https://orangematter.solarwinds.com/2021/01/11/new-findings-from-our-investigation-of-sunburst (accessed 13 January 2023).

Raulin, N. and Gendron, G. (2017). Piratage : l'équipe Macron sur le pont. *Liberation* (10 August). https://www.liberation.fr/france/2017/08/10/piratage-l-equipe-macron-sur-le-pont_1589281 (accessed 13 January 2023).

Reuters Staff (2014). North Korea complains to UN about film starring Rogen, Franco. *Reuters* (9 July). https://www.reuters.com/article/northkorea-un-film-idUSL2N0PK1FX20140709 (accessed 13 January 2023).

Reuters Staff (2017). Cyber attack hits 200,000 in at least 150 countries: Europol. *Reuters* (14 May). https://www.reuters.com/article/us-cyber-attack-europol-idUSKCN18A0FX (accessed 13 January 2023).

Reuters Staff (2018). Russia denies British allegations that Moscow was behind cyber-attack. *Retuers* (15 February). https://www.reuters.com/article/us-britain-russia-cyber-kremlin-idUSKCN1FZ102 (accessed 13 January 2023).

Reuters Staff (2021). 'Flattered' Russian spy chief denies SolarWinds attack – BBC. *Reuters* (18 May). https://www.reuters.com/technology/russian-spy-chief-denies-svr-was-behind-solarwinds-cyber-attack-bbc-2021-05-18 (accessed 13 January 2023).

Riley, M., Elgin, B., Lawrence, D., and Matlack, C. (2014). Missed alarms and 40 million stolen credit card numbers: how Target blew it. *Bloomberg BusinessWeek* (17 March). https://www.bloomberg.com/news/articles/2014-03-13/target-missed-warnings-in-epic-hack-of-credit-card-data (accessed 13 January 2023).

Ritchie, R. (2019). Maersk: springing back from a catastrophic cyber-attack. *I – Global Intelligence for Digital Leaders*. https://web.archive.org/web/20200910203253/https://www.i-cio.com/management/insight/item/maersk-springing-back-from-a-catastrophic-cyber-attack (accessed 10 March 2023).

Rodriguez, R.J. (2017). Evolution and characterization of point-of-sale RAM scraping malware. *Journal of Computer Virology and Hacking Techniques* 13 (3): 179–192.

Rrushi, J. (2015). A quantitative evaluation of the target selection of havex ICS malware plugin. *Industrial Control System Security (ICSS) Workshop*. https://www.acsac.org/2015/workshops/icss/Julian.Rrushi%20et%20al-%20Manuscript.pdf (accessed 13 January 2023).

SC Staff (2014). Target vendor, Fazio Mechanical, confirms being victim of attack. *SC Media* (6 February). https://www.scmagazine.com/news/security-news/target-vendor-fazio-mechanical-confirms-being-victim-of-attack (accessed 13 January 2023).

Schneiderman, E.T. (2017). *Investigation by Eric T. Schneiderman, Attorney General of the State of New York, of Target Corporation. Assurance No.17-094*. Attorney General of the State of New York Bureau of Internet and Technology. https://ag.ny.gov/sites/default/files/nyag_target_settlement.pdf (accessed 28 March 2023).

Seal, M. (2015). An exclusive look at Sony's hacking saga. *Vanity Fair* (4 February). https://www.vanityfair.com/hollywood/2015/02/sony-hacking-seth-rogen-evan-goldberg (accessed 13 January 2023).

Secureworks Counter Threat Unit Research Team (2017). NotPetya campaign: what we know about the latest global ransomware attack. *Secureworks* (28 July). https://www.secureworks.com/blog/notpetya-campaign-what-we-know-about-the-latest-global-ransomware-attack (accessed 13 January 2023).

Sharma, V. (2011). An analytical survey of recent worm attacks. *International Journal of Computer Science and Network Security* 11 (11): 99–103.

Shrivastava, A. and Thomas, M.A. (2014). Target announces technology overhaul, CIO departure. *Reuters* (5 March). https://www.reuters.com/article/us-target-security-idUSBREA241DE20140305 (accessed 13 January 2023).

Siegel, T. (2013). Seth Rogen to direct, star in 'The Interview' for Columbia Pictures (Exclusive). *The Hollywood Reporter* (21 March). https://www.hollywoodreporter.com/news/general-news/seth-rogen-direct-star-interview-430224 (accessed 13 January 2023).

Siegel, T. (2014). Sony altering Kim Jong Un assassination film 'The Interview' (Exclusive). *The Hollywood Reporter* (13 August). https://www.hollywoodreporter.com/news/general-news/sony-altering-kim-jong-assassination-725092 (accessed 13 January 2023).

Smart, W. (2018). Lessons learned: review of the WannaCry Ransomware Cyber Attack. Chief Information Officer for the Health and Social Care System. https://www.england.nhs.uk/wp-content/uploads/2018/02/lessons-learned-review-wannacry-ransomware-cyber-attack-cio-review.pdf (accessed 13 January 2023).

SolarWinds Government (2021). IT management and monitoring solutions for government. https://www.solarwinds.com/federal-government/it-management-solutions-for-government (accessed 13 January 2023).

Soldatov, A. and Borogan, I. (2011). Russia's very secret services. *World Policy Journal* 28 (1): 83–91.

Solon, O. (2016). Hacking group auctions 'cyber weapons' stolen from NSA. *The Guardian* (16 August). https://www.theguardian.com/technology/2016/aug/16/shadow-brokers-hack-auction-nsa-malware-equation-group (accessed 13 January 2023).

Solon, O. (2017). WannaCry ransomware has links to North Korea, cybersecurity experts say. *The Guardian* (15 May). https://www.theguardian.com/technology/2017/may/15/wannacry-ransomware-north-korea-lazarus-group (accessed 13 January 2023).

Spring, T. (2016). Meet the cryptoworm, the future of ransomware. *Threat Post* (12 April). https://threatpost.com/meet-the-cryptoworm-the-future-of-ransomware/117330 (accessed 13 January 2023).

Strobel, W. and Walcott, J. (2018). Fewer Russian spies in U.S. but getting harder to track. *Reuters* (28 March). https://www.reuters.com/article/us-usa-russia-spies-idUSKBN1H40JW (accessed 13 January 2023).

Symantec (2018). VPNFilter: new router malware with destructive capabilities. *Symantec Threat Intelligence* (23 May). https://symantec-enterprise-blogs. security.com/blogs/threat-intelligence/vpnfilter-iot-malware (accessed 13 January 2023).

Symantec Threat Intel (2017). Can files locked by WannaCry be decrypted: a technical analysis. *Threat Intel* (15 May). https://medium.com/threat-intel/ wannacry-ransomware-decryption-821c7e3f0a2b (accessed 13 January 2023).

Talos (2017). New ransomware variant 'Nyetya' compromises systems worldwide. *Talos Intelligence* (27 June). https://blog.talosintelligence.com/2017/06/worldwide-ransomware-variant.html (accessed 13 January 2023).

Talos (2018a). New VPNFilter malware targets at least 500K networking devices worldwide. *Talos Intelligence* (23 May). https://blog.talosintelligence.com/2018/05/ VPNFilter.html (accessed 13 January 2023).

Talos (2018b). VPNFilter III: more tools for the Swiss army knife of malware. *Talos Intelligence* (26 September). https://blog.talosintelligence.com/2018/09/vpnfilter-part-3.html (accessed 13 January 2023).

Target Corporation (2013). 2012 Annual report. https://investors.target.com/ static-files/cd005867-9956-49b9-a69a-421e3f966030 (accessed 13 January 2023).

Target Corporation (2017). Annual Report Pursuant to Section 13 or 15(d) of the Securities Exchange Act of 1934. For the fiscal year ended January 28, 2017. https://www.sec.gov/Archives/edgar/data/27419/000002741917000008/ tgt-20170128x10k.htm (accessed 13 January 2023).

ThaiCERT (2021). APT Group: Equation Group. *Threat Group Cards: A Threat Actor Encyclopedia*. Digital Service Security Center, Electronic Transactions Development Agency. https://apt.etda.or.th/cgi-bin/showcard.cgi?g=Equation%20 Group&n=1 (accessed 13 January 2023).

The Associated Press (2014). Timeline of the Sony Pictures Entertainment hack, 18 December. https://apnews.com/article/61710d966ec94721881faa84dd05f57c (accessed 13 January 2023).

The White House (2008). National Security Presidential Directive NSPD-54. Homeland Security Presidential Directive HSPD-23. https://irp.fas.org/offdocs/ nspd/nspd-54.pdf (accessed 13 January 2023).

The White House (2018). Statement from the press secretary. https:// trumpwhitehouse.archives.gov/briefings-statements/statement-press-secretary-25 (accessed 13 January 2023).

Thomas, T.L. (2019). *Russian Military Thought: Concepts and Elements*. The Mitre Corporation. https://www.mitre.org/sites/default/files/publications/ pr-19-1004-russian-military-thought-concepts-elements.pdf (accessed 28 March 2023).

Thomson, I. (2017a). Script kiddies pwn 1000s of windows boxes using leaked NSA hack tools, 21 April. https://www.theregister.com/2017/04/21/windows_hacked_ nsa_shadow_brokers (accessed 13 January 2023).

Thomson, I. (2017b). NotPetya ransomware attack cost us $300m – shipping giant Maersk. *The Register* (16 August). https://www.theregister.com/2017/08/16/notpetya_ransomware_attack_cost_us_300m_says_shipping_giant_maersk (accessed 13 January 2023).

Tierney, S. (2017). WannaCry and Jaff: two different ransomware attacks with a common goal. *Infoblox* (17 May). https://blogs.infoblox.com/company/wannacry-and-jaff-two-different-ransomware-attacks-with-a-common (accessed 13 January 2023).

Tills, C. (2018). Case Study: A.P. Møller-Maersk and NotPetya. *Clear Security Communication*. https://www.clairetills.com/post/2018/05/20/case-study-ap-møller-maersk-and-notpetya (accessed 13 January 2023).

Trend Micro (2017). Malware using exploits from Shadow Brokers leak reportedly in the wild. *Trend Micro Security News* (26 April). https://www.trendmicro.com/vinfo/pl/security/news/cybercrime-and-digital-threats/malware-using-exploits-from-shadow-brokers-in-the-wild (accessed 13 January 2023).

Tung, L. (2021). Microsoft: SolarWinds attack took more than 1,000 engineers to create. *ZDNet* (15 February). https://www.zdnet.com/article/microsoft-solarwinds-attack-took-more-than-1000-engineers-to-create (accessed 13 January 2023).

Turton, W. (2020). At least 200 victims identified in suspected Russian hacking – Bloomberg. *Bloomberg* (19 December). https://www.bloomberg.com/news/articles/2020-12-19/at-least-200-victims-identified-in-suspected-russian-hacking (accessed 13 January 2023).

UK National Cyber Security Centre (2017). *UK Internet Edge Router Devices: Advisory*. National Cyber Security Centre. https://www.ncsc.gov.uk/information/uk-internet-edge-router-devices-advisory (accessed 28 March 2023).

UK National Cyber Security Centre (2018). Russian military 'almost certainly' responsible for destructive 2017 cyber attack. *National Cyber Security Centre News* (14 February). www.ncsc.gov.uk/news/russian-military-almost-certainly-responsible-destructive-2017-cyber-attack (accessed 13 January 2023).

Umland, A. and Kinder, A. (2015). Political risk insurance for FDI in Ukraine: how the Eastern European pivot state can be saved. *Harvard International Review* 37 (1): 31–45.

United Nations (2014). *General Assembly Adopts Resolution Calling upon States Not to Recognize Changes in Status of Crimea Region*. United Nations, Department of Public Information. https://www.un.org/press/en/2014/ga11493.doc.htm (accessed 28 March 2023).

US Cybersecurity & Infrastructure Security Agency (2014). Alert (TA14-353A) targeted destructive malware. https://www.cisa.gov/uscert/ncas/alerts/TA14-353A (accessed 13 January 2023).

US Cybersecurity & Infrastructure Security Agency (2016). *Alert (TA16-250A) the Increasing Threat to Network Infrastructure Devices and Recommended Mitigations*. Cybersecurity & Infrastructure Security Agency. https://www.cisa.gov/uscert/ncas/alerts/TA16-250A (accessed 28 March 2023).

US Cybersecurity & Infrastructure Security Agency (2017). *Alert (TA17-181A) Petya Ransomware*. Cybersecurity & Infrastructure Security Agency. https://www.cisa.gov/uscert/ncas/alerts/TA17-181A (accessed 28 March 2023).

US Department of Justice, Office of Public Affairs (2018a). *North Korean Regime-Backed Programmer Charged with Conspiracy to Conduct Multiple Cyber Attacks and Intrusions*. US Department of Justice. https://www.justice.gov/opa/pr/north-korean-regime-backed-programmer-charged-conspiracy-conduct-multiple-cyber-attacks-and (accessed 28 March 2023).

US Department of Justice, Office of Public Affairs (2018b). *Justice Department Announces Actions to Disrupt Advanced Persistent Threat 28 Botnet of Infected Routers and Network Storage Devices*. US Department of Justice. https://www.justice.gov/opa/pr/justice-department-announces-actions-disrupt-advanced-persistent-threat-28-botnet-infected (accessed 28 March 2023).

US Department of Justice, Office of Public Affairs (2020). Six Russian GRU officers charged in connection with worldwide deployment of destructive malware and other disruptive actions in cyberspace. https://www.justice.gov/opa/pr/six-russian-gru-officers-charged-connection-worldwide-deployment-destructive-malware-and (accessed 13 January 2023).

US Department of the Treasury (2021). *Treasury Sanctions Russia with Sweeping New Sanctions Authority*. US Department of the Treasury. https://home.treasury.gov/news/press-releases/jy0127 (accessed 28 March 2023).

Vilmer, J.B.J. (2019). *The 'Macron Leaks' Operation: A Post-Mortem*. Atlantic Council & Institute for Strategic Research. https://www.atlanticcouncil.org/wp-content/uploads/2019/06/The_Macron_Leaks_Operation-A_Post-Mortem.pdf (accessed 28 March 2023).

Voreacos, D., Chiglinsky, K., and Griffin, R. (2019). Merck cyberattack's $1.3 billion question: was it an act of war? *Bloomberg Markets* (3 December). https://www.bloomberg.com/news/features/2019-12-03/merck-cyberattack-s-1-3-billion-question-was-it-an-act-of-war (accessed 13 January 2023).

Wilsher, K. (2017). French media warned not to publish Emmanuel Macron leaks. *The Guardian* (6 May). https://www.theguardian.com/world/2017/may/06/french-warned-not-to-publish-emmanuel-macron-leaks(accessed 13 January 2023).

Xiao, C. (2015). Novel malware XcodeGhost modifies Xcode, Infects Apple iOS Apps and hits App Store. *Unit 42, Paloalto* (17 September). https://unit42.paloaltonetworks.com/novel-malware-xcodeghost-modifies-xcode-infects-apple-ios-apps-and-hits-app-store (accessed 13 January 2023).

Zetter, K. (2014). The malware that duped Target has been found. *Wired* (16 January). https://www.wired.com/2014/01/target-malware-identified (accessed 13 January 2023).

Zetter, K. (2016). Inside the cunning, unprecedented hack of Ukraine's power grid. *Wired* (3 March). https://www.wired.com/2016/03/inside-cunning-unprecedented-hack-ukraines-power-grid (accessed 13 January 2023).

Index

Cyber Threat Intelligence, First Edition. Martin Lee.
© 2023 John Wiley & Sons, Inc. Published 2023 by John Wiley & Sons, Inc.

Printed and bound by CPI Group (UK) Ltd, Croydon, CR0 4YY

27/10/2024

14580673-0002